Sustainable Fashion

Sustainable Fashion

What's Next?

A Conversation about Issues, Practices and Possibilities

Second Edition

Janet Hethorn
Connie Ulasewicz

FAIRCHILD BOOKS

NEW YORK · LONDON · OXFORD · NEW DELHI · SYDNEY

FAIRCHILD BOOKS
Bloomsbury Publishing Inc
1385 Broadway, New York, NY 10018, USA
50 Bedford Square, London, WC1B 3DP, UK

BLOOMSBURY, FAIRCHILD BOOKS and the Fairchild Books logo are trademarks
of Bloomsbury Publishing Plc

First edition published 2008
This edition first published 2015
Reprinted 2019 (twice)

Cover design: Anna Perotti | www.bytheskydesign.com
Cover image © iStock

Library of Congress Cataloging-in-Publication Data
Sustainable fashion : what's next? : a conversation about issues, practices
and possibilities / Janet Hethorn, Connie Ulasewicz. — Second edition.
pages cm
Includes bibliographical references and index.
ISBN 978-1-62892-531-9 (paperback)
1. Clothing trade—Environmental aspects. 2. Clothing trade—Moral and
ethical aspects. 3. Fashion design. 4. Sustainable design. I. Hethorn, Janet. II.
Ulasewicz, Connie.
TT497.S97 2015
746.9'2—dc23
2015004180

ISBN: PB: 978-1-6289-2531-9
       ePDF: 978-1-6289-2533-3
       eBook: 978-1-6289-2532-6

Typeset by Saxon Graphics Ltd, Derby
Printed and bound in the United States of America

To find out more about our authors and books visit www.fairchildbooks.com
and sign up for our newsletter.

SECTION III

The Environment, the Planet, and the Materials Used in Fashion Making   265

Fashion is a Verb
William McDonough

Fashion, to most people, is an ephemeral expression of culture, art, and technology manifesting itself in form. But fashion is also a verb: to fashion is to make. We fashion things—we make and remake—and the world is physically affected by our choices of materials and how we use energy and water and how we treat each other, too. As an architect, I fashion buildings. When I design clothing, I fashion garments. Together, we all fashion a world we want to live in.

Today, we are Earth's dominant species in the Age of the Anthropocene and design, therefore, is the first signal of human intention. While fashion is generally considered an expression of our current culture and what we find beautiful right now, it can also be seen as signifying our intention for the many generations to follow ours. With the wealth of transparent and detailed information we now have about the world around us, why not utilize our intelligence to fashion a more beautiful future? What does it mean to be beautiful if the rivers of China run black while we and our grandchildren are clothed in hazardous substances? Is this our plan, our intention, our design—our fashion?

This is not an exaggeration; it's happening around the world. In China's Hunan province, toxins in the water and soil are making it impossible to grow food safely. Do cheap clothing and consumer products have to cause contaminated soil, water, and air? The common "sustainability" call today is for reduced energy and water use, and even avoiding a relative few of the many hazardous substances involved in textiles, but, as laudable as this call might be, it is insufficient to solve our bad problems because just being less bad is still being bad—by definition. We have a huge design problem. It's time to fashion deep, abiding, and principled solutions and we have examples of how they can be done and we know they can be cost-effective. So, while we valiantly attempt to reduce our badness, let us also delightfully refashion our way of making things toward more goodness with positively defined beneficial systems. It's time to be fierce, intergenerational, intentional, and beautiful. It's time to wage peace with the world and each other by fashioning an endless total beauty in the abundance of materials to use and reuse and reuse and reuse …

This book, in its second edition, is a call to action for the fashion industry and all citizens who engage it—all of us who design, make, buy, wear, and dispose of garments. Janet Hethorn and Connie Ulasewicz began this conversation and continue it today. They see the value of connecting how people live with issues of sustainability, global economics, and the realities of the fashion industry. Their compendium highlights key advances as well as barriers. It renders visible an "essay of clues" that we can all hope leads to a collective, realistic optimism for a positive future. It is an important, inspiring guidepost for fashion in practice.

In the Cradle to Cradle® framework I developed with chemist Michael Braungart, we articulated three key design principles: eliminate the concept of waste, use clean energy flows, and celebrate diversity. Everything we make can be upcycled endlessly—biological nutrients can be returned to the soil and technical nutrients can be repurposed. The framework holistically addresses five attributes: materials as nutrients, material reutilization, renewable energy, water stewardship, and social fairness. When I was a child growing up in Asia, it appeared to me that US society started planned obsolescence for products in order to "churn" the economy, and its people began to live as though there might be no tomorrow—because, thanks to the atom bomb, there actually might not be. Now is the time to put the fear aside, plan for delightful obsolescence, and design for the tomorrow we know is possible. That's why our first textile design with DesignTex, made in the mid-1990s, was beautiful, durable, and cost-effective, but it had other values and qualities too: It saved money, was safe enough to eat, had trimmings that nourish gardens, and converted its mill from one that was polluting water to one that was purifying it.

So, what's next for fashion is, in fact, exactly that: *what's next*—and not just one season. We can creatively define what is next for that garment and its materials, use after use, in beautiful patterns of safe and endless resourcefulness. The fashion industry is both the demand side and the supply side of its business—and it is in the nature of the business to be creating the unusual. So it can certainly apply its charms to refashioning itself to business as unusual. As we practice our commerce, let's remember to ask and answer simple questions: How can something be beautiful if it destroys children's health or the environment? How beautiful can we fashion it as we humbly provide healthy, safe and beautiful abundance as love for all the children of all species for all time?

WILLIAM MCDONOUGH, FAIA, INT. FRIBA, is a widely recognized designer, sustainable growth pioneer, and business strategist. For more than four decades he has defined the principles of the sustainability movement (through his companies: McDonough Innovation, William McDonough + Partners, and MBDC), creating its seminal buildings, products, and writings. He is currently Chair of the World Economic Forum's Meta-Council on the Circular Economy. McDonough is co-creator of the Cradle to Cradle® design framework, and is author of *The Hannover Principles: Design for Sustainability* (1992) and co-author of the influential *Cradle to Cradle: Remaking the Way We Make Things* (2002) and *The Upcycle: Beyond Sustainability—Designing for Abundance* (2013). McDonough has received the Presidential Award for Sustainable Development and the US EPA Presidential Green Chemistry Challenge Award. In 2009 he led the founding of the non-profit Cradle to Cradle Products Innovation Institute to donate the Cradle to Cradle Certified™ Products Program to the public realm. In 2012 he began a collaboration with Stanford University Libraries on a "living archive" of his work and communications. Cradle to Cradle® and C2C® are registered trademarks of MBDC, LLC.

Our Invitation to You to Join the Conversation Now

As you prepare for, or engage in, some aspect of the fashion industry, do you consider how your actions impact sustainable fashion outcomes? Do you think about how fashion can hinder or enhance people's sense of self and their relationships with others? Have you pondered innovative processes and alternative materials that will lend improvements? Are you reluctant to resign yourself to fashion's status quo of unsustainable ways?

If you answered *yes* to these questions, then you are concerned about fashion and sustainability and this book is for you. Within these pages, a conversation continues. The ideas behind it started through conversation; we then invited many writers to join us, and we now invite you to participate.

Addressed within this book are the issues and consequences that consumers, marketers, designers, and product developers engage in as they look for sustainable fashion futures. It features an exploration of systems that facilitate the least burden on the environment with the most benefit to people. Yes, this is complex and involves all aspects of the fashion industry. Anyone involved in any dimension of fashion, from design through product development and promotion, will benefit from reading, discussing, and putting these ideas into action. The time is now for taking action toward sustainability through fashion. Join in the conversation and together we will take action and be a part of what is next.

The format of this book is an anthology, divided into three sections, each focused on an in-depth exploration of sustainable opportunities that we have identified as people, processes, and environment. This innovative model is explained in the introduction and then expanded upon throughout the book. Our model provides an interconnected and circular way to explore these issues that is not possible through old, linear models of understanding the fashion industry. A new and different approach is needed now and as we move forward to what is next.

We begin each section by introducing the overall concepts, issues, and practices that arise within each section's five chapters. Each chapter stands alone, yet together they form the conversation. They may be read in any order. You may come back to some often and skip over others, depending on your current concerns and interests. Within each chapter you will find sidebars, *Ideas in action*, with interviews, case studies, or profiles of professionals, etc. At the end of each chapter there are discussion questions designed to help you think through what you have read and, more importantly, highlight the issues and implications for further development. Included at the end of each section is an example of best practices that businesses or individuals are actively engaged in, as a way to show application of the issues raised within that section. Throughout your reading, please formulate your own challenges and responses to the question "What's next?"

We have invited fashion academics, practitioners, and scholars, each with their own unique knowledge and expertise, to write the chapters that contribute to this dialogue. These contributing writers provide many diverse voices and writing styles, making for lively conversation. The writing is in varying levels of depth and perspectives. And, as with any important conversation, there are conflicts and agreements. Because of the variety in both content and viewpoint, this book is appropriate for graduate and undergraduate students, as well as for people working to bring about change within the fashion industry. It is also important reading for consumers of fashion. We are all in this together. So, thank you for picking up this book. Welcome to the conversation.

New to this Edition

Although considered a second edition, the entire book has been updated, and new topics have been added. Our first edition knitted the terms of sustainability together and presented it as a "Why Now?," yet so much conversation and engagement has taken place in this field since our first edition that the emphasis in this edition is on "What's Next?" Particular examples include:

- Five new contributing writers with five new chapters including new images, diagrams, and points of view:
  Chapter 4: *Social Media as a Tool for Social Change*
  Chapter 5: *Issues of Social Responsibility and the Challenges Faced by the Decision Makers and the Decision Doers*
  Chapter 10: *Technology and Sustainable Futures*
  Chapter 12: *Designing for the Circular Economy: Cradle to Cradle® Design*
  Chapter 15: *Challenges and Propositions: Alternative Approaches to Design and Engagement*
- An emphasis through all chapters on social justice and corporate social responsibility at the people, process, and environmental levels.
- Sidebars within chapters, *Ideas in Action*, focus on an expansion of real-world applications and include interviews, case studies, and profiles of professionals.
- New *Best Practices* at the end of each section reflect applications of the issues raised within that section and include:
  ○ *The Filippa K Story*
  ○ *Sri Lanka: A Model of Sustainable Apparel Industry Initiatives*
  ○ *Peg and Awl: To Make Things out of Other Things*
- Discussion questions at the end of each chapter are designed to help students and professionals think through what's been read and more importantly, highlight the issues and implications for further development.
- The book is sustainably printed on certified paper.

Resources
Sustainable Fashion STUDIO:
- Features online self-quizzes with results and personalized study tips for students.
- Offers videos to bring chapter topics and concepts to life.

Instructor's Resources
- Instructor's Guide.
- Image bank features full-color versions of images that appear in the book.
- Fairchild Books offers STUDIO access free with new book purchases (order ISBN 9781501395383); it is also sold separately through Bloomsbury Fashion Central (www.BloomsburyFashion Central.com).

Terms such as *eco-chic, green,* and *clothing with a conscience* were just developing in 2007 as we sought to answer the question of "Why now?" in the first edition of *Sustainable Fashion.* We were at the forefront of the movement, pulling together the questions to ask and getting the conversation started. We continue to ask whether it is okay to use the word "sustainable" alongside the word "fashion." Most would agree that "sustainable fashion" is somewhat of an oxymoron. After all, sustainability is about longevity, and fashion is about change. Other areas of design activity are quite comfortable with sustainability, yet *sustainable* is a concept not fully embraced by all in the fashion industry. How do we resolve this?

How do we design, develop, produce, wear, and reuse fashion in sustainable ways and still participate with fashion? We must embrace the wide-ranging complexities of sustainability that fashion can address.

"What's next?" By asking the question "sustaining what?" within the context of fashion, we have identified three venues within which to explore sustainability: people, processes, and the environment. Within each segment, we guide you to consider what's next.

People. People consume clothing. They have basic needs that fashion can address. Sustainability works both ways here: as people can sustain the environment by addressing their clothing choices, fashion can also sustain people in various ways. People also make clothing. New to this edition we embrace the social context, the responsibility we have to the social well-being of the people in our global garment industry.

Processes. Processes, both production and economic, continue to have a major impact on the directions that sustainability takes. The way we approach the making of fashion guides the resulting ecological footprint and well-being of society. In this edition, we will also consider the ways that processes can be changed and sustained in relation to new ways of approaching fashion.

Environment. Environmental concerns and opportunities are closely tied to fashion. Since garments are made of materials (e.g., fibers, fabrics, notions), there are direct physical environmental impacts connected to the use, reuse, recycling, resilience, and sustainable actions that surround fashion.

Approaching a Model of Interconnectivity

These segments are interrelated; they do not operate independently, yet each has its own topical focus. By purchasing and wearing clothing, people express choices about their own ecological footprint. Production processes have a major impact on the planet. Clothing has the potential, when designed thoughtfully, to better connect and sustain people as they go about their everyday lives.

The materials available from which to produce fashion items may be unfamiliar to consumers; thus, choices may not be well informed. How do these connections work? We present new ways of thinking about our next steps; yet understanding the expanded and interconnected model is a beginning. How can we, as designers and producers of clothing, impact the many possibilities for sustainable outcomes? How do we take responsibility for informed choices and actions?

This book addresses the issues and consequences that consumers, marketers, designers, and product developers engage in as they move toward and develop sustainable products. It features an exploration of

A model for sustainable fashion: Interconnecting people, processes, and environment. The potential to have a large impact on sustainable issues *through fashion* can be realized when we explore how fashion interacts within all three interconnected areas. Since fashion is more than the materials that garments are made of, we have broader opportunities to explore. The possibilities are much greater when this concept is core to our thinking. (Concept developed by Janet Hethorn and Connie Ulasewicz; illustrated by Joseph M. Sipia)

systems that facilitate the least burden on the environment with the most benefit to people. We are continually reminded of the words written by Yvon Chouinard in his Foreword to our 2008 edition, "There has never yet been, nor is there now, a sustainable business or sustainable fashion on this planet ... We all need to do everything we possibly can to reduce the harm we do to the environment in our work lives as well as in our personal lives." We believe that progress has been made and we seek to engage you, the reader, in a deep exploration of what's next.

Engaging in the "Conversation"

The chapters, interviews, and introductory segments collectively form a conversation. Your reading of these ideas draws you into the conversation too. Through the diverse voices that come together in this book, we investigate, in a broad and meaningful way, what sustainability means alongside fashion. We examine ways of understanding the concepts, as we explore the issues that designers and product developers confront as they go about their business of creating clothing and fashion. We examine practices in all stages of the development process from design through production, retail distribution, consumption, and beyond. Our intention in creating this conversation is to develop a sense of possibility and provide new directions that will allow designers and product developers to work in sustainable ways for sustainable fashion futures.

Understanding Sustainable Fashion

As we contemplate the complexities involved in sustainable fashion, several questions seem to underlie our exploration. The following are a few of these questions, followed by our responses. We feel this will help provide the background to our thinking and approach.

What is Meant by Sustainability?

This question comes up in relation to our book for two reasons. First, it seems that there is some confusion around the term, as it is used so differently in different contexts; and second, it isn't usually a term that is followed by the word "fashion." So let's take a moment to look at where it came from and how we are using it here.

Sustainability, or *the ability to sustain*, is used in conjunction with other terms in order to craft the commonly referred-to definitions. For example, *Our Common Future* (World Commission on Environment and Development, 1987), frequently referred to as the "Brundtland

Report," defines sustainable development as "development that meets the needs of the present without compromising the ability of future generations to meet their own needs." More recently, the Sustainable Apparel Coalition, a group of sustainability leaders from global apparel and footwear companies, was formed with a vision of a sustainable industry that "produces no unnecessary environmental harm and has a positive impact on the people, and communities associated with its activities" (www.apparelcoalition.org).

Fashion has a perhaps surprising, yet quite powerful, role to play in sustainability. Fashion is a process, is expressed and worn by people, and, as a material object, has a direct link to the environment. It is embedded in everyday life. Thus, fashion is ripe for sustainable action on all fronts. So, taking into account broad definitions of sustainability and the unique potential of fashion, sustainability within fashion means that through the development and use of a thing or a process, there is no harm done to people or the planet, and that thing or process, once put into action, can enhance the well-being of the people who interact with it and the environment it is developed and used within.

Most importantly, what does sustainability mean to you? Really think about this and how you might take action related to your answer. It is up to each of us to sort out our own unique course, given our individual passions and possibilities. Through individual introspection, followed by collective action, we will create sustainable futures together.

What is Unique about Fashion that Allows Us to Look at Sustainability in Innovative Ways?

Everyone wears clothing; thus, people have a link to possible improvements toward sustainable fashion and a resilient future. Certainly the people who design, produce, market, and consume and recycle or reuse fashion must be informed and be a part of the larger conversation on sustainable issues and practices. The solution is as close as the clothes on their backs! Fashion provides a major opportunity to broaden sustainable concepts. Fashion provides an opportunity of awareness for sustainability. It is embedded in a system of communication, and it is everywhere.

Fashion is deep and goes directly to who we are and how we connect to one another. Some may think of fashion as frivolous, but it is at the root of the conversation that guides people to respond to the changing world around them. Just consider how massive change could be once the potential of sustainable fashion is realized.

What is also unique to fashion, more so than other sustainable pathways, is that it is a large vehicle. Our industry continues to grow, and in 2012 our global apparel market was valued at US$1.7 trillion and employed approximately 75 million people (www.fashionunited.com). There are many opportunities to purchase and wear clothing, and at many price points and product classifications. People have opportunities to behave in sustainable ways every day when they get dressed, and fashion, when created within a broad understanding of sustainability, can sustain people as well as the environment. People have a desire to make socially responsible choices regarding the fashions they purchase. As designers and product developers of fashion, we are challenged to provide responsible choices. We need to stretch the perception of fashion to remain open to the many layers and complexities that exist. The people, processes, and environments that embody fashion are also calling for new sustainable directions. What a fabulous opportunity awaits!

What's Next for Sustainable Fashion?
Globalization has opened channels of international communication and allowed us the opportunity to question how design, textile, and clothing production decisions affect people and the planet that we all share. The manufacturing of clothing has moved to areas of our world where the lowest wages are paid and we must be concerned about the

air and water pollution created by textile fiber, yarn, and fabric production, and for the people that breathe and wash in these unhealthy environments. Sustainable fashion—what's next permits us to think more creatively about our current fiber and garment production practices and to acknowledge that what we have created in the name of fashion is not okay and needs to change. Preserving the environment is only part of the puzzle. Sustainability is about seeking solutions while maintaining healthy economies and solving social inequities. Fashion connects to all of this. The idea is that creating and consuming fashion uses resources, some renewable and some not. We should use these resources to meet our own needs today while ensuring that future generations will also be able to meet their needs. That's "what's next."

Designers, product developers, retailers, and consumers must continue to model best practices and contribute to the vision of sustainable fashion. We must rethink the processes, and generate new ideas to produce or reproduce garments with a sense of ethics, using appropriate resources and manufacturing them in humane conditions that together sustain the planet and the people that design, produce, retail, and purchase them. The interconnected model of people, processes, and environment that guides this book represents a necessary way of thinking. Fashion is relevant and pleasurable. Together let us realize the sustainable power that can be harnessed by taking the necessary steps asking and embracing the necessary question, "What's next?"

Reference

World Commission on Environment and Development. (1987). *Our common future*. Oxford: Oxford University Press.

ACKNOWLEDGMENTS

Our connections to sustainability began on separate paths but our efforts and commitment quickly aligned. Interactions with our students via projects, debates, and discussions continue to be pivotal to the development of our thinking, and we are thankful for them. It was the energy from these conversations—united with our own passion, commitment, and encouragement from friends, family, and colleagues—that spawned and continues to give life and energy to this project. We thank the contributors for their willingness to join in these growing conversations and craft the vision of sustainability together with us. This book is vibrant due to their diligence and expertise. To the many people at Fairchild who have worked with us to bring this project to you, we are very appreciative. Particular thanks are due to Charlotte Frost (Production Editor), Kiley Kudrna (Editorial Assistant), and Edie Weinberg (Art Development Editor).

The publisher wishes to gratefully acknowledge and thank the reviewers of the first edition whose feedback was invaluable in planning this second edition: Martha Hall, University of Delaware, USA, Melinda K. Adams, University of the Incarnate Word, USA, Hae Jin Gam, Illinois State University, USA, Kim Hiller, Kansas State University, USA, Karen Steen, Cazenovia College, USA, Jennifer Prendergast, Manchester Metropolitan University, UK, and Beverly Bothwell, University of Bedfordshire, UK.

Connecting with People on Sustainable Practices

INTRODUCTION

Looking at sustainability through the lens of fashion provides unique opportunities. Since fashion is both a verb and a noun (i.e., something that is created, expressed, and worn by people), fashion offers myriad opportunities for people to take sustainable actions. By focusing on *people*, their behaviors, their uniqueness, and their interests, this section uncovers exciting possibilities that aren't often considered in contexts of sustainability. These new insights provide an exciting potential for positive change. Real opportunities for change in sustainable practices will occur when the contributions that people make and actions that people take are put into motion. This is an untapped realm to consider when asking the question, "What's next?"

People are the driving force behind sustainable practices. It is really the people, working as designers, retailers, manufacturers, and consumers, living in countries throughout the world, who have power to act in ways to create the most impact, both positive and negative. People are intimately connected to fashion, so we must think about how they behave, what they want, and what might improve their lives and well-being. People are the stakeholders; we are in the unique position to maintain, improve, or destroy our environment through the choices we make. By being smart about these choices and including this knowledge of how to improve the lives and well-being of people through design, product development, and retail decision making, we have interesting opportunities for sustainable outcomes.

We begin this section with an overview of how sustainability as a concept has evolved throughout history and how people have either advanced it or restricted it through their actions and desires. Linda Welters, in Chapter 1, tells this story, beginning in the sixteenth century when clothing was very precious and continuing to the era of overconsumption that we live in today. She weaves together movements and trends in textiles and fashion, laying a beautiful foundation for understanding the history of sustainability in the garment industry and why we need to make changes now.

Recognizing that people are interested in personal and social change, Connie Ulasewicz writes in Chapter 2 about how consumers look to manufacturers and retailers in the sewn products industry to integrate more sustainable practices in the products they market, promote, and sell. She explains how people can become social entrepreneurs by investing in the transformation of the apparel industry through their purchases and monetary contributions to sustainable causes. She lays out simple choices that individuals can make in altering their lifestyles toward sustainability.

Furthering our knowledge about the connection between sustainability and people, in Chapter 3 Janet Hethorn embraces the notion that it is possible to actually sustain people through the vehicle of fashion, as both process and product. Clothing and its expression can figure into providing for and meeting basic needs, including the physical, social, and aesthetic. Toward this end, she encourages us to implement user-centered design thinking as a way to create innovative solutions, thus enhancing sustainability and individual well-being.

Domenica Peterson, in Chapter 4, explores ways that social media can be implemented as a powerful tool for engaging in the sustainable fashion movement. As a millennial herself, Peterson explains the amazing impact that her cohorts, as well as all users of interactive online information, have on industry practices. She provides examples of companies that are successfully engaging consumers via social media, creating transparency and information surrounding social and environmental endeavors. She emphasizes the need to overcome negative practices that advance fast fashion and instead use social media for good.

Chapter 5 completes this section by looking at how clothes are produced, specifically at the people who labor to create the clothes we wear. Connie Ulasewicz identifies and discusses the interconnectedness of the individuals making up manufacturing networks and the challenges they face, in order to help us achieve a greater awareness of "the hands" that bring us what we wear.

What's Next?

- Envision a sustainable consumption model that replaces the outdated overconsumption of clothing. Much more fashionable!
- People need to realize and implement the power to support with their purchases the growth of sustainable practices of retailers and manufacturers.
- Sustainable fashion can enhance the physical, emotional, and psychological well-being of people.
- People are the driving force behind sustainable choices in the fashion industry.

LINDA WELTERS, PHD, is professor in the Textiles, Fashion
Merchandising, and Design Department at the University of Rhode
Island. She has published on European folk dress, archaeological
textiles, American quilts, and American fashion. Her most recent
publication is *The Fashion Reader*, 2nd edition (Berg, 2011), which
she coedited with Abby Lillethun. With Patricia Cunningham, she
coedited *Twentieth-Century American Fashion* (Berg, 2005).

CHAPTER **1**

The Fashion of Sustainability

Linda Welters

To answer the question "What's next?" for sustainable fashion,
we must first look to the past. How has sustainability come and
gone throughout the history of modern fashion, from 1600 until
today? This chapter revisits various movements and trends in fashion
history as they relate to sustainability. Where did these movements
and trends originate? What inspired them? What is currently moving
them forward? An exploration of these questions will lead to an
understanding of why the time for sustainable fashion is indeed now
and what can be done next.

Sustainability: From Necessity to Choice

Sustainability is not a new concept in the history of fashion. It has been
part of the fashion repertoire, albeit in various guises, since the 1960s,
when the counterculture rejected mainstream styles. Yet, long before
the overabundance of goods available to consumers today, economical
use of resources was a way of life.

In the preindustrial era, it took a long time to produce fabrics; thus,
only the elite could afford to participate fully in fashion. Even the
wealthy saved fabrics, remodeled clothes, and sold unwanted items in

the second-hand market. Over the course of four centuries, the concept of sustainability has gone from being a way of life during preindustrial days to a choice in our contemporary era of plenty.

This chapter provides a history of sustainability related to fashion since early modern times. It is divided into three time periods—preindustrial, industrial, and postmodern—which together trace the history of fashion from 1600 to the saturated market we are experiencing today.

Preindustrial Era to Early Industrialization: 1600–1860

Prior to the Industrial Revolution, conserving resources was habitual for the vast majority of humanity simply because of the cost and labor it took to produce the basic necessities of life. Fibers, the raw materials for textiles, came only from nature and were processed into fabrics through laborious, time-consuming processes. For example, flax, the world's oldest fiber, required many steps to go from the mature plant to a fine linen fabric suitable for a gentleman's white shirt. The plant was pulled from the ground and retted to loosen the fibers from the stalk. The sequential processes of braking, scutching, and hackling extracted the strands, which were then combed to straighten them out and to separate long fibers termed *line* from short fibers called *tow* (Coons, 1980). The line was then spun into yarns, woven into *linen* fabric, and finished by bleaching the yardage white. For fine linen fabrics, a finishing process called beetling (i.e., pounding with a wooden mallet-like device) imparted a luster to the fabric. If the fabric was to be dyed, additional steps occurred. The short tow fibers did not go unused. They were processed into coarse fabrics for sacks, mattress covers, and rough workwear. The other major natural fibers besides flax (e.g., wool, silk, and cotton) underwent similar labor-intensive processes to become fabrics.

The Preindustrial World

Textile production was not evenly distributed around the world, resulting in limited fabric choices for consumers despite trade between distant markets. For example, northern Europe's climate was ideal for flax cultivation, but the growing season was too short for cotton cultivation. As a result, Europeans did not wear cotton until the English and Dutch commenced trade with cotton-producing India around the year 1600. Cotton was indigenous to India, where skilled artisans had been painting and printing fine cotton cloth for centuries (Harris, 2004). When the colorful cottons first appeared in Europe, they became the rage among those who could afford them. Their popularity threatened the domestic wool industry in England and the silk industry in France, resulting in legislation against the importation and wearing of Indian painted cottons until the mid-1700s.

Luxurious Apparel for the Wealthy

As a result of the labor involved in production, textiles had high monetary value. Specialized techniques for making luxurious fabrics (e.g., embroidery, lace, brocade, and velvet) further increased prices. Costly raw materials such as silk or gilded thread added additional expense. Conversely, the labor needed to cut and sew fabric into garments was cheap. Thus, the quality of the fabrics in wearing apparel marked a person's status more than its style. Only the aristocracy and the gentry could afford beautiful fabrics and trimmings. They had their clothes made by specialists, who took inspiration from the leading courts of Europe. Portraits that survive from the seventeenth and eighteenth centuries show how elaborate and colorful fashion became in this period. Aristocratic men followed fashion just as closely as women, embellishing themselves with ribbons, bows, and lace. By the eighteenth century, merchants and others of the "middling sort" also sought fashionable clothing as a conduit to higher social standing.

Precious Few Clothes for the Common Folk

Less often depicted in paintings are farmers and laborers, who donned dull-colored clothes of coarse, plain fabrics. Some of these wearers made both the fabric and the clothing themselves. Sometimes neighbors in farming communities bartered rather than paid cash for both raw materials and services such as spinning, weaving, cutting, and sewing (Miller, 2006).

Most people in Europe and North America owned just a few sets of clothes; thus, they had no need for closets. They hung their everyday apparel on hooks and stored seldom-used clothing in trunks. Women altered their best dresses to reflect changes in fashion. People repaired clothes repeatedly to extend wear. A pair of handwoven cotton work trousers in the Historic Textile and Costume Collection at the University of Rhode Island has been patched twenty-four times on the knees and seat (Figure 1.1).

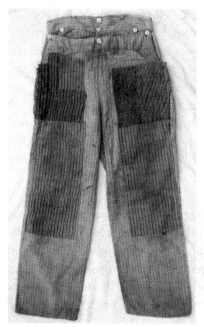

FIGURE 1.1. All but one of the numerous striped and checked fabrics used to repair these cotton work trousers was handwoven. A total of twenty-four patches were used to repair these circa 1830–40 pants from New England. (Photo by Linda Welters. Trousers courtesy of Historic Textile and Costume Collection, University of Rhode Island)

Old but still usable clothes were sold at local markets and through traveling peddlers. Even rags had value, as evidenced by the *ragpicker* of nineteenth-century literature. Clothes were so precious that they were often stolen from laundry baskets or off the backs of drunks leaving taverns and pawned for cash (Lemire, 1990). People named specific clothing items in their wills, as evidenced in the probate documents of the widow Ellinor Quayle Bridson, who died on the Isle of Man in England on April 19, 1764. Bridson carefully enumerated who should receive her unused fabrics as well as specific items of clothing. She bequeathed "unto her eldest son William as much medley [woolen fabric] as will make him a coat and britches," "unto her daughter Jane her red dominey [cloak], a shag hat, best bodys [corset] & stom-anger [stomacher] & her blue calamankey [calimanco, a shiny worsted wool fabric] gown," "unto her daughter Catherine a blue camlet gown & nine yards of poplin for a gown," "unto her two daughters all the check for aprons & all her shaped linen," "unto her mother a new bed gown … , a drugget petticoat, a pledden [probably plaid] petticoat, and a blanket," "unto her maidservant a drugget stripped quilted petticoat," and "unto Jane Bridson Gibdle all the worsted that she had for a gown, the warp double, and the weft single." The remainder of her clothes she bequeathed to her four children "for them to wear" (Will of Ellinor Quayle [als Bridson], 1764). It is worth noting that the fabrics described are mostly wool or linen, which would have been locally available in towns throughout the United Kingdom.

Early Industrialization

During the second half of the eighteenth century, creative minds in Great Britain, France, and America invented devices to mechanize the processing of fiber into fabric (Wilson, 1979). First, John Kay invented the flying shuttle in 1733, which sped up the weaving of cloth. Next, attention turned to the spinning of yarn. In 1767 James Hargreaves developed the spinning jenny, and in 1769 Richard Arkwright invented the water-powered spinning frame. In the 1780s, Edmund Cartwright developed a power loom that could weave cloth by water-powered mill wheels, and in the 1790s Eli Whitney built a machine that ginned cotton. About that same time, Thomas Bell patented the first engraved cylinders to print cloth; previously, printers had stamped the patterns on the cloth with flat copper plates or wooden blocks. This sequence of inventions set the stage for the industrial production of textiles. The Industrial Revolution itself began with innovations in the textiles sector; indeed, Richard Arkwright is remembered as the "father of the Industrial Revolution" (Wilson, 1979, p. 200).

Emergence of Factory-Made Cloth
By the 1820s, factories on both sides of the Atlantic began producing cloth mechanically, which increased supply and reduced price. Farmers stopped cultivating flax for linen and raising sheep for wool. The abundance of inexpensive, factory-made cloth allowed more people to dress well than at any previous period in history.

Introduction of the Fashion Periodical
The same engraved cylinders that printed coloring agents onto textiles could also rapidly print onto paper; soon the inexpensive fashion periodical appeared. Interested women no longer had to rely on letters and word of mouth to learn the latest styles in Europe's fashion capitals. They could subscribe to magazines such as the long-running American periodical *Godey's Lady's Book* (1830–98). Men could peruse the latest trends in publications such as *The Gentleman's Magazine of Fashion* at their favorite tailors. The rate of fashion change accelerated. Local dressmakers and tailors quickly translated printed illustrations into fashionable clothing for clients. Wardrobes, not surprisingly, increased in size, necessitating the inclusion of closets in the building of homes. Textiles for the home also proliferated.

Early Industrialization, the Environment, and Social Responsibility
Early textile manufacturers did not consider the effects of pollution. Textile wet finishing processes used chemicals that were discharged into nearby rivers and streams. Often, neighbors could tell what colors were going onto the cloth because of the residual dye emptied out into the stream adjacent to the local dyehouse or printworks. Also of concern should have been the mordants used to bind coloring agents to the cloth, namely iron, tin, chrome, and copper. Today, mills remove dyes, pigments, and mordants before discharging the spent dyebath into the environment.

The textile industry was not much concerned with fair labor practices, either. Manufacturers looked for the cheapest labor, just as they do now. They employed children, young women, and immigrants, sometimes exploiting their lack of recourse over unfair labor practices. Long hours and fluctuating pay scales characterized the industry in the early years. Conditions in the mills were also problematic. Lung diseases such as tuberculosis spread easily in the moist, lint-laden air. Additionally, the machinery, powered by a system of belts and pulleys, did not stop immediately when turned off. Thus, when clothing or a limb got caught up in the works, serious injuries often resulted. Not all textile manufacturers maintained such inhumane working conditions, however. Some mill owners constructed housing, schools, libraries, and local meeting halls for their employees.

Components of the Mechanized Apparel Factory in Place
Although textile production was mechanized in the first half of the nineteenth century, apparel production was, for the most part, not. Until the invention of the sewing machine in 1846, all sewing was done by hand. Small apparel factories did exist, however, and ready-made clothing was sometimes sold in retail stores and through mail-order catalogs. In the eighteenth century, for example, workers in English factories produced ready-to-wear quilted petticoats for export to the

American colonies (Lemire, 1994). Tailors in American seaside towns stitched jackets and trousers and sold them to sailors on shore leave for just a day or two; the clothes were called *slops* and the stores *slop shops*. Prior to the Civil War, mills in Rhode Island and Massachusetts produced rough fabric known as "negro cloth," which was sewn into crude trousers by local women, then shipped to the South for use by slaves on cotton plantations. However, most apparel was still custom-made in the 1850s. The development of the full-fledged apparel factory depended on the mechanization of textile production. By 1860, all the components were in place.

Industrialization: 1860–1960

In this section, the technological and social developments that affected both the production and consumption of fashion are explored. These include the birth of the couture system, changes in the social system, and the growth of the ready-to-wear industry. These developments paved the way for proliferation of fashionable goods and set the stage for the problem of overabundance that we currently face.

Couture and the Fashion Plate

The couture system was developed in Paris when Charles Frederick Worth, a transplanted Englishman, opened a dressmaking establishment in 1857 that featured a predesigned collection from which clients ordered custom-made copies. This shifted the design function to the dressmaker, whose label now appeared in the garment. It also solidified Paris as the fashion capital of the world for women's dress. For men's dress, England led the way. London's Savile Row gained prominence in establishing trends among the elite for both town and country clothes. The wealth created through the Industrial Revolution ensured a healthy client base for both Paris couturiers and London tailors.

While those at the top of the social strata displayed their status through acquisition of prestigious fashions made in the world's style capitals, the rising middle class wanted to be in style too. They aspired to move up the social ladder with the help of a respectable appearance. Fashion plates in the proliferating number of women's magazines and tailoring guides allowed everyone to follow the latest fashions from Europe, close facsimiles of which could be obtained through local dressmakers, tailors, or retail stores. The development of the paper pattern industry in the 1860s gave those with sewing skills the opportunity to assemble fashionable garments at home (Emery, 2014). Ebenezer Butterick of Sterling, Massachusetts, began selling tissue paper patterns for boys' and men's wear in 1863. His business expanded rapidly to include patterns for women's fashions. Soon women's magazines included paper patterns too. *Harper's Bazaar*, founded in 1867, published trends for clothes, accessories, and hairdos as well as pattern supplements so that enterprising subscribers could recreate the fashions for themselves.

Technology, Manufacturing, and Retail in the Late Nineteenth Century

Technological developments continued to occur in textile manufacturing. By this time all types of textiles, including the laces, velvets, and patterned silks that previously constituted the most expensive fabrics, were made by machine. Synthetic dyes were introduced after William Perkin discovered mauve in 1856, ushering in a period of bright purples, pinks, blues, and oranges in fashion fabrics.

The second half of the nineteenth century also saw the development of the apparel factory, where multiples of prevailing styles were made in a range of sizes. Several factors contributed to America's rapid leap forward as a producer of manufactured clothing. These factors included the lower cost and greater availability of textiles; the invention of the sewing machine; the standardization of sizing for menswear due to advances in the production of military uniforms during the Civil War;

and immigration, both as a source of skilled labor and as a market for ready-to-wear apparel. Jewish immigrants from Europe often came with experience in the garment industry as tailors, peddlers, and shop owners (Goldstein & Greenberg, 2012). They played an important part in developing the apparel and the retail industries in North America.

Technological advances (e.g., vertical knives to cut multiple layers of fabric, electricity to power equipment, and steam pressers) improved production (Kidwell & Christman, 1974). The new, ready-made clothes were distributed through a novel retail venue, the department store. These emporiums brought manufactured goods to the middle classes in stylish settings, first in major cities like London, Paris, New York, Boston, and Chicago, and then in smaller cities. The development of department stores occurred in the second half of the nineteenth century at the same time that the Industrial Revolution produced increasing amounts of manufactured products (Figure 1.2). Distribution to areas far from urban centers expanded with the railroad. Mail-order catalogs made fashionable ready-to-wear clothing available to farmers and ranchers who had settled in the Midwest and western territories of the United States and Canada.

A significant textile and apparel production complex developed in America and Great Britain after the sewing machine sped up clothing and shoe assembly (Kidwell & Christman, 1974). As the nineteenth century drew to a close, factories produced all manner of menswear and children's wear as well as certain women's garments that did not require a customized fit. Women's dresses, because of the close-fitting bodices that dominated fashion, continued to be made to order until styles changed in the first quarter of the twentieth century.

Women's ready-to-wear apparel expanded rapidly after French designer Paul Poiret introduced new, loose-fitting tunic dresses in the late Edwardian period (circa 1908). Copies of his simplified styles could be successfully sized for a range of body types and manufactured as ready-to-wear garments. Dressmakers decreased in number, while women's designers and brands proliferated.

FIGURE 1.2. In this March 1921 illustration, "Along Fifth Avenue," from *Harper's Bazaar*, a maid is removing a hat from a hatbox as her mistress, dressed in a negligee, looks on. The woman's negligee is from Bonwit Teller, an exclusive New York City department store. Three dresses hang in the closet, suggesting greater choice than in the past, thanks to less expensive, mass-manufactured clothing for women. (Illustration courtesy of Historic Textile and Costume Collection, University of Rhode Island)

Paris labels were much desired. Coco Chanel, Madeleine Vionnet, and Jean Patou were just some of the designer labels to flourish in the years between World Wars I and II. American apparel manufacturers both legally and illegally copied designs from Paris couturiers and manufactured them in the United States for sale at a fraction of the price of the originals. Companies scattered throughout the country created attractive, wearable fashions for style-conscious Americans.

New York City was known for women's dresses and coats. California, with its casual lifestyles, excelled at manufacturing sportswear. Chicago and Kansas City were home to menswear companies, while a cluster of cities north of Boston, made shoes.

World War II and Fashion

World War II cut off Paris from the rest of the fashionable world. British and American firms began to highlight their own designers, which strengthened the identities of non-Parisian labels. Leading department stores promoted home-grown designers in window displays, advertising campaigns, and award ceremonies. Consumers balanced personal style with patriotism and the practical need to send scarce resources to the front lines. Nylon, for example, went into parachutes, not stockings. Some women, early social entrepreneurs, drew seams down their bare legs to simulate fashionable stockings. Sustainability may not have been the goal, but, as with the movements to come in the 1960s, social consciousness demonstrated the ability to control consumption, ergo production.

After the war, Paris once again rose to dominance with the opening of Christian Dior's couture house in 1947. Dior's New Look influenced women's fashion for more than a decade and reinstated France to its former position as fashion's world leader. Fashion once again followed the decrees of French designers. Americans, Europeans, Australians, South Africans, and many other nationalities wore Parisian-inspired styles, discarding the old and donning the new as fashion changed.

Introduction of Manufactured Fibers

From the late nineteenth century through the mid-twentieth century, numerous types of manufactured fibers appeared in the marketplace. Artificial silk, first produced commercially by Count Hilaire de Chardonnet in 1891, was renamed rayon in 1924 and took off in the marketplace for women's hosiery and silk-like dresses. Rayon's close relative, acetate, soon followed. Nylon made its debut in 1939, just before World War II began. Fiber research accelerated in the postwar era when attention turned away from military needs and toward consumer products. Acrylic and polyester were introduced for a variety of apparel products. While rayon and acetate came from regenerated cellulose, or wood pulp, which is a renewable resource, the new synthetic fibers (e.g., nylon, acrylic, and polyester) came from fossil fuels (e.g., oil, gas, and coal), which are non-renewable resources. This disparity would become an issue for the environmental movement later in the twentieth century.

Glimmerings of an Anti-Fashion Movement

As the nuclear age dawned, rumblings of dissatisfaction surfaced in America and Europe. Many people feared the atomic bomb. Some young people began to resent the social conformity expected during the postwar era and formed subcultures. In the 1950s, a subculture known as the Teddy Boys and a group of playwrights and writers dubbed the Angry Young Men appeared in Great Britain. In the United States, the Beat Generation grew from a handful of writers and poets into a full-blown youth phenomenon by 1959. Subcultural heroes appeared on the silver screen (e.g., Marlon Brando in 1953's *The Wild One* and James Dean in 1955's *Rebel Without a Cause*), foreshadowing the youth revolution of the 1960s. The clothing choices of these groups revealed a tendency to reject fashion in favor of blue-collar workers' clothing, specifically blue jeans, T-shirts, and boots. Old army jackets and second-hand clothes were also featured in their wardrobes. The glimmerings of an anti-fashion movement had appeared on the horizon, a movement that would profoundly influence the direction of fashion in the following decade. This was a pivotal moment for the rejection of the old ways of producing and consuming fashion, ushering in an era of exploration for a more sustainable future.

Postmodern Times: 1960 to the Early Twenty-First Century

This section explores how fashion production and consumption changed in the postmodern era. During the 1960s, England and Italy joined France as fashion centers. As the first of the babies born after World War II grew up, youthful fashions took center stage. Novelty in fashion was much desired in order to mirror rapid social changes. Department stores, which experienced a three- to six-month lag time from placing orders until the merchandise arrived in stores, faded in popularity. Instead, boutiques with new styles appearing daily became the retail darlings. Throwaway fashion, cheap and disposable, replaced the classic styling of the 1950s and early 1960s. This was epitomized in the paper dress. New fibers and fabrics appeared with rapidity. Spandex, vinyl, saran, polyethylene, and polypropylene emerged from the chemists' laboratories. Couture designers soon incorporated these new materials into mini dresses, jumpsuits, coats, shoes, boots, and hats. Paco Rabanne, for example, made dresses out of linked plastic or aluminum disks (Lehnert, 2000). The decade itself was characterized by swift change influenced by political unrest and social protest. Civil rights and the anti-war movement caused liberals to rethink the status quo. It was also the era of urban renewal, during which developers razed old neighborhoods and downtowns in the name of progress.

The space race contributed to an aura of futurism that pervaded the 1960s. In 1968, the crew of the Apollo 8 command module took the first photograph of Earth as seen from space. Space exploration inspired fashion designers. André Courrèges, with his otherworldly styles, was dubbed the "space age" designer.

Emergence of the Counterculture

In 1962, Rachel Carson's *Silent Spring* raised awareness of the damage done to the environment as a result of the increased use of chemicals. The culprits included cotton growers, who used large amounts of pesticides and fertilizers to achieve greater crop yields, as well as textile manufacturers, who discharged chemical-laden water from their mills into local rivers and streams. Leather tanners were especially oblivious to the problems they created using old-fashioned production methods. The 1998 motion picture *A Civil Action* tells the story of one such company in Woburn, Massachusetts, where an unusually high number of children developed cancer as a result of toxic waste dumped in a pond near the factory. Those concerned with the environment began the ecology movement, the forerunner of today's efforts toward creating a sustainable future for our planet. Over the years, the issues have ranged from pesticides to nuclear power, acid rain to ozone depletion, and deforestation to global warming.

At the end of the 1960s, a counterculture developed among youth in a number of Western countries that rejected the values of their parents' generation, including the way their elders followed fashion. The sixties youth wore jeans, workshirts, personalized tie-dyed T-shirts, love beads, and old-fashioned items acquired in second-hand stores. Women wore their hair long and gave up makeup, in effect rejecting the beauty industry. Men stopped cutting their hair and shaving, which introduced the word "unisex" to the lexicon, as both sexes looked alike in their long hair and jeans. A group of art students at Pratt Institute in Brooklyn, New York, embraced fiber as an art form (Dale, 1986). They crocheted yarns of natural fibers into textured, organic garments that could just as easily be displayed on a wall as worn on the body. The art-to-wear movement had begun.

By 1970, the counterculture had profoundly influenced fashion. Old rules of etiquette that dictated correct attire for specific occasions broke down. People did not need to dress up any more; consequently, they adopted casual attire for everyday wear. Jeans made their way into everyone's wardrobe. Consumers developed an aversion to synthetics, preferring the *natural* look. The back-to-the-earth movement was born (Figure 1.3). Color palettes showed a preference for tan, brown, gold, and avocado green. Even footwear got into the act. While hand-crafted leather sandals had been a favorite of the hippies in the 1960s, hiking boots became the footwear of choice for the back-to-the-land crowd. In Denmark, Anne Kalso developed the Earth Shoe™, based on negative heel technology. Advertisements claimed that it was like walking on the beach, leaving footprints in the sand (The Kalso Story, 2014).

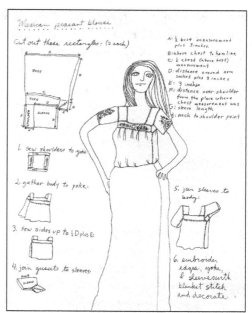

FIGURE 1.3. This drawing, "Directions for Making a Mexican Peasant Blouse," appeared in Alicia Bay Laurel's *Living on the Earth*, which was published in 1971. Laurel lived on Wheeler Ranch in Sonoma County, California, in the 1970s. She wrote and illustrated the book for others living on communes. *Living on the Earth* sold 350,000 copies and appeared on the *New York Times* Bestseller List. (Illustration copyright Alicia Bay Laurel)

The Link between Consumption and Conservation

Ecology was the buzzword, and natural fibers rebounded. The link was drawn between consumption and conservation. Debates about which fibers and fabrics depleted resources took place—to wit, while cotton, a natural fiber, was renewable, it was not as durable as polyester, meaning that it would require replacement more quickly. It also took longer to dry in the clothes dryer, using up more energy than quick-drying synthetics. Additionally, it needed ironing. Double-knitted polyester, on the other hand, a favorite of the early 1970s, earned a reputation for being too "plastic" as the decade progressed. Synthetic fiber manufacturers responded to these debates with modifications to make their products more wearable and more environmentally friendly. Fiber producers built grooves into the fibers to improve wicking of moisture away from the skin. In the United Kingdom, researchers looked for more environmentally friendly methods to produce rayon, which resulted in the new fiber lyocell in the 1990s. This regenerated cellulose fiber is marketed under the trade name Tencel®. Although chemically identical to rayon, the solvent that is used in lyocell production is more easily recovered than the solvents involved in the production of rayon. Research into improving synthetic fibers continued in the 1980s, and in 1990 the high-denier microfiber was introduced to the marketplace. "High-tech" fabric developments have occurred regularly in recent decades, inspiring fashion designers to create new styles using these fabrics.

Emergence of Environmentalism and Social Consciousness

In the meantime, production of fashion items began moving out of countries with mature economies to developing nations in the Caribbean and in Asian countries. Low labor costs reduced the price of apparel to the point where the average family could buy clothes more often than in the past. Shopping became a national pastime. Malls proliferated. Outlet stores and off-price retailers appeared as a venue for manufacturers to get rid of overstock.

Consumers themselves began to consider how to dispose of unused clothes. They purged their closets to get rid of clothes and shoes no longer worn yet still in good shape. Church rummage sales and yard sales were one method of finding a second life for apparel and other goods. But these venues were not enough. Soon Goodwill, The Salvation Army, and other purveyors of second-hand clothes were inundated and no longer disposed of their stock domestically. They started shipping bales of used clothing to Third World countries, particularly in Africa. In those countries, indigenous textile and apparel industries sometimes suffered the consequences of decreased demand in the face of cheap used clothing from America and Europe sold in local markets. Karen Hansen (2000) has studied this phenomenon in Zambia, while Pietra Rivoli (2005) investigated the used clothing markets of Tanzania.

The 1980s saw an increase in the acceptability of wearing "used" clothing by fashionable young people in developed countries, although for the most part as a fashion choice and not with an eye toward conservation. Movies such as *Desperately Seeking Susan* in 1985 showed how stars like Madonna borrowed old items to create new looks. The punk movement, a subculture that first appeared in Great Britain and spread internationally, endorsed the mixing of old clothes with new, edgy garments. "Vintage" entered the fashion scene, and used clothing found a new market. Upscale used clothing stores opened across the United States with names like Second Time Around and Elite Repeat. By the 1990s, actresses began donning vintage designer gowns on the red carpet in an effort to distinguish themselves from the competition.

Some brands incorporated socially conscious advertising to promote their products, although critics argued that the companies were just capitalizing on these issues. Still, these advertising campaigns once again proved how social consciousness can affect consumer behavior. Leading the way was Benetton, an Italian firm that produced knitwear. During the 1980s and 1990s, their controversial ads explored issues of racism, religion, and gender. The company has continued its commitment to social causes by focusing on world hunger and human rights.

In the 1990s the consumer's consciousness was raised again, this time under the banner of *environmentalism*. Organic cotton and Sally Fox's naturally colored cottons (e.g., FoxFibre®) drew attention, as did hemp, which can be grown without fertilizers (Figure 1.4).

A new link had been made between conservation and the environment, but organic cotton did not fare well with consumers at the time, who were more concerned about price than the environment. Wellman Inc., a New Jersey company, began recycling PET polyester soda bottles for fiber. Some of this fiber, labeled Fortrel® EcoSpun™, appeared in the new fleece fabrics. Other companies began researching renewable raw materials, such as soybeans and corn, for fiber.

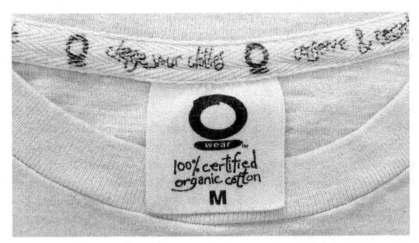

FIGURE 1.4. Label for a 1994 organic cotton T-shirt by O Wear. The twill tape around the neck is printed with the phrases "change your clothes" and "conserve & recycle." (Photograph by Linda Welters)

The Conscientious Lifestyle and its Challenges

Environmentalists and those sympathetic to environmental issues developed a conscientious lifestyle. Healthy eating, regular exercise, and fuel-efficient cars characterized this segment of the population. They also signified their values through their appearance. They wore comfortable "classic" styles and socially conscious brands. Companies associated with outdoor clothing such as Patagonia and L.L.Bean became favorites of environmentalists. Small companies offering hemp clothing emerged. As handcrafted sandals and Earth Shoes had before them, a new brand of footwear from the German company Birkenstock gained cachet within the environmental movement.

Meanwhile, the drive to lower prices for apparel resulted in labor abuses and unsafe working conditions in apparel factories both in the United States and abroad. Illegal immigrants to the United States sometimes found work as operators in apparel factories, where long hours and unsafe conditions were standard operating procedures. Low-wage countries in the Caribbean Basin and the Far East expanded their production. The National Labor Committee exposed conditions in sweatshops that manufactured clothing lines by television talk-show host Kathie Lee Gifford in the 1990s. Consumer pressure on big-name companies connected to sweatshops such as Nike affected sales; the companies responded with programs that certified fair labor practices in their factories. Yet the consumer still wanted the cheapest price, and problems persisted in the global apparel business. Labor abuses spring up in new places every year in the apparel industry. Unsafe working conditions surfaced in Bangladesh in 2012 and 2013, where 118 workers died in two separate factory fires and 1,129 workers died when a building collapsed. The textile industry also began moving offshore. High labor costs were one reason, but the increased expense of meeting environmental legislation was another. Developing countries with lower wages and less stringent environmental regulations took up the slack. In effect, industrialized countries exported their environmental problems to countries eager to develop the manufacturing sector of their economies.

Now Is the Time for Sustainable Fashion

The early twenty-first century is an era of overabundance. Well-designed clothes are available at all price levels, including mass merchandise chains such as Target, H&M, and Zara. New styles are presented so frequently that the industry has labeled this sector *fast fashion*. Everyone can afford to be fashionable and to change his or her wardrobe regularly. Fashion is again disposable. And consumers want variety in their wardrobes. Ours is an era when women have different handbags and shoes for each outfit. Space is needed to store all the clothes and accessories necessary to maintain a fashionable appearance. This means that large walk-in closets are standard features in new homes. For the consumer goods that do not fit in our homes, storage units are available.

Interest in fashion is at an all-time high. Cities in all corners of the globe, from Tokyo, Seoul, and Shanghai to Sydney, Dubai, and Sao

Paulo, have joined the ranks of world fashion capitals. Educational institutions are expanding to serve students from throughout the world who seek to pursue careers in fashion. Fashion, with its propensity for change, is not going away anytime soon. How future generations deal with overabundance, fair labor practices, and environmental concerns is of paramount importance to the well-being of the planet.

The time is right for the fashion industry and consumers to embrace sustainability. The many advances being made in the technology sector are ripe for development. Increased awareness of the damage caused by greenhouse gases calls for stricter environmental controls for the industry, particularly in developing countries. In an era of fast, disposable fashion, designers must consider the problem of post-consumer waste as well as the working conditions of the people who actually make the clothes. Consumers themselves have a growing awareness of practices that lead to sustainable living. The interest in and potential for sustainability in the production and consumption of textile and apparel products is unique to our times.

Conclusion
This chapter explored the development of fashion from 1600 to the present in terms of sustainability. Textiles were scarce in the beginning of the period, requiring laborious processes to produce usable cloth; consequently, people had few clothes. Both clothes and fabrics had value and were passed on to heirs. People practiced sustainability without realizing it. The Industrial Revolution ushered in an era of abundant fabrics, followed by the mechanized production of apparel. Fashionable apparel became available to all classes of people in industrialized countries, sometimes at the expense of the environment and through unfair labor practices. Over the past few decades, however, a growing awareness of environmental issues in the production of textiles and apparel has resulted in some improvements.

We still have a long way to go. The solution lies with researchers, designers, regulators, and consumers who conceive of and choose to wear safer, healthier, and more environmentally sound fashion in the future.

Discussion Questions

1 How did Americans and Europeans dispose of clothing in 1750? How do we dispose of clothing we no longer want today?
2 A case study by the Harvard Business School (9-703-497) on Zara, the Spanish fast fashion firm, included a quote that the company designed fashions with "reasonable but not excessive physical quality: clothes to be worn 10 times" (Ghemawat & Nueno, 2003). How many times on average do you wear clothing items? What might designers and consumers do to improve this picture?
3 What are some benchmarks in the history of fibers? Are natural fibers or manufactured fibers more sustainable?

References

Coons, M. (1980). *All sorts of good sufficient cloth: Linen-making in New England, 1640–1860*. North Andover, MA: Merrimack Valley Textile Museum.

Dale, J. S. (1986). *Art to wear*. New York: Abbeville Press.

Emery, J. (2014). *A history of the paper pattern industry: The home dressmaking fashion revolution*. London: Bloomsbury Academic.

Ghemawat, P. & Nueno, J. L. (2003). Zara: Fast fashion. *Harvard Business Review*. Retrieved July 23, 2014, from http://hbr.org/product/zara-fast-fashion/an/703497-PDF-ENG.

Goldstein, G. M. & Greenberg, E. E. (Eds.) (2012). *A perfect fit: The garment industry and American Jewry, 1860–1960*. Lubbock: Texas Tech University Press.

Hansen, K. T. (2000). *Salaula: The world of secondhand clothing and Zambia*. Chicago: University of Chicago Press.

Harris, J. (Ed.) (2004). *5,000 years of textiles*. Washington, DC: Smithsonian Books.

The Kalso Story. (2014). Retrieved July 23, 2014, from http://www.earthbrands.com/kalsoearthshoe/kalso-the-kalso-stor.

Kidwell, C. B. & Christman, M. C. (1974). *Suiting everyone: The democratization of clothing in America*. Washington, DC: Smithsonian Institution Press.

Lehnert, G. (2000). *A history of fashion in the twentieth century*. Cologne, Germany: Könemann.

Lemire, B. (1990). The theft of clothes and popular consumerism in early modern England. *Journal of Social History, 24*(2), 255–76.

Lemire, B. (1994). Redressing the history of the clothing trade in England: Ready-made clothing, guilds, and women workers, 1650–1800. *Dress, 21*, 61–74.

Michelson, M. (2007, April). Project green all-stars. [Electronic version]. *Outside*, 76.

Miller, M. (2006). *The needle's eye: Women and work in the age of revolution*. Amherst: University of Massachusetts Press.

Rivoli, P. (2005). *The travels of a T-shirt in the global economy*. Hoboken, NJ: John Wiley & Sons.

Will of Ellinor Quayle (als Bridson) (1764). Retrieved July 23, 2014, from http://www.isle-of-man.com/manxnotebook/famhist/wills/1764_eq.htm.

Wilson, K. (1979). *A history of textiles*. Boulder, CO: Westview Press.

CONNIE ULASEWICZ, PHD, is an international consultant focusing on issues of socially responsible manufacturing practices and product reuse. She engages with students as a professor at San Francisco State University and with industry professionals through PeopleWearSF (www.peoplewearsf.org). "Fashion is about change," she says. "If sustainable design and development are our goals, then let us engage thoughtfully and intelligently as we participate in changing what is considered fashionable."

CHAPTER **2**

Social Responsibility and Innovation in the Sewn Products Industry

Connie Ulasewicz

Consumers are looking to manufacturers and retailers to offer more responsible clothing manufactured using socially and environmentally sound methods that enable them to tread lightly on Earth. Pairing their passion for style with a passion for positive change, consumers are increasingly becoming agents of change— social entrepreneurs who invest not only in a transformation of the fashion industry but in the welfare of society and the planet that we all share.

> *It's got to be fashion and not what people perceive as "organic fashion"—those hippie, oatmeal type of clothing—they have to be gorgeous clothes. Otherwise, no one would buy them.*
>
> —Katharine Hamnett, *DNR*, August 8, 2005

Sustainable Fashion: Trend or Mandatory Movement?

The ongoing overexploitation of natural resources and the destruction of the environment have pushed many consumers of fashionable products to question their purchases. We read that the clothing, footwear, and textile industries are second only to agriculture in consuming the most water and contaminating waterways with chemicals for bleaching, dyeing, and finishing fashion products (Chouinard & Stanley, 2012). We hear the terms "sustainable design," "second life," "slow fashion," "ecouterre" and wonder whether these terms are a trendy response to this environmental degradation or a necessary movement within our industry.

Looking at the food industry, one can find an interesting parallel. Environmental journalist Michael Pollan writes about how the present food system is "unsustainable" because of its dependence on fossil fuels and the price in human and environmental health that we can not afford (Pollan, 2011). He explains that normally a sharp distinction is made between people's actions as citizens, in which they are expected to consider the well-being of society, and their actions as consumers. As a consumer we may look at the price as the deciding factor when purchasing food or apparel products, while as a citizen we may consider the seeds, where and how the ingredients were grown, fertilized, and harvested, and the water and air the farmers and community breathe and drink in the process of production.

The sustainable apparel shopper appears to be struggling and pushing to reconcile the roles of being a conscientious consumer and a conscientious citizen. We are actively looking for clothes that we consider "responsible," that make us feel like we are treading lightly on Earth by practicing consumerism with a conscience. Some of us push our expectations for positive change and our passion for style by searching for garments made from fibers whose production respects the environment, sold by retailers with a strong ethical component. We question the sustainability of natural fibers (e.g., cotton or wool) and synthetic fibers (e.g., nylon or polyester) as we learn about new fibers and fabrics like Eco-Spun, a sheepskin-like fabric made from recycled soda bottles; Lenpur, a cashmere-like fabric made from wood pulp of white pine trees; soya, a silky and soft cotton-like fabric made from soybeans; and sasawashi, a cotton or linen-like naturally absorbent fabric made from a mixture of kumazasa bamboo with washi, a type of rice paper. Some of us also look beyond the brand or designer label and seek substance with our style, purchasing products that give a percentage of sales or profits back to the environment or support social causes such as breast cancer or heart disease. Social responsibility in this context relates to the raw materials, design, production, merchandising, retailing, consumption, and disposal of textile and apparel products (Dickson & Eckman, 2007; Ulasewicz & Baugh, 2013).

This chapter focuses on the needs and desires of the consumer, the retailers, and the manufacturers who work together to create and are a part of conscious consumerism. Each of us has the option to choose where, when, and how we spend or choose not to spend our money, on a particular brand, line of clothing, or style of T-shirt. More and more, we are acting like socially responsible agents who desire personal change and respond as social entrepreneurs by investing in the transformation of our industry, society, and planet. At the same time, retailers and manufacturers are increasingly embracing this movement of social entrepreneurialism by launching cause marketing campaigns that promote products through philanthropic activities that give back to the community in order to align themselves with our desires to be good citizens. Exemplary retailers and manufacturers are highlighted throughout the following pages. The chapter closes with some suggested guidelines to follow as we act as conscientious citizens and consumers making honest evaluations of new products, processes, and the myriad of issues that surround sustainable choices in our textile and apparel industries.

> *Consumerism even when it tries to embrace "sustainable" products, is a set of values that teaches us to define ourselves, communicate our identity, and seek meaning through accumulation of stuff, rather than through our values and activities in our community.*
> —Annie Leonard, Stuff activist, *yes!* Fall 2013

Consumers as Social Entrepreneurs and the Power of New Ideas

I like to think of consumers, you and me, as agents of change; we push fashion corporations and businesses to make the right decisions that reflect the needs of the time. My theory is based on the idea that textile and apparel businesses are launched by people who are inspired with design ideas and impassioned to see their ideas become reality. The US domestic textile industry, fueled by the entrepreneurial visions of New England mill owners such as Samuel Slater and Francis Lowell, pushed the Industrial Revolution forward in the eighteenth century. These entrepreneurs pioneered the domestic textile industry with their cloth-producing factories and mill systems (Dunwell, 1978). Apparel design and production followed a different path. In the mid-nineteenth century, Charles Fredrick Worth, an English-born fashion designer, made his mark in Paris by creating what has been termed *haute couture*. He turned his dressmaking practice into a seasonal line of dresses from which his patronesses would choose a design for him to custom fit. It was not until many years later, in the twentieth century, that French designers no longer dominated fashion and an international industry was launched (Cosgrave, 2000). In 1938, *Vogue* published its first annual American issue, highlighting the creations of Claire McCardell, Norman Norell, Mainbocher, and others who birthed another revolutionary concept by designing American sportswear. These individuals, self-motivated by their design-based product ideas, envisioned themselves and their products as engines of change as they launched new textile and apparel industries in the twentieth century. Who are the visionaries, the system reimaginers, and what will be the best practices of the twenty-first century?

Social Entrepreneurialism in the Twenty-First Century

The spirit of entrepreneurialism that fuels change in our industry is different today than in the days of Samuel Slater, Charles Worth, or American sportswear designer Claire McCardell because the challenges are different. Today, we produce and purchase fashion products, including fabrics, trims, and accessories, that inflict damage upon our planet and our people, thereby creating significant social problems. The new entrepreneurs in our industry must have the ability to solve social problems on a large scale. Called "social entrepreneurs," they must be able to persuade, enlighten, touch hearts, shift perceptions, articulate new meanings, and move new concepts through the fashion system. Social entrepreneurship scholars and authors David Bornstein and Susan Davis (2010) describe contemporary social entrepreneurs as transformative forces. These are people who are relentless in pursuit of their visions, who will not take no for an answer, and who will not give up until they have created the change that they believe needs to happen. The term "social entrepreneur" is now spearheaded by individuals as well as companies made of individuals working together with other companies and individuals along the supply chain. The term refers to changemakers, as Beverly Schwartz describes, and what is needed to survive in a world increasingly defined by change are collaborators, or "collaborative entrepreneurships" (2012, p. xiii). Consider the following simple definition of the social entrepreneur or the socially entrepreneurial organization working collaboratively (Garlow & Tafel, 2013):

- tenacious leadership with pragmatic vision;
- the solution addresses a clear social problem;
- the solution changes systems, not symptoms of the problem;
- the model prioritizes social impact over financial gain.

In the twenty-first century, social entrepreneurs are looking for new strategies to benefit society. One such strategy might involve using both charitable contributions and private investment capital—a focus on the needs of the consumer or people on the planet rather than the needs of a company.

One example of such a strategy, first launched in 2005 by Paul David Hewson, or Bono, the activist and Irish singer in the post-punk band U2 and his wife, Ali Hewson, is the global fashion brand Edun (or *nude* spelled backward). Instead of bringing charity to Africa by donating

FIGURE S2.1. A portion of the sales of each EDUN ONE tee goes directly back to the Apparel Lesotho Alliance to Fight AIDS, which provides lifesaving care to factory workers and their families. (Photo courtesy of Adam M. Lee)

money, Edun brings manufacturing jobs that pay living wages to people, thus building sustainable growth opportunities. For spring 2014, 85 percent of the Edun Collection was produced in sub-Saharan Africa. Equally, Edun acts as a voice to encourage the fashion community to do business in Africa as a means to bring the continent out of extreme poverty. Another part of Bono's commitment was the cofounding of the ONE campaign in 2004 with Bobby Shriver. The ONE campaign is a unified effort to rally people, one by one, to fight the emergency of global AIDS and extreme poverty in Africa. In 2006 Shriver and Bono founded (PRODUCT) RED, mobilizing manufacturers, retailers, and consumers to produce, market, and purchase PRODUCT (RED) goods, raising more than $250 million for HIV/AIDS programs in Africa since it was founded.

Behavior Shift in Reuse

As we begin to recognize and acknowledge that fiber, fabric, and design innovations are required by our industry to design, manufacture, and retail sustainable products, we begin to better appreciate the work of the social entrepreneurs who have the passion to move us forward. Social entrepreneurs in our industry are required to shift behavior patterns and perceptions. Some question who initiates the change, the manufacturers and retailers or the consumers, and who responds to the change, again, the manufacturers and retailers or the consumers. Try visualizing the process as a symbiotic relationship—consumers and apparel companies holding each other accountable for their actions. This pushes the sustainable momentum forward. The rise of social entrepreneurship can be seen as a development that has occurred across the world over the past three decades with the emergence of millions of new citizen organizations (Bornstein & Davis, 2010). Organizations inspired by individuals who create new models to promote social well-being restore the environment and create wealth, thereby continuing the cycle of promoting social well-being.

FIGURE 2.1. Clothes collection bins placed in convenient locations that people can remember make it easy for citizens to recycle. The average American consumes 70 pounds of textiles a year. More than 85 percent of this is discarded with the trash. (Photo by Adam M. Lee)

The social need for clothing consumption stems from planned obsolescence; the very function of fashion fuels the excessive need for change, and the continual replacement of garments leads to a rising volume of textiles in landfill .

—Tullia Jack, *Fashioning Use*, p. 124

New Processes to Continue the Clothing Lifecycle

Consider for a moment when you design, make, or purchase an article of clothing or any textile product, such as sheets or towels. Is it a need or a want? And consider what you do with the product when you no longer use it. Do you pitch or sell it or even think about what happens to it when you are finished with it? Reuse, repurpose, upcycling, and recycling are practices aimed at keeping pre- and post-consumer market goods (such as fabrics, trims, clothing, bedding, linens) from ending up in landfill sites as solid waste materials. In 2012, discarded textile products were estimated at 14.3 million tons, or 3.6 percent of all municipal solid waste collected by garbage services in the United States (USEPA, 2012). Less than 16 percent of all textile waste placed in the garbage was recovered (reused or exported) (USEPA, 2012). The remaining 85 percent goes to landfills (SMART, 2012). For every ton of textile products diverted from landfill and reused, an estimated 20 tons of CO_2 emissions are eliminated from the atmosphere (Hunt, 2011, p. 14).

> *The responsible company owes its customers safe, high-quality products and services; this applies to both basics and high end goods. Goods should be well made, durable, and easily repaired. Whatever comes to the end of its useful life needs to be recycled or repurposed into something new.*
> —Yvon Chouinard & Vincent Stanley, *The Responsible Company*, p. 29

Manufacturing previously used fabric into new products provides an opportunity to keep fabric out of the waste stream and remain in a new, secondary fiber/textile supply chain, a cradle-to-cradle model (McDonough & Braungart, 2002). A key to the success of a circular economy or closed loop process is the donation or bringing back of unwanted goods to a collection site, charity organization, or the retailer/manufacturer from whom the goods were purchased. Companies such as Patagonia, Eileen Fisher, Nike, and H&M have begun the process of asking for and taking back products, some offering money for the collection of goods (Figure 2.2). Other US secondhand stores such as Goodwill Industries or Salvation Army have an additional

FIGURE 2.2. Reuse-a-Shoe is a key component of Nike's long-term commitment to waste elimination. Nike collects worn-out athletic shoes of any brand, not just Nike. Shoe materials are ground up to make sports surfacing products used in athletic fields. (Photo by Adam M. Lee)

social and community benefit, or local loop (http://sfgoodwill.org/mission/for-planet/). The shirt or pants donated in a bin or at a drop-off location must be sorted, tagged, and repacked, a process that keeps jobs in the local economy. The San Francisco Goodwill diverts over 20 million pounds from local landfills annually, with more than 80 percent of its revenue coming from the sale of these donated goods; it provides employment for over 1,000 individuals (SFGoodwill, 2013).

The New Ethical Dilemmas of Social-Conscious Businesses
The new standard of corporate performance envisioned by the social entrepreneurs encompasses both financial and ethical dimensions, regardless of the size of the company. A consideration of a textile and apparel company's ethical attributes includes investigating its environmental and social practices. An example of what may be considered an ethical dilemma encountered in our industry revolves around the definition of what makes a fiber choice ecologically correct or sustainable. In 2004, Paris hosted the first Ethical Fashion Show®· Founded by Paris designer Isabelle Quéhé, the European event was centered on ethical fashion, promoting designers using fibers and dye processes that supported the environment. The fashion presented at the Ethical Fashion Show® aimed for a fair balance between creativity, quality, and price, with products manufactured with raw materials and dyes not harmful to the environment. Held in Berlin in 2014, during the Berlin Fashion Week, the show continues to represent socially responsible fashion exhibitors, and has become a platform for information and networking regarding sustainability in the textile industry.

> *Consumers are becoming increasingly inquisitive and critical. They want to know from which materials and under what conditions their clothing is made—the right time for a professional trade show, which represents contemporary eco-friendly and socially responsible fashion. If you do it right it will last forever.*
> —Ethical Fashion Show Berlin, ethicalfashionshowberlin.com

As mentioned earlier, social entrepreneurial companies consider the new standard for corporate performance one that encompasses financial and ethical dimensions for all companies, no matter their size. Many companies are not new to this consideration. Consider the following:

- Los Angeles designer Linda Loudermilk, considered a pioneer in the ecologically friendly couture design arena, aims to hit people at a gut level by capturing the soul and raw beauty of people and nature in her designs. The garments in her collections emphasize our universal connectedness and our responsibility to take care of each other and the Earth (Loudermilk, n.d.). Each season, Loudermilk creates a theme that she features on T-shirts. For spring 2006 her theme was "Water is a Human Right," a message still purchasable today, with 17 percent of the proceeds donated to worldwide water initiatives.
- English designer Katharine Hamnett believes the effect of change in the clothing industry will have more impact on climate change "than if the entire world signed the Kyoto agreement" (Epiro, 2005). She is known as a supporter of political causes, designing T-shirts to bear, for example, the simple words "Education not Trident" (British nuclear weapon system), or "58% Don't want Pershing" (a type of war missile) (Hudson, 2013).
- Levi Strauss & Company conducted a lifecycle assessment of several products in 2007, looking particularly at the use of water in all stages—from growing the cotton to production to consumer care. In 2011 it began offering a denim collection that reduced the average amount of water in the finishing process from 11 to 4 gallons per pair (Critchell, 2011). Further, the company updated its care tags after finding that their customers were responsible for 45 percent of the total water usage, typically washing their 501s 100 times on average over the life of the jeans (Berfield, 2012).

- Marks and Spencer (M&S), the British retailer with more than 700 stores located throughout the United Kingdom and 360 stores worldwide, is recognized for its progressive approach to sustainable business practices (Marks and Spencer, n.d). In 2007 it initiated Plan A, a commitment to work with its customers to reduce carbon dioxide (CO_2) emissions. As a part of this plan, M&S launched a new care label campaign to encourage consumers to reduce their impact on the environment by lowering their clothes washing water temperature. The reminder "Think climate—Wash at 30°C" was imprinted on the clothing labels of all M&S products. Under Plan A, by 2015 M&S products aimed to become carbon neutral, sending no waste to landfill, extending sustainable sourcing, and improving ethical trading (Bowers, 2007). One year ahead of plan, over 50 percent of its products meet at least one of these goals (Marks & Spencer, 2014).

Linda Loudermilk, Katharine Hamnett, Levi Strauss, and Marks and Spencer provide us with examples of small and large companies acting and responding as social entrepreneurs as they choose to support and promote the use of sustainable practices in their products and with their customers.

Marketing and Good Citizenship

The basic tenet of sustainable design requires that the needs of the current generation must be met without compromising the needs of future generations (World Commission on Environment and Development, 1987). My belief is that most of us want to be socially and environmentally conscious but find it difficult to identify the important issues. Not having a framework to assess and analyze the sustainable issues and choices we face in our industry can be daunting. It is challenging to make informed decisions and move forward. As consumers change their perceptions of brands because of new respect or diminishing respect for a company's culture or business practices, they force companies to reassess and understand that corporate social responsibility must be a part of a business's corporate culture. According to the 2014 US Consumer Perspectives & Trends in Sustainability report from the US National Marketing Institute, more consumers are willing to pay more for environmentally friendly products, while there is increasing concern about genetically modified organisms (GMOs)—think cotton seeds (NMI, 2014).

In 2005, retail companies gave away 1.7 percent of their profits before paying taxes, compared with 0.9 percent for companies in other industries, according to the Committee to Encourage Philanthropy (CECP) (Barbaro, 2006). A coalition of CEOs whose mission is to create a better world through business, the CECP reported that in 2013, of the 261 companies who participated in the giving numbers, giving was up across industries with 1.95 percent of pre-tax profits increasingly given to community and economic development programs. Gradually, corporations are tying their brands to non-profit causes, while non-profits are competing with corporations for consumer attention and consumer dollars. Clearly, causes sell; they touch human emotions and create deep allegiances to experiences and quite possibly to products. In fact, non-profit organizations are spending big dollars on media, public relations, advertising, and communications, according to exclusive research by Changing Our World, Inc (n.d.). In many cases, it's the non-profits that are driving the message recognition by branding philanthropic causes, and they are spending billions doing it.

But with all of the new campaigns and products, it can often be very confusing to choose the right cause to support. It's difficult to be sure that marketing tools and advertising campaigns designed to make us aware of the choices are truthful and honest. Does the money collected go to the correct cause, and do the products promoting that cause actually have any relationship to it? The practice of linking specific products to charitable donations, or *cause marketing*, continues to be a

The Certified B Corporation Model

Maryland was the first state in the United States to support the new for-profit business model termed the Benefit Corporation or B Corporation, with twelve more states supporting as of 2013. Created by changemakers and social entrepreneurs driven by the desire to create social and environmental value as the primary core of their existence, consider the following from Amy Kincaide of Change Matters (2014) for where that value exists:

- the thing (product or service) that you do or make;
- the way you do it (being different from the typical way that others do it in your industry); or
- the people with whom and the place in which you do it.

In a B Corporation a company's performance is based not on the financial performance alone, but rather on the qualitative performance or achievement of positive impact on the community and/ or the environments as stated in the corporation's goals. Annual reports are posted on a company website supporting full transparency to the community. Accreditation status is garnered from an organization called B Labs, and is given to companies that meet standards and expand local recognition (Chouinard & Stanley, 2012). The B Corp logo helps consumers identify these changemakers, supporting their products and services, further extending and becoming a part of using business as a force for good in our global economy.

FIGURE S2.2. Benefit Corporations or B Corps are visionary organizations with the mission of using business to solve social and environmental problems.

FIGURE 2.3. Awareness ribbons are folded into loops and are used by the wearer to make a subtle statement of support for a cause or an issue. The meaning behind the awareness ribbon depends on its color.

popular method for corporations to attempt to clean up their image while contributing to charity. The abundance of ribbon campaigns (e.g., pink for breast cancer awareness, red for AIDS awareness, mint for abuse awareness, and dark red for Mothers Against Drunk Driving) are intended to raise the conscientious consumer's awareness, and yet sometimes the abundance of the products produced in the color or carrying the ribbon logo just confuse and irritate potential consumers (Figure 2.3).

Brand Names and Cause Marketing

In the twenty-first century, there is little hesitancy about linking brand names with a cause because the response from the consumer to pioneering companies that have tried to do so has been so positive. The trend can be traced back to 2004, when millions of people bought $1 Livestrong bracelets to benefit the Lance Armstrong Foundation (Barbaro, 2006). Consumers not only wanted to support a charity but also wanted to broadcast their philanthropy to the world with a yellow plastic bracelet worn on their wrist.

Cause marketing is created when a for-profit business and non-profit business join to create a marketing partnership to support a social cause. At its best, cause marketing is a win–win–win proposition.

The cause wins by being both promoted and funded, the consumer wins by feeling good about making a positive choice, and the retailer wins by making the sale and presumably feeling good about being an agent of positive change. As retailers engage in cause marketing, they put philanthropy at the center of their products and campaigns and develop year-long sustainable models.

For the past twenty years, Cone, Inc., a Boston-based strategy and communications agency, has researched American perceptions and behaviors toward corporate support of social issues and has found that, more than ever before, companies must get involved with social issues in order to protect and enhance their reputations. As reported in its 2013 Cone Corporate Community Social Impact Study (www.conecomm.com):

- 9 in 10 Americans say they look to companies to support social or environmental issues in some capacity;
- 43 percent of Americans believe that companies should prioritize issues that affect the quality of life locally, more so than nationally 38 percent, and globally 20 percent;
- 91 percent of Americans want to see more products, services, and retailers support worthy issues, an 8 percent increase from 2010.

Causal Campaigns Can Help a Business and its Product
Causal marketing campaigns that can build trust with consumers will be more sustainable for businesses. Gaining consumer confidence will be imperative. Marketers know that appealing to sustainability values will not overcome a fundamental weakness in a product, but sometimes a weakness can also be a strength.

Great campaigns exist, but consumers may not know about them:

- Go Red for Women, the American Heart Association's campaign, began in February 2004 to raise awareness that heart disease is women's number one killer. The first Friday in February is National Wear Red Day, and in 2007 an entire website was devoted to providing consumers with products to purchase to support the cause (Shop Go Red, n.d.). Macy's is a corporate sponsor of the National Wear Red Campaign and supports and promotes this cause throughout the year. Since its inception, the awareness campaign reports that 21 percent fewer women are dying of this disease and 23 percent of women report knowing that heart disease is the number one killer of women (https://www.goredforwomen. org/get-involved/national-wear-red-day/national-wear-red-day/).

- Timberland, a global leader in the design, engineering, and marketing of premium quality footwear, launched a causal marketing campaign in 2006: a three-section "nutritional label" on each box intended to educate consumers about the products they purchase. The manufactured section gives the name and location of the factory where the product was made. The environmental impact section reports how much energy is needed to produce the footwear and how much of Timberland's energy is generated from renewable resources such as the sun, wind, and water. The community impact section reports on issues of social responsibility. Timberland is enhancing its brand image with the intent that it will see an increase in sales as it demonstrates its respect for the environment through socially responsible business practices. Its CEO, Jeff Swart, is, "re-imagining every aspect of its business practices so our children will not be confronted with irreversible damage" (Michelson, 2007).

- Yvon Chouinard, founder of Patagonia, Inc., and Craig Mathews, owner of Blue Ribbon Flies (which sells fly-fishing equipment), launched One Percent for the Planet, an alliance of more than 370 companies from the United States, Canada, Europe, Japan, the South Pacific, and South America in 2001. The alliance recognizes the true cost of doing business and donates 1 percent of its sales to environmental organizations worldwide. This environmental alliance is designed to help members become sustainable businesses.

- Nau, a Portland, Oregon company with a new message, emerged in 2007. Hailed in the press as a "transformational" clothing company, Nau melds social responsibility and good outdoor clothing and gear. Nau states that it is "committed to radically altering the landscape of corporate philanthropy, so much so that we'd like to change that ungainly phrase. We prefer community partnership" (Nau, n.d.). Customers are able to direct 5 percent of every sale to an environmental, social, or humanitarian charitable organization of their choice. By inviting the customer to determine where the company donations are directed, the consumer will in essence be able to participate in choosing where they would like to effect change.

Where Do We Go from Here?
I would like to include you, the reader, as a participant in this movement of social good. I would like for us to decide together how we can be socially conscious fashion consumers. The ideas of fashion sustainability and "slow fashion" need to move from the fringe to the mainstream, and, to do that, they must be skillfully marketed before they will shift people's perceptions and behaviors. We need to collectively find a common voice and respond by: (1) purchasing products that come from renewable resources; (2) actively supporting the reuse or recycling of products; and (3) ensuring that manufacturing processes are safe for human ecological health in all phases of the product lifecycle. The path to engage in these three activities is challenging as new business models demanding that manufacturers, retailers, and consumers act together in making sustainable choices are developing. If we act as both good citizens and good consumers, we will send a consistent message all the way back up the design supply chain asking for new processes to be followed (Figure 2.4).

The US Federal Trade Commission (FTC) first developed guidelines in 1992 for the use of environmental marketing claims, with the latest revision in 2010 stated on its website (Federal Trade Commission, n.d.):

FIGURE 2.4. The Tablecloth Project takes discarded tablecloths from the San Francisco Hotel industry and repurposes them into shopping bags, diverting them from the waste stream while creating an environmentally appropriate manufacturing model. (Photo by Connie Ulasewicz)

These guides apply to environmental claims included in labeling, advertising, promotional materials, and all other forms of marketing, whether asserted directly or by implication, through words, symbols, emblems, logos, depictions, product brand names, or through any other means, including marketing through digital or electronic means, such as the Internet or electronic mail. The guides apply to any claim about the environmental attributes of a product, package, or service in connection with the sale, offering for sale, or marketing of such product, package or service for personal, family, or household use, or for commercial, institutional, or industrial use.

The guidelines are not legislative rules and are therefore unenforceable, yet they are still very helpful and informative as guiding principles for eco-savvy companies to promote and market their products. Over time, as more clothing companies engage in environmental practices, the labeling will become clearer so that we can make informed consumer choices.

The University of Cambridge study "Well Dressed," in 2006, set out a different type of model than the FTC and a vision of a sustainable clothing industry that would offer new opportunities to retailers and manufacturers. "The key to change is to ensure that the government, industry, and consumers work together to achieve a more sustainable clothes and textiles industry" (Allwood, Laursen et al., 2006). The research supported the concepts of conscientious consumerism and put forth the idea that to reduce environmental impact and promote social equity within our industry, the consumer would need to demand more choices. Its suggestions included the following:

- Buy secondhand clothing when possible.
- Buy fewer and more durable products.
- Lease or rent clothing that would otherwise not be worn to the end of the garment's natural life.
- Wash clothes less often at lower temperatures, using eco-detergents, hang dry, and do not iron.

At first, these findings may seem challenging for the fashionable consumer to support, but fashion is about change. Design entrepreneurs can turn these possibilities into fashionable realities. The designer is the central connection between the manufacturers that produce the goods and the consumers who buy them.

Conclusion: What Can You Do?
If sustainable design and sustainable development is our goal, then we must engage thoughtfully and with knowledge as we participate in the socially responsible consumption of fashion. With the awareness that there is a pro and a con to all decisions, consider the following five actions for conscientious consumerism, and remember that every act of consumption is a vote for the type of world in which you wish to be a part:

- Do question marketing campaigns, but do not dismiss a product because of the campaign.
- Do read clothing labels, support locally made products, try new fibers, and ask questions.
- Do fix, mend, alter, and reuse clothing to extend the natural life.
- Do think twice before you purchase, and do buy fewer and more durable products.
- Do pass clean unwanted garments back to the manufacturer or to an appropriate reuse or social collection center.

Look beyond the surface appearance, and consider the total life span of the fashionable products you purchase. Remember, it is a symbiotic relationship between the consumer and the manufacturers and retailers from which we purchase, and what seems like radical or unusual fashion today may well be considered acceptable and mainstream tomorrow.

Discussion Questions

1   Research an apparel company that gives back to the planet and/or people. How is this social giving a part of their mission statement and company philosophy?
2   With a partner or in a group, develop a cause marketing campaign for a product you like. Search for an organization or group in your neighborhood or city that would most benefit from the campaign and interview it as to its needs. Develop a flyer, website, or product that explains the marketing campaign. Have a day when each group will present and discuss their campaigns and the class will decide which ones were the most effective and why.
3   Find a garment in your closet that you can recreate, mend, or alter in some manner that makes it fashionable and wearable. If you cannot "update" it, work with a partner or other class member who can. Take before and after pictures and add them to your portfolio.

References

Allwood, J. M., Laursen, S. E., Malvido de Rodriguez, C. & Bocken, N. M. P. (2006). *Well dressed: The present and future of clothing and textiles in the United Kingdom*. Institute for Manufacturing, University of Cambridge.

Barbaro, M. (2006, November 13). Candles, jeans, lipsticks: Products with ulterior motives. *New York Times*, p. 33.

Berfield, S. (2012, October 18). Levi's goes green with waste less jeans. Bloomberg Business Week. http://www.businessweek.com/articles/2012-10-18/levis-goes-green-with-waste-less-jeans.

Bornstein, D. & Davis, S. (2010). *Social entrepreneurship: What everyone needs to know*. New York: Oxford University Press.

Bowers, J. (2007, January 14). M & S promises radical change with L200m environmental action plan. *The Guardian*. http://www.theguardian.com/business/2007/jan/15/marksspencer.retail.

Changing our World website. (n.d.). http://www.changingourworld.com.

Chouinard, Y. & Stanley, V. (2012). *The responsible company: What we've learned from Patagonia's first 40 years*. California: Patagonia Books.

Cone Corporate Community Impact Study. (2013). Website: http://cone comm.com.

Cosgrave, B. (2000). *The complete history of costume and fashion*. Facts on File.

Critchell, S. (2011, January 11). Soft and dry? Levi's launches "waterless" denim. http://www.nbcnews.com/id/41023951/ns/business-going_green/t/soft-dry-levis-launches-waterless-denim/.

Dickson, M. & Eckman, M. (2007, July). Social responsibility: The concept as defined by apparel and textile scholars. *Clothing and Textiles Research Journal*, 24(3), 178–91.

Dunwell, S. (1978). *The run of the mill*. Boston, MA: David R. Godine.

Edun website. (n.d.). http://www.edun.ie/one.asp.

Epiro, S. (2005, August 8). Woman on a mission. *Daily News Record*, 35(32), 18.

Ethical Fashion Show. (n.d.). Retrieved from http://www.ethicalfashionshow.com/ efs_va.htm.

Federal Trade Commission Guide for the Use of Environmental Marketing Claims. (n.d.). Retrieved July 27, 2012, from the Federal Trade Commission website: http://www.ftc.gov/bcp/grnrule/guides980427.htm#260.7.

Garlow, E. & Tafel, R. (2013, May 22). Social entrepreneurship: The power of a simple and inclusive definition. *Stanford Social Innovation Review*.

http://www.ssireview.org/blog/entry/the_power_of_a_simple_and_inclusive_definition.

Hudson, K. (2013, March 27). New Katharine Hamnett anti-Trident designs. Campaign for Nuclear Disarmament.

Hunt, L. (2011). Charities suffer as criminal gangs target lucrative clothing recycling sector. *Ecologist, 40*(21), 14–16.

Jack, T. (2013). Fashioning use: A polemic to provoke pro-environmental garment maintenance. In M. A. Gardetti & A.L. Torres (Eds.), *Sustainability in fashion and textiles: Values, design, production and consumption* (pp. 123–33). Sheffield, UK: Greenleaf Publishing.

Kincaid, A. (2014, May). What social value is your business creating? Change Matters. www.changematters.com.

Loudermilk website. (n.d.). www.lindaloudermilk.com.

Marks and Spencer website. (n.d.). www.corporate.marksandspencer.com/.

Marks and Spencer (2014, June 5). *Plan A Report* launches new 2020 eco ethical plan for M&S. http://corporate.marksandspencer.com/media/press-releases/2014/plan-a-report-launches-new-2020-eco-and-ethical-plan-for-mands.

McDonough, W. & Braungart, T. (2002). *Cradle to cradle.* New York: Farrar, Straus and Giroux.

Michelson, M. (2007, April). Project green all-stars. [Electronic version]. *Outside,* 76.

Nau. (n.d.). www.nau.com.

NMI. (2014). http://www.nmisolutions.com/index.php/syndicated-data/segmentation-algorithms-a-panels/lohas-segmentation/nielsen-collaboration.

Pollan, M. (2011, October 6). Michael Pollan answers readers' questions. [Electronic version]. *The New York Times Magazine.* http://michaelpollan.com/articles-archive/michael-pollan-answers-readers-questions/.

Schwartz, B. (2012). *Rippling: How social entrepreneurs spread innovation throughout the world.* San Francisco: Jossey-Bass.

SF Goodwill Annual Report. (2013). http://sfgoodwill.org/wp-content/uploads/2014/02/sf-goodwill_annual-report_2013.pdf.

Shop Go Red. (n.d.). http://www.shopgored.org.

SMART (Secondary Materials and Recycled Textile Association). (2012). Donate recycle don't throw away. www.smartasn.org.

http://www.epa.gov/osw/nonhaz/municipal/pubs/2012_msw_fs.pdf.

Ulasewicz, C. & Baugh, G. (2013). Creating new from that which is discarded: The collaborative San Francisco tablecloth repurposing project. In M. A. Gardetti & A. L. Torres (Eds.), *Sustainability in fashion and textiles: Values, design, production and consumption* (pp. 164–81). Sheffield, UK: Greenleaf Publishing.

USEPA (United States Environmental Protection Agency). (2012). Municipal solid waste generation, recycling, and disposal in the United States: Facts and figures 2012.

World Commission on Environment and Development. (1987). *Our common future*. Oxford: Oxford University Press.

JANET HETHORN, PHD, is professor of art and design, and dean of the College of Communication and Fine Arts at Central Michigan University. Her current research and writing projects examine how viewers respond to expressions of visual style in everyday situations and the issues that emerge from these responses. As a designer, her approach maintains a focus on user-centered innovation and the implementation of methods that leverage collaboration and integration of diverse perspectives.

CHAPTER 3

User-Centered Innovation: Design Thinking and Sustainability

Janet Hethorn

Sustainable fashion begs the question, "Sustaining what?" One important answer is "people." This chapter explores the myriad ways that designers and product developers can apply user-centered innovation practices as a strategy to positively meet people's needs through fashion. When a designer focuses on the needs of the individual, the individual's sense of self and sustained well-being significantly improves. This significance emerges as we look at examples that include the relationship between clothing and the body, and the power of fashion to express meaning and identity. Sustaining people through clothing is not a new concept. Most will agree that clothing is a basic need, much like food and shelter. What is suggested here are ways to place these ideas as central components within the design process.

The Power of Design

This chapter is about ideas and opportunities for innovation. It's about thinking of people, the users of clothing, in ways slightly different from what traditional design practices dictate. To create sustainable outcomes, we must start by critiquing the way we design and how our practices best serve consumers and meet their desires. Design has the power to change our perception, action, and mind-set. It is our responsibility as designers to shift our thinking and put our ideas into action in order to tap into this power. Design thinking allows us to do just that. Simplified, design thinking (or thinking as a designer) is a method of problem solving that focuses on applying a human-centric approach to problem finding and solution building. Through both divergent thinking that expands explorations, and convergent thinking that allows for honing in on correct solutions, this approach guides us to innovative results. Idris Mootee (2012) explains design thinking as "a framework for a human-centered approach to strategic innovation and a new management paradigm for value creation in a world of radically changing networks and disruptive technology."

People as a Focus in the Design Process

The first shift that needs to be made is to simply visualize the end result in a new way. Instead of considering the object, the *garment*, as the focus of your design activity, visualize someone wearing and moving and enjoying his or her life in the garment that you design. Move your focus away from the object to the *person*. In that way, the shift toward sustainability can begin. The opportunity exists to create fashion that sustains people and creates a sense of well-being for the wearer as an individual.

Our traditional design process runs counter to this way of thinking. We think abstractly about people from the get-go. We follow trends and directions that are derived from abstractions of target markets, and from reports of what they purchased in the past along with projections of future buying. Then we generalize these target markets, creating stereotypes of who they are. In pattern development, we use fit models that are perceived by the particular apparel company to represent this market, thus building in problems with garment fit from the start. People are abstracted further as we design through sketches and illustrations that are drawn mostly as front views. Fashions are communicated through magazine images that are static abstractions of what is considered as ideal people wearing your designs. Even real garments, displayed on mannequins in stores, are pinned and tucked to form an ideal silhouette, and the clothing inevitably looks different when seen on moving, breathing people.

As we rethink fashion, we need to start visualizing people, individual people, interacting with their garments in ways that are healthy and meaningful. Truly sustainable fashion should address the emotional, expressive, and physical qualities that garments can provide for consumers. In addition to meeting needs and desires, the resulting satisfaction leads to greater use and a longer functioning cycle. Think about your favorite garment, perhaps a T-shirt or an old sweater, that may be threadbare or faded but is still a part of your core wardrobe because of your emotional attachment to it, and think about how you feel when you wear it. Imagine a world where everyone is wearing clothes that fit well. The fabric is comfortable and enhances, not hinders, their performance. The ideas and identity the wearers express through their appearance feels just right to them. They can move through their days with no annoyance or uncertainty generated from their clothes. Furthermore, they look great. Together, these qualities generate a sense of overall well-being. We have done our job.

Getting There: Moving from Target Markets to Individual Consumers

As introduced above, designers and marketers traditionally think of consumers as "targets." In fact, it is critical for you, as a designer, to consider your target market. Who are you designing for, and how do you create garments that they will want to buy? Marketing firms and merchandisers focus on creating profiles and lifestyle analyses as guidelines for product development. I am not suggesting that we drop this perspective entirely, merely that we consider a more fruitful path for sustainability. If we are to sustain people, we need to look more closely at individuals—who they are, what they want to wear, and what they need. By thinking about people as a group, the opportunities for sustainable design narrow. In fact, I would argue that a goal for hitting the center of a target market breeds waste. It means that there are many people on the fringes whose needs are not met, perpetuating many fashion items that are unacceptable, flawed, or left for discounted secondary choices.

Individuals often reflect this narrow target market approach by finding flaws in themselves because they constantly compare themselves to the ideal and come up short. If something doesn't fit, it is their fault. "My seat is too flat," "my legs are too long," or "if the waist fits, my hips are too big"; these are comments that reflect a self-critique instead of something that is wrong with the garment (e.g., a sizing problem or other flaw). No wonder body images are tattered and self-concept diminished when people see themselves as different from the idealized target markets that are the goal of fashion design. What are they comparing themselves against, and who is taking the responsibility for creating this dynamic? Again, innovation can be realized through expanded attention on the user and going deep into the factors that influence the choices they have and make.

A downside of a generalized target market is the possibility of being so focused as to create a stereotype, perhaps missing other nuances that a focus on the individual would possess. We think of people in groups, we label these groups, and these groups are categorized as departments in stores. As consumers, we are accustomed to this; we shop based on categories. It helps us find things and keep an organized system. But the balance has gone too far. I am simply suggesting that we add back in the focus on individual people who wear clothes and have desires related to those clothes and their total appearance.

As part of the design process, it is critical to get inside the consumers' individual heads and not their collective heads. What would happen if we designed for individuals with individual needs and desires? Now you might think we are already doing that. However, if that is truly the case, then design has failed. We aren't designing for individuals if over 60 percent of people report that they can't find clothes that fit and consumers often complain that they have a hard time finding styles that they feel and look great in.

What if we turn this around? Instead of targeting the consumer, how about *listening* to them? We could find out what they want in order to best represent their aesthetic preferences. We could discover the full range of performance needs they will encounter and how their clothing might address them. What makes for comfortable clothing? How are these concepts different for different individuals? How are they the same? Consider undertaking methods and observations that can uncover the issues that present themselves in what people are currently wearing and what they might wear instead to better meet their needs. A helpful resource that introduces several approaches for learning about human experiences is *Innovating for People: Handbook of Human-Centered Design Methods* (LUMA Institute, 2012). As we move further into this chapter, issues and strategies will be identified to help us move in this direction. Let's get started.

Well-Being: A Basic Concept of Sustainability

Whether within the realms of the social, the economic, or the environmental, sustainability is based on the concept of well-being. We diminish environmental well-being through waste and pollution, and we can improve it through lowering carbon emissions and improving bio-friendly practices. This is easy to grasp and generally acceptable. Not so clear, but still important, is the potential to diminish or enhance the well-being of people through the garments and fashion we create for them. And, when we consider people as the focus of our sustainability efforts, the idea of well-being allows us to open our creativity to embrace meaningful problem solving within the fashion process. Think about a time when you felt absolutely fabulous in what you were wearing. What were the characteristics and features of the clothing, the situation? Then, recall the opposite, a situation when you were at odds with your clothes. Once again, what were the elements that were the culprits? By doing this brief exercise, you can rather simply notice the garment qualities that can be manipulated to impact the relationship between successful design and a sense of well-being. There are many levels of potential success or failure in clothing design. For a garment to fully realize success, and thus enhance the feeling of well-being of the person who is wearing it, the design must meet his or her total needs. Put simply, this means that it should be aesthetically and functionally appropriate for the person and the situation of use. Often designers focus on one or the other of these qualities, functionality *or* aesthetics, but I would argue that both dimensions are addressed and integrated in all successful designs. Let's take a look at what this means for design potential:

- *Aesthetic* refers to all of the visual and expressive elements of a garment, and, more inclusively, the total look.
- *Function* is all about what the garment needs to do, how it performs for and with the body to meet various activities and movements.

When aesthetic and functional concerns are fully addressed within the design process, the possibility for fashion to sustain people comes into focus. In addition, fashion is embedded within social and cultural contexts, and people are constantly searching for and providing meaning within these contexts through what they wear and the resulting visual communication. So, if we are to take full advantage of the opportunity to create fashion that sustains people, we must expand our thinking of how to meet the desires of people who wear clothing, the "user" in design thinking approaches. We must go beyond general notions of markets and focus instead on designing for individual well-being.

Approaches to Discovering Design Opportunities

To create meaningful and desirable designs, a successful strategy for inspiration is to go right to the source. Find out what people need and

then use what you learn as a basis for your design strategies. Watch
them in action, walking down the street, sitting on a subway car,
engaging in a sports activity, or any place at all. Instead of just focusing
on fashion magazines, trend reports, and shopping the market for what
everyone else is designing, simply open your eyes to *how* people are
wearing what they currently put together in everyday situations, and
analyze what is working and what is not. Take photographs, write
notes, talk with them. Here are some specific strategies.

Observations

Position yourself in a location that allows you to watch people and what
they wear. Go to public spaces, parks, shopping malls, street cafés, and
pay attention to how individuals have put together their looks. See how
they arrange items in combinations and how they present themselves
through movement and expression. Notice the entire experience and
how the context in which you are viewing it impacts how you see and
interpret the visual information. Also, be sure to question how you select
what to view. The richest information comes from going past what you
like or see as the next trend. Look carefully at what blends in, as well as
what stands out. Then, document your observations by writing notes,
drawing pictures, and taking photographs. In this activity, you must
remember that you are the "outsider." You are seeing what is present in
the visual field and making your own meaning out of it. This may be
different from what the wearers, or the "insiders," are thinking they are
expressing; their sense of what their clothing means to them is not
always obvious. By developing a combination of approaches, you can
better assess individual users' desires and needs.

Participant Observations

Involve yourself in the activities of what the people for whom you are
designing are doing. Firsthand experience is a great teacher. I often

have my students do fieldwork related to their design goals. If they are designing for people who need clothes for strenuous outdoor activities, I have them wear their best guess at the appropriate outfits and go for a hike in the woods. They go in teams and discuss their findings as they are engaged. What may seem simple, such as the need for clothing that doesn't catch on branches, is immediately obvious, while other findings, such as the need for garments that keep the wearer warm while at the same time allow for changes to cool as the body warms from exercise, really hit home when they experience them directly. With the mind-set of discovery, the ideas for solutions come quickly. I have also sent students to bowling alleys, group yoga classes, and even to shooting ranges. The "walk a mile in my shoes" perspective can go a long way.

Interviews

There are two basic kinds of interview strategies that work well in gaining design insight: individual and group. People love to talk about their clothes and what they would like to see developed differently, so a structured interview can be a beneficial tool. Develop a series of questions, and take along a digital audio recorder. The key to a successful interview is to really listen to the issues that are raised. Be open to allowing the interviewee to express his or her opinions. You may find that the most informative interviews do not answer all of the questions on your list, but the details revealed through conversation uncover findings that your plan didn't anticipate. Ask questions that do not lead to a "yes" or "no" response. Then follow up with additional questions to dig deeper into what you are finding. You could do a series of short interviews, two to five minutes, but also consider conducting longer interviews lasting up to half an hour or more. If you can gain access to a group of people who share similar interests or needs, a focus group interview may be helpful. It's best to limit the group to fewer than eight members in order to allow everyone to feel comfortable and be able to bounce ideas off of each other easily. You can even ask them to bring examples of clothing, perhaps their favorite as well as their least favorite, in order to have real items that will spawn discussion. Or, select a range of photos or images from magazines as a visual starting point for generating reactions. A group of students I worked with were charged with designing wrestling singlets for a client. They invited the university wrestling team to our studio and had a lively discussion, complete with demonstrations. The wrestlers brought their current garments and couldn't stop talking about the problems they were experiencing. As a result, the completed informed designs went beyond the client's expectations. Along with the earlier mentioned *Innovating for People: Handbook of Human-Centered Design Methods* by LUMA Institute (2012), *The Sage Handbook of Qualitative Research* (Denzin & Lincoln, 2005) is a good source of information on interviews, participant observation, as well as other helpful methods.

Data Management and Assessment

Beyond the basic observations and interviews, consider how you are going to manage all the photographs you have taken and then how you might further analyze them for useful design inspiration. Remember, the focus of this data collection is to gather the user's perspective and visual support of their preferences. Searching for visual patterns is a useful strategy. Consider the complete image of the body, the clothing, and the interaction among the contexts (e.g., garment to body, body to surroundings) as you analyze your images. Look for visual structure, both layout and surface, as well as how the visual definers such as line, shape, color, and texture are interacting. A good reference for this process is *The Way We Look* (DeLong, 1998). If you develop an image database or image management system, you will be able to track the evolution of visual information as well as combine it with other text-based responses, either from your own analysis or from interview transcriptions.

Beyond your own image collections, there are many sources you could explore to gather visual knowledge from particular individuals and groups. Flickr, Instagram, Pinterest, and blogs that focus on fashion topics are great resources of images and descriptions. You could also set up your own blog to post questions and gather responses. A class of mine that was designing warm-weather gear for female hunters used this strategy and found access to women they had difficulty finding otherwise. A lively dialogue pursued that included images posted and detailed descriptions of consumer need.

Creating Well-Being through Design

So far, I have introduced the need to focus on individuals and I have described ways to identify their needs and desires, aesthetic and functional, as a basis for creating a sense of well-being through design. Next, I will highlight various ways to hone in on specific elements that, when combined, address user needs through fashion. As mentioned earlier, clothing and fashion looks have aesthetic, or visually expressive, qualities and functional qualities that allow for movement and performance. The pieces that come together that embody these qualities are fabric and bodies. Obviously the combinations are almost limitless. So, design development along with consumer choice narrow down the selection for what is possible to wear.

Going back to the notion of discovering what people want, think about what all that encompasses. What does clothing do for people? How does fashion work in their lives? Simply put, people want clothes that help them look good, feel good, and work for them in various situations.

Looking Good: Expressing Visual Style

You are familiar with the saying "beauty is in the eye of the beholder." It is also in the eye of the expresser. Certainly the person wearing and projecting a look is actively expressing a visual presence, and this is connected to a direct sense of self and beauty. Seeing and making sense of a fashion form is a two-way street in which the designer plays an important role. The clothed body is a visual expression that can generate a range of responses that are not the same for every viewer. Also, what looks good to, or on, one person may be less than ideal for another. The designer is not the *giver* of taste and the consumer simply a receiver. This is not a sustainable model. Instead, think about being the *interpreter* of visual desire for the person (and people) for whom you are designing. This concept is often at odds with design philosophy. Many designers see themselves as the "all knowing" when it comes to what is considered beautiful. In fact, some designers actually feel that their work is put out there for people to buy, like it or not, with little consideration of what the consumer might actually desire as beautiful. In order to design with sustainability in mind, you must develop a relationship between interpreting visual desire and professional visual creativity. Once this mind-set is put into place, it becomes possible to develop fashion that holds meaning for consumers, projects a sense of identity, and connects them to a larger cultural community within which visual relationships are developed. The result of this effort can provide the wearer with improved self-esteem, sense of identity, and respect of place within cultural meaning.

There is no shortage of reading on this topic. Many books have emerged recently that focus on understanding perception and the senses, as well as on recognizing the importance of visual knowledge and design as a holistic process, taking into account objects, users, and contexts of use (Caplan, 2005; Nelson, 2003). As amplified in the book *Make Design Matter* (Carlson, 2012), for design to be relevant to the human condition, it has to have a value beyond its purchase price and style, a lasting value that relates to human existence; significant, timeless, affective, ethical, and sustainable, enhancing our lives and identities.

The opportunities to instead create fashion that is relevant and represents visual meaning and cultural connection for consumers are wide open. As stated by George Nelson (2003), "The pursuit of design is not about the way things appear, but rather about the way things give meaning and relevance to the human experience."

People are constantly creating visual references, changing preferences, and creating new ways of expressing their fashion outlook. Fashion is a powerful form of communication and a meaningful way for individuals to connect to groups, together constructing cultural meaning (Figure 3.1). For further understanding of these complexities, see *Fashion and Cultural Studies* (Kaiser, 2012).

In addition to the design research methods described earlier, it may be helpful to look at the process of seeing, to document and describe references being viewed and to analyze them in relationship with already accepted aesthetic preferences, articulated both visually and verbally (Hethorn, 2005).

FIGURE 3.1. This group of young individuals share an aesthetic preference. Note the similar way of wearing the pants, the careful details of the fit of the shirts, and shape of shoes and laces. Hairstyles and even posture contribute to the details of viewing and communicating through appearance. Noting the details of a look as expressed in the context of wearing (here, on the street) is a design strategy that can lead to more meaningful product development. (Photograph by Janet Hethorn)

ideas in action

Matrushka Construction

(J. Hethorn, personal interview with L. Howe, September 15, 2014)

Through a conversation with Laura Howe, owner and creator, it is clear that a commitment to individual style and fit, as well as to local production and the local community, is alive and well in Silverlake, a neighborhood in Los Angeles. The clothes available at Matrushka Construction are designed, cut, sewn, and silkscreened right in Silverlake. The styles are simple and classic, yet the fabrics make each garment unique and the mix is constantly changing.

It is definitely a fun experience shopping at Matrushka, due to the lively fabric prints and colors, but the best surprise is being able to find something that looks great and fits. Every time. I asked Laura how she creates dresses to truly address her customer's wants and needs. "I look at what has sold and I cut new stuff, paying close attention to what's trending within our design model. Simple, accessible, interesting." She

FIGURE S3.1 The label states Matrushka's attitude to size. (Photograph by Janet Hethorn)

has a keen eye for fit and for her customer's preferences: "Everyone has a different idea of what fits well." And, as their label states, "size is relative." Then, right there in the shop, the Matrushka team makes any needed alterations in a matter of minutes. "Slight adjustments can take a dress from not fitting well to looking fabulous." Laura states that, "If it's a hem, I can do it in less than five minutes. There is a bit of a wow factor. Most people haven't seen this." Then, to continue the magic, once a purchase is made, they sew up a bag from the fabric stash for you to carry your new dress in.

Fabric is all sourced in downtown Los Angeles and everything is handmade in the neighborhood. "We want to work in-house. We literally do cut and sew from start to finish. That's worked." With this local approach, the responsiveness to individual needs is swift. But it goes even deeper. Laura is involved in community action. She hosts artist openings and events in the shop. She is a founding board member of Friends of Griffith Park, an urban wilderness. Not only is this important, but it gives her customers a feeling of being connected to bigger values. The business they support is also supporting their community, the things that they are participating in. They identify.

For more information on Matrushka's collections, process and values, see their website: matrushka.com.

FIGURE S3.2 Alterations can be made to a garment on the spot. Laura Howe working in sewing studio within Matrushka retail space. (Photograph courtesy of Matrushka Construction)

It is not easy to capture and interpret aesthetic preference for individuals and groups, but it is certainly a worthy pursuit if the goal is to develop products that advance the creation of meaningful cultural connections and celebrate diversity among individuals. Tap into this understanding and the resulting design process will aid in supporting sustainability through individual and cultural well-being.

Feeling Good: Comfort and Fit

Certainly, looking good contributes to a sense of feeling good. However, when talking about feeling good, we can expand our understanding with a concrete exploration of the actual physical relationship between fabric and the body. Many people equate feeling good with comfort. If it feels good, it's comfortable. So, what does that mean? The sensory experience of fabric against the body is part of it, as is how the fabric responds to movement and performance. The body is certainly not static. Even when still, the body breathes and functions physiologically in ways that fabric can both impede and enhance. This is only emphasized with movement. Design possibilities are expansive when an understanding of fabric characteristics and body functions are combined.

There are many innovations in fabric technology that make comfort more achievable, whether it is stretch for mobility, moisture management, stain resistance, or antimicrobial characteristics. And, on a nano-level, even more exciting fabric developments are in the works. Do explore the options here and focus on achieving garment designs that are comfortable. Not only will people feel better about themselves and be able to move more freely, but the environment benefits also. Comfortable clothing gets worn more often and is kept longer. Future possibilities in design efforts toward developing comfortable environments will require a strong understanding of both textile (i.e., fiber and fabric) properties as well as the anatomy and physiology of the body. The design process for fashion needs to become more complex and holistic in order for sustainability to be realized. The usual way of developing products must change.

Nothing needs to undergo more change than the way we address garment fit. Fit underlies comfort, and the apparel industry has a long way to go in order to actualize satisfactory fit for a range of bodies. Bodies are not standard, and standard sizing is a myth (Figure 3.2). The sizes assigned to particular ranges of patterns and garments are not at all standard across apparel companies. Our current system of sizing is based on an inconsistent interpretation of body measurements and proportions. Fortunately, there are many design scholars and industry efforts working toward solutions. This, along with advances in technology, provides promise.

Again, start with the individual user and consideration of his or her needs. The majority of consumers are unhappy with the selection of fit options in the marketplace. They would be more than thrilled if

FIGURE 3.2. Personal fit preference and fashion can direct how tight or loose a garment fits, yet the real problems in fit are generated from the differences in how real body shapes vary from the ideal for which patterns are generated. Recognizing fit and misfit with a knowledge of how to make the technical pattern corrections remains a challenge. (Photograph by Janet Hethorn)

solutions were implemented that allowed them to consistently find clothing to fit their bodies. There are several reasons that explain how we got here, but now we should focus on finding solutions. Advances in understanding body shape and dimension are being realized through body scanning and new exploration of categorizing data to represent real bodies (Ashdown et al., 2004). Technical advances in 3-D visualization and computerized pattern development will provide designers with a new approach for creating the shapes necessary for real bodies. Efforts such as these are leading the way toward exciting and hopeful technical solutions.

Design solutions also can be developed that address fit from a different angle. Think about designing garments that are adjustable for comfort and variations in wearing. Creating garments that expand and contract as the body changes is another sustainable solution, reducing the need for separate garments or sets of clothing so as to cover fluctuations in body size dimensions. Meagan Edmond addressed this through her collection, which marks size sustainability (see Figure 3.3). Through adjustments in structural design details, the garments can cover a range of sizes.

There is still the issue of recognizing and correcting fit during sample development (Bye & McKinney, 2010). Garments should be tested on bodies in motion as opposed to static dress forms, and more training is needed in the visual identification of misfit, in order for designers and product developers to make appropriate decisions and corrections. I have often explained to my students that providing people with clothing that fits well is a step toward world peace. When they look amazed, I go on to remind them that when they are wearing something that doesn't fit like they would prefer, is slightly off and bothersome, they go through the day knowing something isn't quite right. If we could get rid of that annoyance, if people wore clothes they felt fabulous in, perhaps they would be nicer to one another. Think about it. Fit and comfort are basic.

FIGURE 3.3. Through design details such as embedded lacing and dimension flexibility, the wearer's clothes can follow her size as it expands and contracts; this is a mark of size sustainability. (Design by Meagan Edmond)

Working Well: Meeting Wearing Requirements

Beyond looking good and feeling good, consumers also desire their clothing and fashion expressions to do what they are intended to do, such as keep them warm and safe, allow them to move more easily, and perform at their best. These qualities represent the most basic level of sustaining people (i.e., life) through fashion by protecting and enhancing body functions. Some of the best design ideas here can be found in the technical areas of sports design and military wear. Looking to these designs for inspiration can be a place to start when thinking of improving everyday clothing for consumers. For example, the sleeve designs in mountaineering jackets can be adapted for casual wear to allow for the arm to move more smoothly and not disturb the hang of the torso covering. Advances in protection and ballistic impact strategies may find their way into urban outerwear and children's sportswear.

In today's world, protection can take on many meanings. Clothing can also aid in protecting us from harmful biological and chemical agents, and can carry needed tools for survival. The surface colors and patterns of a garment can reflect, stand out, or blend into various environments. It can be a creative challenge to think about sustaining people through innovative protective design strategies, and not just for extreme situations. You only need to consider all the possibilities of where people might find themselves and the various needs that surface when considering the demands we put our bodies through. The Nomad Coat (see Figure 3.4) was designed for survival and is the one coat that would be grabbed on the way out the door if there were only

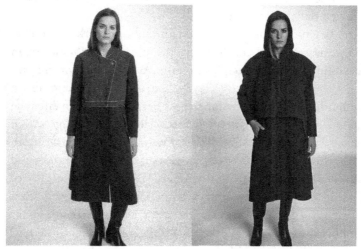

Nomad Coat #1   Worn with or without protective hooded vest. Layered wool with couched trim embellishment and vintage metallic piping on edges. Interior pockets hold tools for survival.

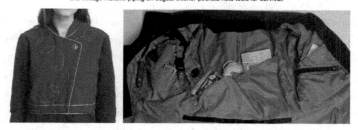

FIGURE 3.4. The Nomad Coat is an outer garment that can be layered for weather variation. Inside pockets are strategically placed and contain everything needed for urban survival. (Photographs by Kathy Atkinson. Coat design by Janet Hethorn)

emergency, where the coat would need to provide the shelter and tools to assist basic survival and travel. At the same time, the wearer a few minutes to pack up and leave, not knowing when, or if, return would be possible. The situation might be a natural disaster or other would need to blend in and feel comfortable in a variety of possible environments, both social and physical. The exterior of the coat was designed with inspiration from nomadic folk cultures, and the interior is fully lined with pockets to carry matches, tools, a flashlight, whistle, and an assortment of other survival necessities. There is enough ease between the body and the garment to allow for wearing a camelback water pack or a bulletproof vest.

Once you begin to think about how clothing can work for people, beyond the expressive and comfort qualities, many possibilities open up for sustaining people through clothing. As a near environment, clothing is a shelter, a protective layer next to the skin, and also a vehicle for holding and transporting necessities. Clothing can enhance health and wellness, through carrying needed items, or through actual bio-delivery systems on the fiber level. Energetic symbols, amulets, and charms also provide many people with a sense of protection and well-being (Figure 3.5). Historically, there are many examples of warriors going into battle wearing a shirt that they designed from dream information or spiritual guidance, and you don't need to go far for contemporary examples of people wearing their lucky shirt in their favorite color, embellished with a meaningful motif, when they think they need to be brave or to bolster self-confidence.

So, yes, opportunities abound for innovative design strategies to help clothing better meet user need and desire. Engineers and architects are looking to "biomimicry," the inspiration from nature and systems, to inform new approaches to building. Learning from the natural world is a problem-solving approach that is rich in supporting the development of sustainable solutions toward meeting human needs (Harman, 2014). There are many reasons why fashion could benefit from this kind of investigation and design application. The study of biological systems

FIGURE 3.5. Della Reams' original design for the Dia Jacket, made of cotton/rayon jacquard woven fabric, was influenced by Chinese herbal medicine packaging and imbued with healing energy. (Photograph by Lori Recca. Jacket design by Della Reams)

that have sustained life in nature certainly can provide inspiration for new ways of thinking about how designs in clothing structures and systems can assist in sustaining life for people. We are designing for living, breathing organisms, individuals with particular needs. Through applying design thinking approaches and expanding our creative thinking, we can better address our sustainable options.

Beyond Development and Into Use

Really successful companies know what consumers want and are willing to change to meet their needs (Tisch & Weber, 2007). This chapter has provided suggestions and potential directions for shifting the design and development process in order to create user-centered innovation as a sustainable practice. Clearly garments have the potential to sustain people, but the way they are used can also have an effect on environmental sustainability, specifically through how they are cared for and in the length of time they are in use. Therefore, as a person designing and developing a product (e.g., clothing, fashion), you have the responsibility to think about the life of this product as it is being used.

How Will It Be Cleaned?

You can select materials and garment labeling practices that will lessen the environmental impact of water use and pollutants. As the producer of the garments, you are the expert, and the consumer is the novice. You know all about what has gone into the finished product and how it can best be maintained. It is your responsibility to communicate these ideas clearly to the consumer.

What Might Extend the Garment's Time of Use?

By engaging in a design process that addresses user needs, as this chapter has focused on, the design professional will create garments that will be kept and used longer. That is already a step toward lessening environmental impact, but think about the opportunities to take this further. How about setting up a system where consumers can return items for repair? This is common in some outerwear companies, and is a growing practice in others. I recently purchased a pair of denim jeans at Imogene and Willie in Nashville, Tennessee. The team there was involved in finding the right fit and altering if needed (Figure 3.6). They also will "gladly repair normal wear and tear" (http://www.imogeneandwillie.com/repair). What's to stop us from expanding this practice to a broader range of fashion items? In addition to extended garment life and happier consumers, knowing what and where things break is a first step toward avoiding future problems.

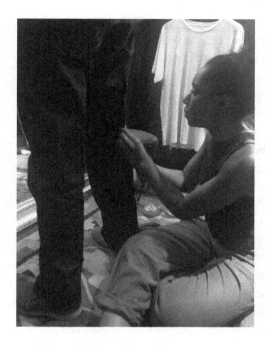

FIGURE 3.6. By paying attention to individual fit and comfort, in addition to vintage style, Imogene and Willie have created perfect jeans, designed and made locally. They do in-store fitting and on-site alterations when needed.

Feedback as Helpful Co-design

Many consumer products have stringent quality control and testing labs in-house at the production level. Think about automobiles and appliances. Clothing, as a product, often relies on the feedback from consumers for much of the information about quality and use problems. When a garment has a problem, people either return it, discard it, or don't purchase it in the first place. The manufacturer receives the information about problems through an indirect communication channel. Why not set up a system of direct feedback from the consumer? Put contact information on labels and obviously placed on websites. Invite feedback and use this information to continually improve the products you develop. The people who use your designs have intimate knowledge of fit, feel, sizing, and performance. This is useful. Tap into it. A sustainable fashion process requires open communication.

Conclusion

We all know that clothing should fit comfortably, that people would be happier if they felt good about how they looked, and that garments that perform well are better than those that don't. Connecting these ideas to sustainability also makes sense. But what are we doing about this? Has the real-world fashion practice met these goals? The textile pipeline fiber-to-consumer model has not invited action toward embracing the sustainability options regarding people. When consumers are at the end of a linear process, they are left to choose from what is pumped out, including garments that fall short of their desires. I have suggested that consciously putting the end user in the center of the conversation in order to meet their needs and provide well-being is a more sustainable model. Finding innovative solutions through design thinking and a focus on user-centeredness through the design and production process should be just as essential as choosing the correct fabric for a garment. Fashion innovation is a powerful process when we expand our thinking about what is possible.

Yes, fashion does provide pleasure, and it can provide even more if we get it right. This is a good thing. I keep imagining a world where people are leading happy and meaningful lives. They are wearing clothes that support this direction. They are wearing clothes that represent who they are. Instead of creating stereotypes and generalized looks, we are creating a clothing environment that supports and sustains individual well-being. Knowing that people have needs and designing toward those needs is core to sustainability.

Discussion Questions

1   What does "well-being" have to do with sustainability?
2   In what ways does design have power in shaping people's lives? How is this power used positively in fashion design? Are there examples of it being used negatively?

3   During the design process, how does focusing on individual people rather than on target markets enhance sustainability?

4   What is the connection between well-being and understanding of visual style that defines an individual or group? How might this understanding enhance sustainability?

References

Ashdown, S., Loker, S., Schoenfelder, K. & Lyman-Clarke, L. (2004, summer). Using 3d scans for fit analysis. *Journal of Textile and Apparel, Technology and Management, 4*(1).

Bye, E. & McKinney, E. (2010). Fit analysis using 3-D and live fit models. *International Journal of Clothing Science and Technology, 22*(2/3), 88–100.

Caplan, R. (2005). *By design.* 2nd ed. New York: Fairchild Publications.

Carlson, David. (2012). *Make design matter.* Amsterdam, The Netherlands: BIS Publishers and David Carlson.

DeLong, M. R. (1998). *The way we look: Dress and aesthetics.* New York: Fairchild Publications.

Denzin, N. & Lincoln, Y. (2005). *The Sage handbook of qualitative research.* 3rd ed. Thousand Oaks, CA: Sage Publications.

Harman, Jay. (2014). *The shark's paintbrush, biomimicry and how nature is inspiring innovation.* Ashland, OR: White Cloud Press.

Hethorn, J. (2005, spring). Understanding aesthetic preference: Approaches toward improved product development. *Journal of Textile and Apparel Technology and Management, 4*(3).

Proceedings of the 2nd IASTED/ISMM Conference on Distributed Multimedia Systems and Applications. Stanford, CA.

Kaiser, S. B. (2012). *Fashion and cultural studies.* Oxford: Berg Publishers.

LUMA Institute. (2012). *Innovating for people: Handbook of human-centered design methods.* Pittsburgh, PA.

Mootee, Idris. (2012). *Design thinking for strategic innovation.* Hoboken, NJ: John Wiley & Sons, Inc.

Nelson, G. (2003). *How to see.* Oakland, CA: Design Within Reach.

Tisch, J. & Weber, K. (2007). *Chocolates on the pillow aren't enough: Reinventing the customer experience.* Hoboken, NJ: John Wiley & Sons, Inc.

DOMENICA PETERSON is a garment industry executive whose positions have concentrated on building coalitions within the sustainable fashion industry as well as educating companies and consumers about the opportunities available for a more sustainable world through better practices in apparel production and consumption. In 2010 she cofounded the non-profit Global Action Through Fashion (GATF) with the vision to create a more equitable and sustainable world through fashion, and in 2014 Domenica launched Averti, a luxury loungewear and lingerie line hand made in Los Angeles, California.

CHAPTER 4

Social Media as a Tool for Social Change

Domenica Peterson

Social media enables seemingly unrelated people around the world to organize around common interests to bring about social change. It allows customers to have a public dialogue directly with companies and hold them accountable for their actions. Social media has also played a major role in the sustainable fashion movement. This chapter explores social media and how it can be used as a tool to make the fashion industry better and change the way we communicate with companies. Social media is the way of the future, especially since it is an integral part of the lives of millennials and will continue to expand and grow with younger generations. These pages examine the meaning of social media, and how non-profits, companies, and celebrities are utilizing it for positive change in the industry. Social media can have a truly wonderful impact on the world, but it is also used to promote bad products and ideas and make problems worse, so it must be explored as a whole.

What is Social Media?

Traditionally, media has consisted of information being presented by an official source, where information travels in one direction. Social media, on the other hand, is a shared experience. Users are presented with information from any variety of sources on the Internet and then have the ability to interact with that information by sharing it or inserting their feedback. With mobile technology, people have access to social media almost everywhere and any time, making information sharing faster and more frequent than ever before. On the Web, social media consists of all that is shared and public; users often don't even realize just how much they engage with social media (see Table 4.1).

Social media, or Web 2.0, has been traced back to around 2004–2005. Although the origins of social media could be tracked even further to Tom Truscott and Jim Ellis's Usenet (a public message forum founded in 1979) and Bruce and Susan Abelson's Open Diary (an online Diary community founded in 1998), Web 2.0 marked the change from individual publishing toward platforms that could be continuously, collaboratively modified by a community of users and the creation of social networking sites like Myspace in 2003 and Facebook in 2004 (Kaplan & Haenlein, 2010).

Prior to the social media era, traditional media consisted of print, television, radio, and independent web sources. In the fashion industry, historically two fashion collections, spring/summer and fall/winter, were presented each year to buyers and press, and consumers read about those collections and trends when they were published in newspapers and magazines or on television. With social media, the speed of information is now instantaneous. Consumers are able to watch live streams of the fashion shows on Style.com, see commentary from fashion journalists and bloggers in real time via their social media channels (Figure 4.1), and get instant updates from companies on new products and styles. With this increased exposure, companies are able to create new trends in short periods of time and sell more and more clothing. There are now too many seasons and fashion shows to keep track of and fast fashion retailers receive shipments of new styles every day.

TABLE 4.1. A few of the many forms of social media

Social networks	Facebook, Myspace, LinkedIn, Google +
Blogs	Wordpress, Squarespace
Microblogs	Tumblr, Twitter
Wiki	Wikipedia, Wikia
Music	Spotify, Pandora
Video	YouTube, Vevo
Internet forums	Gaia, Womens Health
Virtual worlds	World of Warcraft
Podcasts	Planet Money
Social curating	Pinterest
Review and rating platforms	Yelp, Epinions
Social marketplaces	eBay, Etsy, Airbnb
Content sharing	Google Docs
Picture sharing	Instagram, Flickr
Ride sharing	Lyft, Uber
Social news	Reddit, BuzzFeed

FIGURE 4.1. A blogger takes a snapshot of the action backstage at Paris Fashion Week, September 2014. (Photo courtesy of Domenica Peterson)

Why is Social Media Important?

According to the Pew Research Institute, 50 percent of social network users share or repost news stories and 46 percent discuss news issues or events via social media (Mitchell, 2014). Smartphones and social media also give people the tools to participate in real-time eyewitness news reporting. Many users end up seeing news while using social media that they didn't go looking for. According to Pew, "Half of Facebook users get news there even though they did not go there looking for it. And the Facebook users who get news at the highest rates are 18-to-29-year-olds."

As a millennial, social media has been a part of my entire adult life. Since entering the sustainable fashion field upon graduating from college in 2008, media and the way we access information has changed dramatically. There are more than 80 million millennials in the United States, generally considered to be born between the early 1980s and the early 2000s, making up more than 25 percent of the US population (Gualtieri & Seppanen, 2012). If brands and non-profits want to connect with a millennial audience, social media is imperative. According to a 2014 study by SDL, a customer experience software and services provider, five out of six millennials connect with companies on social media networks; social networks and customizable news feeds dominate content discovery. The average millennial checks his or her smartphone 45 times a day (SDL, 2014). The top three channels where millennials discover online information are Facebook, Twitter, and YouTube, with customizable news feed sites surpassing traditional news sites and email for content discovery.

Millennials and all consumers have a tremendous impact. Our actions and consumption habits influence corporate behavior and policy. When we buy Fair Trade and environmentally responsible products, we are sending a message to companies that we believe in fair wages, healthy working conditions, and preserving the planet. Never before has the voice of the consumer been so important, thanks to social media. The last few years have marked a significant change in the sustainable fashion movement as the rise in social media has given millions of people across the globe the ability to organize around common interests and impact corporate decisions, policy, and politics on a huge scale.

The Negative Power of Social Media

While social media has become a powerful tool in the sustainable fashion movement, it has also become a powerful tool to fuel consumption and the fast fashion movement. Through social media, we are constantly bombarded with images of new trends, real-time images of who-wore-what-where, and highly targeted advertising like never before. For the most part, people can click right through from these images to purchase.

Of the many problems associated with the fashion industry, it could be argued that overconsumption is the largest. Right now, the growth of the fast fashion movement, aided by social media, is outpacing the growth of the sustainable fashion movement. This has to change. Fast fashion giants like Forever 21, Zara, and H&M have millions of followers on social media, where they communicate multiple times daily with their customers. They've tapped the rise of street style and selfies, encouraging their customers to become advertisers by posting pictures of themselves wearing the retailers' designs. Their followers are constantly bombarded by new products, beautiful images, and calls to action by brands in a strategic method to get them to buy more. A 2010 study conducted by New York City officials to determine the state of the fashion industry in New York showed fast fashion getting faster, with H&M, Uniqlo, and Forever 21 growing 13, 23, and 25 percent respectively, while specialty retailers grew only 2 percent over the same time period (Mau, 2012).

As Elizabeth Cline points out in her book *Overdressed* (2012), throughout history clothes have been expensive and highly valued. In 1929 the average middle-class man in the United States owned six outfits and the average woman owned nine, and now the average person in the States buys on average 64 items of clothing per year (Cline, 2012). The challenge for sustainable fashion advocates, moving forward, will be to convince consumers not only to buy better, but to buy less, and to utilize ever-growing social media for good.

Campaigns for Social Change in the Fashion Industry

There are several challenges that make consumer-driven change difficult, including complexity around the issues and limited access to more ethical or sustainable options. It is up to companies and activists trying to change consumer behavior to communicate simply and clearly in a way that is empowering, not overwhelming. Some companies are using social media brilliantly, with increased transparency. An example is a company using YouTube to take the consumer directly into their factories to meet the workers and see how their clothing is made. Three of these positive actions are highlighted in the following pages.

Greenpeace's Detox Fashion

One of the most exciting campaigns that has benefited from social media (what they call #peoplepower), in the sustainable fashion space, is Greenpeace's Detox Fashion campaign. Starting in 2011, Greenpeace published a series of reports on the toxic chemicals used to make clothes and in the clothes themselves. Their first report, *Dirty Laundry* (2011, July 13), exposed the links between textile factories using toxic chemicals and water pollution in China. The fourth report was titled *Toxic Threads: The Big Fashion Stitch-Up* (2012, November 20). This report expanded the original *Dirty Laundry* study to include twenty global fashion brands like Armani, Levi's, and Zara (Figure 4.2). Greenpeace purchased 141 items of clothing from popular stores in 29 countries and tested them in a laboratory. They found toxic chemicals in two-thirds of the clothing items, including nonylphenol ethoxylates, also known as NPEs, which break down to form toxic nonylphenol (a persistent chemical with hormone-disrupting properties that builds up in the food chain, and is hazardous even at very low levels), phthalates, azo dyes that can release cancer-causing amines, and more.

Greenpeace has called on the public to spread the word and put pressure on companies to commit to eliminating the use of the most hazardous chemicals by 2020. Greenpeace has targeted individual companies, starting with Adidas and Nike and most recently focusing on luxury brands. Now over twenty global brands have committed to detoxing, more than half a million people have signed up to join the campaign, and millions of friends and followers have been exposed to the campaign via social media. When individuals sign up to volunteer for the campaign, Greenpeace asks them first to share the Detox

FIGURE 4.2. Image from the Fashion Victims Studio Shoot accompanies the launch of Greenpeace's *Toxic Threads: The Big Fashion Stitch-Up* report. (Photo © Lance Lee / Greenpeace, rights obtained by Domenica Peterson)

campaign on Facebook and tag their friends, share on Twitter with the hashtag #Detox #Fashion, and email the video link to all their contacts.

When Greenpeace decided to focus its campaign on Zara, the world's largest clothing retailer (Hansen, 2012), in late November 2012, people took to social media outlets en masse. Twitter alone saw 43,800 mentions of Zara and the Detox campaign; 300,000 people signed up to join the campaign to Detox Zara; tens of thousands of people emailed and tweeted directly to the company for an ambitious Detox commitment; and over 700 people in eighty cities in twenty countries held live protests in front of Zara stores. Within a week, Zara committed to detox and to eliminate the worst chemicals in its supply chain even earlier than asked, by 2015.

After publishing their sixth report, *Toxic Threads: Under Wraps* (2012, December 5), about the textile industry's role in polluting Mexico's rivers, Greenpeace channeled its energy toward Levi's, the main perpetrator in the report. Within 36 hours, 100,000 people joined the campaign. Mexican actor Gael Garcia made a video calling for Mexicans to demand better practices, activists in Copenhagen performed a vertical catwalk next to one of their stores, seventeen activists unfurled a 110 meter long arrow pointed at one of the pollution sites, and in Tel Aviv a number of "Mexican brides" turned up at a Levi's store asking for a real "commitment" from the brand—in all, over 700 people in eighty countries got involved in one weekend. On Twitter, activists and Detox supporters reached 4,493,777 friends and followers around the world. Eight days after the launch of the report, with hundreds of thousands of people demanding that they "Go Forth and Detox," Levi's committed to the Detox program.

The campaign continues to grow and Greenpeace now not only produces new reports targeting new companies, but also monitors the progress and potential "greenwashing" of those companies that have already committed to #Detox. Greenpeace is also working to change policy—for example, the Taiwan Toxic Chemical Substances Control Act (TW-TSCA), which represents a huge step forward toward a toxin-free Taiwan.

Interview with Robin Perkins, Communications Coordinator, Detox Greenpeace

What drew you to the Detox campaign?
I think the Detox campaign is a bit of a dark horse in Greenpeace. When the campaign began three years ago it was really a front-runner in reaching out to a whole new audience of fashion fans, and creating a wave of change in an industry where the problem was not a priority beforehand. It is inspiring to see how a diverse movement has galvanized around the campaign's demands, with millions calling on big brands to give us toxic-free fashion, leading to Detox commitments from twenty major fashion companies like H&M and Adidas.

What is the most exciting thing about the Detox campaign?
Perhaps one of the most exciting and inspiring things about the Detox campaign is the fact that we are working as part of a global movement united in calling for change in the way our clothes are made. It really is a testament to people power. We have seen global stripteases, mannequin walkouts, millions of names on petitions, Twitter storms and support from well-known designers and celebrities. We have seen how people can make brands listen and commit to acting on behalf of our planet and our children's future. Even more exciting is to see these companies turn their pledges into action, taking responsibility for the hazardous chemicals they use and taking concrete steps to help solve the urgent environmental issue of toxic-water pollution.

Greenpeace has a long history of educating and rallying the public around environmental issues. Do you think social media has changed the way Greenpeace does this?
Undoubtedly. Social media has transformed the way we campaign as an organization but also the way that people around the world can connect and unite behind a cause. Hundreds of thousands of people can come together and take action instantly, news can be shared faster than ever

and, as an organization, we are able to mobilize, inspire, and talk to our supporters like never before. As we have seen with Detox, the movement is much closer and more involved in our campaign—something that makes us so much stronger. For example, supporters taking to the social media channels of their favorite brands to call on them to commit or thousands of people helping the Detox message reach an audience of millions by sharing our videos or our photos.

Greenpeace is all about #peoplepower. Millions of people got exposure to the Detox Fashion campaign through social media posted by friends and trusted sources. How are you able to organize and inspire so many people to share your campaigns and get involved?
I think sharing inspiring, engaging, and clear messages with our supporters and audiences is crucial. We want people to understand the gravity of the issue: our global waterways are being severely polluted with hazardous chemicals that can impact our health, our planet, and our future. However, we also want people to feel empowered to be able to change this. We have seen time and time again how thousands of small actions combine into a force to be reckoned with. In addition, we laid down a challenge to global fashion brands to become environmental leaders. It wasn't about painting them as the enemy but giving them the opportunity to show their customers what they were made of and work with us towards a solution. Why can't your favorite brand also be one of the greenest? This idea that anyone, anywhere in the world CAN really make a difference and feel involved is inspirational, especially when you see concrete outcomes and on-the-ground change.

Social media is a powerful tool for positive social change, but at the same time social media pushes the consumption of harmful products like never before. Does the positive impact of social media outweigh the negative?
I think there is no doubt that social media represents an incredibly powerful tool for good. From transparency, sharing, and movement building alone it has transformed the way we as a global community act

and interact across borders. It is also worth emphasizing the increasingly important relationship between the offline and the online worlds. For example, we are now able to live tweet from a protest while activists are standing in front of stores, something that remains a very powerful tool for us, while activists can share photos with their networks or journalists in an instant. Whilst it might have meant more advertising or more opportunities for brands to reach consumers, I think the positives far outweigh the negatives.

Greenpeace has had specific goals and outcomes to create better legislation and get companies to commit to clean up their policies. What will you tackle next?
We definitely want to ensure that people are aware of the problems surrounding the fashion industry, for example the huge issue of water pollution from industry in production hubs like China but also regarding the solutions, for example, supply chain transparency, reducing waste or designing products that are made to last. However, this has to be matched with concrete actions from corporations and strong legislation from governments. I think these three elements are ultimately interlinked and only when we have all three can we ensure a toxic-free future for the generations to come. As for what is next, you will have to wait and see!

Rana Plaza & Fashion Revolution Day

Another exciting example of the power of social media was the Fashion Revolution Day campaign. In sixty countries around the world, tens of thousands of people participated in the first Fashion Revolution Day on April 24, 2014, turning an item of clothing inside out and asking the question: "Who made your clothes?"

On April 24, 2013, the collapse of the Rana Plaza garment factory in Bangladesh became the deadliest disaster in recent years in the apparel industry. The poorly constructed factory came crashing down on workers making clothing for global brands like Children's Place, Benetton, Gap, and many more. While these types of disasters happen multiple times a year in the factories that produce our clothes, Rana Plaza's high death toll stood out, at 1,133 with 2,500 injured. Thanks to social media, news of the event and graphic images of the accident and victims went viral online.

As a response, Carry Somers, a Fair Trade pioneer based in the UK, founded Fashion Revolution Day to turn the momentum around ethical fashion into a long-standing campaign to improve practices in the fashion industry. The goal of the campaign was to get as many people around the world to wear their clothing inside out, asking the question "Who made your clothes?," and post a photo of themselves online via social media with the hashtag #Insideout on April 24, 2014, the one-year anniversary of the event (Figure 4.3). Getting involved was simple: spread the word. They worked with colleagues and friends to build country chapters of dedicated volunteers to activate the movement in their countries. They encouraged people to host events in advance and reached out to international press.

People from sixty countries around the world ended up participating in Fashion Revolution Day. #Insideout was the number one global trend on Twitter, followed by #RanaPlaza second and #Fashion RevolutionDay third. In the UK, every major fashion magazine covered the story, such as *Harper's Bazaar* and *Marie Claire*. British *Vogue* even ran an #Insideout street style gallery on April 25. The British High Commissioner to Bangladesh spent half his speech on April 24 talking about Fashion Revolution Day to an audience of heads of mission, NGOs, and including the Deputy Director General of the International Labour Organization. He finished by telling them all to check out the hashtag #Insideout! Finland organized thirty-two events, over 2,000 attended Barcelona's outdoor catwalk event, Kenya held a spoken word and poetry competition on the subject of Who Made Your Clothes?, and Argentina reached 35,000 viewers on social media alone. (Statistics obtained from Fashion Revolution Day: http:// fashionrevolution.org/, May 19, 2014.)

FIGURE 4.3. Official image from the Fashion Revolution Day #InsideOut Campaign. (Photograph by: Keiron O'Connor, for Fashion Revolution Day. Model: Portia at Storm. Corset: Katharine Hamnett. Jeans: Komodo. Bag: MAITRI. Stylist: Stevie Westgarth. Make-up: Jo Frost. Hair: Eliot Bsilla)

Planet Money's Travels of a T-Shirt

In April 2013 Planet Money, a joint project of National Public Radio (NPR) and *This American Life* that focuses on coverage of the global economy, launched a Kickstarter campaign to sell T-shirts that would fund covering the story of what it took to create that T-shirt. Inspired by Pietra Rivoli's book, *The Travels of a T-Shirt in the Global Economy*, Planet Money wanted consumers to understand what really goes into the creation of a T-shirt and how many people around the world are a part of that process.

Social media enabled them to fund the project by crowdfunding on Kickstarter. They surpassed their goal of $50,000 by raising $590,807 from 20,242 people. They then set off around the world, starting with a cotton farmer in Texas, to a spinning facility in Indonesia, to a knitting facility in Bangladesh, to sewing facilities in Bangladesh and Colombia, and back to you in a shipping container. They filmed and recorded the journey of creating the T-shirts. The story was then made available online through podcasts and videos on their website and YouTube. As of 2014, the Planet Money T-Shirt project had over 893,000 page views and total downloads from the Planet Money podcast episodes about the T-Shirt project came to 3,011,219. (Statistics obtained from email conversation with Jess Jiang, Production Assistant at NPR, on September 25, 2014.)

Successful Marketing Campaigns: Capturing Consumers' Attention

Consumers have a louder voice as a result of social media, and companies are realizing that consumers care about social and environmental issues and are willing to put their money behind it. A 2011 Pew survey found that millennials were more supportive of stricter environmental laws, more likely to attribute global warming to human activity, more likely to favor environmentally friendly policies such as green energy development and tax incentives for hybrid vehicles, likely to pay more for responsibly made products and roughly 80 percent want to work for companies that care about their impacts.

As Kaplan and Haenlein wrote, "Historically, companies were able to control the information available about them through strategically placed press announcements and good public relations managers. Today, however, firms have been increasingly relegated to the sidelines as mere observers, having neither the knowledge nor the chance—or sometimes, even the right—to alter publicly posted comments provided by their customers" (Kaplan & Haenlein, 2010, p. 60).

Communicating complex issues around sustainable fashion can be challenging, but companies are learning that utilizing social media as a tool for transparency, honesty, and communicating their social and environmental endeavors can be powerful marketing.

Interview with Jasmin Malik Chua, @jasminchua, Managing Editor of Ecouterre

A 15-year veteran of the publishing industry, Jasmin joined Ecouterre from TreeHugger, where she wrote about sustainable fashion and beauty. She has an MS in biomedical journalism from New York University—she was a founding fellow of the literary reportage program—and a BS in animal biology from the National University of Singapore. In addition to stories published in online and print publications like *Alive*, *Plenty*, *The Huffington Post*, and *Sprig*, Jasmin has been quoted as a green expert by such publications and outlets as *The New York Times*, BBC Radio, *BusinessWeek*, *Newsweek*, and *People*.

You have been writing about sustainable fashion online for a long time! How did you start? What was it like when you started?
I first started writing about sustainable fashion at TreeHugger, back when no one else was covering it. When Jill Fehrenbacher of Inhabitat spun off Ecouterre—a response to complaints from readers who didn't want the so-called "frivolity" of fashion mingling with their architecture and design stories—she asked me to be its founding managing editor.

How has it changed?
People are definitely more aware that fashion, as an industry, has its flaws. When we first started, you couldn't read an article about sustainable fashion without at least one mention of "hemp sacks"; now there's a deeper understanding that mindfully produced clothes can be just as luxurious or trendsetting as their conventional counterparts. The Rana Plaza building collapse in April 2013 also brought the issues of forced labor and poverty wages to the forefront. The Internet age has allowed movements to crystallize and ideas to cross-pollinate to a degree they haven't before.

How do you think social media has played a role in the sustainable fashion movement?
Real-time conversations have allowed us to mobilize with unprecedented speed and efficiency. We're not just gawping into the void any more;

dialogs happen 24/7. In the online space, anyone, regardless of race, gender, or political or religious beliefs, has a voice.

What are your tips for communicating complex issues around sustainable fashion, in a way that engages and helps change consumption patterns?
It's true that a picture is worth a thousand words. Visuals are more effective than walls of text—that one iconic image of the couple clutching each other in the rubble of Rana Plaza, even in death, communicated the magnitude of the situation more effectively than any 1,000-word screeds did.

What sustainable fashion companies or non-profits utilize social media the best, in your opinion?
Greenpeace and PETA are masters at using Twitter and Facebook to further their campaigns.

FIGURE S4.1. Photograph by Taslima Akhter, a Bangladeshi photographer and activist. He wrote in the May 8, 2013 edition of *Time* (TIME Photo Department, 2013), "I have been asked many questions about the photograph of the couple embracing in the aftermath of the [Rana Plaza building] collapse [in Bangladesh]. I have tried desperately, but have yet to find any clues about them ... Every time I look back to this photo, I feel uncomfortable—it haunts me. It's as if they are saying to me, we are not a number—not only cheap labor and cheap lives. We are human beings like you. Our life is precious like yours, and our dreams are precious, too."

Tell us about Ecouterre!
We're the leading website dedicated to sustainable and future-forward fashion. While we don't shy away from reporting the darker aspects of the fashion industry—the environmental pollution, the human cost, etc.—we do try to balance it with stories about progressive designers and brands who are making real differences. In other words, we're equal parts carrot and stick.

What is the power of a blog compared to conventional media like newspapers and magazines?
Immediacy—magazines have three-month lead times; newspapers at least a day. With blogs, we can report on news as it happens. We can also produce multimedia packages that interact with the reader on multiple levels. Print is important, but it's a static medium.

Everlane

One example of groundbreaking marketing is Everlane. With a motto of "Radical Transparency," Everlane believes in showing customers where their clothes are made and what the true cost of that clothing is. It does this by providing that information right next to each product on their website. For each product you can see pictures, and sometimes video, of the factory where that product was made. They also provide an infographic for each item, breaking down its cost into materials, labor, shipping, and Everlane's markup (Figure 4.4).

Everlane is an online-only boutique and depends completely on social media, press, and word-of-mouth for sales. As Adam Tschorn of the *Los Angeles Times* reports,

> Everlane taps into the conscious consumerism zeitgeist by not only serving up the locations and descriptions of its supplying factories— which span the globe from eastern China to northern California— but also by attempting to forge a deeper, more emotional connection by including details such as real-time weather conditions and the local time of each locale. The resulting effect on a jaded e-customer is not unlike that when one stumbles into an honest relationship after dating a string of serial cheaters. (Tschorn, 2014)

Everlane keeps its branding simple: luxury basics direct to consumer at a lower-than-market price because they cut out the middlemen. The About section on their Facebook page, where they have nearly 80,000 followers, reads simply, "Know your factories. Know your costs. Always Ask Why." Their visual identity is elegant, clean, and minimalist with natural-looking models against plain backgrounds. In addition to promoting their products and story via their Twitter, Tumblr, and Facebook accounts, they invest in social media with strategies like inviting fashion bloggers and press to tour their factory in Los Angeles. They also partner with celebrities to launch certain pieces. For example, Everlane recently collaborated with Ernest Hemingway's great-granddaughter and model Langley Fox to design two sleeveless cotton T-shirts, which made their debut in July 2014. Over 2,000 of the tanks sold the day they launched.

Everlane's model of "radical transparency" is inspiring and leading a shift in company behavior, proving that a model of honesty and transparency is profitable. As of September 2014, Everlane is on track to do 2.5 times more business than it did last year (Tschorn, 2014).

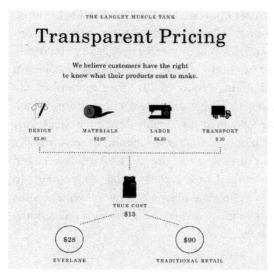

THE LANGLEY MUSCLE TANK

Transparent Pricing

We believe customers have the right
to know what their products cost to make.

DESIGN	MATERIALS	LABOR	TRANSPORT
$2.80	$2.65	$6.90	$.20

TRUE COST
$13

$28
EVERLANE

$90
TRADITIONAL RETAIL

FIGURE 4.4. Everlane's Langley Drape Tee price breakdown infographic. (Screen Capture by Domenica Peterson)

A Shift in Conventional Fashion Media

Conventional fashion media have undergone a huge shift toward digital media outlets. The Condé Nast media company (which includes *Vogue*, *Glamour*, *Allure*, and *Lucky*, among others), for example, is in the middle of a major digital expansion. In 2013, Condé Nast launched an online video network, starting with channels for its publications *GQ* and *Glamour*, and recently introducing *Vogue* and *The Scene*, which sources content from all their media outlets and partners (Condé Nast, 2014).

The conventional fashion world has changed the way it perceives sustainable fashion. While "eco," "ethical," and "sustainable" might not have previously been in the high fashion vocabulary, they are now. Fashion magazines like *Elle*, *Marie Claire*, and *Harper's Bazaar* are featuring sustainable designs. *Vogue* has a regular "Style Ethics" column featuring companies like SUNO, a New York-based women's wear label working with artisans in Kenya, India, New York, and Peru, celebrating unique textures, prints, and embroideries; Maiyet, founded by human rights activist Paul Van Zyl and designer Kristy Caylor to promote sustainable employment to keep people out of poverty; Christopher Raeburn, who uses upcycled fabrics; Costello Tagliapietra, who use AirDye technology; Alberta Ferretti's Pure Threads eco collection; Warby Parker, one-for-one model for eyeglasses; and more.

The CFDA (Council of Fashion Designers of America) has begun promoting sustainable fashion initiatives. In 2012 they established the CFDA/Lexus Eco-Fashion Challenge, an award competition which celebrates and rewards the leaders in sustainable design practices. Past winners include Natalie Chanin of Alabama Chanin, an eco-friendly company that focuses on preserving the unique USA traditions and crafting techniques and is rooted in the slow-design movement. In 2013 they launched the CFDA Sustainability Committee, which "aims to inspire members to work in more eco-friendly ways via educational seminars and other programs."

The Power of Celebrity

Celebrities have played an important role in increasing the visibility of sustainable fashion. The most influential celebrity in the sustainable fashion movement has been Livia Firth. Firth founded the Green Carpet Challenge in 2009, a blog on *Vogue* UK's website, to feature sustainable designs on the red carpet. Working with designers and A-list celebrities, the Green Carpet Challenge's goal was to raise awareness of the problems in the fashion industry and show that sustainable fashion can be glamorous. Via the blog and social media, photos of celebrities wearing "green" gowns and tuxedos have gone viral and helped to raise demand for, and awareness of, sustainable fashion.

Through the increased visibility resulting from the Green Carpet Challenge, Firth has realized opportunities to expose designers to more sustainable materials and production methods. Her behind-the-scenes consulting company Eco Age works with companies to guarantee sustainable excellence with strict criteria. Other celebrities, like Emma Watson and fashion models Lily Cole, Amber Valetta, Liya Kabede, and Christy Turlington, have all championed sustainable fashion, spreading the word about their and others' causes via social media, among traditional outlets.

What's Next for Social Media?

Media is changing. As discussed in this chapter, social media is providing groundbreaking new tools for social change around sustainable fashion. It is helping to connect people to where their clothes come from in a complicated global supply chain and gives consumers a voice to speak up and be heard by companies. At the same time, social media is giving companies the opportunity to drive consumption like never before. The fashion industry moves faster than ever from one season and trend to the next, and as a result of this constant exposure consumers are desperate to keep up.

The challenge moving forward will be to utilize the power of social media for good: to put consumer pressure on companies to clean up their social and environmental impact, to put pressure on governments to make better laws protecting workers and the environment, and to get consumers to buy less instead of more. Right now in the social media race, fast fashion and bad practices are winning. We have the power to create change, so let's continue to speak up and speak louder than ever before! It is apparent that companies are beginning to see the value of increased transparency and deeper conversations with their customers, and it will be stimulating to watch this unfold. I leave you with a guide produced by the non-profit Global Action Through Fashion that I cofounded in 2010. Our mission, then and going forward, remains to create a more equitable, environmentally sustainable world through education about socially and environmentally conscious fashion. Social media has been a focus since we first started and we plan to continue to utilize the power of social media and the Web even more in order to educate consumers and companies about best practices.

"How to Be a Sustainable Fashion Consumer," by Global Action Through Fashion

1   *Wash Better and Make Your Clothes Last*
    Did you know that two-thirds of the environmental impact of a piece of clothing happens when you wash and dry it?
•   Use non-toxic laundry detergents. Look for products that are non-toxic, biodegradable, do not contain phosphates and contain natural ingredients. Most household laundry detergents consist of petroleum, phosphates, and synthetic chemicals that are unhealthy to breathe in, leave residue on our clothing and are harmful to our air and waterways.

- Wash in cold water! Hot water requires energy to heat. The cold water will also prevent bleeding or fading of colors.
- Turn apparel inside out to prevent the outside from being worn out.
- Repair and tailor your clothes. Small fixes on you clothing, like a button being replaced or making the fit better, can prolong the life of your clothing tremendously. Take a minute to sew on a button and find a good tailor.
- Consider energy efficient machines.
- Hang dry your clothes! Avoid using a tumble dryer. Tumble dryers age clothing and use unnecessary amounts of energy.

2 *Upcycle and Recycle*
- Make new clothing from old or used clothes to make an updated look and utilize already produced pieces. The most sustainable product is one that already exists.
- Buy vintage or second-hand clothing, or have clothing swaps with your friends. This is also super affordable!

3 *Shop Ethically*
- Invest in fewer, high quality garments that will last you a long time (as opposed to lots of cheaper, poor quality pieces).
- Think about who made your clothing; try to know the origin of what you are buying.
- Know the fibers you are looking at and buy fibers that are not harmful to the environment (stick to better options like hemp, lyocell, organic cotton, recycled polyester, and linen, to name a few).
- Buy Fair Trade.
- Buy locally.

Discussion Questions

1   What is the most successful campaign currently in the sustainable fashion movement? In what ways does that campaign utilize social media to create concrete improvements in the fashion industry?

2   What differences can you make in your own life to improve your consumption habits? How can you engage and educate others to do the same?

3   Individual consumers make a difference, but we must also take collective action to create serious change. Are there any legislation initiatives aimed to make the fashion industry better in your state or country? If not, is there anyone pushing for better regulations, and who might be trying to stop them?

References

A Final Embrace: The Most Haunting Photograph from Bangladesh | LightBox | TIME.com. (2013, May 8). Retrieved September 29, 2014, from http://lightbox.time.com/2013/05/08/a-final-embrace-the-most-haunting-photograph-from-bangladesh/#1.

Cline, E. (2012). *Overdressed: The shockingly high cost of cheap fashion.* New York: Portfolio/Penguin.

Condé Nast (2014, April 29). Condé Nast Entertainment unveils second phase of digital expansion. http://www.condenast.com/press/press-releases/2014/04/29/conde-nast-entertainment-unveils-second-phase-digital-expansion.

Gualtieri, W. & Seppanen, S. (2012, January 1). The millennial generation research review. Retrieved September 25, 2014, from http://www.uschamberfoundation.org/millennial-generation-research-review.

Hansen, S. (2012, November 10). How Zara grew into the world's largest fashion retailer. Retrieved September 25, 2014, from http://www.nytimes.com/2012/11/11/magazine/how-zara-grew-into-the-worlds-largest-fashion-retailer.html?pagewanted=all.

Kaplan, A. & Haenlein, M. (2010). Users of the world, unite! The challenges and opportunities of Social Media. *Business Horizons, 53*, 59–68. from http://www.michaelhaenlein.eu/Publications/Kaplan,%20Andreas%20-%20 Users%20of%20the%20world,%20unite.pdf.

Mau, D. (2012, April 11). NYC releases fashion report: Fashion Week, fast fashion see biggest growth. Retrieved September 25, 2014, from http://fashionista.com/2012/04/nyc-releases-fashion-report-fashion-week-fast-fashion-see-biggest-growth.

Mitchell, A. (2014, March 26). State of the news media 2014. Retrieved September 25, 2014, from http://www.journalism.org/2014/03/26/state-of-the-news-media-2014-overview/.

SDL. (2014). New SDL study shows millennials are 56 percent more likely to discover marketing content on social networks than via search engines or email. SDL. (2014, March 19). Retrieved September 25, 2014, from http://www.sdl.com/aboutus/news/pressreleases/2014/new-sdl-study-shows-millennials-are-56-percent-more-likely-to-discover-marketing-content-on-social-networks-than-via-search-engines-or-email.html.

Tschorn, A. (2014, September 5). Everlane's "radical transparency" is e-tailers' strong suit. *Los Angeles Times.* http://www.latimes.com/travel/fashion/la-ig-everlane-20140907-story.html.

CONNIE ULASEWICZ, PHD, is a professor at San Francisco State University with over 30 years of industry experience in global product development and manufacturing. Her current research and writing projects examine the need for greater transparency in all parts of the global supply chain of the sewn products industry. She integrates her findings through her teaching and community engaged scholarship.

CHAPTER 5

Issues of Social Responsibility and the Challenges Faced by the Decision Makers and the Decision Doers

Connie Ulasewicz

> *People are far removed from the production of clothes that they wear. The average High street shopper will never experience 20 years of picking cotton in sweltering heat or work in a polyester factory in Zhejiang. This gives the impression that clothes exist independently both of people and nature. The fashion industry is adept at hiding the human labour behind its wealth and power; it is even better at hiding the materials that go into producing our clothes.*
>
> —Tansy Hoskins, *Stitched Up*, p. 97

Have you ever thought about the people that sewed your clothes, dyed the yarns, grew the cotton, or sheared the sheep for the fiber and yarn that were used in your clothing? Our industry is consumed by social responsibility challenges faced by two often opposing forces: *decision makers*, who decide how, what, where, and how much to produce, and those that take the orders, the *decision doers* that must meet the demands requested of them. Might you be a culprit of fast fashion (defined as the ability to find and purchase new styles and silhouettes that are replenished weekly or monthly), because the cost of them is so affordable to you and the true value of the work—the growing of the fiber, spinning of the yarn, and sewing of the parts—is undervalued or undercosted?

Our apparel industry relies on human labor, the physical hands of many to get the work done. We were made shockingly aware of the toils of the industry when we heard, in 2013, of the collapse of an eight-story commercial building, the Rana Plaza, in Dhaka, Bangladesh where more than 1,100 garment workers died and another 2,500 were injured, some of them permanently, because of the unsafe structure in which they were forced to work (Eidelson, 2014; Mantle, 2013). Were you aware of the importance of the garment manufacturing industry to the country of Bangladesh and its people? In 2011, over 23 percent of Bangladesh's GDP (gross domestic product) was in ready-made garments, representing 4.8 percent of global garment exports and 24 percent of their workforce (www.ilo.org). Why are people allowed to work or why do they choose to work in unsafe facilities making a wage that cannot sustain them? We have lost sight of what Dickson, Loker, and Eckman (2009) call out as the labor issues related to the hands that produce our textiles and apparel:

- forced labor;
- low wages;
- excessive work hours;
- discrimination;
- health and safety hazards;
- psychological and physical abuse;
- lack of awareness of workers' rights;
- lack of worker representation for negotiations with management.

A community of people, most often distributed around the world, produces a garment yet rarely have a connection to each other or the part they had in creating the shirts, jackets, or pants that we are wearing. This community of people is connected through a complex global supply chain of textile and apparel trade, government regulations, and national and international trade associations who together must meet the demands of the consumer—that is, you and me, the ones who vote with our dollars. For now, let us focus on the hands of the people, the globalized supply chain that came together to create that shirt, jacket, or pair of pants that you now wear or plan to purchase.

Consider that there are four networks of people in the textile and apparel supply network: (1) raw material; (2) intermediate goods; (3) production; and (4) sales and marketing. Each of these networks has between two and four classifications of jobs within it, for a total count of fifteen (Table 5.1). For now, let us assume that each part of the network has at least one person involved. Yes, at times there may be many more than one person or at times it may be a machine run by one or more people, but at a minimum there are thirty hands that touch each one of our garments, before our own two hands. Think about it!

The intent of this chapter is to bring you closer to those hands, and to gain a greater awareness of the responsibilities and decisions involved in the steps of the supply network of apparel manufacturing before that product gets into your hands. Further, we want to visualize the hands of the workers, whether they are the youthful hands of a young sewing machine operator, or the rugged hands of an elder farmer. Visualize the texture and color of the hands of the sewer in Malaysia or the cutter in New York City or the dyer in Portugal. The increased mechanization, modernization, outsourcing, and global manufacturing of our textile and apparel supply network led to the fragmentation of the connection of these hands, and a lack of understanding of the people behind the hands, their working or labor needs. Please read on for a brief historical context and a greater understanding of the when and the why of the disconnect of the hands. Then, at the end of the chapter, you will be asked how you and I can connect those hands together again.

TABLE 5.1. The textile and apparel supply network (Illustration by Connie Ulasewicz)

Raw Material Network	Hands
Soil preparation	
Growing of cotton	
Picking of cotton	
Cleaning of cotton	
Intermediate Goods Network	
Yarn spinning	
Weaving or knitting	
Finishing fabric: dyeing, printing, washing	
Production Network	
Storage and spreading of fabric	
Making of marker	
Cutting of garment	
Sewing of garment	
Printing or embroidery of graphic	
Final inspection at factory	
Sales and Marketing Network	
Shipping/delivery to store/warehouse	
Unpacking/selling/repacking	

Historical Highlights of Industry Challenges

The challenges we read about today concerning labor standards and working conditions for the hands involved in making our textiles and apparel are, unfortunately, not new. Many date back to the days of the Industrial Revolution in Great Britain and the United States. An 1832 parliamentary investigation in England, the Sadler Committee Report, documents the appalling working conditions in the textile mills: 14-hour days, beginning work at the age of eight, and being beaten and chastised for arriving late to work and with little time for eating of meals. The excerpts that follow are from the 1832 report:

What were the hours of labour in that mill?
—My master told me that I had to produce a certain quantity of yarn; the hours were at that time fourteen; I said that I was not able to produce the quantity of yarn that was required; I told him if he took the timepiece out of the mill I would produce that quantity, and after that time I found no difficulty in producing the quantity.

How long have you worked per day in order to produce the quantity your master required?
—I have wrought nineteen hours.

Your labour is very excessive?
—Yes; you have not time for any thing.

Suppose you flagged a little, or were too late, what would they do?
—Strap us.

Are they in the habit of strapping those who are last in doffing?
—Yes.

Constantly?
—Yes.

Girls as well as boys?
—Yes.

Have you ever been strapped?
—Yes.

Severely?
—Yes.

Could you eat your food well in that factory?
—No, indeed I had not much to eat, and the little I had I could not eat it, my appetite was so poor, and being covered with dust; and it was no use to take it home, I could not eat it, and the overlooker took it, and gave it to the pigs.

These unjust working conditions continued in the northeastern region of the United States where factories, "centralized buildings for large scale cooperation of people and machines embodied new concepts of space, time work" (Dunwell, 1978, p. 24). In the early nineteenth century, Lowell, Massachusetts was the place for the textile mills, where, rather than depending on child labor as in England, they relied on the hands of the farm women for their labor force, who lived in boarding houses surrounding the mills. A writing in the 1842 *Lowell Offering*, a magazine written by the mill girls, highlights a similar discontent as in the 1832 Sadler Report:

I am going home, where I shall not be obliged to rise so early in the morning, not be dragged by the factory bell, nor confined in a close noisy room from morning to night. I shall not stay here ... Up before the day, at the clang of the bell,—and out of the mill by the clang of the bell—into the mill, and at work in obedience to that ding dong of a bell—just as though we were so many living machines (Dunwell, 1978, p. 49).

These unreliable labor conditions persisted in the northwestern region of the United States, in San Francisco. In the later part of the nineteenth century, Chinese workers were a growing workforce of the local sewing trade. Chinese men actually dominated over women in the sewing machine operator workforce until early in the twentieth century (Lai & Jeung, 2008). This extract explains their predicament:

> … workloads at any one factory were not consistent. Workers would go from one factory to another as work was available. Workers were usually paid a set price per dozen. Hours were long and the pay substandard. (Lai & Jeung, 2008, p. 3)

Why the social inequities and human indignities? The mass production of clothing was achieved by the automation of the spinning of the yarns, the weaving and knitting of fabrics. The movement away from custom to mass production brought with it a seemingly new freedom of less expensive garments for a desiring consumer. Yet the sewing of a garment still took the hands of a worker, a doer to operate a sewing machine. The labor compliance issues, the sewers' need of a living wage, earned in a safe working environment, may have moved to different regions of the world, but these issues remain with us today (Figure 5.1).

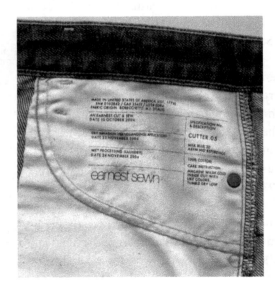

FIGURE 5.1. How different would it be if there were a signature of the maker of each part of our clothing on our clothing? Would we each, the wearer and the maker, feel more connected to the process? (Photo by Janet Hethorn)

Twentieth-century Quota and Free Trade Movements

The mass production of apparel continued to grow throughout the twentieth century and, until the 1970s, was generally predictable, with seasonal collections produced closer to the final US or European city destination and shipped to meet anticipated consumer desire. In 1973, a quota system—or allocation by fiber and garment type of manufactured clothing products exported from particular developing countries and imported into the United States and the European Union—was imposed. The quota system was designed to be a method to defend against unfair competition from developing countries and safeguard domestic production. In reality, it opened up trading and allowed access to an expanding global market for American and European designed clothing, cut and sewn in regions of the world where the labor prices were cheaper. The sourcing hunt was on for garments to be cut and sewn for the lowest possible costs. The disconnect between the thirty hands from the growth or manufacturing of the fiber, to the spinning into yarn, weaving or knitting into cloth, cutting and sewing, grew, as did the social inequities of the people behind the hands.

In 1994 the United States Congress adopted the North American Free Trade Act (NAFTA), which realigned production and free trade with Canada, Mexico, and the United States (Gould, 2009). There was no quota or regulation by fiber or garment type, and several more trade policies followed as globalization continued to profoundly impact the garment industry. The free trade alliances in many ways increased the reliance of consumers in the United States on cheap "foreign" labor to keep the cost of goods at a minimum (Esbenshade, 2004). In 2004 the United States signed the Central American Free Trade Agreement (CAFTA-DR) with the five Central American countries of Costa Rica, El Salvador, Guatemala, Honduras, and Nicaragua, plus the Dominican Republic. This agreement promotes social responsibility and a transparency between the hands of the doers and the hands of the decision makers. There are requirements within the agreement regarding the farmers and the workers who manufacture the finished products—the doers or laborers—and their standards of work (Office of the US Trade Representative, CAFTA-DR).

Manufacturer vs. Contractor

As the outsourcing of garment production increased to regions of the world far removed from company headquarters, the terms "manufacturer" and "contractor" gained new meaning. A manufacturer is the owner or the creator or the ideas person behind a label or brand (Bonacich & Applebaum, 2000). Most garment manufacturers do not manufacture the clothing in their line or collection; rather they purchase the fabric and have it delivered to a location, possibly another continent or region of the world, for production. The cutting and sewing of the garments, the production of them, is done by independent contractors who hire and manage local workers to cut and sew for them. This system enables the manufacturer of the clothing to reap the benefits of fine cutting and sewing without having any direct relationship with the doers, the garment workers (Bonacich & Applebaum, 2000). The manufacturer pays the contractor with the understanding that the contractor will pay the workers; the manufacturer is not legally responsible for the doers, the contractor is.

Who, then, is responsible for setting the pay for the workers, providing them with working machines, proper working conditions, and setting their hours of work? When will "sweatshop," the term for the exploitation of production workers in the garment industry (Esbenshade, 2004), no longer be used? What is the social responsibility that the contractor, the manufacturer, the retailer, and we the consumer have for the conditions in the garment factories? We still have workers, government officials, and anti-sweatshop crusaders coming together to ask questions about why the working conditions are inhumane and why codes of conduct are not followed.

ideas in action

During the 1980s I was a production manager for the San Francisco manufacturing company Esprit, in particular the Esprit Collection. My department was responsible for orders and timely delivery for all knitted and woven garments that we contracted through our agents outside of the United States. My travel schedule included visits to all cities and regions of the world where I, the Decision Maker, had placed orders for the production of our clothing. My job was to check on the process or stages of the Doers' work and to make sure we were on schedule for timely deliveries. A typically seasonal trip would begin in San Francisco, with many stops to inspect and meet with factory owners and fabric representatives in cities within Portugal, Italy, India, Hong Kong, Macau, Taiwan, Japan, and Singapore. We were developing sales plans 6–12 months in advance to secure the quota for production.

FIGURE S5.1. Travel to cities outside of New Delhi, India, where the yarn was transported by bicycle to the weaving huts. The workers were glad to see us. (Photo by Connie Ulasewicz)

Did I witness what has been termed child labor, long working hours, and unsafe working conditions? Reflecting back, yes. But at the time, we were building the economy and providing a place for people to work, in an industry they knew. Did I meet workers, continually, and did they appear unhappy? No. We were providing them with work, and, yes, we were paying them in a timely manner for that work. They were appreciative of our visits and our willingness to work together. In many ways, they were honored that we traveled to them, connected with them, and in essence monitored their work from afar. To this day I am so appreciative of each of their hands, and the ability to see the skill and work they provided for our customers.

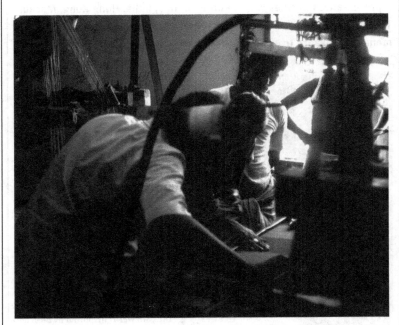

FIGURE S5.2. Inspecting the weaving, making sure it was in progress. (Photo by Connie Ulasewicz)

Codes of Conduct

Codes of conduct are "lists of principles that manufacturers develop to guide the conditions of production in their contracting factories" (Esbenshade, 2004). The codes usually include issues surrounding hours of work, minimum working age, and, more recently, health and safety codes and compliance with the local laws (Bonacich & Applebaum, 2000). The inherent purpose is to guarantee that a manufacturer's products are made meeting the standards they have given the contractor and that they have agreed to follow for the conditions of the workers. The codes of conduct are written documents, signed by the contractors. The terminology and methodology used to ensure that these codes are met is termed "monitoring."

Monitoring Systems

Monitoring is the process by which a manufacturer visits the contractor at his or her shop or facility where the clothing is being produced. Terms such as "compliance" or "human rights" divisions are used for the monitoring departments within large manufacturing companies, such as GAP Inc., Nike, or Reebok. Monitoring may also be conducted by an organization or group outside of the manufacturer or contractor, hired for their ability to give an unbiased analysis of the contracting facilities. In 1998, the Fair Labor Association or FLA was formed with the purpose of improving workers' rights worldwide in many industries such as coffee, electronics, apparel, and footwear. The FLA monitors the working operations and the hands of the doers, the workers who plant and harvest the fibers, and who work in the facilities where the spinning, fabric production, garment cutting and sewing and finishing take place. As stated on the Fair Labor Association website (www. fairlabor.org/), "Unfortunately, many of them [garment industry workers] work in deplorable conditions."

Sometimes the workers themselves go on strike if their managers do not pay them. Why would they not be paid for completing the work? One of many examples occurred in 2012: textile workers in Indonesia were not paid for over a year, because their employer fled the country (Kasper, 2012). A second example occurred in August of 2014, in Bangladesh. Garment workers went on hunger strike for the three months of back pay they did not receive when their manager was imprisoned on charges of negligence and homicide for the 112 workers who died in a factory fire in a local factory in 2012 (Monitor Global Outlook, 2014).

Industry Support Groups

The plight of the workers in our industry and the social injustices they suffer while cutting and sewing our clothes are well documented. Over time, organizations and associations have erupted, often out of tragedy, focusing on different constituencies or groups of people. One group, the United States Against Sweatshops (USAS), founded in 1998, is a coalition of youth and students whose initial focus was on university branded apparel, fighting for the rights of the workers, the doers creating the T-shirts, sweatshirts, and sweatpants sold in university bookstores. Their push continues to be for labor codes of conduct that set minimum standards for collegiate wearing apparel, a "sweat-free" solution.

In 2000, USAS founded the Worker Rights Consortium (WRC), an independent monitoring organization to investigate the labor conditions in factories producing collegiate apparel around the world (Merk, 2014). Universities actually pay a membership fee to belong to the WRC and some join because of protests brought on their campuses by their local USAS student chapters (Dickson, Locker, & Eckman, 2009). In 2014, 175 universities and colleges in the United States and Canada were affiliated with the WRC.

Joining Hands to Engage in Responsible Manufacturing

In a world where robots walk on Mars, the underwear you are wearing can only be produced by human hands. Because of this, fashion and human labour are inseparable. Everything we wear is the direct result of detailed, repetitive human toil.

—Tansy Hoskins, *Stitched Up*, p. 69

At the beginning of the twenty-first century, a reawakening and requestioning began. Possibly the movement is pushed by technology, the speed at which data, photographs, and video clips of those thirty-plus hands and the conditions in which they are working are instantly brought to our attention. In the twenty-first century, the social meaning of how, why, and where products are designed and produced has gained momentum (Binkley, 2010). As consumers begin to ask those questions, the value of the brand or label lies in the conscious choice of country, state, or city of origin for each component and method of production.

There is a new breed of design manufacturers with a new business sense of the interconnectedness of the hands of the decision makers and the hands of the decision doers. Yes, these may be the smaller start-ups, the social entrepreneurs, but the movement is in gear. The Ethical Fashion Initiative is a UN initiative, "changing the way that international fashion business works." Fashion is used as the connector—of the hands of the sewer or the beader, or the cutter or the weaver. The artisan doer living in Africa or Haiti works for and with the product designers. Artisans living in Africa or Haiti are paid a wage that allows them to live a dignified life; through the work of their hands, they create finished goods, not component parts. The programs are monitored and evaluated to document the impact the initiative has not just on the workers, but also on the community in which they live; the monitor is the Fair Labor Association.

Interview with Rosemary Robinson, co-owner of Portland Garment Factory

What makes your factory unique?
We are a full-service factory, established in 2007 in Portland, Oregon, specializing in the start to finish of an item, from development to production. All of our services are offered under one roof: design consultation, pattern making, sourcing, sample making, cutting, and full line production. We have low minimums and capacity for high-volume productions, making Portland Garment Factory an ideal manufacturer for large companies like Nike and Levi's as well as independent designers like Creatures of Comfort and Poler. We can produce knits and wovens, wedding dresses, sportswear, and accessories.

Do you have a hard time finding customers?
The demand for domestic production is getting stronger every day. Companies are understanding the benefits of producing or developing their goods on-shore, such as faster turnaround times, better control of quality in finished goods, more efficient communication with the factory,

FIGURE S5.3. Portland Garment Factory co-owner Rosemary Robinson and Vicente Maya, the production cutter, work together to move rolls of fabric for spreading and cutting. (Photo by Britt Howard)

FIGURE S5.4. Portland Garment Factory is a full-service manufacturing company where samples and prototypes are cut by hand and then sewn for fitting and sales. (Photo by Britt Howard)

and overall peace of mind of knowing their product is in good hands. Over 90 percent of the clothing we purchase in the United States is made overseas, and at Portland Garment Factory we are proud that the products we make at our factory have a sustainable and conscientious history.

How would you describe the culture of your workplace?

We have a very tight-knit dream team with over 210 combined years of experience in the garment industry. We celebrate all of our cultures, with Vietnamese and Chinese New Year parties and Ukrainian and Mexican food buffets. We have double-dutch jump rope breaks, shop bikes, and company parties at the park. Each person on our team brings a unique expertise. We are lucky to say that most of our employees have been with us since the beginning and we are all propelled by new challenges. Our team gets really connected to our customers and helps them become successful. Our sewers love to see the photo shoots from the designers we work with, go to their runway shows, and watch episodes of TV shows or commercials where their work is being featured! Seeing our work in the world keeps us motivated.

What Part is Made Where?

In cities around the world—New York, Los Angeles, London, and Milan—designers are looking to contract out their work to a factory not in another region of the world, but rather across the floor, street, or a different part of the building in order to have a conversation with their cutters and sewers. The goal of these design manufacturers is to provide fair and equitable working conditions for their workers with the understanding of the importance of their hands, all hands, in the growth of the company. Their focus is based on a decision to manufacture their products where they are designed (Roberts, 2013), because of the value that local production or manufacturing brings to their product. In the twenty-first century, as defined by Chouinard and Stanley (2012), a responsible company owes a return to its employees, customers, communities, and nature. It is in their definition of community that they include suppliers of all parts of the garment, from cutting to sewing, to fiber, trim and fabric suppliers:

> to know who does what and where enables a company to work with its suppliers more intelligently and productively—and to improve the working conditions that underlie its products .... Companies will have to work as true partners with their suppliers, in a climate of trust. Profit will not come from taking advantage of each other, but from efficiencies gained by understanding each other's problems and meeting each other's needs. (Chouinard & Stanley, 2012, pp. 29, 32)

San Francisco—Will We Have an Apparel Boom?

It has been documented that the garment manufacturing industry in San Francisco, California is on an upward swing (Roberts, 2013). During the 1970s the garment industry was at its peak with over 1,000 sewing factories that contracted with large manufacturers such as Esprit and the Gap. By 1994, high-volume orders were contracted out

Interview with Britt Howard, co-owner of Portland Garment Factory HouseLine

How did you start your line?

After establishing a solid foundation for Portland Garment Factory [PGF] we decided to take it the next level and set out to design an in-house line of women's wear, aptly titled HouseLine. Our designs showcase Portland Garment Factory's talents in fit and finishing. As modern designers we strive to make ethical and conscious decisions when it comes to fabric choice, design longevity, and our customer's lifestyle. We focus on natural fibers and take care in designing garments that are durable and will last forever. Our designs don't have a timestamp of trend or seasonality.

Is it difficult to convey the fact that US factory owners design HouseLine?

It is very important to us to get the message across that PGF is a domestic manufacturing company first and that HouseLine is a showcase for our

FIGURE S5.5. Lead pattern maker and head seamstress together doing a fitting on a HouseLine jumpsuit. (Photo by Britt Howard)

factory's expertise. We decided to brand HouseLine within PGF rather than separate them, because they would not exist without each other in the same capacity. For instance, our hangtags always say Portland Garment Factory HouseLine.

How many people are involved in making a design come to life?
Starting with the initial design, the garment is ushered into the shop to the pattern maker, materials sourcing person, cutter, sample sewer, quality control person, shipment person … it could be upwards of 6–7 people for a perfect sample! In a small shop like ours, we are able to have daily meetings about design specifics and details. We are old school face-to-face type of people, but for clarity there is always a paper trail.

FIGURE S5.6. Logo of Portland Garment Factory

to areas of the world where labor prices were lower, brought about by the passing of NAFTA and CAFTA (Demicheva, 2013). In 2014, there are an estimated twenty-five factories, including a growing number of manufacturers who have their own sew shops. The terms "Local Manufacturing," "Locally Made," or "SF Made" are in the news (Roberts, 2013), sought out by consumers, and there is a new local aesthetic that resonates with the resourcefulness required (Ioakimedes, 2011) to manufacture in and around the city by the bay, San Francisco. Customers seem to be willing to pay for products with the "Made in San Francisco" label (Frojo, 2014).

Those who are here have a new model, more specialized work, often retailing at higher price points, less inventory, and more just-in-time delivery, as the speed from the design to cutting and sewing is greatly reduced with a walk or short ride to the production facility. As an industry supporter, I was very curious to determine how to increase the demand for strategies that would enhance the San Francisco industry's sustainability and competitiveness (Ulasewicz & Vouchilas, 2008). My goal was to record oral accounts of those involved in the business of local manufacturing, to document what threats the garment manufacturers and contractors faced, and how they envisioned the local community's ability to be competitive in a global market. My research commenced in the fall of 2013. Special attention was given to what interviewees said about the variables that continue to have an impact on the local production, such as government regulations, wages, benefits, social justice issues, and market cycles.

After listening to over 100 hours of responses from people who were designing and manufacturing in San Francisco, it became apparent that these people were driven by the need and very strong desire to support the locals, because that was the "right thing to do." They wanted to "know who's producing my goods ..., everything about how it's being made." They were inherently aware of the higher costs required for a "Made in S.F." label, but forged forward nevertheless because of their convictions and beliefs. As one respondent explained:

> My consumer loves us and has the loudest voice in keeping us here. "Made in America" is very big with the consumer, and "Made in SF" is very important, that is why we are not leaving here. San Francisco is a wonderful platform for emerging designers. People care about the craft of your skill, when you have it made in San Francisco it goes a long way. But our customer has really contributed the most to making us successful.

The business challenge that was expressed by over 90 percent of my fifty-plus interviewees was twofold: first, the cost of labor, the high minimum wage, and second, an inability to find the doers—the sewers who can or want to do the work. The outsourcing or relocating of garment industry jobs that began in the 1970s to countries with cheaper labor had a major effect on the view by the workers of the stability of the industry, and the perceived value of their work (Adachi & Lo, 2008). As one of my interviewees who owns her own sewing shop advised, "Our workforce, traditionally Asian, raised their children to do well in school, go to college, and get better paying jobs outside of the garment industry. It is unclear who the next group of workers will be." San Francisco is not alone in its challenge to find workers and support the resurgence of locally made products. Save the Garment Center (STGC) is an organization in New York City founded in 2007, to support the designers, the factory owners, the workers, the suppliers, and the importance of the jobs this industry creates for the city of New York. There is a growing movement by American retailers to increase production in the United States (Ellis, 2014).

In Conclusion and Back to the Beginning
Had you ever really thought about the many hands of the people involved in the processes of producing the clothing you wear? Each of us does have a vote on what we purchase, what clothing companies, brands, and labels we choose to support with our purchasing dollars. Are you more curious about the process of production and the person who sewed your pants or shirt together? Where in the world they are sitting, how many hours they are working today, and what they will be paid to stitch together that shirt you plan to buy? If you would like to be a part in the reconnection of the hands that make our clothing, please consider the following:

- Ask questions of those from whom you purchase clothing about the hands engaged in the production of the clothing they are making and selling. Where in the world are they located?

- Consider a clothing label that lists the location for each part of the textile and apparel supply network, from fiber to fabric to sewing to finishing to selling.
- Purchase from clothing brands and labels that are transparent in keeping consumers aware of their compliance and involvement with the labor issues of those who use their hands in each stage of the production of the clothing they sell.

Please think about these hands, because the more you do, the greater will be your part in connecting them together.

Discussion Questions

1   Take a garment of clothing you own or are about to buy. Make a chart of the hands and the regions of the world for each part of the textile and apparel supply network. Count how many blank spaces you have. Make a few phone calls, do some research. How many can you fill in?
2   Is your college or alma mater a contributing member of the Worker Rights Consortium? Interview someone involved in the purchasing decisions of the college logo merchandise promoted in your bookstore.
3   How much are the sewers paid in the town/city/country where you were born? Develop a wage chart, compare it with classmates, and develop a global wage chart.

References
Adachi, D. R. & Lo, V. (2008). Made in Chinatown: The decline of San Francisco's garment industry. *Chinese America: History and Perspectives*, 51–9.
Binkley, C. (2010, July 22). How green is my sneaker? *The Wall Street Journal*, pp. D1, D6.

Bonacich, E. & Applebaum, R. (2000). *Behind the label: Inequality in the Los Angeles apparel industry.* Los Angeles: University of California Press.

Chouinard, Y. & Stanley, V. (2012). *The responsible company: What we've learned for Patagonia's first 40 years.* Ventura, CA: Patagonia Books.

Demicheva, V. (December 30, 2013). San Fran's apparel boom. *Women's Wear Daily,* p. 1.

Dickson, M. A., Loker, S. & Eckman, M. (2009). *Social responsibility in the global apparel industry.* New York: Fairchild.

Dunwell, S. (1978). *The run of the mill.* Boston, MA: David R. Godine.

Eidelson, J. (July 28, 2014). A year after the deadly Bangladesh factory disaster, how much has changed? *Bloomsbury BusinessWeek.* http://www. businessweek.com/articles/2014-07-28/a-year-after-deadly-bangladesh-factory-disaster-how-much-has-changed.

Ellis, K. (11 June, 2014). Made in USA gains, but China still key. *Women's Wear Daily,* pp. 1, 9.

Esbenshade, J. (2004). *Monitoring sweatshops: Workers, consumers and the global apparel industry.* Philadelphia, PA: Temple University Press.

Fair Labor Association. http://www.fairlabor.org/our-work.

Frojo, R. (14 February, 2014). Made in San Francisco: Manufacturing a comeback. *San Francisco Business Times.* http://www.bizjournals.com/ sanfrancisco/print-edition/2014/02/14/made-in-san-francisco-manufacturing.html?page=all.

Gould, D. M. (2009). Has NAFTA changed North American trade? http://dspace.cigilibrary.org/jspui/bitstream/123456789/717/1/Has% 20NAFTA%20Changed%20North%20American%20Trade.pdf?1.

Hoskins, T. E. (2014). *Stitched up: The anti-capitalist book of fashion.* London: Pluto Press.

International Labor Organization Mission and Objectives. http://www.ilo. org/global/about-the-ilo/mission-and-objectives/lang--en/index.htm.

Ioakimedes, N. (2011, September). Made in S. F. *San Francisco Magazine,* pp. 105–15.

Kasper, A. D. (February 15, 2012). US university pressures Indonesian companies to compensate workers. *Jakarta Globe.* http://thejakartaglobe. beritasatu.com/archive/us-university-pressures-indonesian-companies-to-compensate-workers/.

Lai, M. L. & Jeung, R. (2008). Guilds, unions and garment factories. *Chinese America: History and Perspectives*, 1–10.

Mantle, B. (July 12, 2013). UNITE HERE, International labor rights forum, and Bangladeshi garment workers president announce American Eagle's latest retailer to join Bangladesh safety accord. Unite Here. http://unite here.org/unite-here-international-labor-rights-forum-and-bangladeshi-garment-workers-president-announce-american-eagle-as-latest-retailer-to-join-bangladesh-safety-accord/.

Merk, K. (September 25, 2014). United students against sweatshops hosts Alta Garcia workers. *Daily Nebraskan*. http://www.dailynebraskan.com/news/united-students-against-sweatshops-hosts-alta-gracia-workers/article_d1c93 f06-4468-11e4-abff-0017a43b2370.html.

Monitor Global Outlook. (August 5, 2014). Bangladesh protests underscore labor risks. http://www.monitorglobaloutlook.com/Briefings/2014/08/Bangladesh-protests-underscore-labor-risks.

Office of the United States Trade Representative, CAFTA–DR (Central America RTA–Dominican Republic). http://www.ustr.gov/trade-agreements/free-trade-agreements/cafta-dr-dominican-republic-central-america-fta.

Roberts, C. (March 3, 2013). Designs for a fashion mecca. *The SF Examiner*, pp. 4–5.

The Sadler Report (1832). http://history.hanover.edu/courses/excerpts/111sad.html.

University Students Against Sweatshops. (USAS). http://usas.org/campaigns/garment-worker-solidarity/.

Ulasewicz, C. & Vouchilas, G. (2008). Sustainable design practices and consumer behavior: FCS student perceptions. *Journal of Family & Consumer Sciences, 100*(4), 17–20.

The Filippa K Story

Kerli Kant Hvass, PhD Fellow, Copenhagen Business School, Denmark

Filippa K is a leading Scandinavian high quality fashion brand started by Filippa Knutsson and Patrik Kihlborg in 1993 with the ambition to design, manufacture, communicate, and sell timeless fashion. Filippa K operates in twenty markets around the world with seven core markets in Scandinavia and Europe. The company stands for style, simplicity, and quality. As expressed by the founder, Filippa Knutsson, "We interpret fashion into wearable, aesthetically balanced pieces that stand the test of time." Instead of following the fast trends in the fashion industry, the company's cornerstone is being a champion of long-lasting fashion by offering timeless design and premium quality, prolonged selling opportunity in stores, fitting services, repair, and second life through reuse and recycling.

The company has a holistic view of its business: everything they create, produce, and sell is part of an ecosystem of the business, as well as of the natural ecosystem. This is further supported by a caring corporate culture where employees care about each other, about Filippa K products, and about their broader macro environment. Hence, the company's business model focuses on moving from a linear, take–make–waste rationale to a circular production and consumption model, where toxic substances and waste are eliminated throughout the production process, which is further supported by working with reuse, repair, remake, and recycle principles. I had the privilege of visiting the company and interviewing several people at Filippa K, and was allowed to attend internal meetings and discussions in order to discover more about their exploration and practices when working with sustainability, with a focus on prolonging the life of their garments through reuse.

Filippa K Second Hand

According to their sustainability manager, one of the biggest impacts the business has is in the consumer phase, and therefore they are trying to implement practices to help consumers make more conscious choices when it comes to consumption, use, and reuse. In pursuing this, and to encourage a longer life for their products, they opened their first Filippa K Second Hand store in Stockholm in 2008. This was done in collaboration with a local entrepreneur who had successfully run another female consignment store in the neighborhood, Judit's Second Hand. The Filippa K Second Hand store sells exclusively Filippa K garments and accessories for females and males and is operated as a consignment store where customers bring back their used Filippa K clothes, shoes, and accessories to be resold. The customer retains the ownership of the product until someone else purchases it. Once the product is sold, the profit is split equally. If not sold, the product goes back to the owner or is donated to a local charity. In addition, over the years the store has also been used as a sales channel for collection samples.

Opening a single-brand second-hand store is not very common and requires strong brand awareness and market maturity to ensure that there are enough products circulating among consumers and loyal customers. All this is something that Filippa K aims for through their products and business operations, and the opening of a second-hand store is proof of these preconditions. One of the informants interviewed at Filippa K described it in a very straightforward way: "to make a second-hand store with one brand is not easy. But if we can do that, it shows that we are really serious about our values. It's really a quality stamp."

The Filippa K Second Hand store has been both popular and profitable. Demand has been higher than supply—proof that there is consumer interest and a positive business case. The store has not been very visible in Filippa K's external communication since the company is both modest and subtle when it comes to communicating its innovations. However, according to a customer survey carried out by Filippa K, 60 percent of the respondents are aware of the second-hand store and 87 percent would consider shopping there.

One thing that surprised me during the interviews was the internal unity across the organization about the second-hand concept. All nine informants whom I interviewed during my research, and who represent different functions (e.g., design, retail, finance, wholesale, logistics, merchandise) at the company, supported and were proud of the second-hand concept. They regarded it as a very natural and logical step for Filippa K to pursue since the brand stands for timeless design and premium quality. It is ideal for Filippa K to capture the value from its pre-owned garments, while at the same time offering a wider selection, better prices, and sustainable shopping choice for consumers. This organizational unity clearly makes it easier to integrate the second-hand concept into the existing business model in order to scale up the concept and expand to other markets, which is something that the company is currently evaluating.

Consumers are Suppliers and Co-creators of Value

A business model based on a circular value chain of products involves a new collaborative relationship with the end consumer. The way customers use, care for, reuse, and discard their clothes becomes a direct interest for fashion companies. Consumers can no longer be regarded solely as economic agents who buy end products but should also be seen as valuable suppliers of merchandise for the second-hand market. At Filippa K they have clearly defined and emphasized that customers are seen as users and active parts of a garment's life cycle before the garments are returned to Filippa K. The company describes its customer as "someone who has passion for modern style but is not a slave to fashion and fast trends. It is a person that is confident enough to wear the label on the inside and values simplicity in the design as well as high quality." These characteristics are very important for the second-hand concept. Customer loyalty and a company's ability to build and maintain this loyalty, together with building a closer relationship with the consumer, is critical for the success of Filippa K's reuse and recycling initiatives since the brand is reliant on consumers both to bring back their unwanted clothes and to buy used Filippa K products. The challenge is to find new ways of engaging with customers, and to discover new narratives and incentives to make consumers become co-producers of the post-retail fashion value.

At the very least, in Stockholm, Sweden, where the second-hand store is currently located, the readiness for Filippa K Second Hand is strong. According to the internal customer survey Filippa K carried out in 2013, 70 percent of the respondents said that they have Filippa K garments, shoes, or accessories at home that they would consider selling at the second-hand store, and more than half are also willing to shop Filippa K Second Hand. With the second-hand retail concept, Filippa K is not aiming to push more consumption but rather to encourage and facilitate reuse-based consumption in the market, and to expand their customer base to other customer groups, for example those who cannot afford Filippa K first-hand products.

New Competencies

Reuse and recycling initiatives create opportunities for new value propositions, but they also require companies to acquire new skill sets in order to professionally capture and benefit from these opportunities—for example, good knowledge of second-hand markets, which in many aspects operate differently than first-hand markets, including garment and accessory sorting, pricing, and customer engagement and education. For companies, customer engagement and education through general awareness raising and in-store communication is an essential part of the success, since people are often not aware of the textile reuse and recycling opportunities and the value their used garments may possess.

Furthermore, second-hand retailing is closely linked to an understanding of the local shopping culture, local culture for reuse and recycling, and local brand awareness. Hence the aim of the partnership with Eva Billing, the founder of Judit's Second Hand, has been to test the market for Filippa K's second-hand concept and learn about the second-hand business from an experienced and successful entrepreneur in the local market. While the home market in Sweden is mature and ready for the concept, the case may be different in other countries. Therefore, an engagement with local country managers, wholesale partners, and store personnel is important when considering expansion of such a concept.

Production and Economic Processes in the Global Economy

INTRODUCTION

There are many ways to think about how fashion is manufactured and the impact of production and economic processes on sustainability. Clearly, in order to bring about change we need to examine our thinking and actions. For example, fashion goods are consumable, thus waste is inevitable—or is it? What processes might we develop and implement that can reduce or eliminate the consequences of overproduction and overconsumption? We continue to produce more to sell more in order to keep the economic engine behind fashion functioning, yet we need to recognize that this is unsustainable and in need of a serious and thoughtful overhaul.

It is time to approach production and economic processes from a different perspective, adjusting not just the ways of doing but also our ways of thinking. The traditional linear concept of beginning to end leaves many issues unsolved. From beginning to beginning is a more sustainable model.

This section of our book starts with a provocative discussion in Chapter 6 on the disconnect between production and consumption. Using metaphors to help us understand the complexities, Susan Kaiser encourages us to think in new ways about processes of putting together more flexible supply chains for environmentally sensitive apparel production. Using Patagonia as a case study, and drawing on an interview with their director of environmental analysis, Susan submits the proposition that sustainable fashion requires a flexible mix of metaphors.

In Chapter 7, Paul Gill, an international trade executive, explores the dynamics of decision making and questioning the possibilities of sustainable product development as we participate in global production and trade. Through his own experiences with the 1973 United States imposed quota system—the numerical limitation by fiber and garment style that could be imported from particular countries to other trade agreements—he provides a context for understanding a changing world of mass production and the demands of these global processes.

Taking the stance that sustainable design action is possible on a production level, Timo Rissanen introduces zero waste fashion design in Chapter 8. With a zero waste approach, the fabric that garments are cut from is all utilized in the garment, as opposed to having leftover fabric that turns to waste. He explains methods for increasing fabric yield and reducing fabric waste through the design process and innovative pattern making. These approaches suggest a possible future that combats our current situation in which we generate massive waste within our industry and consumption practices.

What is the process for reusing the waste that is created? Jana Hawley writes in Chapter 9 about the hidden industry of apparel and textile recycling. She poses the question: if most post-consumer waste is recyclable, then why is such a high percentage of textiles and clothing products dumped into landfill? Jana reviews the economic impact of the textile recycling process and the global challenges faced throughout the world in addressing this challenge.

Lucy Dunne closes this section in Chapter 10 by looking at how technology is implemented as a tool in creating sustainable products and processes. She shares her pioneering research on how technology can encourage sustainability in consumption. Acknowledging that waste exists in home wardrobes, these processes are poised to produce alternative solutions and "smart wardrobe" decisions.

What's Next?
- Address the challenge: Textiles are nearly 100 percent recyclable, and yet textile and apparel products are still sent to landfills.
- Implement processes to design and develop garments with lower fabric consumption.
- Seek solutions: The manufacturing of clothing has moved to areas of our world where the lowest wages are paid and where little concern is shown about the air and water pollution created by the production of textile fiber, yarn, and fabric.
- Use technology solutions in identifying consumer wardrobe management to lessen production need.
- Think more creatively about our current fiber and garment production practices.

SUSAN B. KAISER, PHD, is professor of textiles and clothing, as well as women and gender studies, and interim dean (humanities, arts, and cultural studies) at the University of California, Davis. She is a fellow and past president of the International Textile and Apparel Association and serves on the editorial board of *Fashion Theory*. Her research revolves around the interplay between fashion theory and feminist cultural studies, with a particular focus on issues of place/space, the production–consumption interface in textile and apparel systems, and (re)constructions of masculinities through style and fashion.

CHAPTER **6**

Mixing Metaphors in the Fiber, Textile, and Apparel Complex: Moving Forward

Susan B. Kaiser

Various metaphors are commonly used to interpret the fiber, textile, and apparel complex: pipeline, value chain, upstream versus downstream, and even bathtub. A sustainable fashion system, however, requires moving beyond comparisons based on binary and linear frameworks. Drawing on industry case materials, this chapter introduces alternative, circuitous, web-like, and "transparency" alternatives, submitting that sustainable fashion requires a flexible mix of metaphors.

(De)constructing Metaphors

In 2006, Suzy Menkes, reporter for the *International Herald Tribune*, declared that green was the "new black." As fashion followers know, every season there is a new fashion color. Although green, like any other color, never completely goes out of style, some colors are hotter than others in any fashion season. However, Menkes meant the concept of "green" more broadly: She was using green metaphorically to refer to the idea of sustainable fashion—as a connector between short- and long-term goals. She meant "green as the new black" as a metaphor—or cultural mood (Kaiser & Ketchum, 2005)—for rethinking the ways in which materials are processed, marketed, and used by consumers fashionably, alongside a critical eye toward more sustainable (i.e., environmental, ethical, economic) practices.

Metaphors provide words or images that represent abstract concepts; metaphors suggest analogies that enable us to visualize and understand concepts that might otherwise be difficult to grasp. Metaphors also have their limits, however; they break down when analyzed critically and creatively. For example, "green is the new black" does not work as well today as it did in 2006, because although green never goes completely out of style, it could not continue to be the "new black" for more than one season.

Yet "green," if not the latest fashion color, is still a metaphor for sustainability. The concept of sustainable fashion recognizes that there is a tension between short- and long-term goals. What's next, and what are the consequences of bridging the gap between the latest season and longer-term goals for people, the planet, and profitability?

This chapter explores various metaphors that have been used to make sense of the fiber, textile, and apparel complex. The larger questions at stake are: How have metaphors enabled or hindered the possibility of sustainable fashion? How can we analyze the metaphors used to capture the fiber–textile–apparel complex critically and creatively? How can we begin to imagine, analyze, and compare alternative metaphors?

As helpful as metaphors may be, they do have their limits. Even illuminating metaphors that help us make new connections eventually break down when we push or press them persistently. Feminist philosopher Marilyn Frye (1996) indicates that we can learn a lot by pressing helpful metaphors and by exploring their limits. By understanding where and why metaphors break down, we can realize where and why they may actually *limit* our ability to think critically and creatively, or to envision new possibilities. Frye (1996) argues that we need a variety of metaphors to understand complicated phenomena and to envision new ways of seeing and experiencing the world. She suggests that it is not only okay, but also instructive, to *mix* metaphors. The development of multiple metaphors requires diversity of thought, thereby affording us multiple perspectives and possibilities for the future. Such diversity enables us to reap the benefits of any single metaphor while also gathering additional metaphors from which we can select when the limits of the first one have been reached: "What we are about is re-metaphorizing the world. We need as many and various perceivers as possible to mix metaphors wildly enough so we will never be short of them, never have to push one beyond its limits, just for lack of another to take up where it left off" (Frye, 1996, p. 42).

Exploring Metaphors for the Fiber, Textile, and Apparel Complex
In the textiles and apparel field, various metaphors have been used to describe the fiber, textile, and apparel complex and its material flows. These have primarily derived from the modern, Western ways of knowing associated with industrial capitalism. Often these metaphors have either referred to a *binary*, or either/or, opposition between production and consumption (i.e., the production versus consumption metaphor) or to a one-dimensional, or *linear*, flow of materials from production to consumption (i.e., the pipeline or value chain metaphors). The remainder of this chapter is organized around these and other, circuitous, web-like, and "transparency" metaphors associated with the modern industrialization of the fiber, textile, and apparel complex, with a focus on the implications for sustainability.

Throughout the chapter, I use the clothing company Patagonia as a case study to illustrate the various metaphors employed. I am especially indebted to Jill Dumain, director of environmental strategy, for the more circular metaphors in the later sections. She graduated from the University of California at Davis in 1991 but has worked at Patagonia since 1989 in various capacities, from an intern to a fabric development specialist to an environmental analyst to her current position. Over the years, and beginning with her time as a student at UC Davis, Dumain has influenced my thinking in many ways. Her ability to connect the dots in the fiber, textile, and apparel complex and her commitment to issues of sustainability are remarkable. This chapter draws heavily on an initial interview with her (Dumain, 2007), as well as other updates and more general information about Patagonia and its environmental mission and strategies.

Binary Metaphors

Binary metaphors (e.g., production *versus* consumption) contribute to binary thinking, or thinking in *twos* with an oppositional mind-set (see Figure 6.1). Binary or oppositional thinking emphasizes differences *between* two categories and minimizes differences *within* each category. Although binary metaphors provide a certain kind of clarity as they simplify reality, they ultimately limit our ability to envision new possibilities. Binary thinking restricts us from considering, for example, three or more categories; new ways of forging alliances; and relationships in general that are more flexible, multiple, overlapping, and complicated than binary metaphors can contain.

The following two sections consider two sets of binary metaphors, both of which have roots in modern industrial thinking and practice.

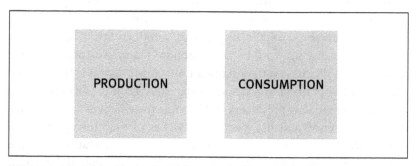

FIGURE 6.1. A depiction of the production/consumption binary metaphor.

Production and Consumption

Prior to the industrialization of the fiber, textile, and apparel complex that occurred between the late eighteenth and early twentieth centuries, production and consumption were basically connected through activities in the home or village. Only the wealthy could afford to have many clothes; materials were expensive. Working with natural fibers, individuals and families spun yarn, wove or knitted fabrics, and sewed them into garments. They either wore them to the point of threadbare materials or they passed them on to family members, friends, or servants. Once the garments were worn, they might be cut into scraps for rags to be used around the home for cleaning or occasionally worked into a quilt or a rug.

This connection between producing, or *making*, and consuming, or *using* (i.e., wearing), began to break down with processes of industrialization. Beginning in the latter part of the eighteenth century, textiles became the first industrialized product, with the development of the cotton gin and later with mechanized spinning, weaving, and knitting processes. With the advent of the sewing machine around the middle of the nineteenth century, clothes could be mass-produced as well, although garment production remained a labor-intensive process, as it still is today.

An oppositional system, or binary way of thinking, emerged between production and consumption. Production became conceptualized as an orderly, mechanized, and rational process of making goods for the purpose of profit. In contrast, consumption became understood as the opposite of productivity. Consumption involved "using up" products or goods. Cultural studies scholar Raymond Williams (1980) described how consumption is based upon the metaphor of the stomach and the digestive system; consumers take the goods created by producers and become the channels "along which the product flows and disappears" (p. 43). Because clothes are worn on the body rather than eaten, there are some limitations to the consumption metaphor. Yet the majority of people are seen as consumers rather than producers: "We are the market, which the system of industrial production has organized" (Williams, 1980, p. 43).

Advertising and cultural processes create what Williams (1980) described as a magical system through which clothing consumption becomes a process of human desires. These processes create a disconnect between the *material* side of production, resource use, and textile and clothing properties; and a *magical* world based on a sense of promise, pleasure, and power: "You do not only buy an object: you buy social respect, discrimination, health, beauty, success, power to control your environment. The magic obscures its real sources of general satisfaction because their discovery would involve radical change in the whole common way of life" (Williams, 1980, p. 47).

Because users tend to buy more than "an adequate supply of personal 'consumer goods,'" Williams argues that the larger needs of society are denied. He critiques the "consumer ideal" to the extent that "consumption tends always to materialize as an individual activity" (p. 43). In many ways, consumption, as a process, boils down to the purchase and use of products by sufficient numbers of individual consumers. How, in this context, can consumption be critiqued from a cultural point of view? If there is a philosophy of "to each his or her own," then how can the larger needs of society and the environment be understood, beyond a capitalist framework?

Since at least the late 1970s and early 1980s, the global restructuring of capitalism has fostered a disconnect between production and consumption. In the 1990s, the media spotlighted the consequences of this disconnect through issues ranging from environmental degradation to sweatshops. By this time, some apparel companies were already exploring ways to enhance their social responsibility by addressing these issues directly in their own production practices and those that preceded theirs (i.e., fiber, yarn, and textile production). Among the many challenges associated with these explorations were those spawned by global capitalism: larger, multinational corporations; rapid change in apparel fashion; an increasing "speed to market" to meet consumer demand; a "race to the bottom" for lower labor costs; and lower prices for consumers in a highly competitive global marketplace. These factors fostered the idea of fast fashion, or the production and purchase of new, inexpensive clothes every couple of weeks. As one consumer cited in a *New York Times* article noted, "If it falls apart, you just toss it away!" (Rosenthal, 2007). These discarded clothes do not simply disappear, however. Research has suggested that fast fashion consumers may have positive attitudes toward the environment, but these attitudes do not necessarily correlate with participation in end-of-life garment recycling (Joung, 2014). Fashion's materials have to end up somewhere, and it appears that this often happens to be in a landfill; hence, fast fashion contributes to the large and worsening source of the carbon emissions contributing to global climate change (Allwood et al., 2006).

Thinking about production and consumption as distinctly separate entities has its limits, materially as well as metaphorically. Ultimately, the limitations of understanding production and consumption as opposites of one another can be realized through the environmental and social issues associated with globalization. Just one of many tragic examples of this disconnect in social terms is the collapse of an eight-story building with five garment factories in Bangladesh in 2013; this collapse killed more than 1,134 workers (Kenney, 2013). As in the 1990s (with the media attention to sweatshop conditions in factories in developing nations), the public became aware of the implications of the relatively low and competitive prices consumers pay for clothing: manufacturers' "race to the bottom" for the lowest labor costs in the world. In times of such tragedies, labor conditions—typically invisible to most consumers—garner moments of visibility and foster an awareness of the conditions under which clothing is actually made.

Just as it is generally difficult for consumers to imagine or know who made their clothes (and where, and under what conditions and what kind of compensation), it is difficult for consumers to understand the environmental consequences and complexities associated with the processing and distribution of their clothing. The process of fast fashion has intensified garment and environmental challenges that are associated with global competitiveness in the fiber, textile, and apparel complex.

Rather than thinking about production and consumption in separate, either/or terms, there is a need for both/and thinking that acknowledges contradictions and connections (Kaiser, 2012). As an example of this kind of thinking, Jill Dumain talked about one of many experiences at Patagonia in which she encountered the important linkages between production and consumption, described in the book *Let My People Go Surfing* by Yvon Chouinard (2005), founder and owner of Patagonia. She was wearing a dress made from a fiber that she saw produced firsthand (Dumain, quoted in Chouinard, 2005, p. 116):

"How to seed a dress": We have been driving for several hours up winding roads high into the mountains of China's Shaanxi Province. I am here to visit the fields where our hemp is grown [see Figure 6.2]. Hemp farming is complex and difficult to understand without seeing it firsthand. At the end of this long, isolated road I expect to see no more than one field with a farmer. I am surprised to find an entire village in a flurry of activity ... Most of the villagers are busy getting the hemp ready to be delivered to the mill that weaves our [Patagonia's] fabric. Bundles of hemp stand in the field to dry. Seeds are being separated from the stalks, which are then carried to the river and submerged for retting (a process that loosens the fiber from the woody pulp) ... Later in the seasons, when the retting is complete, the stable fibers will be separated from the stalks and delivered to the mill. I am amazed to witness an entire village working to produce the dress I am wearing today—from a seed.

FIGURE 6.2. A field of growing hemp, which will be harvested, delivered to a mill, and woven into fabric. (Photo courtesy of Patagonia)

Dumain's story reveals how, despite the disconnect between global production and consumption, it is possible to make connections, but it takes some effort. Her experience is relatively unique. Rarely do many of us have or take the opportunity to trace the clothes we wear back to the raw fibers from which they are made. Dumain's story is a helpful reminder that it is possible and important, at least, to imagine the connections.

Upstream and Downstream

Metaphors derived from nature have been used to describe how materials flow like water from production to consumption. Downstream is used to represent the movement of produced goods in the direction of the consumer, whereas upstream references earlier stages of production, back to the raw fiber or natural resource required.

Like production and consumption, the upstream and downstream metaphors are based upon binary opposition, or thinking in twos. The difference is that at least there is some sense of movement or flowing associated with upstream versus downstream, as compared to production versus consumption.

The focus of industrial capitalism was production for the sake of downstream profit, in the direction of the buyer, or consumer. By the end of the century, cultural critics such as Thorstein Veblen (1899) expressed concerns about a society based on "conspicuous consumption" and an ethos of wastefulness. Production and consumption became less connected as the processes of growing fibrous materials and making them into clothing moved from the home or local studio into factories.

When pushed to their limits, the downstream and upstream metaphors raise the question: Who gets to decide which way is up and which way is down? Are the dynamics about physical gravity, or cultural power, or both? Presumably, the consumption end of the equation has more gravitational pull, downward, but in many ways the oppositional metaphors prioritize production as being on a higher cultural plane. Indeed, the upstream/downstream metaphor seems to belie the ambivalence (i.e., the "both/and" rather than the "either/or" feelings) that underpins fashion and capitalism alike.

Pushing the metaphor a bit further, there is no feedback mechanism (i.e., some way for consumer issues to get back to those producing for them) for communication between downstream and upstream. From an environmental point of view, one can imagine waste materials (e.g., affluent dyes and other chemicals) floating downstream, possibly polluting rivers and streams. This kind of imagery brings to mind the need to delineate the stages of production. What occurs at each stage, from the initial use of natural resources to their processing and fashioning for their ultimate consumers? And, what consequences do these stages have for the concept of sustainable fashion?

Linear Metaphors

Many of the metaphors used to visualize and understand the fiber, textile, and apparel complex are linear and one-way in terms of material flows. Linear thinking, like binary thinking, is a legacy of modern industrialization. Since the environmental movement of the late 1960s and early 1970s, the idea of linear industrial thinking has been critiqued (McDonough & Braungart, 2002, p. 26):

> Neither the health of natural systems, nor an awareness of their delicacy, complexity, and interconnectedness, has been part of the industrial design agenda. At its deepest foundation, the industrial infrastructure we have today is linear; it is focused on making a product and getting it to a customer quickly and cheaply without considering much else.

Pipeline

The pipeline metaphor is based upon the movement of gases or liquids (e.g., oil, natural gas, water) along a series of pipes that have become fused together so as to become seamless. The whole idea is one of movement: keeping the goods flowing (see Figure 6.3).

The pipeline does help to interpret how materials generally flow from one stage to another: fiber producer to yarn spinner to fabric maker to garment manufacturer, and then through the distribution process (i.e., marketing and retailing) to the ultimate consumer. However, when we press the metaphor, what do we find? To what extent does the pipeline metaphor bring to mind dumping out processed materials on consumers and anyone else who may be downstream? Where are the feedback loops from producer to consumer? And, perhaps most critically, which parts of the pipeline are visible and which are invisible? To what extent does this still create a disconnect between production and consumption? To what extent is it feasible for consumers (the downstream folks) to be aware of the

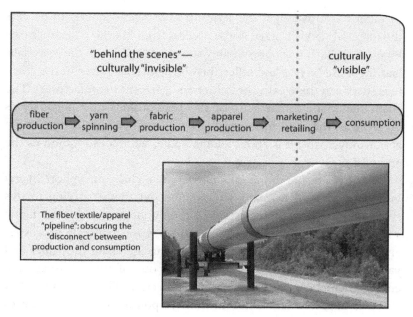

FIGURE 6.3. The fiber/textile/apparel pipeline metaphor, which obscures the disconnect between production and consumption. (Illustration by Erin Fitzsimmons based on a drawing by Susan Kaiser)

conditions of production (i.e., the implications for the environment and for workers' economic situations and human rights)?

Chain Metaphors

The value chain metaphor suggests that every stage of processing or treatment (e.g., from fiber to yarn, textile to apparel product) affords additional value. The chain metaphor, like the pipeline metaphor, is basically linear, but it is not as seamless. Rather, it enables us to visualize the links from one stage of production to another, through production and to the consumer, downstream. The value chain may also be called the supply chain, referring, for example, to an apparel manufacturer's consideration of his or her suppliers. The chain metaphor acknowledges the series of exchanges required to process the materials at each stage in the process from fiber to consumer (see Figure 6.4). Each stage presumably adds further value to the materials, and there are buyers and sellers involved with each link in the chain (e.g., between the weaver or knitter and garment manufacturer). The chain metaphor reminds us of the relationships and negotiations involved in the flow of materials. The whole process is not simply about movement; it is about adding value, with consumption as the end goal.

So, what are the limitations of the value chain metaphor? In my interview with Jill Dumain, she pointed out that according to this system, apparel manufacturers would only interact with their fabric suppliers and retailers and consumers. Hence, the materials, processes, and people involved in earlier stages along the chain (i.e., fiber and yarn production) are "out of sight and out of mind," as are the environmental consequences of these processes. The chain metaphor absolves apparel manufacturers from responsibility for the choices made in cotton production, for example.

As Patagonia made a commitment to research the environmental impacts all along the value chain, cotton became a key focus, Dumain explained. She realized the need to make direct links between sustainable agriculture and apparel production (i.e., to foster the fiber–fashion nexus). She discussed how Patagonia's research led to a policy,

the value chain

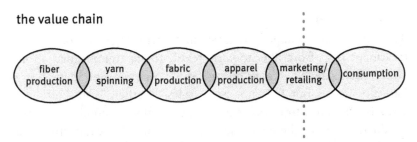

FIGURE 6.4. The value chain metaphor. (Illustration by Jenny Green based on a drawing by Susan Kaiser)

beginning in 1996, of using 100 percent organic cotton to avoid chemical pesticides and defoliants used in industrialized cotton production. She revealed that until about 1991, the value chain model had previously kept the agricultural fields "out of sight and out of mind." Up until this time, Patagonia had been interacting primarily with its fabric suppliers on the left, or upstream, side of the production chain. They realized that if they wanted to fulfill their environmental goals, they needed to look back to the raw material; they felt the need to dig further. The more they learned, the more responsible they needed to become in putting together their own supply chains. Chouinard (2005) describes this process in his book (p. 215):

> Many of our existing fabric vendors refused to participate in our process of switching over to organic cotton, mostly because of a lack of alternative suppliers and their skepticism about the market potential. The staff at Patagonia had to go back all the way to the beginning of the supply chain. We searched out cotton brokers with access to bales of organic cotton. Of all the fabric mills we ended up using for our supply of organic cotton, only two had had prior experience working with it ... Our organic cotton program has been a success, but not just because our customers are making the same choice we made—to pay more now for organics rather than pay the hidden environmental costs down the road—but because our designers and production people now have to begin their work with a bale of raw cotton and follow it all the way through the process of becoming a finished garment.

Bathtub: Stock and Flow

Nearly fifty years ago, clothing economist Geitel Winakor (1969) observed that the problem with the chain metaphor, which she described as marketing-based, was that the consumer can only be seen as a customer. In fact, there are three processes associated with consumption: acquisition, inventory, and discard. The first process, acquisition, may be described as a flow from retailer to consumer (e.g., as a purchase), or as a flow from one consumer to another (e.g., as a gift or a hand-me-down). The second process involves consumer inventory, or stock management. Inventory involves use or wear, care, and active storage. The third process is that of discard (e.g., the act of literally discarding, disposing, donating, or recycling). Discard refers to the stage at which the garment leaves the possession of the individual. Like acquisition, discard constitutes a kind of flow (out of the closet). Winakor used the economic metaphor of a bathtub to visualize her stock-and-flow model of clothing consumption. In this metaphor, water flows in through a faucet and then is stored for a period of time in the tub (i.e., the wardrobe). The tub can only become so full before it overflows (i.e., experiences wardrobe overload). The process of releasing the water down the drain is analogous to the process of discard. Usually, the flows in and out of the tub are intermittent rather than continuous. The flows depend on how often the consumer shops and discards.

Whereas marketing models of consumption generally prioritize the point of acquisition, Winakor (1969) emphasized that it is usually more challenging "to pinpoint the moment of discard" (p. 631). Why is this so? She outlined a number of reasons. First, the "moment of acquisition" is usually "more pleasurable and more memorable." Second, "the moment of discard" often involves some degree of doubt or uncertainty: Will I ever wear this again? What should I do with this?

A feedback mechanism presumably connects acquisition with inventory and discard in order to maintain a sense of equilibrium. Winakor (1969) called for more clarification of this feedback mechanism. She noted the complex and individualized nature of the overall process: each consumer probably has her or his own equilibrium level. For example, consumers may have guidelines they use when they discard, such as, "Have I worn it in the last year?" Some might have a "shirt in, shirt out" policy: if they buy something new, they get rid of something else. Other consumers just let the closet overflow until they clearly need to do something.

Winakor pointed out the uniqueness of clothing as compared to other basic human needs. Clothing is not as durable as a house, but it cannot be "consumed once and for all like food." Over forty years after Winakor wrote this, Rebecca Calahan-Klein, president of Organic Exchange, comments: "The big joke in the organic advocacy world is that one day we will have a shirt we can eat" (Jana, 2006). Until this day comes, the issue of environmental waste is one that plagues environmentally conscious textile and apparel producers and consumers alike. The contemporary concept of fast fashion and the shorter life cycles of clothes in the inventory phase of Winakor's metaphor contribute to more waste for the discard phase, due to a dynamic and continuous, rather than an intermittent, flow in and out of the bathtub metaphor.

Winakor's bathtub metaphor is helpful, because: (1) it expands our thinking about consumption, which becomes more than the end of a pipeline or chain; and (2) it includes the need for a feedback mechanism. Although it did not fully take environmental issues into account and although it still basically follows a linear model, Winakor's model still enables us to conceptualize consumption in ways that help us to imagine feedback mechanisms and the implications of consumer waste.

Cradle-to-Grave

The cradle-to-grave metaphor calls attention to the complete life cycle of a garment from an environmental point of view. It recognizes that materials come from the earth and ultimately return to the earth. They do not simply appear or disappear according to fashion cycles. Like Winakor's bathtub metaphor, the cradle-to-grave metaphor considers the life of the garment once it reaches the consumer, including how it is cared for, how it is disposed of or recycled, and the like. Such a life cycle analysis is critical, because research generally indicates that the post-sale care of a clothing product causes as much as four times the amount of harm to the environment, primarily through water and energy use, than does the entire manufacturing pipeline (Allwood et al., 2006; Chouinard, 2005).

With an awareness of environmental impacts along every stage of this linear process from birth to death, the negative environmental and social consequences of production, distribution, and consumption can be minimized, or in other words made "less bad." However, there are still major problems with a cradle-to-grave way of thinking: Earth's resources are finite; resources need to become more renewable. Second, Earth's ability to store waste (e.g., in landfills) is limited; waste needs to be minimized. Moreover, our thinking is still constrained by the linear, one-way metaphor.

Cradle-to-Cradle

The cradle-to-cradle metaphor builds upon an environmentally conscious cradle-to-grave metaphor, with a focus on design and product development: the creation of innovative and high quality products that not only generate economic value but also enhance the well-being of nature and culture. A cradle-to-cradle approach conceptualizes products as contributing to what McDonough and Braungart (2002) call the "triple top line": the interplay among ecology, economy, and equity. A cradle-to-cradle approach involves a supply chain with a feedback loop. One product's life cycle becomes connected with a new product's life cycle. Making and consuming clothes becomes transformed into a "regenerative force." The grave of one garment's life cycle becomes the cradle of its own or another product's life cycle. Ultimately, this means producing clothes that will never become waste. Instead, they become the "food" or nutrients for new, high quality products. And here, quality includes vibrant contributions to nature, to individuals (consumers and workers alike), communities, and the economy. Industrial systems themselves help to restore nature and culture.

To develop cradle-to-cradle cycles, McDonough and Braungart (2002, pp. 103–4) say that we can take important cues from nature:

> If humans are truly going to prosper, we will have to learn to imitate nature's highly effective cradle-to-cradle system of nutrient flow and metabolism, in which the very concept of waste does not exist ... It means that the valuable nutrients contained in the materials shape and determine the design: form follows evolution, not just function.

In the cradle-to-cradle metaphor, diversity in design becomes a key idea as the end of the life span of one product may be the beginning of a new life span for that product. The concept of diversity refers both to nature and to culture. Diversity in design includes "not only how a product is made but how it is to be used, and by whom ... [I]t may have many uses, and many users, over time and space" (McDonough & Braungart, 2002, p. 139).

Cradle-to-cradle is the foundation in a larger process of upcycling. In *The Upcycle: Beyond Sustainability—Designing for Abundance*, McDonough & Braungart (2013) argue that it is not enough to "do no harm" to the planet: We need to redesign our activity to improve the planet. "The goal of the upcycle is a delightfully diverse, safe, healthy, and just world with clean air, water, soil, and power—economically, equitably, ecologically, and elegantly enjoyed" (McDonough & Braungart, 2013, p. ix).

As Patagonia began to explore ways of minimizing environmental waste, it analyzed its fleece jackets, manufactured with "virgin" polyester. Working with a company called Wellman, Patagonia developed a process that takes soda pop bottles, which are also made of polyester, and recycles them into raw material for jackets. The process of making a single jacket requires 25 bottles; between 1993 and 2003, Patagonia and Wellman diverted 86 million soda bottles from landfills: "For every 150 virgin polyester jackets that we replaced with post-consumer recycled (PCR), we saved 42 gallons of oil and prevented a half-ton of toxic air emissions" (Chouinard, 2005, p. 212). Adopting the cradle-to-cradle metaphor, Chouinard takes a self-reflexive look at Patagonia's environmental mission (pp. 114–15):

> But we can never be satisfied with our progress ... Recycling some of our wastes and making Synchilla jackets [see Figure 6.5] out of recycled soda pop bottles are not enough. We have to take responsibility for what we make, from birth to death and then beyond death, back to rebirth, what the architect, designer, and author Bill McDonough calls "cradle to cradle." It means making a pair of pants out of infinitely recyclable polyester or a polymer like Nylon 6 and, when it is finally worn out, melting down the pants to a resin and creating another pair from the same resin—over and over again.

FIGURE 6.5.
Patagonia's Synchilla jacket. (Photo courtesy of Patagonia)

Thinking in Circles: Creating Connections, Closing Loops

In my conversation with Dumain, I asked her how she visualizes the fiber, textile, and apparel complex. She replied that she initially had thought of it as linear, but now she finds herself "thinking in circles." The issue, she said, is who needs to communicate with whom; who needs to be connecting; where feedback is required (Dumain, 2007).

From Lines to Loops

As Dumain and I talked further, she clarified how lines begin to "loop over" in unexpected places. She noted how in her years of problem-solving experience with Patagonia, she has come to envision the fiber, textile, and apparel complex in new ways (Dumain, 2007):

> When we embarked [on the organic cotton commitment], we were very linear. We traveled down the line … But the linear approach turned into circles. The [yarn] spinner asked, "What's organic?" He had to come to us, and everybody had to be talking to each other for the success of the program. Everybody needed to have access to each other.

The need to make the necessary connections to achieve longer-term goals for the environment, and to build new relationships as required, demanded a lot of effort. It entailed moving beyond linear thinking toward a process of collective learning, creating, and constructing new, more flexible ways of knowing.

The supply or value chain did not simply materialize for Dumain and Patagonia; rather, if they wanted to make a difference in the environment, they had to build their own and let it take its course in terms of the twists and turns necessary to foster communication and trust (see Figure 6.6). This was no longer a linear process.

So, let's push the metaphor of a linear chain that loops over a bit further. Let's imagine a necklace; it's basically linear, but if one wants

FIGURE 6.6. The "thinking in circles" concept, crossing over and creating loops in the supply chain metaphor. (Illustration by Jenny Green based on a drawing by Susan Kaiser)

to wear it around one's neck, some curving is required. If it is a small or fine chain-link necklace, it is not difficult for unexpected twists or knots to appear as the necklace doubles back on itself. Although this is undoubtedly an annoying occurrence, it can be instructive to think with metaphorically. It reminds us of the need to cross over, to loop back. Twists and turns can point out challenges that need to be addressed.

Sustainability requires thinking more in circles than in a straight line. The supply chain needs to become less rigid, or more flexible, so that crossing over becomes a possibility in order to sustain multiple businesses as well as the environment. Crossing over and developing loops is even more important and possible than ever in the flatter world associated with globalization, wherein new technologies become coupled with local networks (Friedman, 2006). The process of putting together a supply chain for environmentally sensitive apparel production demands forging new connections and closing some loops.

Spiderwebs

Perhaps we can begin to imagine a metaphor that is three-dimensional. A spiderweb is an intriguing metaphor (see Figure 6.7). It encourages us to think in terms of networks rather than lines. Spider silk is a highly

FIGURE 6.7. This drawing depicts the spiderweb metaphor, which encourages thinking in terms of networks rather than lines. (Illustration by Jenny Green based on a drawing by Susan Kaiser)

flexible material, and spiders have a repertoire of at least five different silks. Spider silk is biocompatible and biodegradable; it is eight times more extensible than Kevlar fiber (i.e., the "active ingredient" used in bulletproof vests) and five times tougher. A spiderweb is a highly complex and yet elegantly simple construction. It is a "self-organized pattern formation" (Camazine et al., 2003). And it can be repaired or replaced as necessary.

What is at the center of the spiderweb metaphor for the fiber, textile, and apparel complex? Because a spiderweb is a flexible rather than a fixed structure, it makes sense to visualize different configurations. The center may change from one web to the next. For example, often the consumer will be at the center, with the opportunity for numerous players, not only retailers, to interact directly with her or him. At times, however, a company may want to visualize itself in the center so that it can reimagine its relationship with other players beyond the linear format that keeps some players "out of sight and out of mind" (Dumain, 2007). When Patagonia did a lot of soul searching regarding its environmental mission in the late 1980s, it re-envisioned its supply chain and began to see the need to interact directly with cotton growers, for example (Chouinard, 2005).

Dumain explained in her interview how the center of Patagonia's supply chain can emerge in unexpected places. For example, a yarn spinner became central to the development of a production web in Bangkok, Thailand. The yarn spinner became the "center of the deal" or the "common denominator" who knew a lot of people. The spinner helped to make connections with the organic cotton growers and cotton brokers, as well as with weavers and knitters. Dumain put together the organic cotton web that Patagonia desired by working with the yarn spinner's contacts. As a result, she said, "we became much more effective in our R&D. Otherwise, it would have stopped along the line [or linear chain], at its weakest link." Initially, the fabric supplier would say, "I can't get that [organic cotton and polyester blend] yarn." Dumain asked, "Will you knit it if I can get the yarn?" (Dumain, 2007).

The yarn spinner, accustomed to working with conventional cotton, then set up a separate operation for Patagonia's organic cotton, blended in various percentages with polyester. This yarn spinner had set up his mill with an eye toward the flexibility to handle smaller specialty items. This enabled Patagonia to experiment with different ratios of organic cotton and polyester in small quantities. The spinner then coordinated his timing with weavers and knitters, in the spirit of experimenting through a small-scale R&D effort.

In its commitment to use only organic cotton in its clothing, Patagonia keeps a consistent supply web in place. The web is built on relationships, and enables Patagonia "to do a lot more R&D than would normally be possible for a company our size" (Dumain, 2007). Patagonia also uses organic cotton from California, Texas, New Mexico, Turkey, Africa, and Israel. Dumain stressed the importance of addressing both short- and long-term goals in building supply webs based on trust (Dumain, 2007):

We need both [short- and long-term goals]. One hundred years is very different than 100 days, but the latter is part of our daily world. In the short run, especially with new projects, we need some "wins" at the beginning. It is so hard to do something different. People can then get excited; they see the possibilities ... You just need to start in—to start from scratch—and then short-term wins encourage people in the long term.

The spiderweb metaphor can be useful to imagine short- and long-term "wins" in diverse configurations. No two webs will be identical, just as there is biodiversity in nature. Rather, the web will depend upon the specific project or network required for a specific context or challenge. If we push the spiderweb metaphor, as always, we will find some limits. However, at least it, as do the other circular metaphors, breaks us out of a binary or linear mind-set and opens up new possibilities for understanding relationship building as a vital part of sustainable fashion.

Transparency

Increasingly in recent years, transparency has become an important metaphor in government and higher education, as well as industry. It refers to a culture of openness, disclosure, and accountability. In the environmental context, transparent systems of disclosure intentionally strive to protect the global planet and to reduce harms to it. In recent years, environmental studies scholars such as Gupta and Mason (2014) argue that there has been a "transparency turn," through which the public and private sectors alike are engaging in environmental decision making and strategic planning in ways that can be "seen through," or that are more visible in the spirit of full disclosure.

In the context of the fiber, textile, and apparel complex, the transparency turn involves a move toward more visibility of the various players and partners involved in the production, distribution, consumption, and post-consumer life and possible after-life of a garment. In short, there is a strong desire to reclaim a deep knowledge of the "supply chain" (Chouinard & Stanley, 2012).

Patagonia's "Footprint Chronicles" (http://www.patagonia.com/us/footprint) provide a transparent look at their circuitous supply chain and their interactions with the various factories or partners involved. On the company website, one finds in-depth details about sourced materials (e.g., organic cotton, traceable down, recycled polyester), factory conditions, challenges, and goals. With a sense of self-reflexivity (i.e., what is not perfect, what could be improved, what has the company learned), Patagonia provides a wealth of information to consumers and industry colleagues alike: "The goal is to use transparency about our supply chain to help us reduce our adverse social and environmental impacts – and on an industrial scale. We've been in business long enough to know that when we can reduce or eliminate a harm, other businesses will be eager to follow suit" (www.patagonia.com, 2014).

Conclusion

As Frye (1996) argues, there are advantages to keeping multiple metaphors at hand, and to continuing to create them. Whether the metaphors used to visualize the fiber, textile, and apparel complex are based on binary, linear, circular, web-like, transparent, or other frameworks, they have all made some contributions to our ways of understanding this complex. I write this chapter in the spirit of inviting ongoing, critical, and creative approaches to analyze existing metaphors and generate new ones, in order to foster a more sustainable, and hopefully more equitable, fiber, textile, and apparel system.

At the same time, following Frye (1996), I want to conclude with a call to mix metaphors. Metaphors come in all kinds of colors, shapes, and sizes; sustainable fashion requires a critical and creative mixing of metaphors. As various environmental and social challenges present themselves to producers and consumers alike, it is advantageous to have an array of metaphors available to mix, match, and juxtapose in our collective toolkits.

Acknowledgment

I am most grateful to two graduate students, Ryan Looysen and Jennifer Norah Sorensen, for independently suggesting the spiderweb metaphor, on different occasions, as I was working on this chapter and discussing it with them. Their suggestions really got me thinking outside of the box, or the linear mode, actually, as did my interview with Jill Dumain. I sincerely appreciate all of their contributions and thought-provoking insights.

Discussion Questions

1   To what extent does the pipeline metaphor help to interpret how materials flow from one stage of production to another? What are its limitations?

2   Visit the Patagonia website (www.patagonia.com). Which of the metaphors in this chapter can you link to Patagonia's practices? Does Patagonia mix metaphors? Explain.

3   Why is it important to have a "feedback loop" in the fiber, textile, and apparel system? Which of the metaphors in this chapter have feedback loops? Explain.

4   Why does sustainable fashion require a critical and creative mixture of linear and circular and other metaphors?

References

Allwood, J. M., Laursen, S. E., de Rodriguez, C. M. & Bocken, N. M. P. (2006). *Well dressed? The present and future of clothing and textiles in the United Kingdom.* Cambridge: University of Cambridge Institute for Manufacturing.

Camazine, S. et al. (2003). *Self-organization in biological systems.* Princeton, NJ: Princeton University Press.

Chouinard, Y. (2005). *Let my people go surfing: The education of a reluctant businessman.* New York: The Penguin Press.

Chouinard, Y. & Stanley, V. (2012). *The responsible company: What we've learned from Patagonia's first 40 years.* Ventura, CA: Patagonia Books.

Dumain, J., director of environmental analysis, Patagonia. (2007, January 12). Personal interview.

Friedman, T. L. (2006). *The world is flat: A brief history of the twenty-first century.* 2nd ed. New York: Farrar, Straus, and Giroux.

Frye, M. (1996). The possibility of feminist theory. In A. Garry & M. Pearsall (Eds.), *Women, knowledge, and reality: Explorations in feminist philosophy.* New York and London: Routledge.

Gupta, A. & Mason, M. (2014). A transparency turn in global environmental governance. In A. Gupta & M. Mason (Eds.), *Transparency in global environmental governance: Critical perspectives* (pp. 3–38). Boston, MA: Massachusetts Institute of Technology Press.

Jana, R. (2006, September 29). Green threads for the eco chic. *Business Week Online.*

Joung, H.-M. (2014). Fast-fashion consumers' post-purchase behaviours. *International Journal of Retail and Distribution Management, 42*(8), 688–97.

Kaiser, S. B. (2012). *Fashion and cultural studies.* London: Berg.

Kaiser, S. B. & Ketchum, K. (2005). Consuming fashion as flexibility: Metaphor, cultural mood, and materiality. In S. Ratneshwar & D. G. Mick (Eds.), *Inside consumption: Consumer motives, goals, and desires.* London: Routledge.

Kenney, C. (2013, December 26). The tragic number that got us all talking about our clothing. *Planet Money: The Economy Explained.* www.npr.org (accessed September 28, 2014).

McDonough, W. & Braungart, M. (2002). *Cradle to cradle: Remaking the way we make things.* New York: North Point Press.

McDonough, W. & Braungart, M. (2013). *The upcycle: Beyond sustainability—Designing for abundance.* New York: North Point Press.

Menkes, S. (2006, May 31). Eco-friendly: Why green is the new black. *International Herald Tribune.*

Rosenthal, E. (2007, January 25). Can polyester save the world? *New York Times,* p. G-1.

Veblen, T. (1899). *The theory of the leisure class.* New York and London: Macmillan.

Williams, R. (1980). The magic of advertising. In R. Williams (Ed.), *Problems in materialism and culture* (pp. 170–95). London: Verso.

Winakor, G. (1969). The process of clothing consumption. *Journal of Home Economics, 61*(8), 629–34.

PAUL GILL is a garment industry executive with more than thirty years of experience specializing in areas of global manufacturing, production, scouring, and factory relationships. He is renowned for his work in promoting and resolving issues of fair trade with domestic and international manufacturing firms.

CHAPTER 7

Economy of Scale:
A Global Context

Paul Gill

What can global manufacturing teach us about sustainability? In the early 1970s, a quota system was instituted to control the flow of goods manufactured in developing countries and sold to richer consuming regions like the United States and the European Union. In 2005, that system was removed and a new revolution began. I experienced it all, and in this chapter I lend my personal experience to help us consider the rise and fall of the quota system, the emergence of China as a global trade leader, the move to Bangladesh, Cambodia, Vietnam, and what it all means for developing sustainable sourcing and manufacturing in the twenty-first century.

The Rise and Fall of the Quota System

The history of the textile and apparel industries' quota system provides a framework for an understanding of global manufacturing. For more than thirty years, this system served as a means to control and sustain the flow of goods between countries that are developed (e.g., United States, Europe) and developing (e.g., China, India). Quotas were numerical limits on the number of products in specific categories, determined by the fiber type and garment style, that could be imported from particular countries. Quotas were intended to be a means to sustain and protect domestic manufacturers from what seemed to be unfair competition from other countries. This protectionist idea went down with the quota system with an eye to developing and sustaining a global textile and apparel manufacturing system.

Quotas

In 1973, the United States imposed a quota system for textiles and apparel on its predominantly Asian trading partners, which included Hong Kong, Korea, Indonesia, and Taiwan (Rivoli, 2005) (see Figure 7.1). Japan also had quotas imposed on it because it was seen in those days as a source of low-cost apparel. Each country was free to decide how to distribute its quota, or *allocation*, which was issued according to fiber and garment type. A country's allocations were based on previous years' records of what it shipped in the past. Hong Kong, for example, had been a center of wool sweater manufacturing because many of the factories from northern China had fled to the free market there at the

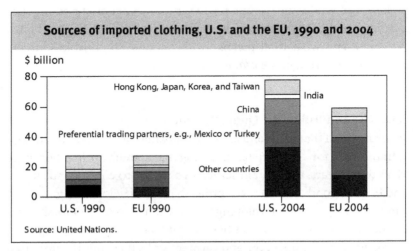

FIGURE 7.1. Sources of clothing imports during the period of the US quota system.

time of the communist revolution in 1948. Thus, Hong Kong had a substantial allocation of wool sweater quota despite its obvious absence of sheep. Fibers that were not significantly imported, such as linen and ramie, were excluded, as was silk. The exclusion of ramie led in short order to the development of ramie/cotton and other ramie or linen blends designed specifically to evade quota requirements (Rivoli, 2005).

The International Quota Trade

I started my first job in the apparel industry in January 1972. The company, Tami Sportswear, was a San Francisco based designer, wholesaler, and manufacturer of medium- to low-priced women's sportswear. By 1972, the company was importing as much as two-thirds of its products, all knit tops, from Hong Kong and Taiwan. (There was no trade at that time between the United States and China.) Domestic production was done at an in-house factory of about seventy sewers and several large local shops. All the workers in the factory and the shops were union members. Tami also had a wholly owned Hong Kong subsidiary that purchased yarn on the open market and stored it in *godowns*, or public warehouses, in Hong Kong. In response to purchase orders issued at the home office in San Francisco, the yarn was sent to Hong Kong dyers and then to knitting factories. The finished products were usually air-freighted to San Francisco to be included in coordinated customer orders that included sportswear made in San Francisco and nylon shirts purchased from Taiwan.

My tasks included the tracking of the Hong Kong inventory from purchases of raw material into finished goods, as well as the tracking of shipments from Hong Kong and Taiwan into San Francisco. I calculated the cost per unit of the styles and made endless worksheets, as there were no computers in those days, comparing the costs to the selling prices. That was a gross margin calculation, although I knew little about cost accounting at that time. The gross margins on the knits from Hong Kong, comparing the wholesale selling price to the landed cost (including air freight), were about 65 percent on average. The margins on the nylon shirts from Taiwan were typically over 70 percent, including air freight.

Quota never had an intrinsic cost. It was a term that denoted the license issued under bilateral agreements that accounted for the total amount of a particular type of garment or textile that was being shipped to the United States in any one year. The United States and its trading partner country agreed to an amount of the category in dozens or kilograms. The licenses giving the right to ship these products to the United States were granted to exporters from the foreign government. The system was designed to create limits, not cost. From the beginning, some countries saw the advantage of allowing the quota to be bought and sold on the open market. This had the effect of ensuring that the allocation would be used most efficiently, as only a factory or exporting company with a profitable order would seek out and buy quota. Then the quota would be used up or, at least, used in the best way. Hong Kong, of course, started an open quota market immediately. Brokers were called farmers, and they did what any broker would do: match buyer and seller at the best price. Prices for quota by category were listed daily in the newspaper just like the price of common stock. Some factories that had received an initial large allocation of quota based on their previous performance got out of the manufacturing business entirely; the cost of their continued allocation from the Hong Kong government was zero, which left the entire selling price as profit.

Other countries, such as Taiwan and Korea, both of which still had command-type economies and military dictatorship governments, made it a crime to sell or buy quota. Nonetheless, factories found a way to trade under the table: one factory might have more orders than its quota allocation permitted and needed to get more quota to fill them, while another factory might not be doing as well and have quota to sell. As a result, in every instance, in both free and controlled markets, quota came to have a cost.

In the following decades, apparel manufacturing infrastructure was built up in many other countries, and therefore import capacity vastly increased (Burke, 2006). Quota was imposed on some of those countries, but not all—this depended on the desirability and suspected trade potential of the country. The US government saw an opportunity to develop trade with some nations and gave these nations a "special introductory offer" (Marshall, Iritani, & Dickerson, 2005). Places like Mongolia, Cambodia, and Nepal became "quota havens." As exporters in Hong Kong and India did not have enough quota, they turned to these regions and quickly established factories and trading partners. The North American Free Trade Agreement (NAFTA) and the Caribbean Basin Initiative (CBI) exempted Mexico and some Caribbean countries from quota and in many cases duty as well. In effect, the textile and apparel industry became a useful tool in trade negotiations and broader foreign policy considerations.

The pretense that the quota system was designed to protect the domestic apparel manufacturing industry should have been dispelled decades ago. It was not operating to protect anything much in the United States, whatever its original intentions (Burke, 2006). It became a system of preferences so that the United States would have bargaining chips for whatever really mattered in trade. Because no other type of product had numerical limits included in world trade, it frequently became the only bargaining chip. But it did nothing to slow the ever-increasing flood of imports. The quota system helped to create an expanding global market for American- and European-designed clothes, as manufacturers and retailers scoured the world looking for the next best and cheapest source. It added cost to the consumer, but did nothing to slow the decline of domestic needle trade or textile jobs (US Congress, 1987).

After Quota

When the quota system ended in 2005, the principal effect was to dislocate production in some less developed countries. For example, India had been farming out production to Bangladesh, Nepal, and Sri Lanka as Indian factories looked for ways to diminish or eliminate quota costs. In 2005, that production was brought back to India because it was far easier to manage and coordinate manufacturing in one place under one set of eyes. Those other countries, especially Bangladesh and Nepal, suffered significant economic losses as the Indian-owned factories closed. Their garment manufacturing businesses could not sustain the changes, and the people, mostly women who had been working in the factories, suffered from a lack of employment. To a lesser extent the same thing happened with China as Chinese factories in Cambodia and Mongolia lost business. This was mitigated by the sudden unilateral imposition of safeguards, or *limits*, on Chinese exports of specific categories by the United States. But this was a short-term issue based on the flood of Chinese production that was impacting other trading partners of the United States in the Caribbean and elsewhere. China was not part of the quota system when that system was implemented. When US trade began with China, quota limits for that trade were established. Imports from China have grown rapidly, and China is now the largest single source of imported apparel (ANZ, 2012). China has a vast impact on the entire textile and apparel market throughout Asia and, increasingly, in other parts of the world as well.

Sustainable China

As the largest and most efficient region where apparel is produced, China can offer us many lessons about manufacturing that can inform our approach toward sustainable fashion. When we think about manufacturing in terms of sustainability, the key concepts are *productivity*, *efficient use of resources*, and *pollution control*.

Productivity

I went to China in 2002 to try to forge an alliance between an American company I was forming that would design and sell children's clothing, and a government agency in a part of Jiangsu Province charged with coordinating the local economy for textiles and apparel (Figure 7.2). The negotiation was successful, and in the summer of 2002 we set up an office given to us by the agency. That summer, I began to visit factories and textile mills in an effort to learn as much as I could about the capability and working methodology of Chinese factories. I had spent much of the prior thirty years in and around factories primarily in the San Francisco Bay Area but also in Los Angeles. Chinese production on the surface was deceptively familiar because of the similar ethnicity of management and employees. This was despite the fact that the language used in Bay Area factories is universally Cantonese and hardly anyone in the part of China where I was could speak or understand a word of Cantonese.

The concept of productivity in making clothes relates to the output per worker in one hour, which in turn relates to the organization of the workplace and especially to the quality of the equipment being used. Why is productivity related to sustainability? As we have repeatedly seen with regard to fuel efficiency or organic farming, to name a couple of obvious examples, no significant shift in production can take place until the costs of the product are competitive. So organic produce need

FIGURE 7.2. Map of Jiangsu Province, where Shanghai is located. (Map courtesy of Volina/ Shutterstock)

not be cheaper than produce grown with chemicals; it may even be more expensive. But the premium that the product can attract cannot be greater than the market will bear. This makes sense. Even in an environmentally conscious community like Berkeley, California, there is a limit on how much more you can charge for eco-friendly products. Productivity is a key element of sustainability precisely because the inefficient use of human labor is wasteful, not economically viable, and therefore not sustainable.

In 1999, I was executive director of an industry-sponsored non-profit in San Francisco called Made by the Bay. I was approached by a top executive of one of the market's largest sellers of men's pants. He had an inside track on a contract with the US Navy for "dress slacks," a part of the uniform. The catch was that the pants needed to be made in the United States because they were part of the uniform, but the company no longer had any facilities in the United States for manufacturing. I embarked on what widened to a national search, and the result was that it was not possible to do this production for the price that the Navy wanted to pay.

Why was it so difficult to find a suitable factory in the United States to make these pants? In the course of my search, I visited a factory in Los Angeles that made private-label men's wool slacks for Nordstrom, which was almost its exclusive customer. The factory had a highly trained workforce, a steady flow of work, and all the expensive equipment necessary to do the job. The owner explained to me that he had made the investment in the equipment as well as in workforce development because the ongoing contractual relationship with Nordstrom made this business profitable. He said that it would be crazy to purchase the type of equipment to do the waistband, pockets, and so forth without that long-term relationship in place because a manufacturer could never recover the cost of the equipment in a short period. A company would never, he said, speculate on buying the equipment, hoping that it could find more business later. The market was far too uncertain, and major customers had supply chains in place.

When I approached several Bay Area factories with the same proposition, I found that he was correct. I could get bids on the work, but the price per unit was far too high because the technical work, such as setting the pockets, was going to be done by machine operators, not with automated equipment. At US labor prices, that added far too much to the cost. Why not buy the machinery? Because the contract was for only 180,000 pairs spread over two or three years. That was not nearly enough to justify the outlay for the equipment, which might have been $1 million. Through contacts in New York, I approached the Union of Needletrades, Industrial, and Textile Employees (UNITE) to see if there was a factory in North Carolina or Tennessee that was capable of this job. I had no luck.

Most discussions of "cheap imports" start and end with a picture of low-paid foreign workers versus US workers. However, the problem is much more complicated than that. When I began to visit Chinese facilities for cut-and-sew, knitting, weaving, embroidery, printing, and so forth, I was struck by the high quality of the machinery in use as well as its ready availability. Chinese workers have an immense advantage because they are highly productive. They not only have a high output relative to their wages, which speaks for their work ethic, but more importantly, I think, the industry as a whole has a very high per-person, per-hour output due to the investment that has been made in modern, efficiently computer-driven equipment. The more work that is done by machinery, the less dependent production is on low-cost labor to remain competitive. China has low-cost labor, to be sure, but it is not as low as that of some Southeast and South Asian countries or Africa. China's competitive advantage is its productivity. In a sense, and in my opinion, the 2005 controversy between the United States and China that resulted in the temporary imposition of safeguards is a complete red herring. There is virtually nothing that would induce an investor in the United States to buy the machinery and train the workers in an effort to become competitive with China. If it hadn't happened after twenty-five years of a full-blown quota system between the two countries, it is not likely to happen now.

In 2006, I accepted a position as import director with a San Francisco based manufacturer of women's and girls' clothing selling to the US department store market. The company is one of the largest branded suppliers (units and dollars) remaining. The shift in the retail market from a model that centered on the middleman as a developer and reseller of fashion to the retailer community to a model that emphasizes private label developed for chain stores (Target, Wal-Mart, H&M, Forever 21, Gap), or private label developed for department stores (Macy's alone has more than a dozen "labels" that it owns), has dramatically accelerated over the past twenty years. The middlemen (wholesalers) that remain as viable businesses are under severe margin pressure to compete with their own customers. The private label chain stores do not buy brands at all. If you see a label at Target, they own it. I was hired largely due to my experience in China during the previous years and my extensive experience in the wholesale business over the previous thirty-five years. Needless to say, the position was a challenge.

At the time I was hired, the company produced garments in China (probably 70 percent), Mexico (about 10 percent), domestically (another 10 percent), and minor amounts in the Philippines, Indonesia, and India. My years of experience working with Chinese manufacturers and exporters were extremely valuable. However, starting in 2006, the Chinese government had allowed their currency (RMB) to slowly increase in value against the US dollar. Without getting too technical, the impact on US importers was a steady increase in prices paid to Chinese factories as the dollar bought less and less. To provide a reference point, today in mid-2014 the dollar has decreased in value against the RMB by about 26 percent since the floating started. For US exporters, this has been a great assistance. For producers of high-tech items (e.g., iPhones), this has been insignificant since the labor content of such an expensive object is not noticeable and in any case the market demand has absorbed the cost increase easily. For private label manufacturers of clothing, the increase has not been burdensome as they are the same entities that set their own retail prices. For wholesalers such as the company employing me, it has been an exit sign—leave China or lose any chance of being competitive.

My first significant change in 2007 was to start to increase our production capability in the Philippines. By 2010 our production in the Philippines had increased by a factor of ten compared to 2006. My second significant change was to explore opportunities for production in Vietnam, where we had had no production previously. We started producing garments in Vietnam in 2008 and it is now at least equal to our production in the Philippines. We also increased our production in Indonesia. By 2012 our imports from China had been nearly eliminated except for machine knit sweaters. The change was rapid, dramatic, and not without challenges. We created a Hong Kong based operation in 2006 to manage logistics and quality control in Asia. In 2007 we added an experienced manager in Hong Kong to interface with a third-party compliance and material testing company. We began hiring local staff in the Philippines and Vietnam in 2008 and now have nearly twenty inspectors in the field reporting daily via Internet link, along with a staff of seven full-time employees in the Hong Kong office.

China has many advantages for garment production: proximity to raw materials (almost all fabric and trims are produced in China); worker experience and skill; infrastructure of roads and ports; and far better and faster ocean shipping to West Coast ports (Figures 7.3 and 7.4). All of those have been sacrificed, to some extent, for better garment prices as none of those advantages translate into better prices offered by retailers to wholesalers. This is a low margin industry under the best of circumstances. Rising costs due to currency plus in-country inflation in every Asian country have put even greater pressure on this industry and especially the wholesaler.

FIGURE 7.3. (RIGHT) A small garment-sewing factory in Nantong city in China's Jiangsu Province. (Photo courtesy of Paul Gill)

FIGURE 7.4. (BELOW) A garment-cutting table in a large Nantong city factory in China's Jiangsu Province. (Photo courtesy of Paul Gill)

Efficient Use of Resources

When I started at Tami thirty-five years ago, we were buying our imported items six months in advance of our season, based purely on projections. Therefore, inevitably we were acquiring hundreds of thousands of unwanted units that needed to be sold off after the season to jobbers, those wholesalers that purchase merchandise at low cost and sell to discounters. All the way back up the line, we had ordered too much fabric, too much yarn, and too much dye; we had used too many boxes, too much fuel for transportation, and so on. Waste is inherently not sustainable, not only because it is damaging to the environment but because it is ultimately not economical. The costs of waste, visible and invisible, inevitably get added to the product.

Western consumer economies, especially the United States, are constructed around the presentation of as many immediate choices for the consumer as possible. When you go to the retail store online or offline to buy a shirt or a suit, you expect that they will have the color and size that you want. Similarly, manufacturers want to buy fabric and trim that is in stock because it significantly shortens the production time and makes it possible to delay production choices (e.g., which styles to cut and how many) until the last possible moment. Retailers try to push the unsold inventory back to the manufacturers; they in turn try to push it back to the suppliers, which try to keep as little raw material as possible in a finished condition, adding little or no value to the raw material until absolutely necessary. Of course this effort to be lean inevitably lengthens the time necessary to fill an order when compared to a fully stocked shelf. Being lean and having happy customers at the same time is the trick. Retailers call this *partnering*, and manufacturers sweat daily trying to be good partners to them because the bigger party is keen on transferring risk to the smaller one. Consultants call it *supply chain management*. Whatever you call it, eliminating waste, both resources and money, is vital to any sustainable production.

Doing business in China is eye-opening in many ways. China is highly productive and technologically proficient; therefore, there is an embracing of lean manufacturing—virtually nothing is in stock. Nothing is wasted in China. When it comes to manufacturing apparel, you do not buy trim except at a bazaar where you can find odds and ends of anything. You do not buy fabric. You do not buy shipping boxes. What you do is place an order for finished garments and provide complete specs including packing instructions. Everything is made to order. The production line is as efficient as possible. There is virtually no waste. There are, however, conditions and consequences to doing business this way:

- Your instructions must be complete and correct at the time you place the order.
- If your instructions are not complete, frequently the factory will not accept the order and you may lose your place in the production line. I have seen this happen, and it is not a pleasant experience.
- You cannot make changes. Once your instructions are delivered, that is it, unless the factory has made the error. Even then, it is difficult to persuade those at the factory that it is, in fact, their error.

Communication is vital with regard to instructions. It must be done in a standardized format, with every piece of information appearing in the same location for every item. The use of terms must be industry standard.

This meeting of culture and production has led to very efficient manufacturing. China, more than any other place, has embraced lean manufacturing in apparel. It is successful because the use of technology and the short supply lines (e.g., raw material factories to sewing factories) have combined so that time constraints are not an impediment. Typically, it only takes three or four weeks to assemble all the materials for a production run, and that means starting from fiber. Actual production time is another three or four weeks. Shipping time to the West Coast is fourteen days. This means that China's products move from factory to port in sixty days or less.

Pollution control

China is terribly polluted. The values of a clean environment have taken a backseat to short-term financial gain. The sky is gray on a nice day. The water is not drinkable even in luxury high-rise hotels in Shanghai. The air quality is terrible. A friend of mine, living in China, wears a breathing apparatus to sleep because of apnea. The device includes a mask that has a changeable filter. The filter should last six months or more, but he must change it every two weeks because it turns black even when sleeping in an apartment with air conditioning.

Apparel manufacturing is no different. I have personally seen chemical dyes running in a rivulet along a street and directly into the Pearl River between Guangzhou and Hong Kong. Factory environments, while physically clean for the most part, are full of toxic chemicals that would be instant OSHA (Occupational Safety and Health Administration) violations in the United States. There is nothing sustainable about garment manufacturing in China from a green perspective.

All the other countries that I have visited in Asia for business practice just-in-time manufacturing as a matter of course. For garment factories, even staple items such as cartons are purchased at the time the garment order is received. In turn, the carton manufacturer does not produce inventory but puts cartons into production once an order is received. Obviously, the supply chain must have a mass of raw material upstream but it is as far upstream with as little labor added as possible. This type of supply chain management reduces waste, although its purpose is clearly to save the cost of carrying inventory.

The major international auditing and inspection companies have added an environmental section to their evaluation of factories. The inspection helps wholesalers, retailers, and the public to evaluate each factory for its commitment to environmental concerns. Table 7.1 lists the auditing points covered in a typical third-party inspection. As major American and European companies have become more concerned about the environmental impact of their businesses, the pressure on their supply chains has dramatically increased. Major retailers annually evaluate their suppliers using a "green" scorecard. In turn, the suppliers demand that their manufacturing sources be more observant of those considerations in order to be included as a consistent resource.

Unfortunately, from what I have seen in India and elsewhere, these unsustainable conditions seem to be a common occurrence in less developed countries. A green environment is more costly in the short run. We demand it of ourselves, or at least we intend to. When our products are made out of our sight, we seem content to look at price and quality and ignore the side effects to the environment that may be included with the product itself. There is nothing sustainable about a dirty environment, and this principle applies to all types of industries operating around the world. Fashion is just one part of that puzzle. Can the developed world insist that China green itself if it wants to continue to export at these levels? That is a serious question that has not been addressed in manufacturing anywhere in the world. The Chinese environment is not sustainable regardless of its industry's quality of efficiency and productivity, because the industry is a huge hazard to the health of the Chinese. The polluted air and water generated by the chemicals, dyes, and glues used in production are literally making people sick. One can assume that this will be addressed in the near future, but it is not likely to be the result of outside pressure (Knappe, 2003).

TABLE 7.1. Auditing points typically listed in an environmental inspection

No.	Checkpoints	Score		N/A	Comments
		Yes	No		
9.1	Does the factory have all permits and licenses required by local law or regulations?	1			Based on document provided for review, the factory got an approval of the local authority on environment protection on 03 Jan 2007 as per local law.
9.2	Is the factory in compliance with local law or regulation regarding wastewater discharge?	1			The factory conducted the environment compliance and reported to the local authority on 22 April 2014 in compliance with local laws.
9.3	Does the factory keep records of waste handling and disposal?			N/A	
9.4	Does the factory maintain a written record of all use and movement of hazardous materials?	1			Based on document provided for review, all use and movement of hazardous materials were recorded accordingly and the records were retained in May 2014.
9.5	Are relevant employees trained in the safe use, handling and disposal of hazardous materials?	1			Based on document provided for review, cleaning workers and relevant employees such as warehouse and cleaners were trained in the safe use, handling and disposal of hazardous materials.
9.6	Have there been any notices of deficiencies issued by government agencies in the past year? If yes, explain.	1			No evidence was identified that there had been any notices of deficiencies issued by government agencies in the past year.

ideas in action

Vietnam has been among the fastest growing economies in the world over the past decade. While far smaller than China, its growth has been "China on steroids." Like many less developed countries, the garment industry has served as an entry point for labor removed from farming and as a vehicle to collect dollars or euro. There has been a vast investment by Korean businesses in Vietnam in all industries from sewing to electronics. There has been a very large investment from Japanese businesses and now even Chinese companies are investing in manufacturing in Vietnam. American investment has mostly come from Vietnamese/Americans with family in the Saigon area—and a lot of that is in the garment industry. Like China (but faster), Vietnam has begun to move away from the low-return garment industry in favor of electronics and other high-tech production. Vietnam has an educated and motivated workforce, especially in the south, and that is attractive to investors. Just as apparel production in China has migrated inland due to costs near the coastal cities and the far better employment opportunities available there, Vietnamese apparel production is migrating away from Saigon. It is not unusual to find new factories being built three or four hours away by car or even further up the central coast. My prediction is that the apparel industry in Vietnam will become less and less important to the Vietnamese economy over the next few years as standards of living improve and the drive for consumer goods among the population brings wages up significantly.

The Philippines is a conundrum. The apparel industry is concentrated in a ring around greater Manila. That part of the Philippines has a generally educated workforce and many (if not most) people speak English. The area is a bewildering mix of neighborhoods and stores, almost comparable to those you would see in America. Yet, many other parts of greater Manila are impoverished, with people living in cardboard or tin shacks. Frequently one can see the tall office buildings and luxury hotels from the impoverished areas. Why? Unlike other Asian countries that have a population migrating from the farms to the cities, the Philippines has one of the highest population growth rates in the world despite the generally high level of education. As a result there is a constant increase in young workers that the more developed parts of the economy cannot absorb. Therefore the garment factories, generally medium sized and older, have trouble finding workers. Change in the profile of the Philippine apparel sector is directly related to a reduction of population growth. This is difficult to predict given the prevailing religious sentiments of the vast majority of the population.

Other countries in Asia that I have visited on business (Indonesia, Bangladesh, India) follow a more typical pattern of using the apparel industry as an entry-level industrial platform. How each country will develop its apparel sector depends on many factors, but it is largely related to population growth and the availability of other areas of employment. Many US and European apparel companies are investigating opportunities in Myanmar. The apparel sector depends on low-cost labor combined with a minimally acceptable infrastructure (electricity, water, roads, ports). The stable platform of doing business in the coastal areas of China, which existed from the mid-1980s until the mid-2000s, is long gone. The industry migrates to low-cost regions even within countries as the price pressure in North America and Western Europe dictates.

Conclusion

Despite its goals to sustain and protect domestic manufacturers from foreign competition, the quota system has not in any way reduced the runaway increases in import of apparel to the United States and the European Union. Whatever trade disputes have arisen or may yet arise between the United States and Europe, on the one hand, and the United States and China on the other, China will be the leading source of US apparel imports for as long as the emphasis on the textile and apparel industry makes sense for China.

As the leading source for the world's apparel, China is unparalleled in its productivity. This is primarily due to the development of China's

FIGURE 7.5. This large garment manufacturing factory is located in Nantong city in the Jiangsu Province of East Central China, on the Chang River, about 30 miles (50 km) from the East China Sea. The center of an important cotton-growing area, Nantong is still dependent upon the textile industry. (Photo courtesy of Paul Gill)

highly technical industry. Chinese factories and workers hold a huge advantage over those in both the developed and developing countries. This is because China pays its workers relatively low wages compared to those in developed countries while possessing an infrastructure technically superior to those in other developing, low-paying countries.

If sustaining life and sustaining the environment are priorities, we must seriously consider how to address our industry production demands in the world. The demand for a better life is overwhelming among the Chinese population. The easiest and most cost-effective, albeit short-sighted, way to achieve that life is to continue development in the same way that development has proceeded since the invention of the steam engine, and that is not eco-friendly. To advocate that China adopt a more costly process of development is unrealistic, at least in the short run. The entire notion of sustainability must take into account both the long- and the short-term costs associated with converting current industrial practices to more sustainable processes. No conversation that skips this issue can be seen as realistic.

Discussion Questions

1   How does a company decide where to go for manufacturing? What are some of the principal issues that go into such decisions?

2   How should a company evaluate changing manufacturing environments? Clearly the locations chosen change in value over short periods of time. What would be some of the tools that could be used to make sure your company stays on top of this issue?

3   Environmental issues are evaluated in compliance audits of factories. However, they are rated with a value of about 6 percent of the total point score. Health & Safety issues are given 25 percent and employee-related issues are given 65 percent of the total. Do you think that is reasonable? If you disagree, explain your reasoning.

References

ANZ. (2012). Commercial banking Asia. Textile & Garment Industry Market Update. Retrieved October 2014, from http://www.anzbusiness.com/content/dam/anz-superregional/Textiles%26GarmentIndustryUpdate.pdf.

Burke, K. (2006, July 27). Guest editorial. *Apparel Magazine*. Retrieved October 2006, from http://www.apparelmag.com/articles/feature052406.shtml.

Knappe, M. (2003). Textiles and clothing: What happens after 2005. *International Trade Forum Magazine*, 2.

Marshall, T., Iritani, E., & Dickerson, M. (2005, January 16). A world unravels. *Los Angeles Times*. Retrieved November 2006, from http://www.latimes.com/business/la-fi-quotaone16jan16,0,3076753.story.

Rivoli, P. (2005). Tangled threads of protectionism—Part 1. Retrieved October 2006, from YaleGlobal Online: http://yaleglobal.yale.edu/article.

US Congress. (1987, April). The U.S. textile and apparel industry, a revolution in progress. Special Report OTA-TET-332. Washington, DC: Government Printing Office.

TIMO RISSANEN is a fashion designer and academic whose design practice and research are deeply immersed in sustainability. His PhD focused on zero waste fashion design. He is the Assistant Professor of Fashion Design and Sustainability at Parsons The New School for Design, and Program Director for AAS Fashion Design and AAS Fashion Marketing.

CHAPTER 8

Zero Waste Fashion Design

Timo Rissanen

With 10 to 20 percent of its fabric swept off the cutting-room floor, the fashion industry is leaving a significant ecological footprint. This waste could be dramatically reduced, however, with some creative design thinking. Zero waste fashion design challenges designers to rethink their relationship with pattern cutters and adopt a process that could result in 100 percent fabric use in the garments that the industry produces.

Pattern Cutting as Fashion Design

This chapter examines an aspect of clothing production that is often invisible and thus not regarded as a problem: pre-consumer fabric waste. Arguably, the perception of fabric as disposable by many in the fashion industry should be questioned. To produce raw fiber and turn fiber into fabric consumes energy, chemicals, and water: fabric is precious. The wasting of fabric occurs in garment manufacturing, but the ability to eliminate fabric waste resides within fashion design and pattern cutting. To eliminate fabric waste, the garment pieces must use up the entire length of the fabric, interlocking like the pieces of a completed jigsaw puzzle. The combined expertise of the fashion designer and pattern cutter can achieve this. The aim in zero waste fashion design is to simultaneously design a set of garment pieces that take up a given length of fabric in two dimensions and the garment in three dimensions. No fabric waste is then created exclusive of the garment. Some fabric may be wasted within the garment, but the potential benefits of that will be discussed further in the chapter. A zero waste garment is designed through the making of its pattern, while ensuring that the resulting garment is aesthetically pleasing, fits appropriately, and is within an acceptable range of cost. Fashion design and pattern cutting are not hierarchically or otherwise distinct activities; pattern cutting is part of the design process.

Precious Fabric and Wasted Fabric

Why should we avoid wasting fabric? Fabrics are increasingly inexpensive, and the amount of waste may not seem worth worrying about. A brief look at the two most commonly used fibers, cotton and polyester, reveals some cause for concern. As a natural fiber, cotton is easily mistaken for an environmentally friendly fiber. Cotton, however, is a heavily sprayed crop; cotton growing takes up 2.4 percent of the world's arable land, yet 24 percent of insecticides and 11 percent of pesticides used globally in agriculture go toward cotton production (Chapagain et al., 2005, p. 19). Cotton is also a "thirsty" fiber, both to grow and to treat to achieve a finished cotton fabric from fiber. Cotton accounts for 2.6 percent of global water use (p. 31). The polyesters used in fashion come from a finite source, oil, and consume considerable energy to produce (Allwood et al., 2006, pp. 13–14). Toxic additives accompany polyester, sometimes unnecessarily (McDonough & Braungart, 2002, pp. 37–8). In a landfill, polyester breaks down slowly. On the other hand, polyester's resistance to physical degradation may be a great advantage. The polyester polymer can be recycled almost infinitely with no degradation to the quality of the fiber.

What happens to fabric waste? The dumping of textiles in landfill is problematic. Natural fibers will decompose but may release harmful chemicals and methane in the process; synthetics may take centuries to decompose. A large industry exists trading in scrap fabric (the real "rag trade") and thus keeps the waste from landfill. Fabric recycling, however, is a difficult issue. McDonough and Braungart (2002, pp. 56–9) use the term "downcycling" to describe the degradation in material quality through recycling. The quality of yarn spun from a natural fiber relies on the length of the fiber. Recycled natural fiber tends to be shorter than "virgin" fiber, and thus not suitable for all uses. Nonetheless, recent improvements in systems and technologies have resulted in higher quality fabrics made from off-cut waste, such as the 100 percent recycled, 100 percent cotton denim by Pure Waste Textiles in Finland.

The production of any fiber and the manufacture of that fiber into fabric consumes energy, raw materials, almost always water, and often chemical additives. Regardless of recyclability, cotton and polyester reveal that fabric arrives at the fashion designer with a significant ecological footprint acquired during its production. Cooklin (1997, p. 9) estimates the average waste to be 15 percent of total fabric used, while Abernathy et al. (1999, p. 136) place the figure at around 10 percent for pants and jeans, but higher for blouses, jackets, and underwear. According to Allwood et al. (2006, p. 16), in the United Kingdom one million tons of clothing is consumed annually. With the waste estimates, it is safe to say that at least 100,000 tons of fabric is wasted to make the clothes consumed in the United Kingdom each year. The much higher global figure and the ecological footprint inherent in all fabrics should justify attempts to drastically reduce the amount of fabric wasted by the industry.

Fashion Creation Methods

To put zero waste fashion design into context, a look at all fashion creation methods available to industry through existing technologies is necessary (see Figure 8.1). In fabric waste creation, three main categories emerge: *cut-and-sew*, of which zero waste fashion design is a

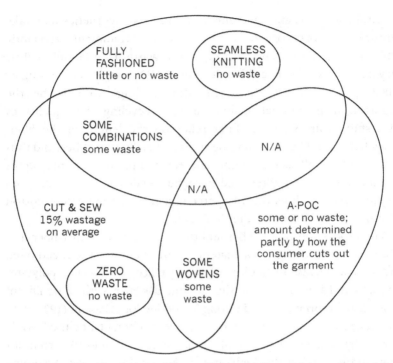

FIGURE 8.1. This illustration depicts fashion creation methods from a fabric waste perspective. Three broad fashion creation methods exist, but combinations of these are also possible. Zero waste fashion design refers to cut-and-sew that wastes no fabric. (Illustration by Jenny Green from a drawing by Timo Rissanen)

part; *fully fashioned*, which includes whole-garment knitting; and *A-POC* (A Piece Of Cloth). The two most common methods of fashion creation in the industry are cut-and-sew and fully fashioned. An introduction to fabric construction is also necessary, as different fabric types have implications for the different fashion creation methods. Three broad categories exist for fabric construction: wovens, knits, and non-wovens. Wovens have yarns interlacing in two directions, warp and weft; knits are rows of looped yarns; and non-wovens are made directly from fiber without spinning it into yarn first, or may not consist of fiber at all (e.g., leather).

Fully Fashioned (Yarn + Knitting + Sewing = Garment) and Whole-garment knitting (Yarn + Knitting = Garment)

Fully fashioned in its true form eliminates yarn or fiber waste, and is commonly used in knits. The garment pieces are knitted individually and then sewed together. Whole-garment knitting eliminates sewing from the process—a machine knits a finished garment (Black, 2002, p. 118). With the technology available to fashion design, a fully fashioned approach is possible in woven and non-woven fabrics through craft methods (e.g., hand-weaving and felting). Non-woven sails made of carbon and aramid fiber by North Sails Nevada show that non-wovens can be adapted for an industrial fully fashioned approach. The sails are made into the exact required shape by specialized fiber-laying machinery (Brown, 2005, pp. 53, 55). To adapt this technology for the fashion industry seems likely as increasingly diverse non-wovens become available. Industrially available technology for fully fashioned weaving has not been developed for use within the fashion industry. The cost of weaving shapes other than long rectangular lengths of fabric may be prohibitive. A recent study predicts that in the future, the highest impact development will take place in non-woven and fully fashioned knit applications (Allwood et al., 2006, pp. 25, 33).

A-POC (Yarn + Knitting or Weaving = Fabric, Followed by Fabric + Cutting = Garment + Fabric Waste)

In the late 1990s, Issey Miyake and Dai Fujiwara launched A-POC (A Piece Of Cloth). In knits, a flat tube of fabric is knitted with the two sides of the tube joined in areas. The wearer buys a tube and, following the lines of the joins, cuts out finished garments (Kries & von Vegesack, 2001). A-POC is similar to whole-garment knitting in that a machine produces a garment that requires no sewing, but the technologies used to produce each are different (Black, 2002, p. 118). How the wearer cuts out the pieces determines partly how much waste is created. Several woven

A-POC garments were developed; for example, Caravan and Pain de Mie from 2000. The latter, a dress or skirt and top depending on how it is cut, can be cut out as finished garments like the knits, while the Caravan jacket requires one row of sewing at the back after cutting (Kries & von Vegesack, 2001, p. 63). Considering the non-woven fully fashioned sail technology, it seems possible to extend A-POC to non-wovens, too.

Cut-and-Sew (Fabric + Cutting + Sewing = Garment + Fabric Waste) and Zero waste fashion design (Fabric + Cutting + Sewing = Garment)

Cut-and-sew is self-explanatory. Garment pieces are cut from fabric and sewed to make garments. Any type of fabric may be used. Conventional cut-and-sew wastes 10 to 20 percent of the total fabric used, while zero waste fashion design refers to cut-and-sew that wastes none.

Unlike fully fashioned and A-POC, cut-and-sew and zero waste fashion design require no reprogramming of machinery to create new garment styles and are suitable for all fabric types. Furthermore, cutting and sewing woven fabrics allows subtleties within a design that may not be possible through other methods. It is therefore likely that cutting and sewing will remain alongside emerging technologies for the foreseeable future.

Garment Design and Making Process

The following sections describe the processes of garment design and make.

Fashion Design

Most fashion designers use sketching to develop ideas, from initial concept to a design that can be pattern-made and made into a sample garment. The benefits of sketching are many: It is fast, ideas become visible to the designer and others quickly, and various elements of design (e.g., silhouette, balance, and line) can be resolved before the costly pattern cutting and construction processes.

Pattern cutting

Pattern cutting, or pattern making, is the making of a pattern for a garment. Usually a pattern maker does this, guided by the designer's sketch. Occasionally the fashion designer makes the pattern, and this chapter proposes, through examples, that pattern cutting can be an effective design tool alongside sketching. Manual pattern cutting using pens, scissors, paper and card is still common, although computerized approaches using increasingly sophisticated CAD/CAM software are on the rise.

Construction: Cutting and Sewing

Using the pattern, a toile is cut and sewed. The toile is a garment prototype in inexpensive fabric, to allow the design team to test fit and examine the design in three-dimensional form. Depending on the design and the amount of required alterations, more than one toile may be necessary before the pattern is made to the design team's satisfaction. A sample cutter then cuts a sample in the actual fabric, which a sample machinist sews.

Production: Grading, Making a Marker, Cutting, and Sewing

Once the designer and pattern maker, and sometimes a buyer or a merchandiser, approve the sample garment, the pattern maker or a grader grades the pattern into the required range of sizes. Grading may be done manually but is increasingly done digitally. A marker maker uses the graded pattern to create a marker. The marker is a cutting layout containing all the pieces of all the sizes to be cut for production. The cutter or an automated cutting system uses the marker as a guide to cut out the garment pieces in fabric. Production machinists, organized for maximum efficiency, make up the garments. Sewing may be segmented; for example, one machinist might only sew side seams while another works on cuffs. Finished garments are pressed, tagged, and shipped to retailers.

Since the early twentieth century, the steps in the process of garment making, from fashion design to production sewing, have been organized somewhat hierarchically. The specialization of each is the result of a search for better efficiencies. The benefits are many; as each role concentrates on fewer tasks, it is likely to result in a higher level of expertise in one area, and garment production also becomes faster. On the other hand, some consequences are problematic. The primary obstacle to fabric waste elimination is the separation of fashion design and pattern cutting on one hand, and fashion design and manufacturing on the other.

In current industry practice, the marker maker is responsible for efficient fabric usage. When creating the marker, the marker maker attempts to place all the garment pieces within the fabric as closely as possible. The motivation is economic; the tightest fit of the pattern pieces uses the least fabric per garment, thereby reducing production costs dramatically. Notably, it is economically affordable to waste 10 to 20 percent of the fabric, even if this is not ecologically sound. Even the latest computer software affords only mild increases in this efficiency, because it is bound by what has already been designed and pattern-cut. Conventionally, garments are not designed and pattern-made with the cutting layout (i.e., the marker) in mind. The amount of waste is determined by garment style (e.g., number and shapes of pattern pieces), the number of garment sizes and garments in one marker, and the marker maker's skill. A more efficient marker is usually achieved by mixing the pieces of several sizes in one marker or by cutting more than one of the same size in one marker.

Contemporary Zero Waste Fashion Design

An investigation into traditional forms of dress as well as fashion history and present fashion reveals many examples where fabric is treated as precious in the making of clothes, and very little or none is wasted. The sheer number of examples and the spread of these over centuries provide us with guidance in moving forward. It helps to examine these examples across broad, overlapping themes. The themes used here are *fabric*, *pattern design*, and *garment design*. With fabric waste elimination as our focus, fabric has some specific implications for design. Similarly, as the making of the garment pattern determines whether the making of the garment wastes fabric or not, pattern design includes issues best addressed during pattern cutting. Garment design refers to aspects that may be addressed prior to commencing making a garment and features that differ from more conventional ways of designing. The themes may seem to contradict an earlier statement that pattern cutting is integral to fashion design, if fabric waste is to be eliminated. The themes assist in building a new understanding about zero fabric waste creation and should not be considered exclusionary.

Fabric

In the simplest examples of fabric waste elimination, fabric equals garment: fabric is not cut into and thus none is wasted. The himation, chiton, and peplos of ancient Greece and the sari of India are lengths of fabric with no cutting, worn draped on the body. The sari yields several variations (Lynton, 1995, pp. 14–16), as does ancient Greek dress (Rudofsky, 1947, p. 137). Different fabric lengths and widths allow further diversity.

In zero waste fashion design, fabric width becomes a design consideration, because the width determines how the pattern pieces may be configured on a length of fabric. Fabric width is a major difference between cut-and-sew and zero waste fashion creation: Rarely does one need to consider fabric width when designing a cut-and-sew garment, while a zero waste garment is fundamentally informed by the width of its fabric. Perhaps the best known garment that wastes no fabric is the kimono of Japan. The narrow width of the fabric used in the kimono determines its horizontal dimensions (Tarrant, 1994, p. 36). Rather than make the kimono in a range of sizes, each is adjusted to the wearer by wrapping and tying on a belt (Van Assche, 2005, p. 7).

For Yeohlee Teng, a contemporary designer in New York, economical fabric use is integral to her work. In a jacket made in 1998, fabric width determines the length of the sleeves, as these are cut in one and perpendicular to the body of the jacket (Major & Teng, 2003, p. 53). The pattern diagram lacks some pattern pieces such as facings, and the amount of waste is difficult to determine. In fact, most pattern diagrams of Teng's work have components missing. The purpose of the diagrams is probably to be broadly illustrative of garment cut, rather than to accurately reproduce the garment pattern.

Zandra Rhodes is an English designer whose fashion is heavily influenced by her textile prints. Rhodes develops a print first, and this informs the garment shape (Rhodes & Knight, 1984, p. 9). A blouse from 1979 demonstrates this approach. The print pattern, Chinese Squares, is engineered to the fabric width. The garment is then developed according to the print; it uses the full fabric width with the possible exception of selvedges (Rhodes, 2005, pp. 34–6). The blouse does create some fabric waste, despite the sleeve and peplum pieces interlocking fully. For complete fabric waste elimination, the fabric selvedges need to be incorporated into the garment somehow. Haute couture sewing, the most expensive level of hand finishing, as demonstrated by Shaeffer (2011, p. 54), provides an example. Selvedge strips can be used internally to stabilize necklines, armholes, and other garment parts, and the technique is easily adapted to ready-to-wear. Selvedge could also be left in the garment as an edge finish, such as a hem or facing edge.

A great variety of fusible interfacings are now available to support parts of a garment (e.g., the jacket front and shirt collar); printed glue bonds the interfacing to the garment fabric. Occasionally the main garment fabric may be used as a sew-in interfacing. For example, in the front neckline of the kimono, surplus fabric in the front neck is pleated inside the collar for support, rather than cut away (Dobson, 2004, p. 54). Often, fusible interfacings are not used with sheer fabrics; where added body is desired (e.g., the cuffs and collar), three or more layers of the garment fabric may be used. This could also make the eventual recycling of a garment easier, as the fiber content of the garment and its interfacing would be the same.

Pattern Design

While rectangular pattern shapes may seem easier to work with in zero waste fashion design, their design potential warrants inquiry. Bernard Rudofsky was an Austrian-American social historian and an ardent critic of contemporary clothing design and manufacture. Following the 1944–45 exhibition and 1947 book *Are Clothes Modern?* (Rudofsky, 1947), Rudofsky incorporated some of his ideas into a range of clothing in 1950 (Bocco Guarneri, 2003, pp. 294–5). The garments in the collection, Bernardo Separates, were made in one size only from rectangular pieces of fabric. Fit was achieved with drawstrings or belts. The aim was a reduction in price through the minimization of sewing. Fabric was the main source of cost. While the pattern diagrams are too simplified to determine whether fabric was wasted, Rudofsky greatly admired fabric-as-garment in ancient Greek dress. The American fashion designer Claire McCardell was Rudofsky's contemporary, and he included her work in *Are Clothes Modern?* (Rudofsky, 1947). The included garments were geometric in cut, not unlike the garments that Rudofsky created a few years later. I have explored geometric shapes extensively in my work, such as in the pajamas from 2011 (Figure 8.2).

Initially, rectangular pattern shapes may seem to only allow basic garment shapes. These shapes can, however, be offset in relation to one another to create three-dimensional rather than flat shapes. Max Tilke was a German ethnographer with an interest in dress from around the world. Whether his depictions of dress are accurate is open to question, but from a fabric waste point of view his work is undeniably interesting. In *Costume Patterns and Designs* (Tilke, 1956, Plate 89: Garments 6 & 7, 9 & 10), a pair of Chinese trousers is made from two rectangles. The offsetting of two rectangles against each other forces the trouser legs to hang "off-grain," on an angle.

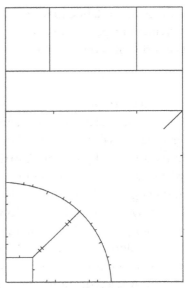

FIGURE 8.2. Pajamas and pattern by Timo Rissanen, 2011. Rissanen designed these using his grandmother's bed sheets from the 1940s, influenced by subtraction cutting by Julian Roberts. (Photograph by Mariano Garcia, patterns by Timo Rissanen)

The Japanese designer Yoshiki Hishinuma has explored similar principles in garments made from equilateral triangles (Hishinuma, 1986, pp. 162–72). For example, he has created a pair of asymmetrical trousers from two triangles. While Hishinuma's garments do not seem to be designed with fabric waste as a consideration, it is possible to engineer the pieces of such a garment to interlock on a fabric width by splitting the equilateral triangle into two right-angle triangles of equal size. These can then be flipped into interlocking rectangles. More recently, Study NY has made extensive use of offset rectangles by way of garments that through buttoning allow the wearer to modify the garment (Figure 8.3).

Similarly, graduated fullness or flare can be achieved through the use of interlocking gores, as demonstrated in European gowns from the fourteenth to the eighteenth centuries (Arnold, 1977 [1966], p. 3; Baumgarten, Watson, & Carr, 1999, pp. 43–6). Rectangular gussets

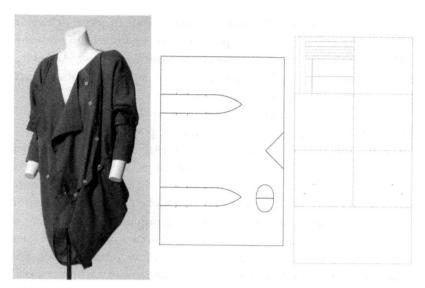

FIGURE 8.3. Dress by Study NY. The company has repeated versions of this dress since its inception in 2009. The dress can be customized by the wearer by altering the buttoning. (Photograph by Thomas McQuillan, pattern by Tara St James)

may be inserted into curved or straight slashes as an alternative to shaped seams to create three-dimensional forms. As the kimono demonstrates, folds may replace straight seams. In knits, even curved edges may be folded rather than cut. Rothstein describes a knitted jacket made of rectangles, where the curved neck and armhole are created through folding under rather than cutting fabric (1984, p. 17).

The 1979 Rhodes bodice and a 1982 hooded cape by Teng (Major & Teng, 2003, pp. 8, 155) show waste occurring from curved pattern edges. Minor modifications to the designs could eliminate most or all of this waste. The sleeve pieces of the Rhodes bodice are squares with a circular cutout in the middle. Straight slashes could replace the circles, and a slash could be offset against another, as described above. In Teng's cape, a more noticeable change would be required to eliminate waste: the cape hem and hood shape could interlock. The text describes the cape as cut "with no waste" (Major & Teng, 2003,

p. 18), while the pattern diagram (155) shows some to occur. Achieving interlocking curves within the pattern to eliminate waste may seem difficult, but Holly McQuillan's work demonstrates that it need not be. When designing curved pattern shapes, one needs to simultaneously determine how to use both sides of the curve.

The largest pattern pieces need to be resolved first, as they will dominate the marker layout (Rissanen, 2013, p. 91). Thayaht, an Italian futurist, designed the "tuta" overalls in 1919; he later worked for Madeleine Vionnet during the 1920s (Chenoune, 1993, pp. 140–2; Stern, 2004, p. 43). The tuta is composed of relatively few pieces: the entire body (e.g., front, back, and legs) is cut from one piece, with slashes for armholes. The pattern diagram (Stern, 2004) includes measurements, so the wasted fabric amount may be assessed accurately. The tuta does waste some fabric, but minor changes would allow full interlocking. For example, the four patch pockets could be redesigned to use up the waste.

In contrast to the tuta, a man's shirt from 1837 (Shep & Cariou, 1999, p. xxiv) has more pieces than most twenty-first-century equivalents. The shirt pieces interlock with no waste, but it is difficult to relate the diagram to the making instructions; the diagram includes fifteen pieces (the main shirt body is not included in the diagram) while the instructions mention nineteen pieces.

Grading

Grading is the incremental change in pattern size to create a garment pattern in a range of sizes. Zero waste fashion design raises the question: Is grading the only way of producing a garment style in a range of sizes? In my PhD research (Rissanen, 2013, pp. 121–31), I identified five pathways to create size ranges of garments:

1   One-size-fits-most
2   Conventional grading
3   Designing each size individually

4   Using a different fabric width for each size
5   A hybrid method

Pathway 1: One-size-fits-most

The need for grading can be eliminated by designing a garment that will fit individuals across a range of sizes. Yeohlee Teng has designed such garments throughout her career, describing them as "the ultimate efficiency" (Luther, in Major & Teng, 2003, p. 18). Teng's skirt in the Yield exhibition (McQuillan & Rissanen, 2011, pp. 12–17) is adjustable to almost any waist size. This pathway is limited to loose, adjustable, or wrapped garments, and occasionally garments made from fabrics with considerable stretch.

Pathway 2: Conventional grading

Grading in the conventional manner remains an option. The benefit of this pathway is the familiarity and speed of the process to industry practitioners; grading remains within manufacture and digital technologies allow for fast grading. The subsequent sizes are likely to create fabric waste; in conventional grading marker planning is not regarded as design. Not all of the garment components necessarily grade, whilst the ones that do, do so unevenly depending on the garment design. Once each component has been graded, it is unlikely that they will configure on fabric in a way that does not create fabric waste. Is it then truthful to claim a garment to be zero waste, if in fact only the original size is?

Pathway 3: Designing each size individually

Each size can be redesigned using the original size as the starting point and a guide. The visual aspects of the designed garment will be retained as close to the original as possible across the resulting sizes while ensuring each size is zero waste. Whilst relative to conventional grading this pathway may be time-consuming, one could argue that this is an example of deeper engagement with fashion design practice than what may be the norm. Instead of handing over the patterns of a garment to a grader to produce patterns for a range of sizes, the fashion designer, working with the pattern cutter and/or grader, is responsible for each size; grading becomes a criterion for fashion design rather than manufacture. Changes to the design are inevitable but these would need to be kept to a minimum, in order to satisfy the expectations of retailers and consumers.

In order to design each size, the designer would first need to determine the garment components that need to grade and by how much. These components may need to be given priority in the redesign process, as they may set the limits for the pieces that do not necessarily need to grade (for example, pockets, tabs, epaulettes, etc.) and smaller pieces that grade in one direction only (cuffs, collars, etc.). When it has been determined which components need to grade, two options emerge for the redesign process, depending on the garment design: changing or retaining the configuration of the garment components in the marker. Each will now be examined:

Pathway 3A: Changing the marker configuration. Once the garment components have been assessed for their need for grading, they need to be examined on the fabric width to see how similarly they may configure in comparison to the marker of the original size. A number of strategies exist to facilitate the redesign process. For example, pattern pieces that can be added or deleted to affect grading are a possibility.

Changing the marker configuration is likely to result in considerable changes in garment appearance. The marker for Endurance Shirt II (created in 2011) is considerably different from the marker for Endurance Shirt I (created in 2009). Although the two shirts (Figure 8.4) are the same size and thus the exercise of adapting a garment from one fabric width to another does not directly relate to grading, it is possible to nevertheless see that changing the marker for each size can significantly impact on garment appearance; the elbow patches from the early shirt were eliminated in the later one. Therefore it would seem that retaining the original marker as much as possible would better facilitate adhering to the criterion of fabric waste in grading.

Pathway 3B: Retaining the marker configuration. A number of possibilities exist for retaining the original marker configuration across sizes.

In some garments where fullness (defined as amount of fabric considerably larger than the body it covers) has been designed into the garment, it may be possible to not change the outline of each garment component to produce a range of sizes. What changes is the relative amount of fullness in a component. Pleats, tucks, darts, and gathers can be employed to control fullness across sizes.

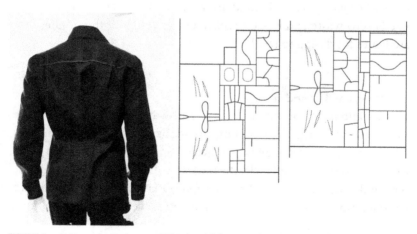

FIGURE 8.4. Patterns for Endurance Shirts I and II (2009 and 2011, respectively). (Photograph by Silversalt, patterns by Timo Rissanen)

The Rhodes bodice discussed earlier breaks some rules about grading in order to maintain the interlocking across a range of sizes. The square sleeve pieces with circular center cutouts do not grade, except for the two cutouts that attach to armholes. The vertical length of the largest-size bodice is the same as one size smaller, so that the pattern fits on the fabric width. The body and peplums are cut on the weft grain, perpendicular rather than parallel to selvedge, to allow conventional horizontal grading. Baumgarten, Watson, and Carr (1999, p. 108) note that in the eighteenth century, shirt size was determined by fabric width, with different sizes cut according to the same pattern configuration. Using a wider fabric made a larger shirt. Weaving a range of fabric widths may be too expensive, but T-shirts without side seams, cut from knitted tubes of various widths, are common.

Pathway 4: Using a different fabric width for each size
Using a different fabric width may be feasible with some tubular knit fabrics like jersey or rib, knitted in a range of diameters. Whether each size is zero waste and exactly replicates the design of the original size are issues for design to resolve.

Pathway 5: A hybrid method
Combinations of the previous four pathways are likely to provide many solutions to grading. Multiple solutions exist, given the variability of garments, varying size range requirements, and variations in grade rules. Garment type and style, the size range that is required, and fabric type and width determine the most appropriate solution. Grading is a consideration for zero waste fashion design as well as for manufacture.

Garment Design

Designing more than one style of garment simultaneously and cutting these from one length of fabric together can reduce the amount of fabric waste, although it does not necessarily do so. The mixing of jacket, trouser, and sometimes vest pieces on one length of fabric instead of cutting each separately is common tailors' practice (Cabrera & Flaherty Meyers, 1983, p. 57). Yeohlee Teng maximized fabric use on a 7-meter length by designing and cutting three different dresses from it simultaneously (Major & Teng, 2003, pp. 80–3). McQuillan similarly designs multiple garments simultaneously. For Yield, McQuillan partnered with textile designer Genevieve Packer to design an outfit of three garments that were seemingly made from dozens of fabrics. The three garments are cut together from one fabric (Figure 8.5). An engineered digital print developed by Packer creates the illusion of multiple fabrics.

To eliminate waste, the technical and visual elements of a garment need to be considered simultaneously; whether they should ever be treated separately is open to question. While considering the appearance or visual aesthetics of a garment, the designer also needs to understand how its pattern pieces may interlock. The garment needs to be considered in two and three dimensions simultaneously. Using design practice as a research methodology, Katherine Townsend (2004) explored the relationship between a two-dimensional textile print and three-dimensional garment form. Like the McQuillan/Packer collaboration above, Townsend's research involved engineering the textile print to work within the flat shapes of the garment patterns as well as the three-dimensional garment. Along similar lines, the English designer Julian Roberts sometimes develops a garment pattern without an exact prediction of the garment itself. The garment form reveals itself once made (McQuillan 2011, p. 85). If designers were open to some degree of trust in such unpredictability, even risk, the adoption of zero waste fashion design could become easier. Zero waste fashion design could not only eliminate waste but perhaps also offer new ways of practicing fashion design.

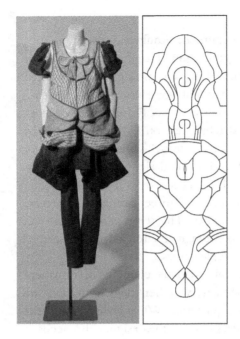

FIGURE 8.5. Vest, dress, and trousers, and their patterns, by Holly McQuillan, with textile design by Genevieve Packer (2011). McQuillan developed the garments and textiles collaboratively with Packer for the Yield exhibition. (Photograph by Thomas McQuillan, pattern by Holly McQuillan)

It may take longer to create a zero waste garment than to create one through more conventional methods, particularly if a designer has not previously worked in such a way. Whether experience over time turns a designer into a zero waste expert is subject to further research. For the time being, evidence shows that at the garment sampling stage more styles are created than are eventually taken to production. According to Waddell (2004, p. 40), "most design houses estimate at least 20 percent wastage at this stage"; the cull is due to limitations in technical or financial feasibility, or because of artistic reasons. The deleted sample garments represent a considerable amount of work by the design team, a cost to the company, and a significant waste of physical resources. Would closer consultation with sales and merchandising, combined with more effective market research and range planning, eliminate some of this waste? If design were subject to more effective research and planning, would more time become available for design?

Study NY

Tara St James is the founder of Study NY, a design studio with a concern for the environmental and human aspects of the fashion industry. St James founded Study NY in 2009, after having worked as the creative director for Covet. St James is the winner of the 2011 Ecco Domani Fashion Foundation Award for Sustainable Design.

Her considered approach to zero waste fashion design and sustained collaborations with artists and textile designers are the key components of her success. St James aims to build upon her brand's sustainability and evaluate the chain of production to see where possibilities exist for further transparency. A believer in open sourcing and information sharing, over the years St James has shared her sources and contacts on her blog. By doing so she supports her suppliers, often smaller, fair-trade textile mills and fashion manufacturers.

St James started Study NY with an entirely zero waste collection for spring 2009 and she has continued zero waste fashion design in subsequent seasons. For example, for spring 2011, St James created a zero waste skirt from a hand-woven silk ikat from Uzbekistan. Zero waste is one of many aspects of sustainability that St James built into the company's core mission. Several times a year Study NY (the company no longer subscribes to the traditional fashion calendar, adopting a slower pace of evolution) repeats a version of a square-cut zero waste dress, which can be worn in a number of ways. This is an efficient example of zero waste fashion design, as a square of fabric with intricately placed buttons and buttonholes allows the wearer to play with the garment and find her ideal way of wearing it. This is a deep engagement with waste elimination; fabric, as well as the experience it creates as a garment, are equally valued.

Conclusion: The End of Fabric Waste

Zero waste fashion design is not good in and of itself; it needs to be examined in a much broader context. Furthermore, entirely new ways of thinking about how the industry could exist and function while allowing humanity to flourish are required. This points toward a new, expanded vision for fashion design: as well as designing and making garments, fashion design needs to design the consumption, wearing, and using of garments, and design collaboratively with other fields the systems in which the wearing and using occurs. A goal may now be set: the fashion industry should aim for 100 percent of the fabric it uses to stay in the garments it produces. To eliminate fabric waste, the often hierarchically distinct areas of pattern cutting and fashion design need to interact more closely. Sketching tends to dominate as the primary design tool, but to eliminate fabric waste, pattern cutting needs to be integral to the design process, not a step following it. Sketching does have its unique advantages as a design tool, but sketching and pattern cutting can and should work in tandem. If fashion designers were to address fabric waste, and evidence suggests they should, sketch-based designing could combine with pattern-based designing. Already fashion schools such as Parsons and California College of the Arts in the United States, Massey University in New Zealand, and LAMK in Finland are teaching zero waste fashion design as part of their curriculum. Some of the initial difficulties of two-dimensional garment pattern design may be overcome by working through draping with fabric; the relationship between flat fabric pieces and three-dimensional form may then become easier to understand. Reflecting on the passion that the contemporary designers covered in this chapter have for textiles in fashion, perhaps fabric- or textile-based designing is more apt a term than pattern-based designing. Fabric is the backbone of fashion and fashion should respect it as such; fabric could positively inform and inspire fashion design in more ways than most current practice suggests.

Fabric waste elimination could foster more carefully considered design and making processes. To adopt more ecologically sustainable fashion creation practices, the industry needs to critically examine its present practices. Currently some of these practices may be taken for granted, such as fabric waste, grading, and the nature of fashion design itself. This is not a call for change for change's sake, but an acknowledgment that change may be justified. More importantly, this is an acknowledgment that change is possible.

When you next design or make a garment, examine the fabric. Try to see how the garment you want to create could use all of it. What is the relationship between the width of the fabric and the garment? If you have the pattern, see where the largest gaps or waste occur between the pieces. How can you adjust the design by incorporating these gaps into the garment? Remember, your creativity and openness to possibility are your greatest asset. Remember also that these can be your greatest limitations. Try to identify what learned rules guide your practice. One useful advantage of rules is that they can help us make sense of things. Once we have learned a rule, breaking it may take us forward. Be brave.

Discussion Questions

1   What factors have contributed to creating the condition where the fabric industry perceives fabric as disposable?
2   If the goal is to eliminate fabric waste, what are the processes that create obstacles to this goal?
3   What opportunities exist for designers for reducing or eliminating fabric waste?

References
Abernathy, F. H., Dunlop, J. T., Hammond, J. H., & Weil, D. (1999). *A stitch in time: Lean retailing and the transformation of manufacturing: Lessons from the apparel and textile industries.* New York and Oxford: Oxford University Press.

Allwood, J., Laursen, S. E., Malvido de Rodríguez, C., & Bocken, N. (2006). *Well dressed? The present and future sustainability of clothing and textiles in the United Kingdom.* Cambridge: University of Cambridge Institute for Manufacturing.

Arnold, J. (1977/1966). *Patterns of fashion 2. Englishwomen's dresses and their construction c. 1860–1940.* London: Macmillan.

Baumgarten, L., Watson, J., & Carr, F. (1999). *Costume close-up: Clothing construction and pattern 1750–1790.* Williamsburg, VA and New York: The Colonial Williamsburg Foundation in association with Quite Specific Media Group, Ltd.

Black, S. (2002). *Knitwear in fashion.* London: Thames & Hudson.

Bocco Guarneri, A. (2003). *Bernard Rudofsky: A humane designer.* New York and Vienna: Springer-Verlag.

Brown, S. (2005). Textiles: Fiber, structure, and function. In M. McQuaid (Ed.), *Extreme textiles. Designing for high performance* (pp. 35–65). London: Thames & Hudson.

Cabrera, R., & Flaherty Meyers, P. (1983). *Classic tailoring techniques: A construction guide for men's wear.* New York: Fairchild Publications.

Chapagain, A. K., Hoekstra, A. Y., Savenije, H. H. G., & Gautam, R. (2005). The water footprint of cotton consumption. *Value of Water. Research Report Series No. 18.* Retrieved October 20, 2006, from http://www.waterfootprint.org.

Chenoune, F. (1993). *A history of men's fashion.* Paris: Flammarion.

Cooklin, G. (1997). *Garment technology for fashion designers.* Oxford: Blackwell Science.

Dobson, J. (2004). *Making kimono and Japanese clothes.* London: Batsford.

Hishinuma, Y. (Ed.). (1986). *Clothes by Yoshiki Hishinuma.* Tokyo: Yobisha Co.

Kries, M. & von Vegesack, A. (2001). *A-POC making: Issey Miyake & Dai Fujiwara.* Berlin: Vitra Design Museum.

Lynton, L. (1995). *The sari: Styles, patterns, history, techniques.* London: Thames & Hudson.

Major, J. S. & Teng, Y. (Eds.). (2003). *Yeohlee: Work. Material architecture.* Mulgrave: Peleus Press.

McDonough, W. & Braungart, M. (2002). *Cradle to cradle: Remaking the way we make things.* New York: North Point Press.

McQuillan, H. (2011). Zero-waste design practice: Strategies and risk taking for garment design. In A. Gwilt & T. Rissanen (Eds.), *Shaping sustainable fashion: Changing the way we make and use clothes.* (pp. 83–97). London: Earthscan.

McQuillan, H. & Rissanen, T. (2011). *Yield: Making fashion without making waste.* New York: Textile Arts Center.

Rhodes, Z. (2005). *Zandra Rhodes: A lifelong love affair with textiles.* [Exhibition catalogue]. Woodbridge, UK: Antique Collectors' Club.

Rhodes, Z. & Knight, A. (1984). *The art of Zandra Rhodes.* London: Jonathan Cape.

Rissanen, T. (2013). Zero waste fashion design: A study at the intersection of cloth, fashion design and pattern cutting. PhD thesis, University of Technology Sydney.

Rothstein, N. (Ed.). (1984). *Four hundred years of fashion.* London: Victoria & Albert Museum.

Rudofsky, B. (1947). *Are clothes modern?* Chicago: Paul Theobald.

Shaeffer, C. B. (2011). *Couture sewing techniques. Revised and updated.* Newtown: The Taunton Press.

Shep, R. L. & Cariou, G. (1999). *Shirts and men's haberdashery: 1840s to 1920s.* Mendocino: R. L. Shep.

Stern, R. (2004). *Against fashion: Clothing as art, 1850–1930.* Cambridge and London: MIT Press.

Tarrant, N. (1994). *The development of costume.* London: Routledge.

Tilke, M. (1956). *Costume patterns and designs: A survey of costume patterns and designs of all periods and nations from antiquity to modern times.* London: A. Zwemmer Ltd.

Townsend, K. (2004). Transforming shape: Hybrid practice as group activity. *The Design Journal, 7*(2), 18–31.

Van Assche, A. (2005). Interweavings: Kimono past and present. In A. Van Assche (Ed.), *Fashioning kimono* (pp. 6–29). Milan: 5 Continents Editions.

Waddell, G. (2004). *How fashion works: Couture, ready-to-wear & mass production.* Oxford: Blackwell Science.

JANA HAWLEY, PHD, is professor and director of the Norton School of Family and Consumer Sciences at the University of Arizona. She has conducted research for more than fifteen years on recycled clothing from a systems perspective that ranges from consumers' discard habits, to policy makers and international trade law, to charitable organizations, and finally to for-profit organizations that search for value-added opportunities for recycled clothing. Hawley believes that recycling clothing is just one of the fundamental solutions needed for building a sustainable future.

CHAPTER **9**

Economic Impact of Textile and Clothing Recycling

Jana Hawley

If most post-consumer waste is nearly 100 percent recyclable, why is such a high percentage of textiles and clothing products dumped into the landfill? To address this problem, we must first understand the economic impact of the textile recycling process. This chapter examines that process, its practitioners, its products, and the challenges it faces in the United States and throughout the world.

A Global System

Textile recycling is a fascinating story that few fully comprehend. In some parts of the world it is part of an underground economy, so in many cases it is not even accounted for in national economy figures. Trade laws prohibit the free flow of used textiles between some nations, citing health risks and negative impacts on fledgling industries as reasons for banning the trade. However, there is no doubt that textile recycling has a positive impact on many entities and contributes significantly to the social responsibility of contemporary culture, including the goodwill associated with environmentalism, charity, and disaster relief that also plays a significant economic role in the global marketplace.

Because textiles are nearly 100 percent recyclable, nothing in the textile and apparel pipeline should be sent to landfills. Rag traders have culled truckloads of used textiles and sorted them for a wide variety of markets. Grateful Dead T-shirts and Harley-Davidson jackets are sent to the Japanese vintage markets. Quality used clothing is sorted in El Paso and sent to developing markets in Central and South America where inexpensive used clothing is needed. Acrylic sweaters are baled in Brooklyn and sent to Italy to be garneted (i.e., the process where textile fabric is shredded back to the fiber stage) and spun into yarns for IKEA stadium blankets. Stained and torn T-shirts are cut into rags in Toronto and sold to furniture makers or machine shops. Old Indian saris are shredded and spun into hand-knitting yarns in Nepal. Mixed damaged clothes are ground into fiber and made into mats to line caskets in South Carolina. The textile recycling industry is a viable industry working diligently to keep waste out of landfills.

This chapter focuses on the economic impact of textile recycling. We begin with an overview of the recycling process, including issues of overconsumption and the resulting recycling processes that occur in the United States and throughout the world. Next, a micro–macro systems model depicts the global textiles recycling processes and their economic impact, particularly as they pertain to post-consumer apparel waste (rather than manufacturing waste). Finally, we look at alternative options for recycling and future trends. My research is based on more than fifteen years of qualitative data collection on apparel and other fashion products consumed and marketed throughout the United States and the world. I have interviewed a myriad of participants along the pipeline of the recycling system both in the United States and globally. Perhaps one of the most interesting things I have learned is that textile and clothing recycling is both a small and grand phenomenon. Many of the rag dealers are small, family-owned businesses that work independently; yet they are tightly knit to a global network that moves used clothing around the world through brokers and to long-time associations that have taken generations to establish. In the past five years, the economic picture of used clothing waste has changed dramatically and will be reflected in the discussion below.

The Textile and Apparel Recycling Process: A Brief Overview

Fashion and the Western lifestyle in general are significant contributors to landfill waste. Not only are products consumed at a high level but Western goods are often over-packaged, contributing even more to the waste stream. As landfill scarcity continues to rise, the costs of dumping will also continue to increase. These escalating costs are of concern for businesses as they seek ways to reduce their overheads.

The Problem of Overconsumption

Fashion itself compounds the problem of overconsumption. Elizabeth Wilson calls fashion "dress in which the key feature is rapid and continual changes of style. Fashion ... *is* change" (Wilson, 2003). But regardless of how dynamic fashion is or how economically viable the fashion industry is, (American) fashion is creating an overabundance of used clothing. Fashion marketers entice us to buy something new every season, sometimes with offerings that are truly new and exciting, but all too often the merchandise is simply a mere twist on last year's successful selling styles, offering the safe bet rather than taking a risk with the shareholders' expectations. Meanwhile, consumers satisfy their whims, often overburdening their closet space and probably their credit cards.

The result is a clothing accumulation that stems from planned obsolescence, the core of fashion. Thus, the essence of fashion fuels the momentum for change, which creates demand for ongoing replacement of products with something that is marketed as new and fresh. In addition, fashion has reached beyond apparel to the home furnishings industry. The result is fashionable goods contributing to consumption at a significantly higher level than need. Without the notion of fashion, the textile, apparel, and home furnishings industries would realize even more vulnerability in an environment that is already extremely competitive. Apparel and home furnishings companies in the United States today have continual fashion "seasons" that constantly capture consumer interest as these companies stimulate sales and profits.

Waste continues to accumulate as consumers continue to buy, which further compounds the problem of what to do with discarded waste of post-consumer apparel and home textile products. Apparel in today's marketplace is different from that of several decades ago, not only in design but also in fiber content. When synthetic fibers were introduced in the twentieth century, textile recycling became more complex for two distinct reasons: (1) fiber strength increased, making it more difficult to shred or "open" the fibers, and (2) fiber blends made it more difficult to purify the sorting process. While for some textile recycling value-added processes concern for the fiber blend does not matter, for others, the fiber content is very important and sorting by blend is a tedious process that requires well-trained specialists.

Textile Recycling Statistics

The textile and apparel recycling effort is concerned with recycling, recyclability, and source reduction of both pre-consumer and post-consumer waste. According to the Council for Textile Recycling (CTR), the average American throws away 70 pounds of apparel products per year (Council for Textile Recycling, 2014). Although textiles seldom earn a category of their own in solid waste management data, the CTR reported that the per capita consumption of fiber in the United States is about 82 pounds per capita with only 15 percent donated or recycled per year (2014). China has surpassed the United States, making China the number one consumer of fiber in the world (Rupp, 2013). Of course, as consumption increases, so will the increase in disposal. Thus, China will eventually become a significant contributor to the textile waste stream if plans are not implemented to salvage the waste from landfills.

It is well established that recycling is economically beneficial, yet much of the discarded clothing and textile waste in the United States fails to reach the recycling pipeline. The United States textile recycling industry annually salvages approximately 12 pounds per capita, but 70 pounds per capita still goes to our landfills (Council for Textile Recycling, 2014). A recently established program, *Wear.Donate.Recycle,* has been established by the Council for Textile Recycling with the purpose of reaching zero post-consumer textile waste entering our landfills by 2037. Companies like American Eagle, J.Crew, and H&M have all initiated donation programs (Sourcing Journal, 2014) and the updated release of the Global Recycled Standard Version 3 has implemented changes that encourage companies to be transparent in the use of reclaimed materials and to be more transparent throughout their supply chain (Lamicella, 2014). This is being made possible in a collaborative effort to empower all entities to make commitments to this important initiative. As an example, even though there are several well-established uses for denim waste, the denim industry still deposits millions of pounds of scrap denim in US landfills annually. However, attempts are being made to create value-added products from denim waste such as Levi's Waste<Less Collection or Bonded Logic's UltraTouch Denim insulation. In 2014, the Environmental Protection Agency (EPA) reported that the recovery rate for textiles was 2.3 million tons in 2012, up from 1.6 million tons in 2006 (Environmental Protection Agency, 2012).

The Textile Recycling Industry

Few people understand the textile recycling industry, its myriad participants, and wide variety of products made from reclaimed textile fiber. As one of the oldest and most established recycling industries in the world, the textile recycling industry reclaims used textile and apparel products and puts them to new and interesting uses. This "hidden" industry (Divita, 1996) consists of approximately 3,000 businesses that are able to divert over 1.3 million tons of post-consumer textile waste annually. Furthermore, the textile recycling industry is able to process 93 percent of the waste without producing harmful by-products or new hazardous waste. E. Stubin, chairman of the Board of Council for Textile Recycling (2014) reports that nearly all after-use textile products can be reclaimed for a variety of markets that are already established. The textile recycling industry partners with engineers, researchers, and industry leaders to search for new viable value-added products made from used textile fiber (personal communication with K. Stewart, July 28, 2014).

Textile recycling can be classified as either pre-consumer or post-consumer waste. Pre-consumer waste consists of by-product materials from the textile, fiber, and cotton industries that are remanufactured for the automotive, aeronautic, home building, furniture, mattress, coarse yarn, home furnishings, paper, apparel, and other industries.

Post-consumer waste is defined as any type of garment or household article made from manufactured textiles that the owner no longer needs and decides to discard. These articles are discarded either because they are worn out, are damaged, are outgrown, or have gone out of fashion. These textile products are sometimes given to charities and passed on to friends and family, but additionally are disposed of into the trash and end up in municipal landfills. Goodwill Industries is able to sell approximately 50 percent of the items it receives in their 2,900+ retail stores, creating more than $3.79 billion, with the remainder sold to used textile dealers and brokers (Goodwill Industries International, July 28, 2014). Figure 9.1 provides a schematic of options for post-consumer textiles.

The Textile Recycling Pipeline

Many essential participants take part in the textile recycling pipeline, including consumers, policy makers, solid-waste managers, not-for-profit agencies, and for-profit textile dealers (Hawley, 2000).

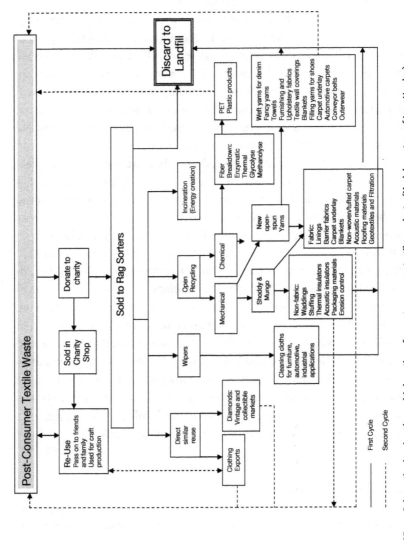

FIGURE 9.1. Schematic showing the multiple options for post-consumer textile products. (Model courtesy of Jana Hawley)

Getting Rid of It

Consumers could make a decision to part with their items by trying to sell them through a variety of channels that include garage sales, consignment shops, and online auctions. Items that do not sell could then be sent through the municipal recycling system, donated to a charitable organization, or thrown away. When consumers finally decide to donate them to a charitable organization, they have made the decision that someone in the world needs their clothing. For many Americans, this step makes them feel good about the donation they are making. For others, giving their things away is a difficult thing to do. One woman said that she would clean out her closets, carry her things in the trunk of her car for several months, and finally be able to drop the things off at Goodwill. The emotional tie that we have to *things* makes it difficult to discard, even at the end of their useful life (McCracken, 1991).

Another woman said that six months after her father died, she had sorted his things, put them in trash bags, taken them to Goodwill, and because Goodwill had so much excess inventory, she watched them put her father's things into a dumpster without even looking in the bags. After sitting in her car crying for a while, she crawled into the dumpster, retrieved her father's things, put them back in her car, and drove away.

Think about things in your own closet. Are there things that you haven't worn for more than three years? Try to analyze why. Are they a size you hope to wear again after you go on that diet? Is it something you simply paid too much for, so how could you possibly *give* it away? Was it a gift from someone dear to you? But if it hasn't been worn for at least three years, isn't it time to give it to charity? As evidenced here, even after consumers make decisions about their things, they may or may not be able to part with them.

Municipal and Charitable Recycling Programs

Most municipalities do not offer convenient, or any, textile recycling options. Curbside pickup of textiles is problematic because when textiles get wet, problems of mold and mildew set in. Some cities have established textile recycling programs where textiles are collected at watertight collection sites. Denton, Texas, reported that when textile recycling was added to the municipal recycling mix, textiles subsidized the costs of the other recycling materials. The EPA reported 16 percent of municipal solid waste was recovered; yet textiles still comprise 11.2 percent of US landfills (Environmental Protection Agency, 2012).

Charitable organizations are the primary option for most consumers when they decide to donate, or *recycle*, their clothing. Evidence reveals, however, that consumers will not donate clothing to charities if they feel the clothing is unwearable (e.g., out of fashion, stained, pilled, etc.). However, most charities cull the things they determine to be saleable at their resale shops and then bale the remainder, which they sell to rag dealers who will, in turn, further process the used clothing for further value-added markets (which will be discussed later in this chapter). It is important here for consumers to understand that all clothing and textile items are recyclable and should be sent into the recycling pipeline. If no municipal recycling option exists for textiles, then charitable organizations are the next best option. Charities are able to reap benefits for their organization from the clothing that is saleable in the retail stores and sell the rest of it to textile graders who in turn obtain their inventory to conduct their for-profit business. In other words, charities and textile graders are interrelated partners in the textile recycling pipeline.

Textile Graders

Each year, textile graders, also called *rag dealers*, *rag sorters*, or *rag graders*, acquire about 80 percent of the excess inventory from charitable organizations and municipal contracts. Clothes come in by the truckload and are offloaded onto conveyor belts where they are sorted for a wide variety of markets ranging from vintage collectibles, exports to developing countries, wipers, and fiber for stuffing. Textile graders account for annual gross sales in excess of $700 million, employing 100,000 workers with over $1 billion wages paid (Council for Textile Recycling, 2014). Recycling International (2004) reported that only 40 percent of the clothes received by textile graders were saleable as clothing. Most textile graders are small, family-owned businesses that have been in operation for several generations (Allenbach, 1993; Shapiro & Sons, 1961). However, start-up entrepreneurs also have opened new rag dealer businesses because they perceive it as a low-cost, easily accessible form of entrepreneurship. What many of the start-ups fail to realize, however, is that this business is highly dependent on global contacts that take years of cultivating clients in overseas markets to sell their sorted goods. As one textile rag dealer told me, "I have spent as much as a year at a time away from my family while I developed and nurtured markets across Africa, Asia, and Latin America. Now that these business contacts have been established, I can pass the contacts on to my son, who will be taking over the business soon." Another rag dealer supported this notion when he said, "Establishing contacts in Africa is particularly difficult. But once those contacts are made, the bond between us has been very strong and full of respect." And an international broker from Europe said the following:

> Buying and selling in Africa is an underground business. The used-textile brokers in Africa are substantially wealthier than many of the citizens who are the consumers of the used clothing. They must hide their wealth in order to maintain credibility among the citizens. One of our buyers has a beautiful burled wood and gilded office that is [hidden away]. When we go to Africa to do business we have to be secretly escorted ... to conduct our business.

Textile recycling companies are often located in large metropolitan areas because it is imperative to keep transportation costs to a minimum and the majority of inventory will come from the urban areas.

Nousiainen & Talvenmaa-Kuusela (1994) reported that transportation and sorting costs were the decisive criteria for profitability for a textile sorting company. Depending on the current economic climate, primarily associated with materials availability, commodity pricing, fuel costs, and current value-added markets, for-profit rag-sorting companies can realize both success and hardship. Although the primary goal of these small businesses is to realize profits, most of the business owners are also committed to environmentalism and take pride in their contribution to waste reduction.

Once sorted, the goods are compressed into large bales, usually 600 to 1,000 kg, wrapped, and warehoused until an order, often from a broker, is received. Several things are considered during sorting for this category: climate of the market, relationships between the exporters and importers, and trade laws for used apparel.

FIGURE 9.2. Used bales of clothing are found on street corners around the world. This photo was taken in New Delhi, India. (Photo courtesy of Jana Hawley)

Grading Used Clothes: Recognizing Economic Opportunities

Textile graders sort for many categories, sometimes as many as 400. Rough sorts (i.e., pulling heavy coats, blankets, plastics, toys, shoes) from the conveyor belts occur first by new employees or employees that do not have the skills to recognize the finer categories. As the clothes move along the conveyor, the higher-skilled employees will sort for the more specific categories (e.g., particular brand names, acrylic or cashmere sweaters, collectible jeans, antique garments). Hawley (2006) provides a complete framework for understanding the sorting process.

Vintage and Collectibles

Of all the categories that graders sort, the most lucrative is vintage collectibles. Many vintage or collectible items have global appeal, as evidenced by the movement of vintage goods from country to country. What might be considered ready for throwaway in one country might be considered hip or cool in another. For example, American items are highly prized in Japanese markets, as I found when I was collecting data at one of the US sites and saw five Japanese buyers rummaging through piles of used clothes to select what they wanted to buy. The owner of the business said that there are many days out of the month when Japanese buyers are in-house making their selections. Japan is the largest importer of used American collectibles and has proved to be very interested in Americana items such as authentic Harley-Davidson clothing, Grateful Dead T-shirts, and Coach handbags. After the September 11, 2001 terrorist attack, the second-hand signature red, white, and blue Tommy Hilfiger goods realized increased interest in some global markets. But perhaps the one item that has had consistent global interest is Levi's jeans, particularly certain older styles. One rag sorter found a pair of collectible Levi's and sold them on the Paris auction block for $18,000. Another rag sorter sold a collectible find for $11,000 to Levi Strauss & Co. A textile grader in the Midwest claimed that he found enough collectible blue jeans to "pay for my three kids' college education." However, it requires a special eye and the ability to forecast trends in order to find the high-value items in the huge piles of used textiles that rag sorters must sift through.

Products considered "vintage" collectibles include the following:

- old rock concert shirts from world famous groups like Led Zeppelin or The Rolling Stones;
- official Harley-Davidson clothing;
- Che Guevara T-shirts;
- 1950s bowling shirts;
- 1950s printed aprons;
- military issue leather bomber jackets;
- original Aran knit from Ireland, 100 percent wool;
- Grateful Dead T-shirts, pre-1995 (death of Jerry Garcia);
- vintage denim (Levi's, Lee, Wrangler);
- vintage collegiate apparel;
- vintage movie apparel;
- Hawaiian shirts;
- smoking jackets, pajamas, robes;
- vintage ties;
- vintage lingerie (slips, sleepwear);
- vintage accessories (belt buckles, scarves, sunglasses);
- bell bottoms;
- swimwear.

The collectible category accounts for approximately one to two percent of the total volume of goods that enter the textile recycling stream, yet this category also accounts for the largest profit center for most textile recycling companies. The manager of the collectible division of a recycling company told me that "when you find the [really good things], they are still diamonds in the rough, but once they are cleaned, pressed, and packaged, they are worth a lot in the marketplace." As a result, many people get into the vintage clothing business, as evidenced by the tremendous number of hits received when "vintage clothing stores" ($n > 9,000,000$) is used as a search string in Google. J. Usatch, a recycling company owner and industry proponent, warned, however, that many people can find and sell vintage collectibles, but it is "the companies that are able to sell the not-so-good qualities to secondary markets [at a profit]" (Recycling International, 2006a, p. 95) that distinguish themselves from the others as successful textile graders.

The word *vintage* is really a misnomer; *collectible* might be more accurate. Items that qualify for collectible status include couture clothing and accessories, Americana items such as Levi's, uniforms such as those worn by Girl and Boy Scouts of America, particular branded items such as Izod, vintage items identified as collectible trends such as old Harley-Davidson T-shirts or 1960s bowling shirts, luxury fibers (e.g., cashmere and camel hair), and antique items, which by the strictest definition means over 100 years old but with regard to clothing usually means 1920s or earlier. Customers for collectibles include well-known designers, eccentric college students, and wealthy celebrities. Retail boutiques featuring vintage clothing can be found in trendy SoHo or Beverly Hills, and the Internet offers a plethora of vintage options.

Vintage shop owners or Internet sellers are often members of the National Association of Resale and Thrift Shops (NART). This Chicago-based association was established in 1984 and has more than 1,000 members. It serves thrift, resale, and consignment shops and promotes public education about the vintage shop industry. TRAID (Textiles Recycling for Aid and Development) is a charity organization that finances itself through the sale of quality second-hand clothing.

Wipers

Another important sorting category for graders is wipers. The wiper market comes from clothing that has seen the end of its useful life as such and may be turned into wiping or polishing rags for industrial use. White T-shirts, sweatshirts, and polo shirts are a primary source for this category because the cotton fiber makes good polishing cloths and absorbent rags. Bags of rags can be found at retail stores such as AutoZone or in Wal-Mart's automotive department. But in some cases, some synthetic fiber, particularly olefin because of its excellent wicking and oleophilic properties, is used where oily spills need to be cleaned up. An industry insider revealed that he sells reclaimed olefin from the sorting process to the oil-refining industry to be used in combinations with hydrophobic fibers as stuffing for "snakes" in ocean oil spill cleanups. Another rag sorter said that he sells rags to washing machine manufacturers for use-testing of machines.

Wipers maintain a fairly stable market over time, yet processing wipers may not be cost-effective. It requires labor to cut the neckband and sleeves from shirts, and also often requires laundering. Both of these add costs to the processing and may not make this category cost-effective, even though the market demand remains stable.

Twenty-Nine Percent Conversion to New Products

Converting used materials to new products is an important category for growth. Companies are partnering with engineers, researchers, and industry leaders to determine value-added products where recycled textiles and apparel can be used. When fiber is cut, shredded, carded, or otherwise machined back to the fiber stage, it is referred to as *shoddy*. Shoddy can be re-engineered into value-added products such as stuffing, automotive components, carpet underlays, casket lining, building materials (e.g., insulation and roofing felt), and low-end blankets. The majority of this category consists of stained, torn, or otherwise unmarketable garments. A textile grader from the Midwest, however, was sorting for 100 percent cotton sweaters because he was selling shredded cotton fiber to mix with sand for use in "Punch-n-Kick" bags made by one of the world's largest sporting manufacture companies. Another informant reports that reclaimed fibers are being used in the production of US currency.

In some cases, mixed fiber from old clothing is made into oil booms and geotextiles for construction erosion because of their excellent strength and wicking properties. GeoHay of Spartansburg, South Carolina is one such company that makes these value-added geotextiles from used clothing. Figure 9.3 shows an example.

A vast number of products are made from reprocessed fiber. Much of this fiber is respun into new yarns or manufactured into woven, knitted, or non-woven fabrications such as garment linings, household items, furniture upholstery, insulation materials, automobile sound absorption materials, automobile carpeting, and toys (Querci, 2000). New yarn producers like those in Prato, Italy, reduce cashmere sweaters to fiber, spin new yarns, and produce cashmere blankets for the luxury market. The blanket manufacturers in Prato also make acrylic stadium blankets for IKEA from acrylic sweaters that are reclaimed from all over the world.

Converting fiber into value-added products is a process that represents an economic and environmental saving of valuable fiber that would otherwise be lost to the landfill. The most unusable and damaged of post-consumer textiles often have the highest level of specifications forced upon it by the end-use industries (e.g., building, auto, aeronautics, sporting equipment, construction materials, and defense).

FIGURE 9.3. Mixed used fibers are made into a variety of geotextiles for construction sites, sewer drainage, or oil spill cleanup. (Photo courtesy of Jana Hawley)

The other category for conversion to new products is the actual redesign of used clothing. Current fashion trends are reflected by a team of young designers who use and customize second-hand clothes for a chain of specialty vintage clothing stores in the United Kingdom. Its offerings include "cheap, chic, and occasional designer surprises" (Ojumo, 2002; Packer, 2002). As another example, a young designer in Dallas, Texas creates new from the old and sells wholesale to various trendy stores such as Urban Outfitters. This concept is common among boutiques with a youth-oriented target market and many examples can be seen on Etsy.com.

Landfill and Incineration for Energy

For some reclaimed fiber, no viable value-added market has been established, so the used goods must be sent to the landfill. Rag sorters work hard to avoid this for both environmental and economic reasons because the average landfill tipping fee in the United States is $44 per ton with a high of $96 per ton in Vermont (Center for Sustainable Systems, 2013).

The incineration of reclaimed fiber for energy production may be another solution to keep textiles out of the landfill. In the United States, early testing reveals that emissions of incinerated used fibers are more than satisfactory, but the process of feeding the boiler systems in many North American power plants is not feasible (Weide, 2004). The incineration of used textiles as an alternative fuel source is more commonly done in Europe than in the United States because European fuel costs have historically been much higher than those in the United States. More research is needed for used textiles to become a viable choice, both economically and environmentally, as an alternative fuel source. As fashion retailers continue to stimulate retail sales and consumers continue to overload closets, however, burning used clothing might become a very viable economic option.

ideas in action

Mitumba—Sweaters of Many Colors

Used clothes arrive in Africa by ship in 600- to 1,000-pound bales and are then opened and sold to brokers and small retailers throughout Africa. In 2003, Tanzania imported more than $60 million of US clothing worn by all social classes (e.g., rich, educated, poor, children, clergy, politicians, old, and young). They call it *mitumba*, a Swahili word that means bale or bundle. When people put on mitumba, you can't tell the rich from the poor.

Because of trade laws, much of mitumba is smuggled through the black markets from Burundi, Zambia, and the Democratic Republic of the Congo. When it arrives in Tanzania, it looks like a plastic bundle the size of a refrigerator. Djibril Duany, the local dealer, cuts open the plastic wrap he bought for about $90 and digs through it to see what great pieces it contains. In it he finds a Cher Farewell Tour T-shirt, a Chicago Bulls jersey, several men's suits, two track suits, and his prize, a Samuel Eto'o jersey. He is thrilled. According to Duany (2006), most mitumba is imported by charitable organizations and intended for the poor, aged, and ill. However, businesspeople can acquire a license to sell mitumba if they pay all pertinent taxes to the government.

Mitumba is often divided based on quality and type. A high demand is placed on shirts, trousers, suits, T-shirts, jackets, and athletic wear. Used suits are of particular value, especially when compared to new suits at substantial prices in boutiques. Prices vary depending on the target market. For rich markets, mitumba can be relatively high.

As mitumba has become commonplace, notions of Western fashion have also become better understood. At one time Tanzanians were draped in vibrant colors and patterns of local industry, but today's Tanzanian manufacturers cannot produce clothing at a cost lower than second-hand clothing. Therefore, mitumba serves an important role to fill the gap. Mitumba is also an important price point for the country's poor. Small entrepreneurs earn a living from selling used clothing in the marketplace. Finally, used clothing provides income in the form of taxes to the Tanzanian government.

> However, there is a negative side to mitumba. Some argue that used-clothing imports have slowed the growth of the fledgling textile manufacturing industry. Used-clothing options are very cheap compared to the handmade cotton goods produced by artisans and the cotton farmers in the area. Others have argued that used clothing contains health risks that could spread skin diseases. And finally, some exporters are shipping clothing that is beyond wearable condition, therefore making Tanzania a dumping ground. Used clothing has been shipped to Africa for years; standards may need to be established where quality goods are shipped so that nothing is left for the dumping ground (Duany, 2006).

Export of Used Clothing

On many street corners throughout the developing world, racks of Western clothing are being sold. I have seen for myself such racks in Thailand, India, Greece, and Mexico (see Figure 9.4). The second-hand export markets compose the largest volume, or roughly 48 percent, of used clothing (Stubin, 2001); most of these goods are shipped to developing countries or used for disaster relief.

Most used clothing from the United States goes to Africa or South and Central America, but markets also exist in parts of Asia, such as India and Pakistan. Most European exports go to either Eastern Europe or Northern Africa. One informant reported that used apparel serves as the largest export from the United States based on volume. The United States exported $149 million in sales of clothing to Africa in 2013 (OTEXA, 2014). One of its primary export sites is Uganda, where a Ugandan woman can purchase a designer T-shirt for $1.20. However, in January of 2005, the East African countries of Tanzania, Uganda, and Kenya imposed upwards of 300 percent import tax increases on used clothing in attempts to shut down the used-clothing imports, citing protectionist measures for their fledgling textile industries. It can be argued, however, that imports of new clothing dumped from China impose more of a threat on the local

FIGURE 9.4. In an open marketplace, such as this one in India, Western clothing is highly valued. Entrepreneurs earn a living selling this used clothing, or mitumba. (Photo courtesy of Jana Hawley)

textile industries than do second-hand clothing from Europe and the United States (Baden & Barber, 2005). These increased taxes gave rise to protests from millions of small businesses who survive by selling used clothing. The protests eventually forced authorities to pay attention, and in early 2006 the tax increases were reversed.

Western clothing is a highly valued commodity and perhaps serves as the only source of affordable clothing in many developing countries where levels of income are so low that food and clean water are the primary concern. Some have argued that the export of clothing to these nations has threatened the traditional dress for many indigenous cultures and at the same time may threaten the young textile and apparel industries of those countries. While this is certainly a sensitive issue that needs consideration, it is also the case that export of wearable, climate-appropriate, and affordable clothing to developing countries is a valuable commodity for most of the population in less privileged areas of the world. It provides not only affordable clothing but also the opportunity for micro-enterprise development of used-clothing stalls throughout the developing world.

Not all used clothing is exported to poorer countries. One textile grader shared that he has a new market in the United Arab Emirates, one of the richest countries in the world. Used clothes in the United Arab Emirates are not intended for the local population but for the immigrant labor from Bangladesh, Pakistan, and Indonesia, because labor jobs do not allow the workers enough discretionary income to purchase the designer labels that are offered in the local shops.

In recent years, rag graders have noted that Africans desire higher quality and more fashion-forward styles. As J. Usatch noted, "Today, selling used clothes to Africa is almost like running a boutique" (Recycling International, 2006b, p. 123). In the past, bales sold to African countries were not graded according to particular style or brand, but today's shipments must be carefully sorted to meet the ever-increasing savvy African consumer demands. This adds value to the bale, which can demand a higher price but also requires higher processing costs.

Even though Africa remains the strongest export area for US exports of used clothing, it is not a consistent market and is affected by the calendar, ever-changing trade policies, and other market forces. For example, November is one of the best months of the year for exports to Africa because many people return to their villages with gifts of clothing for their friends and relatives.

Used-clothing markets can also be impacted by natural disasters such as the 2004 Indian Ocean tsunami, the 2005 Katrina hurricane, or the 2010 Haiti earthquake. In the case of the US hurricanes, Americans often donated their clothing to the hurricane relief projects rather than through their normal channels of donation, significantly altering the supply to rag graders. When the flow of supply changes as dramatically as it did in the case of Hurricane Katrina, it impacts both rag graders and charitable organizations such as Goodwill and The Salvation Army. The truth is, relief agencies often dread the influx of used clothing that inevitably follows a disaster because it requires valuable

ideas in action

When cotton commodity prices skyrocketed in 2010, women weavers of Guatemala could not afford to buy their cotton warp yarns for their traditional back-strap weaving. Mary Anne Wise, of Cultural Cloth, taught the women how to use old clothing to make latch-hook rugs. The village women had a grant to purchase used clothing from the local *pacas* (used clothing stores). With trash bags full of clothes, each of them learned to translate their traditional designs to large-scale patterns in this new art form. In 2014, the rugs were selected for the International Folk Art Market in Sante Fe, New Mexico. By the third day of the market, the rugs were sold

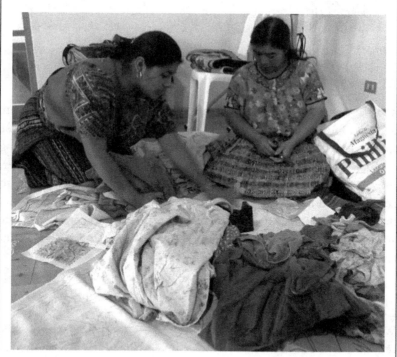

FIGURE S9.1. Guatemalan weavers learn a new art form using old clothes from the *pacas*. (Photo courtesy of Mary Anne Wise)

out and the women were some of the highest earners at the 2014 market. In addition, several of their rugs comprise a permanent traveling exhibition to museums around the globe.

FIGURE S9.2. Latch-hook rug made by Guatemalan weavers of recycled clothing. (Photo courtesy of Mary Anne Wise)

and scarce resources (e.g., time, money, and personnel to sort, clean, and distribute it). Often there is so much donated that warehouse space has to be located in order to manage the huge volume of clothing given. In addition, volunteers or relief workers are diverted from other, more critical recovery activities. It would be better for Americans to continue to donate through their normal charitable channels so that the charitable organizations and rag graders (i.e., the experts) can grade and sort the clothing and ship the appropriate donations to the disaster area as needed.

Conclusion: Future Trends and Directions

We cannot conclude the discussion of the economic impact of textile recycling without also discussing the global nature of the phenomenon. A combination of increased global affluence and lower prices (and quality) of fast fashion goods is causing a significant increase in the plethora of used clothing. While this would seem to provide increased volume for textile graders, that has not been the case. Fast fashion will ultimately have a negative impact on the used clothing trade because the quality of the goods simply does not pass long-term muster. Meanwhile, all other costs to the industry have increased, such as transportation, taxes, labor, etc. In addition, charity shops have recently moved away from apparel, focusing on household goods such as books and furniture (Oakdene Hollins, 2006).

Currently, much of today's market for used clothing is located in the poorest parts of the world. As these countries develop, the desire for used clothing in these poor nations will diminish and be replaced with desire for new goods. At present, these developing countries provide markets where industrialized nations can transform their excessive consumption into useful export.

As landfill space continues to become scarce and costs continue to escalate, so will concerns for environmentalism. Consumers must be provided with easy and informed choices for discarding their used clothing. Policy makers must provide a political environment that allows for the free flow of goods and the easy disposal of recyclable materials.

As environmental concerns continue to rise, consumers must continue to shift their attitude toward the use of recycled goods in the marketplace and embrace recycled goods. At the same time, they need to consider the impact of fast fashion and, instead, purchase higher quality goods that will pass through the second-hand clothing supply chain better. Citizens should lobby their municipalities to add textiles to their recycling options. When we consider the complexity of the textile recycling system and the importance of cooperation among the players, we then understand both the environmental and economic importance of textile recycling. To recycle successfully, everyone must embrace the system and not just make an occasional charitable donation. Meanwhile, arbiters must continue to develop new value-added markets and market the after-use possibilities so that the system functions at full capacity and with commitment from all.

Discussion Questions

1   Consumers often toss worn, stained, out-of-fashion clothing items into the trash, even though they still have value. What strategies could be used to inform consumers that their old things still have value and to encourage them to send their things into the used clothing supply chain?

2   Over time, the collectible value of used clothing changes. Sometimes, it is Grateful Dead T-shirts that have high value; at other times, it is Hawaiian shirts. Make a list of used clothing items that could have value in today's market and discuss why those items are trending now.

3   Used clothing often finds its way into second-hand markets in developing countries. Discuss why certain countries are better target markets for used clothing than other countries.

References

Allenbach, W. (1993, July 3). Making a pitch for textile recycling. *Neighbor, 3.*

Baden, S. & Barber, C. (2005, September). *The impact of second-hand clothing trade on developing countries.* Oxfam.

Center for Sustainable Systems. (2013, October). *Municipal solid waste.* University of Michigan.

Council for Textile Recycling. (2014). The life cycle of second hand clothing. http://www.weardonaterecycle.org/images/clothing-life-cycle.png.

Divita, L. (1996). Missouri manufacturers' interest in textile recycling. Unpublished Master's thesis, University of Missouri, Columbia.

Duany, D., local dealer, United Republic of Tanzania. (2006, July). Personal communication.

Environmental Protection Agency. (2012). Municipal solid waste generation, recycling, and disposal in the United States: Facts and figures for 2012. http://www.epa.gov/epawaste/nonhaz/municipal/pubs/2012_msw_fs.pdf.

Goodwill Industries International. (2014). Our results. http://www.goodwill. org/about-us/.

Hawley, J. M. (2000). Textile recycling as a system: A micro/macro analysis. *Journal of Family and Consumer Sciences, 93*(5), 35–40.

Hawley, J. M. (2006). Digging for diamonds: A conceptual framework for understanding reclaimed textile products. *Clothing and Textiles Research Journal, 24*(3), 262–75.

Lamicella, L. (2014, August 7). Textile exchange releases updated global recycled standard. Sourcingjournalonline.com. http://goo.gl/N2Ebm8.

McCracken, G. (1991). *Culture and consumption.* Bloomington: Indiana University Press.

Nousiainen, P. & Talvenmaa-Kuusela, P. (September 27, 1994). Solid textile waste recycling. Paper presented at "Globalization: Technological, economic, and environmental imperatives," 75th World Conference of Textile Institute, Atlanta, Georgia.

Oakdene Hollins. (2006). Recycling of low grade clothing waste. Defra Contract Reference: WRT152. Nonwoven Innovation & Research Institute.

Ojumo, A. (2002, November 24). Charity shops are beating the high street at its own game. *The Observer,* 5.

OTEXA. (September, 2014). Trade data US imports and exports of textiles and apparel. http://www.otexa.ita.doc.gov/msrpoint.htm.

Packer, G. (2002, March 31). How Susie Bayer's T-shirt ended up on Yusuf Mama's back. *New York Times,* 54.

Querci, U. (2000, July 22). Personal communication.

Recycling International market analysis. (2004, October 4). Germany pleads for recycling levy on clothing. Retrieved November 20, 2006 from http://www.recyclinginternational.com/markets/textiles.aspx.

Recycling International market analysis. (2006a, February 20). Winter weather impacts on supplies. Retrieved November 20, 2006 from http://www. recyclinginternational.com/markets/textiles.aspx.

Recycling International market analysis. (2006b, May 2). Spring collections boost supply. Retrieved November 20, 2006 from http://www. recyclinginternational.com/markets/textiles.aspx.

Rupp, J. (2013). Hong Kong: Center of the fiber industry. http://www.textileworld.com/Issues/2013/September-October/Features/Hong_Kong-Center_Of_The_Fiber_Industry.

Shapiro & Sons, Inc. (1961). *Reclaimed resources: A handbook of textile fabrics and fibres including lists of most important grades*. Baltimore, MD: S. Shapiro & Sons.

Sourcing Journal. (2014). Retrieved September 2, 2014 from https://www.sourcingjournalonline.com/?s=recycling&x=0&y=0.

Stewart, K. (2006, October 22). Personal communication.

Stubin, E., owner, TransAmerica. (2001). Personal communication, July 17, 2001.

Weide. (2004, March 20). Personal communication.

Wilson, E. (2003). *Adorned in dreams*. Camden, NJ: Rutgers University Press.

LUCY E. DUNNE is an Associate Professor at the University of Minnesota, where she is on the faculty of Apparel Design, Product Design, and Human Factors and Ergonomics, and holds affiliate membership in the graduate faculties of Computer Science and Engineering, Electrical and Computer Engineering, and the Institute for Health Informatics. She holds BS and MA degrees from Cornell University in Textiles and Apparel, an AAS in Electronic Technology from Tompkins-Cortland Community College, and a PhD in Computer Science from University College Dublin. Her research is focused on wearability and textile-based wearable technology and she explores new functionality in apparel, human–device interface, production and manufacture, and human factors of wearable products. Dr. Dunne has received the National Science Foundation's CAREER award and the NASA Silver Achievement Medal for her work with functional clothing and wearable technology.

CHAPTER **10**

Technology and Sustainable Futures

Lucy E. Dunne

Introduction

Much of the development in sustainability of apparel has focused on moving levers within the production process, and in end-of-life recycling and/or reuse of apparel. Technology can play a major part in improving the sustainability of apparel production: from fibers produced with fewer water resources, to garments designed to fit an individual body, to virtual garments that eliminate the construction and shipping of samples, to manufacturing techniques that minimize waste.

These changes focus on the ability of the industry to change: the responsibility of apparel producers is to think carefully and innovate to improve the sustainability of things like textile production, waste in the manufacturing process, and recyclability of garments. However, the end user is also a participant in this system, and also has agency to change. In a similar manner, technology can also make it more possible for the consumer to make effective changes to consumption behaviors.

This chapter will focus on the use of technology to encourage sustainability in consumption.

Consumers reliably express interest in making sustainable purchasing decisions, yet apparel is consumed more and more rapidly, in steadily increasing quantities. Figure 10.1 shows the annual garments sold per capita in the USA divided by the total US population for that year. The number of annually purchased garments per capita has doubled since the earliest date data were available, and shows sharp growth between 1998 and 2000, as the fast fashion paradigm took hold in the US market.

As fast fashion practices steadily lower individual garment prices, purchasing decisions can be made with less deliberation. This may mean that consumers become less willing to spend mental energy making sustainable decisions. It may also increase the "error" in purchasing decisions, meaning that consumers may make more unwise impulse purchases that lead to waste in the home wardrobe. Today, the United States is the world's biggest exporter of used clothing, primarily to underdeveloped countries (Rivoli, 2009). Waste from US consumer purchases makes its way to less developed economies, where it can effectively stifle local economic and cultural development. The constant pressure for cheaper and faster fashion has also taken its

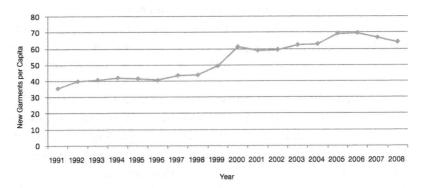

FIGURE 10.1. Annual new garments sold per capita in the USA.

toll on working conditions in the industry as cheap labor is exploited in developing countries (Claudio, 2007). The Western consumer's demand for wardrobe novelty through faster and cheaper consumption has clearly led to an unsustainable consumption level that is having drastic impacts on the environment and society worldwide.

We can see then that there exists a discrepancy between consumer value for sustainability and consumer behavior. This conflict is often perceived as a trade-off, or a zero-sum game, in which a benefit to one side directly leads to an equal drawback to the other side. In other words, if the consumer behaves more sustainably, they must sacrifice some of the satisfaction of buying and owning clothing. One method of encouraging sustainable behavior is to increase consumer awareness of the importance of sustainable consumption, so that it becomes more important to the consumer than the pleasure or convenience of consumption. Another approach is to emphasize the negative effects of consumption, adding guilt into the decision-making process to overcome the drivers of consumption. Without changing any other aspect of the system, this may result in what can be perceived as a "guilt trip" strategy. However, if instead the system as a whole, the nature of the garment, and the drivers of high-volume consumption are investigated in more depth, it may be possible to meet all of the consumer's needs without requiring a sacrifice.

As with many things, technology can be the game changer that moves the apparel consumption process from a zero-sum trade-off between the consumer needs that drive consumption and the desire to act sustainably to a positive-sum game in which both of these goals can be achieved. Two approaches to a positive-sum conclusion that use technology to meet consumer needs will be discussed in this chapter: the use of technology to improve the efficiency of use of the home wardrobe, and the use of technology to facilitate the consumer's desire for variability in apparel.

The Home Wardrobe

The contents of an individual's wardrobe reflect the results of the purchasing, use, and disposal practices of that particular consumer. The apparel supply chain before and after it reaches the home is fairly well documented and understood. By contrast, however, relatively little is known about what happens to apparel products once they enter the home. What happens at home has a strong influence on the individual's purchasing behavior, however. Understanding what's in the home wardrobe and how it is used can help us to determine what the individual is seeking in purchasing new clothing, and perhaps find ways to meet that need without adding more excess clothing to the system.

The first step is to measure the size of the problem. This is a more difficult task than it may seem: for example, while the volume of apparel bought and sold is well documented, the size and variability of the home wardrobe (even for a particular demographic or population) is difficult to describe quantitatively. There are a few studies that have looked at what is in the wardrobe, however. Woodward (2007) completed a study of the entire contents of twenty-seven women's wardrobes. Her participants had an average of 98 items of clothing in their wardrobes, of which they estimated 37 percent were in "active" use on average (worn "habitually or often"), 50 percent were in "potential" use (worn "rarely or sometimes"), and 12 percent were "inactive" (unworn / formerly worn).

In our studies (Dunne, Zhang, & Terveen, 2012), we counted the garments in the wardrobes of eleven individuals (nine women), ages 23–30. In contrast to Woodward, we counted only the garments in the "working wardrobe," which we define as only those garments that the user tells us they "would wear to work." This eliminates the very formal and very casual garments in the wardrobe, hosiery, undergarments, and outerwear, as well as any garments that are kept for emotional reasons or otherwise not regularly worn. When we surveyed consumers (98 women and 33 men, ages 18–55), female participants told us their wardrobes contained 20 to 500 items (average

129), and male participants reported 15 to 300 items (average 72). In our in-home wardrobe catalogs, we counted between 49 and 185 garments in wardrobes of our female participants (mean 98.38, SD 54.35), and between 28 and 31 garments in wardrobes of our male participants.

Of the garments in the wardrobe, female participants across our studies reported on average that 40–45 percent of their wardrobe was in "regular use" (defined as garments worn once per month or more), and male subjects reported 47–53 percent in regular use. By contrast, in a study of the workday dressing patterns of five fashion innovators/opinion leaders over 3–8 months, we counted only 7 percent of the wardrobe worn once per month or more for female participants as opposed to 47 percent for male participants.

It is difficult to define the necessary size of the wardrobe in order to determine what may or may not constitute waste. However, a baseline metric is useful for comparison purposes. Functional necessity may be roughly calculated based on the restrictions of laundering. Assuming an individual may wear an average of three garments per day (a high-end estimate), wears each garment once before laundering, and cleans his/her clothing once per week, the wardrobe would consist of 21 garments. Assuming laundering every two weeks, this increases to 42. (NB: in our research, we find that actual practices do not follow this pattern—garments are worn more than once before laundering, an average-size outfit consists of two garments, and frequency of laundry behaviors varies considerably.) We encompass the average wardrobe size observed by male participants as between 21 and 42 garments. However, we do not reach the lower bound for female participants. This kind of functional necessity baseline is likely to be on the low end when other factors (such as social influences) are accounted for. Further, our "regular use" metric of one wearing per month is somewhat arbitrarily decided, and not based in analysis of social influences and norms. However, in our study of workday dressing behaviors, our female participants could only have worn a maximum of 32–34 percent of the garments in their wardrobes once in a month, even if no garments were worn more than once. (For male participants it was feasible to wear every garment in their wardrobe once or more in a month.) Further, we saw a long-tailed distribution of garment wear frequency, with most garments being worn between one and three times during the study period but a small number of garments being worn as many as twenty-four times. Finally, for female participants only 56 percent of the wardrobe (average) was worn at all during the study period. Even male participants wore only 77 percent of the garments that they self-selected as viable for wearing to work.

While not conclusive, these data indicate that: (1) the size of the wardrobe is likely larger than strictly "necessary" for covering the body in clean clothes; and (2) for all users there exists some percentage of the wardrobe that is disfavored enough to see very little wear. It is important to also point out that all of our users continued to purchase clothing: that is to say, it was not the case that even with this abundance they saw no need to acquire new clothing.

The Dressing Decision

Having established that many consumers own more clothing than they can feasibly wear, and that the excess (particularly the unworn or seldom-worn excess) may represent some part of the waste in the apparel system that reduces its sustainability, it is important to investigate the reasons for this overconsumption behavior. Woodward (2007), in her in-depth interviews with participants, uncovered many emotionally driven reasons that unworn clothing is kept in the wardrobe. Bye and McKinney (2007) similarly found emotionally driven reasons that poorly fitting clothing is maintained in the wardrobe. However, in our studies we looked primarily at the use of the working wardrobe, which eliminates clothing that is kept for reasons other than regular use. Nevertheless, even so, many garments were not worn and a smaller portion was used more frequently. If we can determine why some garments don't get used, it is possible we can use technology to prevent this from happening. This problem has two possible solutions: If it is true that the garments are all "good" but are not being used for some reason (e.g., they have been forgotten about), perhaps we can remind the user in some way. If some garments are not "good" (don't work in the wardrobe), perhaps we can figure out why, and help the user to avoid buying garments that won't be used. Both of these alternatives rely on understanding how people decide what to wear in the morning and where they may be having difficulty with that process.

A frequent theme in discussing the dressing decision is the difficulty and anxiety that the process poses for many users. Guy, Green, and Banim call this the "wardrobe moment," a daily mini-crisis in which the individual's wardrobe management techniques are put into play in a time-restricted problem-solving challenge (Guy, Green, & Banim, 2003). In our survey of 83 participants (23 male), 52 percent of male respondents and 40 percent of female respondents cited having "too few options" as a source of difficulty when dressing—only 4 percent and 13 percent respectively cited "too many options" as a source of difficulty. At the same time, 55 percent of women and 30 percent of men responded that not being able to "think of a good outfit" was a source of dressing difficulty.

Overall for our female respondents, the most significant sources of dressing difficulty were trouble with aesthetics/looking good, finding an outfit that meets today's needs, and having too few options. Male respondents showed overall lower levels of difficulty arising from these variables than female respondents. For male respondents the most significant sources of difficulty were having too few options, finding an outfit that meets today's needs, and not having anything clean. Having too many options was ranked as the least significant source of difficulty for both male and female respondents, despite the reported large sizes of wardrobes. We found that both male and female participants were interested in being comfortable and looking good.

Women were also interested in dressing to flatter their bodies, while men prioritized dressing quickly.

It is important to note, however, that all consumers are not equal in their experience of the dressing decision. The variability in garment features is significantly larger for traditionally female contemporary clothing than it is for traditionally male contemporary clothing. Within cisgenders (http://en.wikipedia.org/wiki/Cisgender), it is well known that consumers do not all share the same level of sensitivity to garment and aesthetic variables, nor the same level of interest. Consumer variability in this area is often characterized using the consumer spectrum, from fashion leader to fashion laggard, as shown in Figure 10.2. Consumers on the fashion leader end of the spectrum typically are more invested in and sensitive to aesthetics in dress, and are more interested in distinguishing themselves or standing out from the crowd. They are typically the first to develop and/or adopt new trends. Consumers on the laggard end of the scale are among the last to adopt new trends, are less interested and invested in dressing, and are more interested in fitting in than standing out.

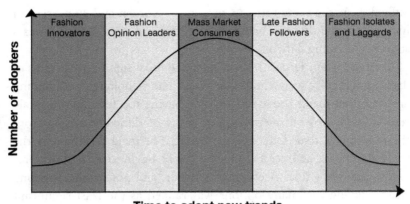

Time to adopt new trends
Interest in assimilating/fitting in
Disinterest/disinvestment with dressing decisions

FIGURE 10.2. The consumer spectrum.

In our survey, some aspects of the dressing decision varied for individuals at different points on the consumer spectrum. For instance, fashion innovators and opinion leaders tended to be more interested in having fun with the dressing decision, and in looking good or flattering the body. Fashion laggards were more interested in dressing quickly.

It is also true that the dressing decision itself is very complex. Given a wardrobe of the average size we measured from our female participants (a wardrobe of 99 pieces, comprised of 60 tops, 8 skirts, 14 pants, 13 dresses, and 4 jackets), with the basic assumption that all tops go with all bottoms and dresses are worn alone, the total number of outfits in the wardrobe can be calculated as:

22 bottoms × 60 tops × 4 jackets + 13 dresses = 5,293 outfits

If some of the tops (say, half) can be worn on top of the other half, the calculation becomes:

22 bottoms × 30 base layers × 34 top layers + 13 dresses = 22,453

Further, in situations where three tops can be worn together (e.g. chemise/tank, shirt/sweater, jacket), the number of possible outfits gets very large indeed:

22 bottoms × 20 base layers × 20 mid-layers × 24 top layers + 13 dresses = 211,213

Imagine considering all 211,213 possible outfits when deciding what to wear! It's clear that that kind of a choice is far too complex for a five-minute dressing process. However, this kind of excessive complexity is in fact true of many decisions that humans perform each day. In any decision where a thorough, objective analysis is either too expensive or too difficult, humans use *cognitive heuristics*, or shortcuts, to speed the process along. The most relevant of these heuristics for the dressing decision is the use of a *satisficing strategy*. Satisficing strategies, as opposed to optimizing strategies, seek to find a "good enough" solution rather than a "best" solution. We evaluate alternatives until we arrive at one that adequately solves the problem, and progress no further (Wickens et al., 2003).

The generation of alternative solutions is also subject to cognitive heuristics. Availability heuristics prioritize easily retrieved solutions. Easily spotted items such as those stored in plain sight or those with attention-grabbing visual characteristics may be more available at the time of decision making. At the same time, the capacity of working memory is generally restricted to 7 ± 2 items (Miller, 1956). Items out of sight and out of mind, so to speak, may be disadvantaged as candidate solutions. All of these strategies work in concert to reinforce a small percentage of the wardrobe, which may comprise that small percentage of "regular use" garments observed in our studies. Further, as that smaller percentage sees disproportionate use, it may engender feelings of boredom and a lack of viable options in the wardrobe. Novelty seeking is a strong driver of hedonistic shopping behaviors, and the lack of novelty afforded by the overused percentage may lead to the acquisition of new garments that provide feelings of novelty.

What emerges from these objectives and sources of difficulty in dressing is a kind of trial-and-error approach in which garments are purchased with the intent of maintaining or improving one's appearance within a set of perceived constraints. If the problem were as simple as just reminding the user of garments they have forgotten, we could easily build a system that suggests a garment on a screen, or a system that rotates the closet (think of Cher Horowitz in the film *Clueless*) so that garments in the back are more visible. Intuitively, however, we know that just being reminded of a garment is not enough. That garment must be effectively integrated into an outfit that is successful as a whole.

Returning to our 211,213 outfits in a hypothetical closet, how many of those outfits are actually wearable? To find out, we asked three fashion and apparel experts to evaluate a random subset of 3,083 outfits randomly generated from an actual participant's wardrobe. These outfits were each made up of 1–4 garments, photographed flat. Our experts found that 2,574 of the randomly generated outfits (83.5 percent) were "wearable," that is, they were a combination of garments that someone could reasonably wear and look appropriate in. The key here, however, is that these were outfits that "somebody" could look "appropriate" in. How many somebodies would look *good* in any of these outfits? How can we teach a computer what makes an outfit good?

The Smart Wardrobe: Reducing Waste through Outfit Recommendations

Based on what has been previously discussed in this chapter, we find that the home wardrobe contains a lot of waste generated by trial-and-error purchase decisions and reinforced by cognitive heuristics employed to manage the complexity of the dressing decision. Further, we also hypothesize that a large part of the difficulty in purchasing and decision making can be outsourced to a computer-aided recommendation system, which can in turn perhaps circumvent novelty-seeking purchasing behaviors by meeting the user's need for novelty through novel combinations of underused garments. At the same time, an effective recommendation system may be able to reduce the "error" in garment purchases by comparing new garments with the use patterns of similar garments in the existing wardrobe, and informing the user of how well the new garment will work with existing garments before the purchase is made. However, in order to build a recommendation system, we first need to understand how outfits are built.

To begin, we use a combination of design principles and outfit properties to identify how garments are put together to form an outfit. We find that an outfit can be defined through some very basic properties (e.g., it covers the body); but how likely the user is to wear that outfit depends also on some higher-level properties (such as how it looks on her body or how trendy it is). Figure 10.3 shows the hierarchy of outfit properties, which parallels Maslow's hierarchy of human needs—beginning with the basic fundamentals like covering the body, and progressing upwards to the more emotional aspects like looking fashionable and aesthetically pleasing. While it may seem that the lower-order qualities are always met before higher-order qualities are considered, as with Maslow's hierarchy this is not always the case: consider, for example, an evening outfit in which aesthetics may be more important than things like dressing for the weather or being physically comfortable.

Lower-order needs like covering the body are simpler to achieve. However, as we move upwards in the hierarchy, it becomes increasingly difficult to teach a computer how to achieve these objectives. Even something like matching requires that the system understands what colors go together, what garments go with what other garments, and in what order they can be layered.

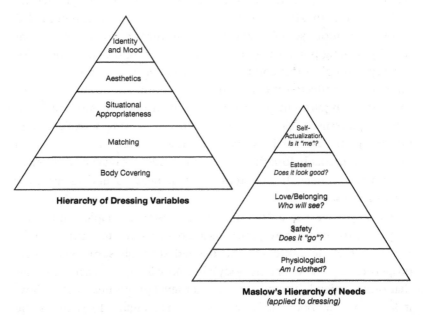

FIGURE 10.3. Hierarchy of outfit qualities.

When considering the more difficult qualities like achieving an aesthetically pleasing outfit, there are many sets of rules and guidelines that have been proposed. For example, consider the "golden ratio" that many design students are taught. This rule suggests that dividing the body into specific unequal proportions usually results in a better aesthetic than other proportions, or than dividing the body into equal proportions. However, Lowe found by evaluating historical fashion plates that in practice this wasn't always the case (Lowe, 1984).

Other prescriptive rule-sets also exist, especially in the popular press and in advice books. These approaches are very varied, but many use either a color-based approach such as the popular "Color Me Beautiful" system (Jackson, 1987) or an approach based on body shape such as the popular TV show *What Not to Wear* (Woodall & Constantine, 2002). Although presented by "experts," most of these approaches have not been scientifically evaluated. However, they may form useful foundations for possible outfit-building systems.

Building a Smart Wardrobe

We have built a rudimentary smart wardrobe system to explore the ways in which people use their clothing and to investigate some of the challenges of automatic outfit-building. In our system, each garment is tagged with a radio-frequency identification (RFID) chip, which looks like a button and is attached to a label or interior seam of the garment. A computer-based system allows the user to either ask for suggestions or select a starting garment themselves, by looking through pictures or scanning a garment RFID tag. It then checks the weather to perform a filter based on temperature, and then checks for a pattern in the garment (more than one color in a single garment). Depending on what kind of garment was selected as the starting point (a top, bottom, dress, etc.), it then offers the wearer suggestions for matching garments to complete an outfit. We use a very rudimentary process, filtering only for garment type and for color when there is a pattern present.

Finally, the system shows alternatives in two rows—the top row shows the five least recently worn garments, and the bottom row shows the five most recently worn garments. In this way we can investigate whether users are simply forgetting about garments they haven't worn recently, or whether they are not useful garments.

In our studies of what portion of the wardrobe is in regular use, we measured the utility of individual garments in the wardrobe. Utility was defined as the number of other garments that a given garment was worn with. For example, a pair of jeans might be a garment with high utility, because they are worn with many different other garments. On the other hand, a specific skirt may only be wearable with one or two tops, and therefore would have low utility in the wardrobe. Figure 10.4 shows the results for our five participants – it is clear that most garments have low utility, but a few have very high utility (Dunne et al., 2012).

This kind of information can be used to help consumers make good purchase decisions. If the system can learn from the properties of garments with high utility, it can look for new garments with similar properties. Further, if the system can learn what garments go together,

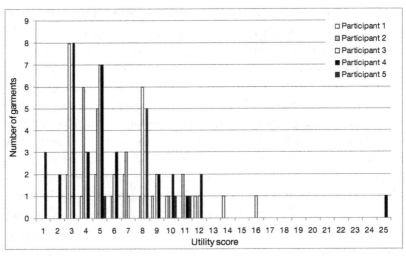

FIGURE 10.4. Utility of garments in the wardrobe.

it can offer the consumer suggestions of garments at home that could be worn with a potential new purchase, allowing the consumer to see how well the new purchase may fit with existing garments before making a decision to buy it.

ideas in action

Building a Smart Wardrobe

One of the most significant challenges to a successful outfit-building recommendation system is the development of the algorithm that builds outfits and selects options to recommend to the user. There are many highly developed recommendation systems out there, such as those used by Amazon.com to suggest products, those used by Netflix to recommend movies, and those used by news websites to recommend articles (Konstan et al., 1997; Resnick & Varian, 1997; Rhodes, 1997; Sen et al., 2006). However, wardrobe recommendations are subtly different from these other domains, and pose different challenges.

Recommender systems generally use historical behavior patterns or user demographics to learn preferences for things like movies, books, or clothing, and then apply these preferences to new items to generate recommendations. These recommendations can be based on the user's data alone, or can use similar users' selections to offer suggestions. Most of the common areas where recommender systems are used involve highly subjective preference, such as movie choices, and focus on a one-time or infrequent problem-solving challenge (such as buying a camera or selecting a movie). The specific recommendation task is similarly complex: most recommendation domains involve ultimate identification of a single good option (e.g., restaurant, movie, product). Dressing requires coordination of multiple subunits into a successful whole, which introduces problems of matching, layering, and evaluation of the resulting whole.

Traditional recommendation techniques typically use either features of the user's decisions (collaborative recommendation, "people who like this

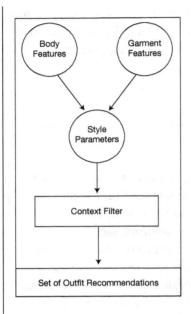

FIGURE S10.1. Influences on outfit recommendations.

also liked ..."), features of the user themselves (personalized or demographic recommendation, "people like you also liked ..."), or features of the product in question (content-based recommendation, "other items like this ...") to locate similar options to recommend to the user (Adomavicius & Tuzhilin, 2005). For the wardrobe, collaborative and demographic recommendations are likely to need the additional influence of a rule set that takes into account the user's body, because a successful outfit relies on the shape of the specific user's body as well as the aesthetics that the user prefers. For example, it may be true that people who like the same style that you do liked a given garment, but it may not be true that that garment will suit your body (depending on how differently those individuals are shaped). Content-based recommendation seeks to find options similar to products (in our case, outfits or garments) the user has previously liked, which may be helpful but narrow.

In order to make content-based recommendations, the system must have knowledge about the features of each item in order to compare it to other items. This set of features is the item's profile. The features included in the item profile can be essential to the success of the recommendation. For instance, in clothing recommendation, garment size may be an easily accessed but not helpful feature. Because there is so much variability in garment sizing, an individual user may wear many different sizes in different brands. For outfit recommendations, the set of useful features that affect quality of the resulting outfit is still unknown.

Acquiring these features for each garment can be accomplished through automated means or through manual tagging. For most garments, a set of quantitative information is known at some point by the manufacturer (in the form of a spec sheet or tech pack for the garment). This information may capture things like garment dimensions, color specifications, and fabrication. Certainly this information would be useful in an outfit recommendation system, and would even make it theoretically possible to avoid using sizing information and instead use garment dimensions directly. In the absence of garment specifications, some information can be gleaned automatically by using image-processing techniques. Some amount of color information and coarse garment dimensions can be extracted (Kalantidis, Kennedy, & Li, 2013).

Other garment features are more difficult to obtain automatically, and may be extremely useful in recommendations. Things like the style or trend category into which a garment fits must be assessed qualitatively, most often by a human, unless that information is also provided by the manufacturer.

In a hypothetical situation in which manufacturers were willing to freely share all data for all garments, a recommender system would have reasonably easy access to a tremendous amount of information. However, detailed information about garments could easily be regarded as proprietary information by the manufacturer, and it is easy to see why access might not be feasible. Without access to the kind of specs that are a by-product of garment production, garment features must be reassembled post facto. This can be a labor-intensive process—measuring garments, capturing color specifications, and manually classifying garment features such as sleeve type, style category, and fabrication.

Variability in Apparel

A system capable of understanding how garments go together into good outfits can help reduce poor purchasing decisions and can help provide novelty through new outfits built of existing garments. However, the large number of garments in the current in-home wardrobe also points to a basic interest in variety on the part of the consumer. It is likely that that interest is both intrinsic (e.g., an interest on the part of the consumer in enjoying variety in their daily outfit choices) and extrinsic (e.g., a perceived societal expectation that the same garment not be worn too frequently), to varying degrees for each consumer. However, this need for variety means that even in a very efficient wardrobe where there are very few unused garments, there will still be a considerable amount of variety.

Another way that technology can reduce consumption without requiring the user to give up their desire for variety is to build variability into the garment itself. Garments that are able to change their appearance can serve the function of multiple garments, and therefore remove the need to purchase additional garments. Further, embedded technology can also increase the value of a garment to the individual, perhaps leading to longer-term use.

In order to use technology for this purpose, it is important to first understand what kind of variability consumers seek in clothing. In the wardrobes we have analyzed, we found that female consumers owned the highest number of tops of any garment in the wardrobe. Within those tops, color and pattern change was an important area of variability, as was sleeve length (Koo, Dunne, & Bye, 2013).

Facilitating Variability

The term "smart clothing" is used to refer to clothing with embedded technology that serves a functional or aesthetic purpose. This technology is most commonly electronic, but garments with functions based on material properties (such as phase change) are also sometimes called "smart." Embedded electronics can be used to achieve a very wide variety of functions, including things like sensing and monitoring the body for medical or sports purposes, aiding the user in communicating with mobile devices or with other users, and providing dynamic protective functions like insulation or impact protection. Electronics can also be used to achieve the kind of transformability that may allow a single garment to function as multiple garments (aesthetically speaking).

Achieving color or pattern change is a difficult task in apparel. One method commonly used in currently available products is to use light-emitting technologies such as light-emitting diodes (LEDs), electro-luminescent (EL) wires or panels, or even liquid crystal displays (LCDs). These techniques produce colors, patterns, and images in a manner similar to a computer screen, and in some cases it makes them easy to program and use. However, there are two significant drawbacks: first, many of these technologies are stiff and bulky, and not easy to integrate into comfortable garments. Advancements are made steadily on this problem, however, and in the near future we may have light-emitting fabric technologies that feel and appear more similar to textiles than current products do. The second obstacle is the visual nature of light-emitting displays. Current apparel is not light emitting, but is instead what would be called "passive" or "non-emissive" display in the computer graphics world, meaning that instead of generating light it reflects ambient light. Changing colors and patterns in passive displays is in some ways a more challenging problem, and fewer technologies exist that make it possible.

One technique for creating non-emissive displays is to use micro-encapsulated charged pigments. This is the technique used by e-ink displays (Rogers et al., 2001). If two pigments with opposite charge are enclosed in the micro-capsule, and an electric charge is applied to the capsule, the oppositely charged particles will be drawn toward the charge and the similarly charged particles will be pushed away (as shown in Figure 10.5). If one set of particles is white and the other is black, for instance, then the capsule becomes a "pixel" and can be used to build words or graphics on a surface. This approach is very effective in building black-and-white or monochromatic images, but is more difficult to use for full-color displays. However, a color filter applied on top of the black/white pixels makes full-color display possible.

Another approach to passive color and pattern change is the use of thermochromic inks and dyes. Thermochromic materials change color with a change in temperature. The Hypercolor clothing popular in the 1980s was the first use of this kind of technology in apparel, but relied on ambient temperature changes or body temperature changes. Electronic technology can be used to induce a color-change on-demand, by running a current through a thermochromic substance, causing it to heat up. Designer Maggie Orth of International Fashion Machines has used this approach to create "Electric Plaid," a textile with a plaid appearance that changes color and pattern on demand (Marculescu et al., 2003).

Drawbacks to thermochromic materials are the relatively long transition time (especially to reverse a color change, when the material must cool down in order to change back to its original color), and the relatively high energy cost. Further, controlling temperature change precisely enough to create specific colors is a challenge, especially when ambient and body temperatures are also changing.

While the ability to change color and pattern would create a huge amount of variability in a single garment (especially in standardized garments like button-down shirts or T-shirts), we observed a considerable

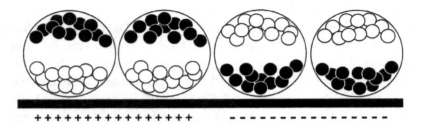

FIGURE 10.5. Micro-encapsulated charged pigments used for passive display.

amount of variability in garment shapes, features, and fits, especially in female consumer wardrobes. Enabling a single garment to transform into many different garment shapes is a much bigger challenge than color and pattern change. However, the early stages of development in this direction do exist.

Most directly, designers have experimented with transformable garments for many decades, mostly through the use of fasteners and creative garment cutting. An example of this approach is the popular Infinity or sarong dress style, which can be worn a nearly infinite number of ways by tying and draping the fabric of the dress.

Embedded technology can also be used to achieve a transformation of garment shape. Designer Hussein Chalayan, in his spring/summer 2007 collection "One Hundred and Eleven," debuted some dramatic shape-changing garments ("Chalayan Spring 2007," n.d.). Some changed from one historical reference to another, and others changed surface appearance. The final look was a dress that was gradually drawn up into the model's hat. These pieces used two of the most common technologies used to create shape changes: motors and mechanical systems, and shape-memory materials.

Motors and mechanical systems are more powerful than many other alternatives to shape change. However, they can be difficult to implement in clothing, since they often rely on rigid structures. The physics of clothing are less easily predicted than the physics of rigid structures, and this can make it difficult to develop moving parts and pulley systems in clothing.

Shape-memory materials, by contrast, are often found in fiber form. Materials like shape-memory alloys (SMAs) are metal wires that can be used in one of two ways: to shorten in length when electrical current is applied, or to remember a shape when current is applied. In the latter case, a SMA wire can be trained into a specific curve or a spring shape, and can be used to pull a piece of textile into that shape. When there is no current, the wire acts like a very flexible thin wire. When current is applied, the wire stiffens into the pre-trained shape.

While SMAs and other shape-memory materials have clear comfort and aesthetic benefits, they pose challenges in other ways. Similar to thermochromic materials, it is the temperature change that causes shape-memory materials to remember a shape. Therefore, they require a relatively large amount of energy compared to other electronics. Further, compared to motors and mechanical systems, SMAs are typically able to provide far less force. Therefore they are easiest to use with very light, flexible textiles.

The future of shape-changing clothing is definitely farther away, but progress continues in the research and design worlds. Truly shape-shifting clothing would enable a tremendous amount of variability, and has the potential to dramatically reduce the number of garments an individual may need to own.

Laundering and Maintenance

Along with increased versatility in clothing comes a new paradigm for care and maintenance. If an individual owns two or three very versatile garments, when are they cleaned? Further, if these garments are made versatile by using fragile and expensive embedded electronics, how will those be laundered?

One possibility is that garments may be designed to require less cleaning. Today, many designers have begun taking into account the energy costs of washing clothing. The amount of energy consumed can be significantly reduced by changing the parameters of washing (lowering water temperatures, air-drying instead of tumble-drying) and by reducing the frequency of washing (Fletcher, Dewberry, & Goggin, 2001).

Fabric technologies can help to reduce the necessary washing of a garment while keeping it clean. Textiles inspired by the natural self-cleaning properties of the lotus leaf have been developed: they shed dirt and contaminants naturally by transporting them along a nano-textured surface (Smith, 2010). Silver fibers (often used to make electrical connections in a garment) have inherent antimicrobial properties, which reduce the build-up of odor-generating bacteria (Dastjerdi & Montazer, 2010). Finally, surface finishes that repel stains and liquids have been developed that can be applied to almost any textile surface (Smith, 2010).

Adding Value

Finally, one additional way in which embedded technology can potentially extend the life span of a garment and increase its versatility is by adding value through electronic functions. Some electronic functions can augment the functions that are traditionally performed by clothing. For example, conductive fibers can be used to generate heat in a garment on demand. A shirt with a built-in heater could function as a lightweight garment for warm weather and as a light jacket for cooler weather, by using electric heat instead of insulation. Other functions enabled by electronics are entirely new to clothing. For example, embedded electrodes and monitoring hardware can allow a shirt to monitor vital signs or to keep track of a potentially emerging medical condition. While clothing has not traditionally been capable of taking on this role, the function may add enough value to the garment that the user is willing to use it more often or for a longer period of time than a traditional garment.

Conclusion

The value of technology to apparel is not necessarily correlated to its complexity. A very simple technology like an RFID chip can allow the user to take control of the dressing decision, and reduce the error and waste that is currently such a large part of our everyday purchasing choices. Similarly, however, next-generation shape-shifting technologies could potentially allow one garment to take the place of an entire wardrobe. The essential factor to the success of any technological approach is its relationship to the needs and wants of the consumer. Understanding what we want out of our clothes (things like variety, expression, and novelty) as well as what constraints currently exist that prevent us from acting sustainably (things like a limited amount of attention and time) can help point designers to the places where technology can be effectively used to overcome a problem. Through the development of this kind of intervention, we can extend sustainable change beyond manufacturing and recycling, to the selection and use phase of the garment life cycle.

Discussion Questions

1   What aspects of the fashion system can be changed to improve long-term sustainability? What are the relative impacts of making changes to these aspects of the system?
2   Who should be responsible for sustainability in the fashion system? Is it more important that industry professionals or consumers make changes to improve sustainability?
3   Think about your own shopping behaviors. What are the most common reasons you buy new clothing? How much clothing do you currently own but not use? Why?
4   If your clothing could be more versatile, how would you want it to adapt? What would you want your "future clothing" to do?

References

Adomavicius, G. & Tuzhilin, A. (2005). Toward the next generation of recommender systems: A survey of the state-of-the-art and possible extensions. *IEEE Transactions on Knowledge and Data Engineering, 17*(6), 734–49.
Bye, E. & McKinney, E. (2007). Sizing up the wardrobe: Why we keep clothes that do not fit. *Fashion Theory: The Journal of Dress, Body & Culture, 11,* 483–98.

Chalayan Spring 2007 Ready-to-Wear Collection. (n.d.). Style.com: Runway Review. http://www.style.com/fashionshows/review/S2007RTW-HCHALAYA/.

Claudio, L. (2007). Waste couture: Environmental impact of the clothing industry. *Environmental Health Perspectives, 115*(9), A448–54.

Dastjerdi, R. & Montazer, M. (2010). A review on the application of inorganic nano-structured materials in the modification of textiles: Focus on anti-microbial properties. *Colloids and Surfaces B: Biointerfaces, 79*(1), 5–18.

Dunne, L. E., Zhang, V., & Terveen, L. (2012). An investigation of contents and use of the home wardrobe. In *Proceedings of the ACM Conference on Ubiquitous Computing*. Pittsburgh, PA.

Fletcher, K., Dewberry, E., & Goggin, P. (2001). Sustainable consumption by design. In M. J. Cohen & J. Murphy (Eds.), *Exploring sustainable consumption* (pp. 213–24). Oxford: Elsevier.

Guy, A., Green, E., & Banim, M. (2003). *Through the wardrobe: Women's relationships with their clothes*. Berg Publishers.

Jackson, C. (1987). *Color me beautiful*. Rev. edition. New York: Ballantine Books.

Kalantidis, Y., Kennedy, L., & Li, L.-J. (2013). Getting the look: Clothing recognition and segmentation for automatic product suggestions in everyday photos. In *Proceedings of the 3rd ACM Conference on International Conference on Multimedia Retrieval* (pp. 105–12). New York: ACM.

Konstan, J. A., Miller, B. N., Maltz, D., Herlocker, J. L., Gordon, L. R., & Riedl, J. (1997). GroupLens: Applying collaborative filtering to Usenet news. *Communications of the ACM, 40*(3), 77–87.

Koo, H. S., Dunne, L., & Bye, E. (2013). Design functions in transformable garments for sustainability. *International Journal of Fashion Design, Technology and Education, 7*(1), 10–20.

Lowe, E. D. (1984). Aesthetic rules in women's apparel: Empirical fact or fantasy. *Journal of Consumer Studies & Home Economics, 8*(2), 169–81.

Marculescu, D., Marculescu, R., Park, S., & Jayaraman, S. (2003). Ready to ware. *IEEE Spectrum, 40*(10), 28–32.

Miller, G. A. (1956). The magical number seven, plus or minus two: Some limits of our capacity for processing information. *Psychological Review, 63*, 81–97.

Resnick, P. & Varian, H. R. (1997). Recommender systems. *Communications of the Association for Computing Machinery, 40*(3), 56–8.

Rhodes, B. J. (1997). The wearable remembrance agent: A system for augmented memory. In *Proceedings of the IEEE International Symposium on Wearable Computers* (pp. 123–28).

Rivoli, P. (2009). *The travels of a T-shirt in the global economy: An economist examines the markets, power, and politics of world trade.* 2nd ed. Wiley.

Rogers, J. A., Bao, Z., Baldwin, K., Dodabalapur, A., Crone, B., Raju, V. R., … Drzaic, P. (2001). Paper-like electronic displays: Large-area rubber-stamped plastic sheets of electronics and microencapsulated electrophoretic inks. *Proceedings of the National Academy of Sciences, 98*(9), 4835–40.

Sen, S., Lam, S. K., Rashid, A. M., Cosley, D., Frankowski, D., Osterhouse, J., … Riedl, J. (2006). Tagging, communities, vocabulary, evolution. In *Proceedings of the 2006 Conference on Computer Supported Cooperative Work* (pp. 181–90). Banff, Alberta, Canada.

Smith, W. C. (2010). *Smart textile coatings and laminates.* Elsevier.

Wickens, C. D., Lee, J. D., Liu, Y., & Gordon-Becker, S. (2003). *Introduction to human factors engineering.* 2nd ed. Prentice Hall.

Woodall, T. C. & Constantine, S. (2002). *What not to wear.* Riverhead Books.

Woodward, S. (2007). *Why women wear what they wear.* Oxford: Berg Publishers.

Sri Lanka: A Model of Sustainable Apparel Industry Initiatives

Suzanne Loker, Professor Emerita, Cornell University, USA

Sustainability of socially and environmentally responsible practices "signifies improving, building upon and overall achieving responsible practices that are maintained over the long term [and then raising expectations]. Sustainability is the ultimate goal of successful socially responsible practices." Its measure of success is the continuous improvement of the lives of workers and their communities and the health of the environment in which they live (Dickson, Loker & Eckman, 2009, p. 37). Businesses set goals but in theory can never reach these goals because the bar continues to rise. Sri Lanka has become a model for socially and environmentally responsible apparel production that is supplier led and focused on building sustainability through worker and community empowerment and public policy partnerships.

Sri Lanka Apparel

Sri Lanka is a small island country located off the southern tip of India, with a population of 21 million, 65,600 sq. km in area, and with 1,700 km of coastline. Similar to other developing countries, Sri Lanka built its export markets on agricultural products such as tea, rubber, and coconut and then moved into manufacturing apparel as that industry globalized. Sri Lanka has over 350 apparel factories and sixteen textile factories. The industry accounts for about 65 percent of the country's industrial production exports and 43 percent of the Sri Lanka export revenue. The industry employs over 350,000 directly (Joint Apparel Association Forum, 2014)—and, in 2013, provided 15 percent of the total labor force (http://www.masfabricpark.com/textile_apparel_industry. html). Over 90 percent of the population is literate; English is the business language, Sinhalese and Tamil are national languages, and all three are widely taught in the schools. This is the setting in which the apparel industry has grown since the 1970s, and especially since the later 1980s when Western countries began the seemingly endless search for low-cost apparel-producing countries. Sri Lanka is no longer the least expensive country to produce in, but it is one of the leaders in socially and environmentally responsible production in South Asia and beyond and provides a country-wide model of sustainable apparel production and socially responsible practices. Based on six factory tours and over twenty-five interviews with industry managers, designers, and brand buyers in 2010 as well as published reports and academic articles about Sri Lanka's apparel industry, four strategies for sustainability used by Sri Lanka apparel were identified: supplier ownership, worker empowerment, environmental sustainability, and public policy engagement.

Supplier Ownership

In the past decade, Sri Lanka's apparel industry members reorganized six separate industry associations into one, the Joint Apparel Association Forum (JAAF), to speak as one voice to the government, non-governmental organizations (NGOs), civil groups, and multinational initiatives and to play a part in setting country policies while initiating JAAF programs. One notable JAAF initiative is the industry-wide Garments Without Guilt (GWG). As suppliers to a number of major EU and US brands and retailers, GWG is unique in its supplier-driven nature.

The principle behind Garments Without Guilt is that "ethical working conditions and environmental sustainability assure that the 'Made in Sri Lanka' label is not only synonymous with quality, reliability but more importantly with social and environmental accountability." Its charter identifies and expands on four "protection" principles that are internationally accepted as the foundation for socially responsible business:

- Free of child labour
- Free of forced labour
- Free of discrimination on any grounds
- Free of sweatshop practices.

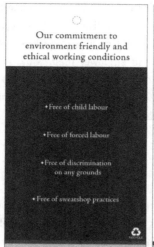

SGS, an international leading inspection, verification, testing, and certification company, developed the auditing system for Garments Without Guilt based on the Ethical Trading Initiative's Base Code and CSR foundations. SGS independently audits factories annually for certification. In 2010, about 105 Sri Lankan apparel factories out of the approximately 200 operating factories were GWG certified. In addition, Sri Lankan apparel suppliers comply with the labor, health and safety, and environmental requirements of each customer, including certifications such as WRAP, SA 8000, Fair Trade, Organic Exchange 100, Global Organic Standard (GOTS), ISO 9001 and 14001, and OHSAS 18801.

The motivation for Garments Without Guilt came from the results of a JAAF-commissioned survey to identify Sri Lanka apparel's competitive advantage. Quality, reliability, and innovation were found to be strong, yet the one thing that differentiated Sri Lanka's industry from others was its ethical practices. GWG was launched to signify Sri Lanka's supplier-led, industry/country-wide approach to sustainable apparel production.

Five "progression" principles are listed by GWG in addition to the "Protection" principles that are monitored for compliance—rural poverty alleviation, women's empowerment, education, environmental initiatives, and better quality of life.

These have been pursued by individual company initiatives, overarching efforts with communities, and contributions to effective public policy. Several exemplars of social and environmental initiatives illustrate GWG's underlying goal: to improve the lives of workers and empower them while retaining a workforce that is ready to work. The sustainability of these projects is aided by Sri Lanka's cultural foundation focused on helping others and commitment to worker engagement in identifying and developing the projects.

Worker Empowerment

Women Go Beyond
With about 87 percent of the workers in Sri Lankan factories in 1998 being young women and over 60 percent of its factories in rural villages (Kelegama & Wijayasiri, 2004), the empowerment of women is at the foundation of many of the industry's social initiatives. MAS Holdings' Women Go Beyond initiative started in individual factories, with educational programs in health, English, computers, and other topics; it recognized women who had overcome some great life challenge and/or achieved in an extraordinary way. The programs were structured at the factory level to identify and address the needs of the local workers and their communities. After several years, the company institutionalized these local activities into company-wide program offerings for skill development, career advancement, and work–life balance, among others, in recognition that the most important resource in the company is the people. The vision is that by investing in people and helping them align with the company goals, sustainability will be achieved. Women Go Beyond champions are selected each year from co-worker nominations at each MAS factory: their achievements are celebrated and they serve as role models to other workers. The Go Beyond initiative was expanded to Eco Go Beyond in 2006, a school-based program in the villages near MAS factories that introduces environmental concepts to children and involves them through self-designed projects for ten-person student teams. Examples include habits of saving, paths to a nutritious lifestyle, and protecting school buildings against soil erosion. The Go Beyond initiatives demonstrate supplier ownership as well as empowerment.

Care for Our Own

In response to finding a widespread need for clean water and sanitation, Brandix initiated this community-based project as part of its social and environmental sustainability program. One manager told the story of women in one community who had to walk an hour each way to get clean water ... twice a day. This meant getting up in the dark for the trip in order to get to work on time. To respond to the need for access to clean water, tube wells and water storage tanks were constructed in communities and desalination plants were built along the coastal belt in post-tsunami locations. Each community project was designed to address the local needs identified by workers and community members, such as digging a well at the road in front of an employee's home to provide community access to water. One of the largest projects was building the Brandix Water Resources Board Centre for Water Conservation and Management in Anuradhapura in partnership with the US retailer GAP. Run by the Water Resources Board, its work is to educate students, teachers, community workers, and the general public on water conservation and management.

Environmental Sustainability

MAS Holdings, Brandix, and Hirdaramani, Sri Lanka's three largest apparel firms, built the first apparel factories in the world to receive LEED certification at the platinum and gold levels (Leadership in Energy and Environmental Design by the US Green Building Council), two as new buildings and one as a renovated thirty-year-old factory. The certification awards points in four areas: sustainable site, water efficiency, energy and atmosphere, and materials and resources, plus innovation in design and regional priority. Continuous measurement of environmental impacts is required and it highlights achieved reductions. For example, on average these three Sri Lankan factories save 40–46 percent on energy consumption, 50–63 percent on water consumption, and have a 48–70 percent lower carbon footprint than the average comparably sized apparel factories. All of the factories have achieved 0 percent waste to landfill. Two smaller firms are also leaders in environmental sustainability: Rakshaa's 250-person factory has been built to most of the LEED certifications and a Star Garments factory has earned the LEED certification.

In addition to these individual firm initiatives, JAAF spearheaded environmental education in line with industry goals: to adopt LEED principles incrementally to improve the environmentally responsible practices expected by GWG. The "Go Green" seminar increased awareness of environmental impacts from apparel production by encouraging adoption of ten factory strategies, some modest and some ambitious. For example, to save energy from lighting, factories could change the light source from tube lighting to small task LED lights on the machines, and the seven types of waste could be reduced for cost savings and sustainable advantage. Building eco-factories and switching to solar or wind power were identified as major undertakings.

Public Policy Engagement

Specific country-wide initiatives addressing the apparel industry and supported by Sri Lanka's government are the 200 Garment Factories (GFP) and Reawakening the North and East. 200 Garment Factories was implemented in 1992 and offered financial incentives for taking work to rural villages and building communities and infrastructure rather than bringing workers to the

urban areas, relocating them away from their families and requiring earnings to be spent on living accommodation. The Reawakening the North and East initiative was sponsored by the government and USAID to help rebuild communities after the 2004 tsunami and the decades-long civil war that ended in 2009 by employing locals and prisoners of war. One example is the Brandix factory in Sri Lanka's rural Punani near the coastal city of Batticaloa, where Tamil, Sinhalese, and Muslim women work together in a modern factory producing garments for Marks & Spencer and Tesco.

Challenges and Conclusions

There are challenges for Sri Lanka and its apparel industry. Tourism is a growing emphasis for development in Sri Lanka and is testing the dominance of the apparel industry, its employee recruitment and retention, and public policy support systems. There has been international concern over human rights violations by the Sri Lankan government during and following the thirty-year civil war, including the suspension of duty-free trade with the European Union in 2010. These accusations are in stark contrast to the Garments Without Guilt initiative and therefore raise questions. Sri Lanka apparel giants—MAS, Brandix, and Hirdaramani—are building the front and backward integration necessary for value-added services beyond production contracting, such as design competence and fiber and fabric innovation and production. These growth steps can stabilize the firms' business but also add cost to the apparel production services that are the foundation of the industry.

Even with these challenges, Sri Lanka's apparel firms have earned numerous national and international awards for both social and environmental achievements in addition to LEED certification, among them American Apparel and Footwear Association's Award for Excellence in Social Responsibility for Women's Issues and for Preservation of the Environment; Nike Outstanding Performance in Innovation, Regional Product Development, Quality, and CSR; International Green Apple Environmental Gold Awards; Market Movers from the World Bank; lead case for UN Global Compact 2007 report "Embedding Human Rights into Business Practices."

The Sri Lanka apparel industry recognizes that the women behind the sewing machines are its most important resource. Initiatives beyond compliance monitoring that empower workers and build healthy communities have been vital to the industry's success, yet there is still much work to be done. Sustainable social and environmental practices and initiatives must continue to be introduced, measured, and improved. They must go beyond the factory floor, engage workers for ideas, and improve the lives of workers, their families, and communities. Sri Lanka apparel is positioned well to use its supplier-led social and economic programs as a competitive advantage as well as an economic development driver.

References

Dickson, M. A., Loker, S., & Eckman, M. (2009). *Social responsibility in the global apparel industry*. New York: Fairchild.

Joint Apparel Association Forum. (2014). Information acquired by email in December 2014.

Kelegama, S. & Wijayasiri, J. (2004). Overview of the garment industry in Sri Lanka. In S. Kelegama, *Ready-made garment industry in Sri Lanka: Facing the global challenge* (pp. 13–45). Colombo, Sri Lanka: Institute of Policy Studies of Sri Lanka.

The Environment, the Planet, and the Materials Used in Fashion Making

INTRODUCTION

Clearly, the time has come to implement strategies that generate environmental improvements for the planet. There is no need to explain this point here. Instead, the chapters in this section look at what is unique about fashion and the everyday components we take for granted. It is the hidden things that may have the most chance for the largest impact. Consumers are aware that hybrid and electric cars are the choice for environmentally responsible transportation, but are they aware that the basic fibers that make up their clothing can also be part of meaningful and significant environmental change?

As you make choices regarding design approaches or sourcing decisions relative to fabrics, design approaches, and production techniques, how important is your awareness of current and future carbon footprints? Some believe that the apparel industry is too large to turn around, that the sustainable segment doesn't have enough consumer acceptance around it to drive change, but how real and embedded are these excuses? We have heard that the consumer is reluctant to pay the higher price for sustainable fashion, or at least not enough of them are committed to the idea to force change. Any alteration in business may result in initial cost increases, but does the price need to be higher in the long run? Many companies have found that there are great savings over time when implementing decisions that assist the environmental goals. A follow-up question to consider is, what are the costs involved with *not* making a commitment to sustainability and lowering environmental impact?

We start the exploration of environmental situations and solutions by questioning the design process and reframing the fashion system into a sustainable system. In Chapter 11, Van Dyk Lewis explores a deeper sense of the complexities involved in the creation of fashion, and proposes that we must interconnect and refurbish if we are to turn around what is not working and embrace sustainability as a possibility. To address the challenges to come, he encourages us to take the leadership necessary to truly think about fashion praxis in ways we have not been open to previously, where the human is with, not separate from, nature.

In Chapter 12, Annie McCourt and Lewis Perkins lead us to a new way of thinking, where positive impact is possible within fashion making. They explain the core principles of Cradle to Cradle, an approach to design and production that actually enhances the well-being of nature, as opposed to depleting it. They then challenge us to take action toward developing products that are Cradle to Cradle Certified™. Introduced also is the Fashion Positive Initiative, in support of collaborations toward an effective circular economy.

Gail Baugh, in Chapter 13, explores new possibilities available to the fashion industry as we consider how to resolve the issue of sustainable fiber supply by using emerging fiber innovations. Environmentally responsible fiber choices are not limited to natural or organically grown fibers; they can also include fibers manufactured from renewable raw materials. Fiber choices are expanding, and this discussion provides a clear description and analysis of how best to understand their design potential and role in sustainable product development.

How are apparel companies addressing ethical, social, and environmental challenges? In Chapter 14, Shona Quinn explains how established sustainable apparel companies proactively reduce risk by encouraging suppliers to look at the entire system of activities and resources linked to their business, including but not limited to management, processes, raw materials, and community. She takes us through the key components to environmental stewardship and shares new models of sustainable sourcing.

Leaving us on a note of possibility, Hélène Day Fraser introduces several new directions and systems as suggestions for designers to investigate, as ways to take action toward creating sustainable fashion. She challenges us to reimagine design processes in order to include elements of renewal, regeneration, and reorganization. With a glimpse at possibilities for engagement, Chapter 15 ends and begins our journey. Inspired by an array of thoughtful processes, we are encouraged to bring sustainable fashion into the realm of excitement and possibility.

What's Next?

- How can we harness and use technology to its fullest to support sustainable action in and with the materials used in creating fashion?
- Customers are curious about how things are made. How do we best communicate information so that environmental action is possible? Can you visualize an ingredient label, like those used in the food industry, listing all of the ingredients used to manufacture a fiber, yarn, and fabric?
- Imagine Cradle to Cradle® intentions as a guide to a sustainable fashion industry. Materials are safe and clothes are designed with end-of-use potential.
- Address the challenge: We all live on one planet and share the same air and water, yet environmental protection regulations and enforcement vary from country to country. There are no global standards.

VAN DYK LEWIS is interested in art, philosophy, design, architecture, and the latent power of fashion as an agent for change in directing mass opinion. He is the director of Cornell Fashion at Cornell University.

CHAPTER 11

Treatise for Fashion Sustainable Thinking

Van Dyk Manasseh Lewis

Sustainable Technology

This discussion considers the idea that leadership in sustainable fashion practice may only occur when fashion design champions sustainable practice instead of the ultimately limiting tropes of beauty, glamour, hipness and luxury. However, these tropes should be understood as means and not ends. Motivation for this conversation lay in the contention that these tropes, especially beauty, may provide value to a wider appreciation of sustainable fashion, a way of penetrating the out-of-step thinking about fashion.

Much of the fashion designer's practice is concerned with concocting influence and demonstrating change. If this view is accepted, then locating fashion potential might be useful in establishing tangible and lasting sustainable fashion practice. This chapter will interrogate what is possible and what may be discovered within the dialectic of fashion (technologies) and anti-fashion technologies.[1]

In *The Operable Man* (2000), Peter Sloterdijk writes that humans have always utilized technology for evolving out of a pre-human state to our current state with an exposure to further creation and manipulation; this is not at all perverse. The conversation about what is considered to be fashion and what is considered anti-fashion provides a contextual frame in which the definition of social fashion and fashion objects and their operation within culture is configured. Current thinking and practice has failed to unite design, fashion, sustainability, and technology: The disposition of these (new) formations is yet to establish a workable hierarchy or philosophical context in which to fulfill the discussion.

The question of symptom or desire for sustainability emerges not from human desire for fashion or sustainability, but as a result of procedural actions in moving toward a functional design prescription for making garments. In any conversation about fashion and how it might be rendered, underlying prompts about sustainability are generally denied. In denial lurks the idea of sustainability that exists alone and free from the aesthetic concerns of the fashion trend, and free from the quickening pace of technologies that will eventually lead everything, including the fiction we call taste.

Discussion of the future, and particularly the future of design education, focuses upon the big pivotal battles which occur between sustainability and technology. Indeed the design school of the future will have to consider the kind of relationship and level of commitment to be shared. How technology will coalesce with soft design fields such as textiles and fashion, and, more profoundly, what will the process be in forming a map of territories owned and managed by practitioners of the ideology of sustainability? What constituents will work together and which ones will be jettisoned?

In efforts to construct an improved future, technologists have mounted new-tech apparatuses on to the human body and occasionally in the human body. The relatively short history of wearables ranges from highly useful applications such as astronauts' suits, to designer bras that sensor heart rate, to tattoos designed to locate hypersensitive body temperature, to trivial applications such as clothes that light up for no reason other than stage entertainment.[2]

Sustainability evokes concentrated functions that are accountable throughout the supply chain with benefits for the individual that include constellations of organic products, handcrafted products, and regimes for the repurposing of clothes.

Polemics proffered by the technologist and the sustainer are in opposition, if not conflict. The notion of "improvement" is contravened by that of "progress"—the former is the province of the sustainer and the latter is the province of the technologist. The sustainer works with existing structures to improve systems of product and wearer experience, while the technologist seeks to innovate by connecting people to interface with electrical networks. Beyond innovation, technologists currently experiment with the possibility that the body and technology might intersect; this is called the *singularity*. Although singularity seems like an idea from a dystopian sci-fi novel, it is both a concept and a technology that could eclipse sustainability as a vital action at this stage of human social and economic development. Not only is it accurate to contend that technologists will not champion sustainable fashion, but the opposite is also accurate. Research has not uncovered a third way where sustainable designers practice and experiment with wearables.

In McLuhanesque-speak of a hot–cool dialectic (McLuhan & Fiore, 1967), technologists move forward quickly while fashion designers practicing sustainability seek to slow down, stall, and possibly invoke homeostasis. All of this division seems to prompt even more questions: about teaching and practice, and more importantly, theory to practice, leading to further examination of fashion's multidisciplinary structure. Ultimately this convenes in the question that out-of-field educators and university administrations ponder: How might fashion design best serve society?

Should fashion slow down or speed up, subsume all tangible inventions and interventions, or monitor everything occurring in society while remaining mindful of the foundational relationship between the human body and clothes and the perplexing question of the most compelling and advantageous method of interface for our times?

Speaking about design education, John Thackara (2014), the design writer, comments that design might use an "appreciative inquiry ... rather than compile lists of all the problems that need to be fixed, and the wicked things that have been done, the group [must] focus[es] first on what's working; it then explores how successful ingredients might be used elsewhere, and how." Thackara goes on to draw attention to teaching methods that address our complex world and how individuals might take control of situations by using "a different set of leadership skills."

In general terms, sustainable fashion is an idea that lacks focused leadership. Consultants, trade associations, academia, retailers, and even consumers have not consistently—individually or collectively—composed serious policies or actions that combine to present a way for fashion to become sustainable beyond occasional and superficial demonstration. The fashion industry's latency in developing a shared ideology, emanating from leadership, can explain why any attempt to mount a unified campaign for sustainability simply does not exist.

Latency is a harsh description, yet deserved by an industry that is ever and increasingly attuned to the regime of speed and change. A characteristic of the fashion industry is its rapid metabolic rate of trend creation and disintegration: trends live and die in the virtual world before they ever come to prominence in the real world. The small triumphs of trends in sustainable fashion are often local and silent compared to the mass hyper-conforming trends developed as spectacle and consumption to the masses. The emergence of sustainable trends and their lack of acceptance within mass culture seems to indicate that sustainability is more of a modality of information—a virtual idea—than tangible fact. As Baudrillard (1983) tells us, information produces more information. This is the fallout for information producing more mass, yet the masses do not demand sustainable fashion; they demand the energy of the ephemeral "here today, gone tomorrow" fashion trends.

Although fashion continues a relentless nibbling away at possible actions that might encourage a sustainable fashion industry, transformation from the current fashion system to one that connects with nature is always bound in plasticity. The obsession of fashion is to recreate history and other cultures as themes to be presented as actualism, desires of fantasy rather than accurate renditions.

Much of the designer's work is done in this area; if the designer is to influence society and to offer change focusing upon sustainability, then locating where fashion might exist is a necessary part of creative success. A philosophy of fashion interrogates what is possible and may be discovered within the fashion–anti-fashion dialectic. What is considered to be fashion and anti-fashion provides a contextual frame where one is able to organize:

- a definition of social fashion and fashion objects and their operation within culture;
- the disposition of fashion design in regard to contemporary issues;
- a reconsideration of fashion.

Studio praxis, which is the process of how theory is enacted and realized, applies a "process" design research and design analysis: ideas generation, pattern making, silhouette development, image making, research, and writing. Any thought or form must be different from the last thought or form, and if we continue with this creative determinism we must order and rank our ideas, then isolate those differences and exploit them accordingly. This position is innovative because it bridges the gap between more familiar multidisciplinary expositions of fashion and a very direct interpretation of particular thematics. The thinking here is that fashion design must serve society; as a consequence, designers need to acquire extensive knowledge and perspective:

- Current fashion praxis persists.
- Sustainability fashion design practice is defined.
- Current fashion and sustainable praxis are united.

Failure of sustainable fashion is founded in the promise of an ecological catastrophe sometime in the future; unlike war and disaster, it is not staged in the present and graphically visited in the news media. Sustainability has become a fringe doctrine that has slipped in passively, leaving the populace confused, especially because an actual date for ecological disaster has not been declared. And since realization of the event has not been fermented in the public psyche, it is an undeniably difficult task for fashion companies, and particularly designers, to comprehend while building utility into fashion garments and systems. Importantly, the product life cycle theory states that as one profit center fails, another is uncovered through the invention of new products. Adoption of this theory offers untold opportunity for fashion, although the sustainability movement may struggle with compliance to core tenets.

Cynically, governments, corporations, and consumers catapulted through the Industrial Revolution without plan or panic for the future. Indeed it was artists, romantics, and intellectuals that promoted the idea of man in nature, rather than man separate from nature. The "back to nature" movement—such as the Pre-Raphaelites, and bohemian groups like the pre-World War II German youth group the *Wandervogel* who railed against National Socialists and unbridled consumerism—provided by example an alternative way of living that was in stark contrast to progress.

Even now, natural resources that have taken millennia to form are being eradicated. With only 150 years of coal reserves remaining, we (the rich world) continue with a pattern of rapid consumption, instead of swapping to clean energies like solar and biofuel.

Teleological Sustainable Fashion

The essence of all garments should be their potential to be sustainable. A reconsideration of the garment may include imbuing garments, through design, with teleological conditioning hitherto absent from the fashion design curriculum.

Empowering designers to create garments that are representative of sustainability leads to recovering the nature of the garment in relation to the human body. Consider the small sensory connection between human surface and the garment: the haptic differential is a place of interchange and exchange. One trajectory of the haptic space focuses on the effect of abrasion, time, sweat, and dirt; microscopically, these effects interact to reconfigure the garment so that it reflects the sum of the body's preferred actions. Eventually the garment's shape is reformed to mirror the form of the body while the body continually reinforces a preferred silhouette; movement provides micro changes to the topology. After wearing the garment for any appreciable time, the wearer confers ownership, and simultaneously, in making the garment theirs the amount of fashion (as a value and measure) is reduced. Ownership develops from the garment being almost entirely a formulation of the designer to being a re-enactment of the owner's body; another way of understanding the development of ownership is that the fiction of fashion is replaced with the reality of living. The plastic becomes organic. The fashion wearer is always subject to the fashion system's pertinence: in other words, the fashion system regulates new garments through its orthodoxies of criticism. The various paths and filters used in criticism are conducted via fashion shows, written and verbal criticisms, the display and promotion of fashion objects that provided a template to how fashion objects should be used. This is what determines the latest fashion trend: a conceit for individual ideas and an acceptance of fashion expression determined through this process.

For the wearer, discarding any worn garment is an act of sacrifice, structurally no different to overseeing the death of a living thing. At least if Marxist values theory is applied, then the value of the garment, as a unit of production, is representative of the workers' toil. Further, the garment is a holder of facts, sentimental and interiorized and exteriorized simultaneously; the garment has a life.

Translation of the garment from a fashion piece to a garment conditioned by the body establishes potentials for design and the nature of ownership, the body, and sustainability. Connecting all of these explains much, although more should be said about the garment, function, and body: what should a thing be, what should it do? What parameters should be applied? And if already in place, it may not function well. The connection between body, garment, and sustainability is not sufficiently understood, although if the body is accepted as having auspicious meaning—and clothes are created to provide material ontological properties that mimic or render the body relational—sustainability may or may not function as synthesis to the thesis of the body and the potential thesis or antithesis of the garment.

Garment A includes the function X.

Function X is a sustainable response to sustainable and ethical fulfillment of Garment A's production/use.

Prior responses are not included.

Tropes such as beauty, glamour, hipness, and luxury are represented as F.

A is constant, where X is variable and F is unknown [fashion is too complex to determine].

There was a time when fashion was sustainable, but the modern, postmodern and now hypermodern have all but obliterated the condition and possession of fashion. Certainly the Industrial Revolution, global colonization, and now urbanization have done much to relieve individuals of design control; home workers such as Scottish crofters and Bangladeshi Khādī weavers have long been discouraged from making their own fabric and garments, and therefore their own fashion expression.[3]

The direct function of fashion bridging from F to X moves us closer to discovering a normative sustainable fashion; but the work to do this is based in the adaption and derivation employed in the practical organization of fashion practice. Indeed the true issues of sustainability that ask whether financial profit might be viable are not taught or visioned in everyday conversation. Instead manipulation and untruths have become the background for our staged perspective, and since governments do not (re)enforce prudent behaviors through legislation.

Dennis Meadows and Jorgen Randers (2004) make very astute observations about the hidden and eventual demise of the current system. In their influential text *Limits to Growth* (2004), they sketch scenarios where the longer "expansion of population and physical capital continues, gradually humanity will have to divert more capital to cope with the issues that become evident from a combination of constraints. Eventually so much capital is diverted to solving the problems that it becomes impossible to sustain further growth in industrial output."

If these statements are plausible, especially where the ambition is to uncover positivity and progress for fashion sustainability, we must ask what is to be done.

Ritual Consumption

As free humans, we have deemed a few social actions to be privileges. In North America and in much of the first and second world, voting, driving a motor car, and consuming alcoholic beverages are normal and expected behaviors. If a country does not allow its citizens the rights and privileges to partake in such activities, many of us view this as curtailing freedom; we may even sign a petition demanding that these liberties be bestowed on the citizenry of whatever country has not yet understood the pleasures of postmodern life.

In accepting ritualized freedoms of sex, art, security, religion, and entertainment, even information and punishment have been ritualized, like some kind of prehistory narration; our world is entirely embroiled in the posturing of what is acceptable. After all, ritual is an act of uniformity, of ensuring a "normative order," and, in the everyday sense, shopping and consuming fashion is illustrative of being and acting normal.

Not committing to shopping is deemed to be a poor decision or one that may affect the collective well-being. This was the case in the days and weeks following the 2001 attack on the World Trade Center, when then president, George Bush, told the nation to go out and shop, fearing the sum effect of Americans staying away from the shopping ritual could have a negative effect on the economy.

Shopping is deemed to be an American pastime and is therefore in support of the American way of life. If this is a stretch too far, we should interrogate the plausibility of responsibility in the consumption chain. In every phase from design to manufacture, retail, advertising, and consumption, sustainability is treated unequally. The idea of linking these together instead of partitioning them remains one of the fundamental restraints toward developing an intelligent system, responsive to the emotions and opinions of not only the ritual of shopping but of the teleology of fashion clothes production within the greater space of the nation and the globe.

One can imagine that the next step forward is coming to terms with the cost of designer fashions, but not on a fixed scale, because nothing in our world is fixed. Both human and material costs fluctuate, as does opinion about clothes.

The kudos of who made any item of clothing and what hardships (or pleasures) and risk (and positive opportunities) were taken by individuals in creation and manufacture could counter or contribute to consensus of the item's fashionability. Indeed one understands that fashion sustainability is a two-way educative experience, especially at the lower market level, and that for haute couture we have no exemplar.

Chanel haute couture on sale at local equivalent prices at a Dakar or Mombasa marketplace could be a worthwhile experiment (Figures 11.1 and 11.2). It would say much about the futility of ultra luxury in the conversation and much about the seduction of superlative design. Perhaps such an experiment will help guide us through the maze, oppositions, and the enviable stereotyping of rich versus poor: The

FIGURE 11.1. Food and fashion coalesce at a West African marketplace. (SSPL via Getty Images)

FIGURE 11.2. Chanel supermarket, 2014. (AFP/Getty Images)

out-of-place clothes for the *rich* white women supplanted upon *poor* black bodies does what fashion is supposed to do—in that fashion only exists when there is discord, and clash in the object or the system. Whether it is color, the deconstructed hem, the oversized buttons on an otherwise normally proportioned coat, fashion at its essence is a flirtation of tension, which is precisely where our turgid ideology of fashion consumption undergoes radical change.

To understand the interchange between rich white West and poor black South is to understand the valid deviancy alive in beauty. This brings us to a kind of coup d'état, because like any self-respecting fashion subculture, the clash and tension of not fitting the subscribed natural version is paramount. The unintended wearers of Parisian haute couture do not represent the beauty aesthetic of the codes and ideological categories laid down in tradition. The "unusual" beauty of the African woman represents "that unnatural break" (Hebdige, 1990), the new development in fashion, a primitive reconfigured through hypermodernity, leaping over hands-on inventions of the computer, the Internet, film, and the combustion engine. But what did the African body provide before the invention of these modernistic contributions?

So let us leap into metaphor. If we might place the African black body in the role of the personification of sustainability (something like a mythological goddess) and Parisian couture as the veil of death of all natural things, we are thereby brought to our review of beauty as a trope of transgression and compliance. Together, beautiful clothes and beautiful bodies contribute to the deregulation of fashion, an expressive device that we readily understand as free and disorienting. This is one dilemma of materialistic consumer fashion. Away from the spectacle of accumulation, fashion is concerned with beauty and oppositions that continually clash with beauty to form new types that are both reconsiderations of fashion and instantaneously sought after as aspirational propositions.

This is the very homological inference the punks, motorbike boys, hippies, and other subcultural groups subscribed. The spartan economics of youth during the 1950s, 1960s, and 1970s engendered frugality; their value system operated not through the accumulation of more but through doing more with the few things they had—and for some of these groups the garment form was venerated. Their garments became them and they became their garments, together as object; they became things of exquisite beauty. Signification among members was enjoyed as activity of imposition, working into the form rather than adopting new objects to be experiments eventually beatified into the group.

Once defined as being in the world of the subculture, the object has been appropriated, through a process of reassembly, and thereby made to fit the ideals and distinct values of the group. One might conclude that a problem with conventional and mainstream fashion culture is that no template, form, value, or a sense of imitation exist. Processes of representation in fashion are simply lacking. At every phase from design to manufacture, retail, advertising, and consumption, sustainability is denied as an undertaking, the most wanton being the so-called sustainable company that will allow the consumer to make purchases without tariff or quota.[4]

There are otherwise admirable intentions of first-to-market companies such as People Tree, the fair trade company that networks small artisanal companies from the South with larger companies and designers from the North using admirable fair trade self-regulatory practices. Even this kind of operation is without the tools that encourage sustainability. Fair trade is a strategy of the systems of commodity delivery; it functions by considering producers in areas of rural development, promoting traditional skills, and paying fair prices for commodities. Fair trade makes little commentary about the design of things and neither does the fashion sustainability project. I clarify this with a thought about the way we teach fashion design, which is based upon an idealization of clothes and the wearer as the accessory.

Fashion and Sustainability

Fashion and sustainability are oppositional. Fashion as concept and as industry is based upon excess, and not conservancy. If fashion and sustainability are to coalesce, fashion and sustainability need to operate interstitially, sharing not just context but real linkages of shared values. Sustainability and fashion are, and can only be, in opposition, whereas fashion is of itself, and requires a subject to become functional. Sustainability functions as a valorization of good intention, even though many experts now believe that anthropogenic climate change presents a challenge so great that even if measures are put in place now to mediate or to reverse global warming, the Rubicon has already been crossed.

Sustainability is based upon fact; fashion is counterintuitive to fact and tangible things such as clothes as it is based in production and consumption. The essence of fashion does not possess authority to alter political, economic beliefs, although we will discover that fashion is undeniably oblique (from its reflection in an oblique mirror) and, as such, fashion is both suitably compelling, elusive, and inescapable. Simultaneously, fashion rendering and receiving resonances, that may or may not be beneficial to the sustainability project, scramble meaning and offer clarity, albeit temporarily.

Fashion is global in reach and is well placed to establish any belief or ideology. In reference to Durkheim, fashion, like religion, is both sacred and profane. In terms of the profane, fashion has no value in itself, and the sacred gives reverence to the arrival of fashion which dies as soon as it is born. Fashion and sustainability as interstitial space ushers in new methods of design praxis and systems that have potential for radical change.

However, potentials for the fashion industry have not demonstrated any facility to break away from the mechanism of the social political mediascape, in that fashion remains a concomitant of what the social body recognizes and understands as "truth." If fashion is to provide us with a way of legitimizing ourselves, then those who practice fashion must seek out ways of leading evolutions in thinking.

Marketing, merchandising, and production have begun to dominate and blur the design role that was once how the fashion industry validated itself. To re-establish fashion design's imperative, two things have to occur: one is the system of the fashion industry; the other is that designers must network their capacities into a revolutionary gesture. Like all revolutions, an oppositional ideology has to be identified, then a plan to extinguish the ideology conceived. The notion of coalescing with the oppositional ideology can only be possible in centralized systems.

Method

Historical and ethnographic practices, rather than those of economics and statistics, provide insights into human interactions with fashion. Of late, Fashion Studies has developed into a polyvocal exposition where fashion has begun to be uncovered through an increased number of niche disciplines. However, critics of the area might point to a lost opportunity: Fashion Studies, especially in relation to practice, has not become intertwined with or beneficial to fashion practice. The gap that records what has occurred and what might occur are contrasted, perhaps starkly at times, in the divide between academic journals, academics (in their tribes), conferences, and texts that further confirm expectations of what constitutes new, relevant fashion knowledge.

Consider the United States, which has the largest number of research active apparel faculty of any country. This number is burdened with division stemming from decades of focus on merchandising in the universities, while fashion design has become the unequivocal practice within the art school. Unlike the European educational model, where creative fashion programs rather than technological apparel programs dominate, with foci on organization, marketing, and retail of fashion product the United States has also decentered the borderlines of the fashion system. The reality is that offshore manufacture is the heart of the fashion industry. Deterritorialization of the fashion industry was imperative once the economic system and the cultural structure came into synthesis and agreement that manual labor should be set aside for concomitant others to undertake. Mass cutting, sewing, pressing, and finishing is nothing more than Dickensian sweatshop work. Workers are often employed illegally, work in poor conditions, or are subject to dangerous and life-threatening conditions. They are participants in the fashion system, yet the system does not allow participants the opportunity to enter categories of authorship or spectacular representation within design and show presentation phases of the system.

When fashion became truly global sometime after the 1970s, like other cultural operations it left behind old rigid concepts. Fashion was no longer restricted by the ideological structuralist framework and infrastructure that had governed what could be considered fashion, and, more importantly, the manners deployed in wearing fashion clothes. Democratization of so-called "high fashion" occurred because of the advent of *prêt-à-porter*, and relatively affordable high street fashion was spurred by the growth of the teenager and subsequent youth fashion subcultural socialization. Fashion began to reflect the "real lives" of the masses and not only those of the well heeled. Cheaper airline travel brought an end to the insularity of local histories, local communities, and local productions.

This proposition hints at a new role for design, a design method that is enhanced to locate resource and material savings, extending the life of garments, and establishing praxis that is meaningful in its deliberate shift from a profit-centered motive to a profit and ecological purpose. Successful design is reassessed to embody moralistic creativity as the zenith. The difficulty of such an undertaking is squarely based in the unhinging of pragmatic capitalism. It is not that capitalism is fixed or entrenched in tradition, but we do know that capitalism responds to its environment—although the status quo is retained until an enhanced profit line is delineated. The need for profit is contained in the praxis of making clothes continuously and on demand. If we wish to uphold this requirement, then we must identify ecology in a critical debate. Ecological movements have traditionally been the preserve of leftism and political correctness.[5]

The philosopher Paul Virilio (2007) comments, "They want to put Paris in the countryside. But where do you see Paris on our transparent map? Where do you see countryside? From now on, they no longer exist, any more than 'inside' exists for our prisoner." The prisoner is Don Quixote who mistakes his targets in combat, which is both pathetic and deadly.

The charge of an ecological movement that attenuates sustainability is that change is paradoxical. We learn from Virilio that the project for sustainability cannot keep the topic of fashion intact. Change is inevitable, indeed change becomes the factor of discovery. Drawing on Virilio's account of the missing of the target, planning for change and eventually effecting change may be unfulfilling if not retrograde. In other words, there are no—nor can there be any—guarantees. In the construction of alternatives, revisionary praxis cannot hold the values of life and culture as we know it. In fact, it is the preparation for change that needs to be fundamentally formed before architectonic guide points are established. In preparation we are altered to the kind of topography required.

Change in fashion praxis must include the designer divesting him- or herself of the role as a manipulator of fashion, since it is an impossibility. In its place, the designer must research, analyze, and respond to the job of design as a teleological function. In other words, designers must respond to near-term nature stimulus. This praxis will be antenna-like. Unlike current fashion design praxis, it will not prioritize trend; instead it will create a typology of use, plan for longevity and the true cost of production; and be rudimentary of functional design. So in throwing out the studio design ephemeral dictum, it is replaced with one connected to real-world concerns with goals and driving imperatives, but not necessarily facts. What has hitherto been known as fashion must be relinquished; in its place we must use its capacity for mass persuasion to further the discourse of sustainable fashion. If fashion is the action of playing back human pleasure, sustainability is indeed the antithesis of fashion design; therefore we are no longer involved in fashion design as a consideration. The quest for beauty has to be prioritized. The quest of the aesthetic is the quest to recreate nature and the impulse of human behaviors, which of course are of natural form and encompass every material, color, desire, and role. The problem of any new paradigm for fashion that articulates fashion as sustainable is an undertaking of colossal magnitude. Whether it is possible to unite the two is a project that only a major experiment might test. Because a mass experiment of fashion design and marketing sales, coupled with consumptions and the reaction of the wearers and media, is not possible, an experiment would itself be a final act. So we are left to create a treatise of action of what sustainable fashion might be.

Hacking for a New Fashion Praxis

If a suitable understanding of fashion is to be achieved, we must reject Sapir's social science generalist approach (1931) and his contention that fashion is a discrete solution of the subtle conflicts between the human need to legitimize their personal deviation without laying themselves open to the charge of insensitivity to good taste or good manners. Departure from this structuralist view of fashion advances the idea that fashion must be studied by means of the discipline of fashion and not as a subset or contributory facet. This approach says much about fashion as a self-generative phenomenon that is positioned temporarily and interstitially in manners, objects, moods, impressions, and actions. Fashion is both driver and manifestation of change, and is capable of metamorphosis, appearing in behaviors committed by individuals and communities; it is apparent in anything that might be considered as artificial.[6]

Indeed this notion is an ideal ambition for the designer working with the intention of jettisoning fashion while the activity of design is undertaken. The idea of withdrawing fashion from studio praxis cannot only be undertaken as a temporary measure; as fashion is flux and because fashion is unpredictable, it may not always be decoded. The designer's intention to manipulate fashion can only be undertaken in his mind. Less open to control is the post-design phase where the designed object is accepted by individuals and markets. How the object is received by markets is not a concern of the designer, as he does not have purview of this phase. The hack is an attempt to deterritorialize the design content that designers utilize each time they design an object. Consider the design of a pair of jeans. Design of any fashion object relies upon several known and accepted features; when these are coupled with a blank construction of denim pants, they are declared jeans. However, why this item becomes a pair of fashion jeans is based upon subjective qualities over which the designer has only limited control. Any hack must prioritize a stripping away of features that make the garment recognizable. It is expected that once explained vis-à-vis diagrammatic inference, garment design will relinquish all mimetic actions and replace them with subjectification instead of reproducing known features. The new praxis cuts out the ludic freedom of design from a process that takes clothes design closer to being an information system. With this kind of endeavor, especially where human behaviors in terms of taste are indeterminate and to an extent irrelevant, the designer does not have to contort design. In setting up the opposition of fashion praxis against sustainable praxis, no central order exists.

The first stratum does this well.

Studio Praxis Must Remove Orthodoxy

Amongst other things, sustainable design praxis is achieved via a transformation of an activity system of contrasting inputs into outputs that are controlled by designers.

Since a thinking system is defined as consisting of interrelated parts that cooperate in behaviors when responding to stimuli, biological or cosmological systems, or human social occurrences such as fashion are capable of sustainable thinking. If it was possible to create a fashion design studio system as a thinking system, we would have to overcome the first move in a total paradigm shift. To isolate the extremities of difference in system is to place them in a flexible order (not a hierarchy) of intent. The important thing is to remain mindful about what works best in one system when seen in conjunction with another system. Jettisoning one system for another means the idea of that convergence or attaining the same objectives is not necessary, nor is multi-finality; because the two systems are not interlocked, operations in either of the systems do not affect the other, at least in the short term.

Conclusion

Comprehension of sustainable fashion may require a praxis that draws upon interaction with experts from the margins, those who are planning societies where inclusion is valued. Commercially or academically, this work has not been committed to with the purpose of fashion practice.[7] We have committed to the close study of people from the global South who exist on few artifacts and systems of exchange in communities where lawlessness is not a feature nor is it tolerated. One such community is the Wahgi people of Papua New Guinea. These people have been exposed to the West for about seventy years and were discovered as a stone-using people; they were then introduced to manufactured goods, and eventually fought over the income derived from coffee cultivation as global trade began to affect their social order (O'Hanlon, 1993, 9–10).

The idea of paradise existing within modernity, the concept that missionaries and colonialism necessitated upon the Wahgi, is taken up in the imagining of Jacques Fresco's Venus Project (2012). His idea proposes a sustainable new world, ostensibly organized through design. The ambition of the project is to feed, house, and clothe humans sustainably—the overriding character of the Venus Project is uniformity perpetrated through social engineering and the design of objects. The Venus Project states that it will devolve status and ownership of things.

These two systems are designed with efficiencies and perspectives that transcend the widespread and generally accepted current system where resources are used wantonly. In adopting one or other system, the current social outlook ("outlook" is of course used pejoratively) is replaced with new "social" diktats that question the function of the superstructure: the joined-up system of media, the war machine, education, and the legal system are questions for feasible inclusion in a system that contracts social responsibility as a salutary improvement.

The social continues to exist in both examples; it is just that an inversion takes place, concluding in a logic of not just our toleration of nature but nature's toleration of humanity. Currently we tend to take clothing for granted and expect much from it, but for a moment we should consider how reliant upon clothing we have become. The evolutionary trajectory of humankind may have always been one of the needy human cajoling and manipulating the rest of nature to become resources for our maintenance. What we are and what we have become is a direct result of how clothing as a technology and fashion, as a cathartic stepping stone for personal shortfalls and inadequacies, help humans to survive physically and mentally. This observation goes some way to confirm the hopelessness of the human body to interact successfully with the environment, and indeed humans need clothing not for basic survival but to thrive and progress. If clothing is as essential and basic to progress, it is a condition of progress that representation through rank emerges as a self-regulating condition. And while I do not wish to open up speculation about the speed of human evolution and dependency upon fiber, humans are unable to resist the advantages that basic fiber might provide. How we use fiber and manipulate it directly affects human life. This interdependence of apparel objects and human life are inseparable; progress in one is realized in the other. A slow-down in the development of clothing and fashion may result in impeded human progress. Underconsumption of fashion may result in serious consequences not just for economic systems, but also for human systems by way of decorum, allure, beauty, and social control. If fashion is slowed, uniformity may increase and beauty—and its concomitants allure and decorum—may decline.

The question of sustainability in fashion is one of intention, a clear decisive intention to relinquish the shiny surface of what is branded as fashion by the fashion industry (which is an imitation) for the intention of (re)establishing the human with nature and not separating the human from nature. The concern is that for man the maker (*Homo faber*) it is impossible to constrain our biological urge; indeed it may be that the true intention to undertake meaningful and lasting sustainable practice fundamentally characterizes the human as indistinguishable from nature, although in all of humankind's dreaming, progress, creation of support structures and systems, the need to mold, bend, shape, and fashion is *the* genuine definition of humanity.

Discussion Questions

1   It is impossible to ignore how each of us is entrenched by our material desires, whilst this activity was prompted by modernisms, a phenomenological shift that rejected the idea of individualism for conformity to tradition and spiritual belief. In our hyper-modern existence, desire has become a key topic, commodified, manufactured, presented, and mirrored to us. Is desire problematic within the quest for a sustainable fashion design praxis?

2   Fashion subcultures may challenge fashion sustainability more directly than mainstream fashion's cumbersome orthodoxy. Drawing upon examples of subcultures outlined in the chapter, consider the anatomy of a sustainable fashion subculture.

3   The necessity for designers to use sustainable fashion theory in their work is because theory reflects and instills an intellectual rigor that stimulates a deep cultural and/or human questioning of fashion; this is in opposition to the rather dystrophic aesthetic of trend based apparel design. The failing of trend-based strategies is that it supplies dictates of the moment rather than creative organic speculations. In many ways, theory and practice for fashion design is an attempt to challenge this excepted method. Discuss this with reference to fashion sustainability.

Notes

1   The dialectic of fashion and anti-fashion technologies create a tension between knowledge and the unknown. In the dialectic are the "explosive materials" that are latent and this is where the authentic figure of fashion is detached. W. Benjamin, *The Arcades Projects*, trans. H. Eiland and K. McLaughlin (Cambridge, MA: The Belknap Press of Harvard University Press, 2002), p. 392.

2   The term "wearables" has become a ubiquitous term to explain and include all electronics worn on or in the skin, or on clothes. See "Victoria's Secret unveils heart-rate sensing bra," Sourcing Journal.com, posted December 1, 2014 by Angela Velasquez: "Victoria's Secret dipped its toes into the wearable tech space last month when it announced a partnership with fitness and sleep monitor manufacturer Misfit. From Nov. 4–9, the retailer offered a limited edition VS-branded fitness tracker as free gift with purchases over $200." Also see "Stick-on electronic tattoos," *MIT Technology Review*, posted August 11, 2011, by Kenrick Vezina: "John A. Rogers, a professor of materials science at the University of Illinois at Urbana-Champaign, has developed a prototype that can replicate the monitoring abilities of bulky electrocardiograms and other medical devices that are normally restricted to a clinical or laboratory setting. To achieve flexible, stretchable electronics, Rogers employed a principle he had already used to achieve flexibility in substrates. He made the components—all composed of traditional, high-performance materials like silicon—not only incredibly thin, but also 'structured into a serpentine

shape' that allows them to deform without breaking. The result, says Rogers, is that 'the whole system takes on this kind of spiderweb layout.'"

3   http://www.khadiculture.com/khadi.html.

4   Constance Haisma-Kwok, "Hong Kong firms set green goals," *Women's Wear Daily*, April 23, 2008: "Woo, who is also director of denim maker Central Textile, presented a list of commitments the SFBC is making and enumerated the consortium's goals. 'Many brands are already requesting carbon labeling.' said Woo, describing clothing tags that would inform consumers of the carbon used in creating each garment. 'What's interesting is that these companies are already doing what they've promised to do, but quietly,' (Christine) Loh said. 'Instead of just telling their customers, they're coming out. By making public this commitment, they are showing leadership.'"

5   M. L. Parry, O. F. Palutikof, P. J. van der Linden, and C. E. Hanson (eds), *IPCC Fourth Assessment Report* (Cambridge: Cambridge University Press, 2007). "In the 5.3 Adaptation and mitigation section of the report we find the following, ... There is high confidence that neither adaptation nor mitigation alone can avoid all climate change impacts. Adaptation is necessary both in the short term and longer term to address impacts resulting from the warming that would occur even for the lowest stabilization scenarios assessed. ... There is high confidence that the ability of many ecosystems to adapt naturally will be exceeded this century. In addition, multiple barriers and constraints to effective adaptation exist in human systems." http://www.ipcc.ch/pdf/assessment-report/ar4/syr/ar4_syr.pdf.

6   Architectonics refers to the parts that make up a whole, in terms of the preparation to create and gain artistry or understanding. To utilize the original Greek meaning, architectonics referred to architecture. If we apply architectonics to successful creation of fashion we must strive for understanding and harmonies in all relevant things. If an architectonic is to be developed, a teacher–pupil relationship must be instigated.

7   Currently there are three Master's courses dedicated to sustainability in fashion: California College of the Arts, MA Design Strategy; London College of Fashion, MA in Fashion and the Environment; and ESMOD Berlin, MA Sustainability in Fashion.

References

Baudrillard, J. (1993). *Simulations*. New York: Semiotext(e).

Fresco, J. (2012). *Paradise or oblivion*. A Roxanne Meadows Production, The Venus Project.

Hebdige, D. (1990). *Subculture: The unnatural break: the meaning of style*. Methuen.

McLuhan, M. & Fiore, Q. (1967). *The medium is the message: An inventory of effects*. Penguin Books.

Meadows, D. and Randers, J. (2004). *Limits to growth*. City Green Publishing.

O'Hanlon, M. (1993). *Paradise: Portraying the New Guinea Highlands*. London: British Museum Press.

Sapir, E. (1999). *The collected works of Edward Sapir*. Mouton de Gruyter.

Sloterdijk, P. (2000). *The operable man: On the ethical state of gene technology*, trans. J. Westerdale and G. Sautter. Frankfurt am Main: Suhrkam. http:/web.archive.org/web20050312023320/http:www.petersloterdijk.net/international/texts/en_texts_PS_operable_man.html

Thackara, J. (January 5, 2014). *A whole new cloth: Politics and the fashion system*. doorsofperception.com.

Virilio, P. (2007). *Speed and politics*. Semiotext(e).

ANNIE GULLINGSRUD is a Textile & Apparel Associate at Cradle to Cradle Products Innovation Institute. She works to share her ultimate passion for Cradle to Cradle® and help bring Cradle to Cradle design principles and certification to the fashion industry. Annie was introduced to Cradle to Cradle while at California College of the Arts in San Francisco, CA studying sustainable Fashion Design. This methodology brought endless creativity, optimism, and joy to her work. From then on, she began sharing this ideal solution with the world.

LEWIS PERKINS is a Senior VP at Cradle to Cradle Products Innovation Institute. A long-time advocate for doing the right thing, Lewis Perkins is a champion for sustainability—personally and professionally. Prior to joining the Cradle to Cradle Products Innovation Institute, Lewis consulted to companies both big and small on creating programs and awareness for environmental and social initiatives. He continues to draw on this passion and experience to help advance the Institute's mission of scaling Cradle to Cradle Product Certification worldwide.

CHAPTER **12**

Designing for the Circular Economy: Cradle to Cradle® Design

Annie Gullingsrud and Lewis Perkins

Learning about the environmental impacts of the fashion industry can seem discouraging, overwhelming, and sometimes even hopeless—climate change, resource depletion, impacts on human health, water and air pollution, excessive waste. When every message around us encourages us to "do the right thing," the danger could be that we shut down, and do nothing. How do we do the right thing when there are so many "right" things to do? How do we define right? Where do we direct our attention? There are more than fifteen stages of a garment's life cycle, and we learn that each stage has its own environmental and social impacts. What's the best way to determine how to do the right thing? Lowering the water use, using less fabric, reducing emissions, producing zero waste are all "less bad" solutions that some will try to present. If the goal is less, then the ideal is zero. And when is zero ever an ideal goal? Unless you're designing a hologram outfit to project on the body, you *will* have an impact. It does seem like even the best path to being less bad and zero creates negative side effects, is unrealistic, and can be creatively prohibitive. When we look at the sustainable fashion around us, what we see is not the sophisticated, high-fashion, beautiful design walking down the runway of our favorite designers. Is it possible for sustainable fashion to be beautiful *and* good for the planet?

What if there was a way to create a positive impact? What if there was a way we could be "more good" instead of "less bad?" What if there was a way to create beautiful fashion that is also regenerative for the planet? Believing that there could be a different approach—an approach that doesn't intend to shame or guilt and that allows for beautiful design and sustainable materials—an architect by the name of William McDonough and a green chemist, Dr. Michael Braungart, got together in 1992 to craft an entirely different kind of message.

These two people from very different backgrounds met and discovered they shared a unique and revolutionary viewpoint: in a world in which the design intention of commerce had a micro focus on profits, these two men proposed a design intention with a macro focus on increasing health, happiness, prosperity, and the bounty of nature.

They wrote *The Hannover Principles: Design for Sustainability* at the World's Fair in Hanover, Germany (1992). *The Hannover Principles* were created to inspire an approach to design which could meet the needs and aspirations of the present without compromising the ability of the planet to sustain an equally supportive future. *The Hannover Principles* were the first time that designers were addressed and tasked to make considerations themselves when designing products—because McDonough and Braungart believed that we don't have a scarcity problem, but a design problem.

In 2002, McDonough and Braungart laid out their views in the best-selling book, *Cradle to Cradle: Remaking the Way We Make Things* (Figure 12.1). The book proposed a radical way of looking at the impacts and

FIGURE 12.1. *Cradle to Cradle: Remaking the Way We Make Things* outlines an approach to design that produces regenerative, positive, and beautiful products—inside and out.

possibilities of human ingenuity and ambition. The book proposed a simple set of design principles based on emulating nature. Rather than simply poison the planet and ourselves more slowly or strive for efficiency, McDonough and Braungart proposed a different approach: a model for industrial effectiveness, where companies can produce things in ways that actually contribute to nature's bounty. "We see a world of abundance, not limits. In the midst of a great deal of talk about reducing the human ecological footprint, we offer a different vision. What if humans designed products and systems that celebrate an abundance of human creativity, culture, and productivity? That are so intelligent and safe, our species leaves an ecological footprint to delight in, not lament?" (2002, pp. 15–16).

Cradle to Cradle: Remaking the Way We Make Things outlines the concepts for "The Next Industrial Revolution":

- Buildings which, like trees, produce more energy than they use and which purify their own waste water.
- Factories that produce by-products that are high-quality drinking water.

- Products that, when their useful life is over, do not become useless waste but that can be put into the ground, where they will decompose and become food for plants and animals and nutrients for the soil; or, alternately, which can return to industrial cycles to supply high-quality raw materials for new products.
- Billions, even trillions, of dollars' worth of materials which can be used for human and natural purposes.
- A world of abundance, not one of limits, pollution, and waste.

The book caused a stir amongst design communities. Many designers thought of it as a turning point in their careers. Designing good products for the world could be positive, beautiful—inside and out. Designers could stop worrying about contributing less to the mess, and instead design positive, regenerative products. Designers were inspired, ready to set forth on a path, a new way of thinking and designing—a holistic approach that produced innovation and excitement.

Biological and Technical Metabolisms

The book identifies that all materials of human industry safely and productively flow within one of two metabolisms, biological and technical (Figure 12.2).

Biological nutrients are considered consumption products, those that naturally end up in the environment (biological cycle) during use or post-use, and are made from materials that are inherently safe for the biosphere. Biological nutrients include natural fibers such as cotton, wool, and silk. When considering fabrics as biological nutrients, dyes, finishing treatments, and trims also need to be considered.

Technical nutrients are designed as services and are meant to be continuously captured in the system. Synthetic fabrics, such as polyester, nylon, and acrylic are all considered technical nutrients because they can be continuously recycled.

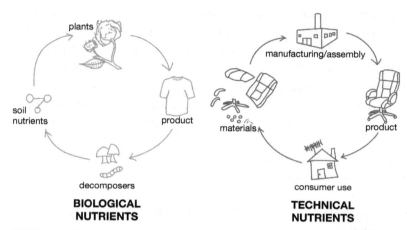

FIGURE 12.2. All materials of human industry safely and productively flow within one of two metabolisms, biological and technical. (Image credit: ©MBDC. Used with permission.)

The book articulated three basic design principles:

1　Everything equals food.
2　Produce with renewable energy.
3　Celebrate diversity.

Everything Equals Food

To illustrate this principle, let's first look to the example that McDonough and Braungart offered in the book:

> Consider the cherry tree: thousands of blossoms create food for birds, humans, and other animals, in order that one pit might eventually fall onto the ground, take root, and grow.
>
> Who would look at the ground littered with cherry blossoms and complain, "How inefficient and wasteful!" Once they fall on the ground, their materials decompose and break down into nutrients that nourish micro-organisms, insects, plants, animals,

and soil. Although the tree actually makes more of its "product" than it needs for its own success in an ecosystem, this abundance has evolved (through millions of years of success and failure or, in business terms, R&D), to serve rich and varied purposes. In fact, the tree's fecundity nourishes just about everything around it.

What might the human-built world look like if a cherry tree had produced it? (McDonough & Braungart, 2002, pp. 72–3)

Everything equals food design principles, as written in *Cradle to Cradle: Remaking the Way We Make Things*:

- Design materials and products that are effectively "food" for other systems.
- Design materials and products that are safe.
- Design materials and products whose nutrient management system leaves a beneficial legacy economically, environmentally and equitably.
- Create and participate in systems to collect and recover the value of these materials and products.
- Manage influent and effluent water streams responsibly, and consider local impact of water use to promote healthy watersheds and ecosystems.
- Promote practices that sequester carbon dioxide (CO_2) in soil rather than in the oceans and in the atmosphere.

According to a study done by the Environmental Protection Agency (EPA), 11 million tons of post-consumer waste textiles are discarded in the United States each year (usagain.com). These textiles could end up in the landfill—sitting, slowly deteriorating (and if synthetic, possibly never decomposing)—and they could also end up in large bodies of water, where they can harm aquatic species and potentially end up back in our food and water. According to a study done by Mark Browne, an ecologist at University College Dublin, microscopic

ideas in action

In 2013, PUMA launched two new collections of lifestyle apparel, footwear, and accessories, both Cradle to Cradle Certified™ Basic. These collections, called "InCycle," include reissues of iconic PUMA styles such as the PUMA Suede sneaker and T7 Track Jacket, along with newly designed windbreakers and sweatshirts and a fully recyclable backpack and shoulder bag (Figure S12.1).

In order to get a full collection that was Cradle to Cradle Certified™, PUMA had to innovate at both micro and macro levels. At the micro level, they looked at what types of pigments and dyestuffs they used in their products, which required them to partner with organizations like EPEA in Germany, who had the chemistry knowledge and could work with their supply base and innovate within their supply chain. PUMA also had to address how they design their products from the beginning. For example, an InCycle T-shirt has been slightly tweaked to make it work within the Cradle to Cradle Biological Cycle, swapping a polyester sewing thread for cotton.

At the macro level, PUMA developed a system within their stores that could take back products and put them into a system where they could be recycled or reused. They also partnered with I:CO to install Bring Back Bins in the majority of their stores that can take products back.

FIGURE S12.1. In 2013, PUMA launched their Cradle to Cradle Certified™ Basic "InCycle" collection.

> The PUMA Bring Me Back program is a product recycling initiative that creates a closed-loop system aimed at diverting products from the landfill. The majority of PUMA locations now have Bring Back Bins that can accept clothes, shoes, and bags. After an InCycle product owner has worn the item to his or her heart's content, he or she can return it to a PUMA Bring Back Bin. I:CO collects the contents of the bins, and takes it from there.
>
> PUMA's cross-functional team worked together to deliver the collection—from sourcing, designers, innovation experts, as well as strategy and marketing—so they could have a 360-degree approach to the collection.
>
> Since the launch of their first Cradle to Cradle Certified™ Basic collection, PUMA has released additional InCycle Collections that are Cradle to Cradle Certified™ Silver.

fragments of acrylic, polyethylene, polypropylene, nylon, and polyester have been discovered in increasing quantities across the northeast Atlantic, as well as on beaches in places as far apart as Britain, Singapore, and India. Do we really want to be eating and drinking our textiles? (Coen, 2011). Now, think of all the energy, time, and non-renewable resources that went into producing that garment. What a loss! It's like throwing away money. No business would intentionally want to do that.

Now imagine a fashion industry that designs with Cradle to Cradle® intention: All clothing is designed with materials that are safe for humans and the environment. The garment is also designed with reuse of materials in mind—there's a strategy for take-back, disassembly, fiber separation, and re-production. Imagine a circular economy of materials that can be endlessly upcycled, not downcycled, an economy where a shirt becomes a pair of trousers becomes a carpet becomes a baby's toy, and so on. Imagine an economy where a designer designs not just for single use, but for a legacy of products with a storyline that has no end.

Produce with Renewable Energy

Let's look to McDonough and Braungart's second book, *The Upcycle: Beyond Sustainability—Designing for Abundance* (2013), for guidance on renewable energy:

> When envisioning what energy could look like in a Cradle to Cradle world, we like to think about Thomas Edison. In 1931, the inventor reportedly said, "We are like tenant farmers chopping down the fence around our house for fuel when we should be using nature's inexhaustible sources of energy—sun, wind, and tide … I'd put my money on the sun and solar energy. What a source of power! I hope we don't have to wait until oil and coal run out before we tackle that." (McDonough & Braungart, 2013, p. 98)

Producing fashion takes energy. Lots of it. While it makes sense to slow down the use of fossil fuels, this is not realistic—or the goal. In a Cradle to Cradle world, all energy would come from renewable energy sources—solar, wind, hydropower, biomass (when not in competition with food supplies), geothermal, and hydrogen fuel—sources that are in no danger of running out.

Celebrate Diversity

Have you ever had a job where you thought you weren't treated properly—you were underpaid, your manager didn't value your work, or you were expected to work additional hours without being compensated? Now imagine that, on top of that, you work in a building with poor ventilation, do not get breaks, and work 15-hour days, all for a couple of dollars a day. Can you imagine the quality of work you might produce?

Now imagine that you're working for an employer who values you, offers a workplace with windows, fresh air, breaks, and compensation you think is fair. The workplace is buzzing with creativity.

Of the two, which scenario do you think you'll be happiest in? And, which of the two do you think you'll be most effective in, producing quality work?

Treating employees properly is just good business sense. When employees are treated this way, they flourish and produce good work. It's that simple.

Technological diversity is key for innovation: explore different options in looking for creative solutions. Materials diversity is also key for innovation. Sticking with materials that are widely known as "sustainable"—such as natural fabrics—can be incredibly limiting, not to mention unrealistic. The fashion industry is a moving train and we're not going to stop it. But we can get on ... we can even be ahead of it! Imagine fabrics that meet performance requirements, can be recycled, and have a positive influence on the environment. Let's look for creative solutions together.

The Book Became a Continuous Improvement Standard

Due to the favorable response that the book *Cradle to Cradle* and its design principles received, William McDonough and Dr. Michael Braungart created an organized framework for quality assessment and innovation: the Cradle to Cradle Certified™ Products program where companies could get their products assessed, certified, and bear the Cradle to Cradle Certified™ hallmark. Today, the Cradle to Cradle Certified™ standard encompasses five certification levels—Basic, Bronze, Silver, Gold, and Platinum—and covers five attributes: Material Health, Material Reutilization, Renewable Energy & Carbon Management, Water Stewardship, and Social Fairness.

Before a product can be certified, it must be assessed by an Accredited Assessment Body, consultancies trained to carry out Cradle to Cradle Certified™ audits and assessments. The Cradle to Cradle Products Innovation Institute, a non-profit organization in San Francisco, CA, audits the Assessment Summary Reports and administers the recommended certification level.

As a designer, while the ideal goal could be Cradle to Cradle certification, we can also look to the goals set out in the Cradle to Cradle Certified™ standard to guide decision making when it comes to fashion design and materials selection. Let's look at each of the five attributes outlined in the Standard for guidance.

Material Health

Design aspiration: Design materials and products that are safe, healthy, and leave positive marks on the world.

To achieve this aspiration, apparel should pose no risk of containing carcinogens, mutagens, or reproductive toxins. Chemicals that could be eliminated include PVC, Teflon, flame retardants, chlorinated hydrocarbons, and phthalates.

Consider:
- Review our Cradle to Cradle Certified™ banned chemicals list: http://www.c2ccertified.org/images/uploads/C2CCertified_Banned_Lists_V3_121113.pdf.
- What type of fabric are you using, and does it contain chemicals that are harmful to people and the environment?
- Is the fabric dyed, and do the dyes contain chemicals that are harmful to people and the environment?
- Is there a finishing on the fabric, such as a water repellent, antimicrobial treatment, anti-wrinkling treatment, or stain repellent? Does the finishing contain harmful chemicals?
- Is the product made of one material type (i.e., 100% cotton or 100% polyester) or multiple? This is necessary in order to easily separate and recycle upon collection.

Material Reutilization

Design aspiration: Design materials and products can be endlessly and safely cycled so they become "food" for new products.

We learned at the beginning of the chapter that we must get rid of the idea of waste and that clothing that sits in a landfill can actually be harmful to our water system and us. Designing clothes for a circular economy takes a simple shift: at the start of the design process, ask yourself, "What will happen at end of use?"

Well, simple, but maybe not easy. Ever since the Industrial Revolution, apparel and fashion has been created without the need to answer this question. Production timelines have gotten shorter, and so has the life span of a garment. Fast fashion companies are quick to respond to trends and produce inexpensive fashion with an intentionally short life span. This can get particularly dangerous when no attention has been given to the health of the materials and chemicals used to make the product. There is a limitless lode of potential impacts here that can last far, far longer than the wearer might wear their garment. And, most synthetic fabrics will take anywhere from 40 to 1,000 years to decompose, or may never go away. Why design products that will *intentionally* end up in the landfill, waterways, or our bodies? Let us instead design products that will *intentionally* end up in new products so that we, as designers, can leave a legacy of good health and beautiful design for generations to come.

This takes a perspective shift and a willingness to confront the reality and the infinite possibility of what can happen next. The good news is that there are many companies emerging internationally who are developing the infrastructure and systems necessary for recovering and recycling materials as the nutrients on a global scale. One of these companies is I:CO, which stands for "I collect." I:CO partners with retailers and cities to make it easy, convenient and rewarding for consumers and businesses to give their unwanted clothing, shoes, accessories such as belts or bags, and other textiles, like linens, a new life. I:CO provides the collection and processing infrastructure to ensure that these old textiles find their next best use and their valuable raw materials enter a closed loop production cycle.

Another is KICI, a European company based in the Netherlands that collects discarded textiles and footwear through community collection containers. The collected textiles and footwear are sorted, based on wearable or non-wearable. The wearable textiles go back in circulation in countries outside Europe or are given to thrift stores or food banks. The non-wearable textiles enter a high-tech process of pulping and recycling, generating fibers for new yarns, relief blankets, or insulation material for housing.

Technology for recycling textiles is relatively basic at this point— not all types of fibers can be recycled, and recycling of fibers that can be recycled can be complicated. Another consideration is when two or more fibers are blended together, particularly a biological and technical nutrient. Take, for example, a cotton/polyester blend. Whereas cotton and polyester can each be recycled or composted on their own, current recycling capabilities are highly limited for separating these fibers and recycling them when they are blended. Since we are designing for the circular economy, we want to envision creating a scalable materials economy where products have many useful lives.

Consider:
*   Is the product made of one material type (i.e., 100% cotton or 100% polyester), or multiple (98% cotton/2% polyester)?
*   If multiple material types, can it be easily separated into individual material types at end of use?
*   Can these material types be recycled via existing infrastructure or processes?
*   Identify partners for using materials in future product manufacturing.
*   How will the garment be collected when the customer's done wearing it?

The Development of Climatex Upholstery

In 1993, Susan Lyons, then Creative Director of Designtex, a New York-based textile company, decided to develop a collection of ecological fabrics. But, at that time, no one knew exactly what a "green" fabric should be. Should it be made of recycled materials, recyclable materials, natural fibers? What was the best direction? Late that year, Lyons contacted William McDonough, an architect and leader in the field of sustainable design, to get his input.

McDonough proposed the concept of "waste=food" as a guiding principle for this (and other) design problem(s). Lyons and McDonough set the goal of making a "consumable" product that, when used or discarded, would turn into soil without any harmful side effects. A partnership then emerged between Designtex, McDonough and his colleague, the chemist Michael Braungart, and the Swiss mill Rohner, to develop a biological-nutrient upholstery that would later be called Climatex®.

FIGURE S12.2. Climatex® upholsteries are designed to safely biodegrade.

Following the "waste=food" principle, the upholstery was designed to break down and return safely to the earth after its useful life. In order to achieve this, every input had to be analyzed, from the raw materials (wool and ramie, a natural plant fiber) to the dyestuffs and other process chemicals used in weaving.

Braungart invited 60 different chemical companies to collaborate on the project. All but one—Ciba-Geigy—declined, reluctant to disclose their formulations to such scrutiny. With Ciba-Geigy's help Braungart analyzed over 8,000 chemical formulations commonly used in textile production, and then selected a mere 38 that he deemed safe for human and environmental health. These were the dyes and process chemicals allowed to be used in the production of Climatex® upholstery.

This optimization of the chemistry caused a change in the mill's waste; the water now flowing out of the mill was actually cleaner than the inflowing water. Other portions of the manufacturing process at Rohner underwent big changes as well. Located in a small farming community in Switzerland, the mill had already been operating under high environmental standards. However, government regulations had recently become stricter, and deemed textile scraps from the weaving process to be hazardous waste. The mill was forced to export the scraps to Spain for disposal, a costly factor of doing business in the region. With the production of the new fabrics designed to safely biodegrade, the mill was able to save the scraps and make them into felt. This felt was used by local strawberry farmers as ground cover for their crops, and the mill was saved costly disposal fees related to previous textile constructions.

Climatex® upholsteries have achieved Gold level certification. Designtex continues to add styles to the Climatex® collection, now woven by Gessner AG in Switzerland.

Renewable Energy and Carbon Management

Design aspiration: Power operations with clean and renewable energy.

Commonly thought of as pollution, carbon emissions summon to mind images of filthy billows pouring out of factory smokestacks or the exhaust pipes of cars; but in fact what we are talking about is one of our most exquisite nutrients. Humans don't have an energy problem. Energy is abundant. What humans have is a materials-in-the-wrong-place problem. People have taken crucial, valuable terrestrial carbon and put it where they can't reach it. Too much of it lingers in the air and water for it to cycle back at its natural rate. It would be like sending gold dust into the sky, or diamonds. Why did they do it? Don't they want it? Now what the heck do they do to get it back? (McDonough & Braungart, 2013, p. 38)

Cradle to Cradle envisions a future in which industry and commerce positively impact the energy supply, ecosystem balance, and community. This is a future powered by current solar income and built on circular material flows. The Renewable Energy and Carbon Management category is a combination of these core principles of Cradle to Cradle design: produce and use renewable energy and eliminate the concept of waste. Renewable energy displaces energy produced from fossil fuels, which emit carbon. Changing the quantity and quality of energy used affects the balance of carbon in the atmosphere and ultimately the climate. Ideally, emissions are simply eliminated, and renewable energy is produced in excess to be supplied to local communities. When emissions do occur, they are managed as biological nutrients and balanced with an equivalent uptake by natural systems.

Consider:

- When sourcing materials and production of apparel, work with factories and mills that source renewable energy for product production.
- How much energy would it take to produce this garment? How far would the inputs have to travel?

Water Stewardship

Design aspiration: Power operations with clean and renewable energy.

While we have the flexibility these days to create ranges of beautiful colors for garment dyeing, from fluorescents to hot pinks to synthetic indigo dyes for blue jeans, these same dyes are creating colored rivers to match. Pink-colored rivers. Blue-colored rivers. Yellow-colored rivers. Now there exists a rainbow of rivers, but they are toxic and are impacting the communities that are relying on them. Water effluents rich with chemicals from the dye or other textile processes can impact receiving water bodies, harm aquatic ecosystems, and contaminate our drinking water.

It is important to know that textile processing that uses less water is not always the best option—water effluent can still be rich in chemicals and released to surrounding water bodies. That's why treating water as a valuable resource means more than using less—it means producing a clean water effluent that can positively impact communities.

Consider:

- Understand and take responsibility for water withdrawals, consumption, and releases within your local ecosystem.
- Work with factories and mills that have water filtration systems already installed, or ask them to install them.
- Work with factories and mills that have not received a significant violation of their discharge permit within the last two years.

Social Fairness

Design aspiration: Honor all natural systems and the people involved in creating products.

Long before the Rana Plaza collapse in Bangladesh in April 2013, apparel factory fires in Bangladesh happened almost weekly. These factories lacked fire exits, had overall unsafe conditions, and were built on unstable foundations. Child labor … excessive work time … poor worker and health safety … chemical exposure in the workplace—sometimes disease-causing. If you knew that the shirt you were wearing was made under these conditions, would you still proudly wear it?

Who would knowingly hire a factory to produce clothing that was being made by workers who were working in conditions that made them highly vulnerable to disease and even death? The keyword here is *knowingly*.

Social fairness ensures that fair practice is taking place. Audits of factories are conducted to ensure that fundamental human rights are being protected.

It is also important for business ethics to go beyond the confines of basic fundamental human rights—to engage responsible manufacturing throughout the supply chain and offer employees the opportunity to work in environments that are beaming with optimism, good management, attractive work environments, and fresh air, and whatever else you can imagine!

Consider:
- Where is my fabric sourced from? Where are the trims sourced from? Where is it being dyed?
- Work with factories that perform social responsibility audits through a third party against an internationally recognized social responsibility program such as B-Corp or SA8000.
- Work with factories or mills that perform social responsibility audits using other programs, using HIGG Index Factory Module, UN Global Compact Tool, or B-Corp.

Fashion Positive

Cradle to Cradle design methodology is a cross-sector approach that has been leveraged for textiles, building materials, cleaning products, home and office supplies, packaging, baby products, and more. To date, over 200 companies have had 2,000+ products certified as meeting or advancing upon Cradle to Cradle design principles.

While Cradle to Cradle design methodology and certification has historically been applied to commercial textiles, the Fashion Positive Initiative was created in 2013 to go deep into the supply chain and assess and certify fashion and textile materials, such as garments, fabric, zippers, buttons, dyes, finishings, and more. These materials will be assessed against the requirements of Material Health, Material Reutilization, Renewable Energy & Carbon Management, Water Stewardship, and Social Fairness, certified, and added to a Library of Materials that designers can trust and access to use in garments and collections as often as they want.

The Fashion Positive Initiative allows for positive and regenerative influence of Cradle to Cradle design methodology to permeate the supply chain and the fashion industry. The Initiative aims to create a positive list of brands, supply chain partners, and producers who are collaborating together to create an effective circular economy. These people represent the heroes of sustainable fashion.

To fund these ongoing projects, the Fashion Positive Revolving Fund has been created to give loans and grants to brands and supply chain partners to spur innovation. Fashion Positive will create long-lasting effects that will have a positive influence on the fashion industry and everyone who wears clothes.

Discussion Questions

1   Look at the contents of your shirt or trousers. Is this a biological or technical nutrient? Or both?

2   Develop a strategy for reuse of this garment at end of use. Would
    you need to redesign the garment to accommodate for a reuse
    strategy?
3   What would be a creative way to collect garments from your
    customers when they are done using them? How could you
    communicate to let them know what to do?

References

Braungart, M. & McDonough, W. (1992). *The Hannover principles: Design for sustainability: Prepared for EXPO 2000, World's Fair*. Charlottesville, VA: William McDonough Architects.

Braungart, M. & McDonough, W. (2002). *Cradle to cradle: Remaking the way we make things*. New York: North Point Press.

Coen, A. (2011). Is synthetic clothing causing "microplastic" pollution in our oceans? *Ecouterre*. Retrieved November 28, 2013 from http://www.ecouterre.com/is-synthetic-clothing-causing-microplastic-pollution-in-oceans-worldwide/.

Let's Use it Again! Usagain. Retrieved November 28, 2014 from http://www.usagain.com.

McDonough, W. & Braungart, M. (2013). *The Upcycle: Beyond Sustainability—Designing for Abundance*. New York: North Point Press.

GAIL BAUGH has extensive senior management experience in the apparel and textile industries, particularly in global product sourcing for large retail chain stores and for Teijin Frontier (USA). Experienced in retail buying, production management, and textile development, Gail has a Chemistry of Textiles undergraduate degree and a Master's degree studying consumers' attitudes toward discarded apparel. "It is my mission," she says, "to focus the apparel industry on fiber innovations to address the environment and conservation of fiber resources. It is the obligation of the apparel industry to responsibly manage fiber resources of the future industry."

CHAPTER 13

Fibers: Exploring Healthy and Clean Fiber

Gail Baugh

Fiber is the basic building block of our textiles industry. Understanding the pros and cons of the interconnectivity of the land, water, chemicals, and energy (Baugh, 2011) involved in producing a particular fiber is the first step to creating sustainable fiber, yarn, and fabric selections. Environmentally responsible fiber choices are not limited to natural or organically grown fibers; they also include fibers manufactured from renewable raw materials and chemically recycled fibers whose characteristics are equal quality to virgin fiber. New and developing technology utilized in fiber development makes fiber choice more complex. The apparel industry has a responsibility to recognize how fiber choice will impact the environment in our global economy. It must explore and evaluate emerging fiber innovations and alternatives to resolve the issue of consistent, cost-effective fiber supply, while reconciling environmental issues such as conserving fiber resources.

Taking the First Step

The apparel industry clings to historical fiber preferences, while the needs of a healthy environment and cleaner, less toxic fiber and textile production methods are forcing different choices on their target markets. With rare exceptions, fashion apparel schools and business models both continue to use the same means to identify fiber choice, disregarding the impact that the fiber choice will have on human health and conservation of resources. Most designers are trained to choose fabrics based on aesthetic considerations alone. The issue of "healthy and clean" is then left to the production teams to source while implementing the designer's vision. Now is the time to ask the decision makers in the apparel industry (e.g., designers, merchandisers, and leaders of corporations) to reconsider their fiber selection priorities, first, for their easily renewable sources and minimal negative impact on the environment, and second, for their aesthetic and performance values. The apparel industry is embarking on a new era in textiles and awareness of new fibers. Future innovations will encourage new product ideas and a new generation of designers and companies to use these new fibers in their collections and assortments. New fiber ideas are emerging more frequently now, as the public policy requirements for more "healthy and clean" fiber increase.

This chapter offers a glimpse of what is here and what is coming, and it is hoped that this information will encourage decision makers in the apparel industry to seek out new fibers, challenge suppliers to produce fabrics using these fibers, and, therefore, change the supply chain from one of creativity and waste to that of creativity, reuse, and renewal.

Is Natural Fiber of Better Quality and Higher Value than Manufactured Fiber?

What do the terms "pure cotton" and "fine wool" mean? The haute couture and other better fashion designers continue to use exclusive fabrics composed of expensive, difficult-to-produce fibers and yarns, most of which use wool and silk as well as cotton and linen fibers. For example, the Coco Chanel suit, reinvented by Karl Lagerfeld for

Chanel, continued to use the wool fabrics inspired by original fabrics from the early twentieth century. New fabric choices were used to recreate the texture and hand of other original suits, and so buyers placed a higher value on a suit produced in the original wool fiber content than one produced in a wool/acrylic blend. But if a fiber occurs in nature, such as the wool fiber in Chanel's example, is it always the best choice for high-fashion products?

Historic Reference

In the past two generations, the fashion industry has promoted the concept that natural fiber (i.e., fiber produced by plants and animals) is superior to manufactured fiber (i.e., rayon or polyester). Natural fiber marketing associations have formed alliances with educators, designers, manufacturers, and retailers to promote their fiber. Meanwhile, manufactured fiber mills imitate natural fiber, reinforcing the perception that natural fiber is superior.

Further emphasizing the use of natural fiber, the hippies of the 1960s and 1970s embraced cotton and wool fiber as a way to reject "establishment values" of that time. Widely popular polyester, nylon, and acrylic fabrics of the late 1950s and early 1960s were rejected by young hippies, who wore cotton T-shirts and jeans to set themselves apart from the new fibers. Natural fibers were perceived as superior, and this new demand led to an increased demand for cotton fiber at all price levels. The popularity of cotton-based, American-style T-shirts and jeans (GAP, Levi Strauss, Guess) has increased the global demand for this fiber.

The designer's priority has been to select fashionable colors and textures in textiles. The priority for fashion manufacturers and retailers has been to have the desired natural fiber available on demand globally, at low prices, to offer timely products at competitive prices.

Now is the time to add fiber choice to the early decision-making process, because it is clear that fiber choice has a significant impact on a healthy and clean environment. And, since the apparel business is global, healthy and clean fiber choice can have a positive influence worldwide. Broadening fiber choice beyond the accepted perceptions of high quality cotton, wool, and silk is important in calling attention to the apparel business's role in making sustainable fiber decisions.

What are the Familiar Fiber Choices in the Industry Now?

Designers and merchandisers, when visiting the textile shows in Paris, Milan, New York, Hong Kong, Hamburg, and Shanghai, continue to focus on the familiar fiber choices (divided into natural fiber and manufactured fiber content and the assorted blends), choosing new textures and colors to reflect the new fashion trends. Below are the familiar groups of fiber that are most often offered to apparel designers at these shows.

Choice 1: Natural Fiber

Most designers will select varieties of linen, cotton, wool, or silk fiber, grown or raised in conventional agricultural methods for the highest yield. Irrigated water, synthetic chemical fertilizers, and pesticides improve the harvest yield of the fiber and generate consistent and predictable fiber quantities. As the chart in Table 13.1 shows, there are other fibers that are commonly used in apparel, and they are listed there as well.

Choice 2: Organic Natural Fiber

The word "organic" is somewhat misleading in describing textile production. In the United States, it refers to standards defined by the USDA Organic Foods Production Act, passed by Congress in 1990, which provides strict guidelines for the production and certification of organic food (Sustainable Table, n.d.). Therefore, the costly adherence

TABLE 13.1. Naturally occurring fiber

Raw material source	Renewable	Water use/ acre	Pesticides/ chemicals	Recyclable/ biodegradable	Comments
Plant Fibers					
Cotton*	Yes	High usage	Yes	N/A / Yes	Most cotton production grown this way.
Chemical-free cotton	Yes	High usage	No	N/A / Yes	Alternative to non-food crop.
Organic cotton	Yes	High usage	No	N/A / Yes	Grown to USDA organic food standards.
Flax* (becomes linen)	Yes	Less than cotton	N/A	N/A / Yes	Flax is more pest-resistant and requires less water than cotton.
Ramie*	Yes	Less than cotton	Resistant to most pests/ diseases	N/A / Yes	Easily grown crop.
Hemp	Yes	Less than cotton	Resistant to most pests/ diseases	N/A / Yes	Easily grown crop. Must have permit to grow in the United States.
Animal Fibers					
Hair fiber*	Yes	Dependent on animal	Yes	N/A / Yes	Domestic animals are dipped in chemicals to remove pests/dirt. Shearing methods designed for mass production. Not humane treatment.
"Organic" hair fiber (sheep only)	Yes	N/A	Non-toxic	N/A / Yes	Toxic chemical dipping is eliminated and replaced with non-toxic methods. Shearing methods are humane and monitored by PETA. Note: Not the USDA guideline definition of "organic."
Silk	Yes	N/A	N/A	N/A / Yes	Requires steam/water during the fiber reclamation from the cocoons. Very labor-intensive production process.

Notes: (a) To be labeled "organic" fiber product, fiber and fabric must conform to the GOTS (Global Organic Textile Standard) guidelines. (b) "Biodegradable" means fibers can technically decompose in moist soil, but the dyeing and finishing processes make this process nearly impossible.
*Commonly used natural fiber today.

to these USDA production standards requires time to provide soil that is defined as organic and farming methods to meet the federal organic farming standards. There are now established certification processes in place to validate a fiber producer's organic fiber claims. The Global Organic Textile Standard or GOTS certification is the globally recognized standard, and the USDA and the Federal Trade Commission (FTC) now recognizes the GOTS for organic labeling related to apparel and other textile products ("Approved Certification Bodies," 2014). So far, organically grown cotton is the only plant fiber that has met the USDA organic standard. Though many apparel companies attempt to use organic cotton fiber, it is clear that the cost and available quantity cannot meet the production requirements. Note that wool, unless produced to the USDA organic standard, is also not considered organic. (See Choice 3 below for an explanation.)

Choice 3: Chemical-Free Fiber

Since organic fiber is not food, the question arises whether it is necessary to produce organic fiber (i.e., fiber produced to the standards of food) or to simply grow fiber without the use of the harmful chemicals used in synthetic fertilizers and pesticides. Unlike the organic standard, producing chemical-free fiber can be done immediately and without time required to certify the soil as organic before planting. Twenty-five percent of all pesticides used in the United States are applied to the cotton crop (Organic Consumer Association, 2014). Chemical-free cotton fiber is available now (BCI fiber), as is chemical-free flax and wool fiber, but the effort to market fiber produced without chemicals is now more widely known. One of the fiber marketing associations, Cotton, Inc., has begun branding and promoting chemical-free cotton (Better Cotton Initiative, BCI). The removal of the harmful chemicals used in natural fiber production is an important step for fiber producers and for providing a healthy and clean alternative to the more costly and less available organically grown cotton fiber. Certification of fiber production practices is required, however.

ideas in action

Recently, the US-based United States Department of Agriculture (USDA) allowed the European Union's GOTS standard for the labeling of apparel using organically grown fiber (USDA, 2011):

1 Certification of organically grown fiber or organic in-conversion.
2 No less than 95 percent of fiber content (organic) or 70 percent in-conversion—labeled as such.
3 Cannot blend with conventional fibers nor be contaminated with prohibited substances throughout the supply chain.
4 Dyestuffs and finishing chemicals must meet the GOTS guidelines.
5 Environmental management must follow national and local processing/manufacturing guidelines.
6 Appropriate worker-related practices as GOTS requirement.
7 Proper record keeping for transparency.

Some wool producers are marketing their fiber as organic, but the wool is actually produced using humane methods, such as eliminating harmful chemicals in the dipping process and administering a sensitive shearing process. Wool labeled organic may not meet the USDA organic standard, but it may actually be chemical-free or reduced-chemical fiber (National Organic Program, 2003).

Choice 4: Manufactured Fiber

Manufactured fiber, produced from a variety of raw materials, has been avoided by most high-priced designers, especially since the 1960s. Viscose and lyocell rayons, polyester, nylon, acrylic, and spandex were not promoted as status fibers. Instead, chemical fiber companies such as DuPont Chemical (producers of Dacron® polyester, Lycra® spandex, and others) or Teijin Frontier, Ltd. (producers of Capilene® polyester fiber and others) have sought mass-market production quantities, targeting moderate-priced retailers and manufacturers. The need and desire for more affordable prices and care-free apparel have become priorities among consumers, so these low-cost, low-maintenance fibers are continuously in demand. Manufactured fiber was originally developed to imitate the more expensive and higher maintenance fibers used by the French haute couture and other designers, so the merchandisers and retail buyers continued to value natural fiber more than the imitating manufactured fiber.

Manufactured fiber is divided into two main categories (see Table 13.2) with a new subcategory now emerging:

1   *Fiber produced using plant-based raw material.* Viscose, HWM, lyocell rayons and acetate fibers are produced using this raw material. Historically, acetate and rayon were extremely toxic to produce. Because of the toxic waste generated during fiber production, which has often ended with polluted wastewater and toxic emissions, these fibers are less available now. Lyocell rayon is the first fiber that uses a closed, recycled production system (i.e., it uses the same chemicals again in further lyocell production) that keeps the toxic chemicals out of the water supply. Tencel® lyocell, by Leizing Fiber, is an example of this generic fiber.

2   *Fiber produced using petroleum-based raw material.* Nylon, polyester, olefin, acrylic, and spandex are the "big five" manufactured fibers that are very important to fabric production. Polyester fiber accounts for over 50 percent of all fiber production. Chemical companies, such as DuPont, used petroleum, a plentiful raw material at the time, as the basis for new fiber development. A seemingly unlimited oil supply meant unlimited fiber production to meet the textile needs of the US economy. The textile industry continues to diversify these fibers to enhance fabric performance.

3   *New category known as bio-based polyester and spandex.* These generic fibers use two components: about one-third plant material and two-thirds petroleum-based products. At the moment, Teijin

TABLE 13.2. Current manufactured fibers

Fiber regenerated cellulosic (plant raw material)	Hand	Luster	Drape	Resiliency	Abrasion resistant	UV resistant	Anti-bacterial	Wicking	Absorbency	Quick dry	Machine washable	Dyeability	Color-fastness	Heat sensitive	Thermo-plastic	Comments
Acetate	Fair	Good	Fair	Fair	Poor	No	No	No	Good	Good	No	Excellent	Fair	Yes	Yes	Easily melts
Viscose rayon	Excellent	Good	Excellent	Fair	Poor	Yes	No	No	Good	Good	No	Excellent	Fair	Yes	No	
Lyocell rayon	Excellent	Poor	Excellent	Good	Fair	Yes	No	No	Good	Good	Yes	Excellent	Good	Yes	No	
Fiber oil-based (petroleum raw material)																
Nylon	Fair	Good	Fair	Very good	Excellent	Poor	No	No	No	Very good	Yes	Fair	Fair	Yes	Yes	Very strong fiber
Polyester	Good	Good	Good	Excellent	Very good	Yes	No	No*	No*	Very good	Yes	Fair	Good	Yes	Yes	*Can be changed to have wicking/absorbent features
Acrylic	Good	Good	Good	Very good	Fair	Yes	No	No	No	Very good	Yes	Fair	Good	Yes	Yes	Very heat-sensitive fiber
Olefin	Fair	Good	Good	Excellent	Excellent	Yes	No	Yes	No	Very good	Yes	Good	Excellent	Yes	Yes	Very durable fiber
Spandex	Fair	Very good	Fair	Excellent	Fair	No	No	No	No	Very good	Yes	Poor	Poor	Yes	Yes	Heat-sensitive

Frontier and Invista are two fiber companies that have produced and marketed these new polyester and spandex fibers. The goal is to reduce petroleum-based fiber composition while increasing fiber production, by adding renewable plant sources that utilize far less energy than the original fiber production. Teijin Frontier's bio-polyester can be chemically recycled into new fiber ("Bio-polyester," 2012). Invista's entry, a bio-based Lycra® spandex, will be available in 2015 ("Invista Unveils," 2014). These new fibers are designed to maintain the original fiber characteristics.

Should the Fashion Industry Stay with the Current Available Choices?

Designers and merchandisers continue to select fabrics produced from the available fiber choices. Are these choices most appropriate for today and tomorrow? There are obvious changes in the world market that are challenging the way fiber is perceived and selected for use:

1   *The interest in "healthy and clean" fiber and textile production.* The environmental impact of fiber and textile production is more visual now. The apparel industry acknowledges the pollution created in both natural fiber and manufactured fiber production (Rainforest News, 2013). With designers making organic fiber choices, leadership is emerging in the apparel industry to rethink the perceived social and market value of fiber.

2   *The reduction of the global oil supply, which produces the key components of polyester, nylon, acrylic, olefin, and spandex.* How will the fiber suppliers react to the shrinking raw material supply?

3   *More demand for fiber production to meet the apparel needs of an increasing global middle-class population.* This pressure has challenged fiber producers to consider alternative easily renewable resources.

The Future Choice of Fiber for the Fashion Industry

What will fashion be like in a post-cotton and post-polyester world? Choosing between a natural or manufactured fiber is no longer simple. Natural fiber, perceived as an "eco" and "pure" fiber, is often being produced with toxic chemicals and large amounts of irrigated water; and manufactured fiber, perceived as unnatural and polluting, can now be produced with minimal toxic processes and reduced CO_2 emissions.

Organic fiber, seen as one possible solution to solve the chemical pollutants used on cotton fiber, cannot fulfill the demand for fiber due to cost and limited quantity. The fiber industry is experimenting with a variety of new ideas to minimize the negative environmental impact and expand raw material fiber sources. These new ideas may be ways to supplement the current fiber supply, either by blending with the new fibers or replacing the currently available fibers altogether. The industry is increasingly turning its attention to fiber sources that are both *easily renewable* and have *fewer toxins/CO_2 emissions* in the production process. Described below are naturally occurring fiber and new manufactured fiber that address both issues.

Naturally Occurring Fiber

Cotton fiber now represents less than 50 percent of globally available fiber. Designers and merchandisers have little to no experience with alternative fibers for cotton. However, there are several fibers that provide similar characteristics. It is important to note that these naturally occurring fibers are not produced in enough quantities to replace all cotton fiber production, but there is enough production to offer alternative choices. It is important for apparel industry decision makers to know the alternatives to cotton fiber, as cotton production comes under increased scrutiny as a high-maintenance crop, questioning its use of toxic chemicals, substantial use of water, and low fiber yields per acre compared to alternative fiber. Below is a review of fibers that are gaining more recognition as viable options to replace or supplement cotton fiber.

ideas in action

Rethinking Cotton Fiber Production

The United States continues to rank in the global top four cotton fiber producers, yet does not produce much yarn or textiles. As an example, the state of California exports more than half its cotton production offshore, so the state water subsidies and federal cotton subsidies benefit few workers and businesses. Cotton requires high maintenance (irrigated water, chemical enhancement) for low yield (one-third of harvest is useable fiber) per acre. Flax and hemp yield is much higher (80–90 percent useable fiber) per acre and require much less water and chemical enhancement to produce the fiber.

The question is, as an industrialized nation, should the US produce cotton fiber when best, highest use of arable land might be for food production, which benefits more people, instead of artificially low-priced cotton fiber? Other developing nations, such as India, China, Pakistan, Peru, and some African nations, can produce needed cotton fiber, and US farmers could concentrate on food or bio-energy production instead.

And with the new "cottonizing" technology from Crailar®, cotton use can be greatly reduced, even among apparel companies that have defined their businesses using cotton fiber, by utilizing the new cotton/flax or cotton/hemp cottonized blends. The environmental benefits are substantial in reducing water and chemicals consumed on cotton fields, by producing flax and hemp fiber instead.

Hanes brand was one of the first companies to obtain a license to use the Crailar® technology in the States, and now offers cottonized flax/cotton blends (Dodes, 2011). There are several advantages of the new fiber blends over 100 percent cotton: (1) they absorb moisture faster yet dry faster (cooler to wear and less energy used in drying); (2) they are lighter weight, even when wet; and (3) they are stronger when wet (more durable in commercial garment washing and consumer care).

It is also very important to note that textile finishing techniques have greatly improved the hand and dyeability of these alternative fibers, making them more desirable fabrics for fashion. Enzyme-related softening and Crailar® "cottonizing" processes can greatly enhance the soft hand of these grass and stem fibers (Borromeo, 2014).

Hemp and flax

Hemp is naturally pest- and mildew-resistant, is easy to grow in many climates, requires less water per acre than cotton, and, including flax, produces much higher yields of fiber per acre than cotton. While flax is the fiber used to produce linen, new finishing processes can provide a cotton fiber substitute. In 2014, the US federal government passed a bill allowing the growing of industrial hemp (NCLS, 2014), a fiber grown without restrictions in other countries. Having almost all the same characteristics as cotton fiber, fiber processing and fabric-finishing techniques have greatly improved, resulting in a final fabric product that is nearly the same as cotton. Using Crailar®'s technique, hemp's and flax's advantage is that they can now supplement or replace cotton as a fiber source. An important step in adding these two cotton-like fiber choices is recognizing the need for inexpensive, naturally occurring fiber that is easily grown without chemicals and without excessive use of water.

Ramie

Ramie is very resistant to mildew, is very absorbent, is quick-drying, and has good strength (Table 13.3). Grown easily in many countries, ramie is often used as a flax substitute for lower-priced linen-like fabrics, or blended with cotton for a similar effect (Figure 13.1). Production and use of ramie fiber could be expanded, particularly with improved finishing technology.

New Developments in Manufactured Fiber

Manufactured fiber is created by extruding strands, or *polymers*, from a chemical fiber soup developed by chemical fiber companies, such as DuPont or Toray. Many chemical fiber companies worldwide have been working on new, renewable raw material sources for fiber manufacturing, and these new fibers are beginning to emerge in the marketplace. These new fibers can be divided into three groups: those

TABLE 13.3. Alternative plant fibers compared to flax and cotton

Fiber name	Absorbency	Abrasion resistance	Machine washable	Wet strength	Drape	Hand	Comments
Compare to flax (linen) and	Excellent	Excellent	Yes	Excellent	Fair	Fair	New finishing techniques are improving the
to cotton	Very good	Very good	Yes	Very good	Good	Good	drape/hand.
Jute	Excellent	Excellent	Yes	Excellent	Fair	Fair	" "
Ramie	Excellent	Excellent	Yes	Very good	Fair	Fair	" "
Hemp	Excellent	Excellent	Yes	Excellent	Fair	Fair	" "

Note: Cotton replaced flax (linen) from the 1940s as the fiber of choice in the United States.

FIGURE 13.1. Ramie grows as a flowering plant to heights of 1 to 2.5 meters and can be harvested up to six times a year. When broken down, the stalk of the vegetable can be used as fiber. (Photo by John Dominis/Time Life Pictures/Getty Images)

manufactured from easily renewable, cellulose-based raw materials, those recycled from protein material, and those produced from other waste products.

Easily Renewable Raw Materials for Manufactured Fiber
Chemical fiber companies, such as DuPont Invista with its Dacron® polyester or Teijin Chemical, realized that oil-based fibers, such as polyester and nylon, could not expand production to meet future fiber needs. The amount of oil devoted to fiber production will continue to decrease as oil costs rise. At the same time, regenerated cellulosic fiber, like rayon and acetate, sometimes uses wood that is not easily renewed, requiring many years before the wood can be harvested. Finding alternative, easily renewable raw material resources to replace oil and wood recently occupied fiber research. Now there are several raw material resources that have successfully been used in creating new fiber that may provide alternative choices to the traditional oil-based (e.g., polyester) and wood-based (e.g., rayon) fibers with which we are so familiar (Table 13.4).

These new fibers, using easily renewable raw materials, seem to offer an alternative to existing manufactured fiber and perhaps another option instead of natural, and especially cotton, fiber. It should be noted that many of these new fiber developments are designed to fulfill a performance function rather than to simply imitate nature (Table 13.5).

The most significant research has been to use existing crops, such as corn, to create fiber. Using a method similar to that in the creation of rayon from wood, INVISTA and Cargill, a chemical fiber company and agribusiness giant, have teamed up to find other cellulose plant materials that can be used to create new manufactured fiber. Corn was one of the first new materials that was successfully developed into a new fiber. A new generic fiber group was formed, PLA (polylactic acid), that described the basic chemical compound of the new fiber polymer. Some of the new, easily renewable, plant-based materials manufactured into textile fiber include the following:

TABLE 13-4. New manufactured fibers compared to petroleum-based fiber

Manufactured Fibers

Raw Material Source	Renewable	Pesticides/Toxic Chemicals	Fibers	Production Method	Recyclable/Biodegradable	Comments
Oil-Related			Petroleum-based			
Petroleum-based	No	No/Toxic chemicals at raw material production stage	Polyester, acrylic, olefin, spandex, nylon	Toxic by-products. Some may enter water supply	No/No	Production methods haven't considered closed cycle procedures, but new ideas are being considered. We like these fibers for their ability to be manipulated at the fiber level for performance.

Regenerated Cellulose Raw Material Source	Renewable	Pesticides/Toxic Chemicals in Fiber Production	Fibers Cellulose-based	Production Method	Recyclable/Biodegradable	Comments
Plant pulp and other wood by-products	Yes	N/A	Acetate, rayon, viscose rayon, cupramonium rayon	Toxic production and by-products into water system	N/A/Yes	Some production methods are now banned due to toxic production methods and waste material.
Plant pulp	Yes	N/A	Lyocell (specific wood crop)	Closed cycle	N/A/Yes	Trees grown especially for lyocell production. Fiber production chemicals do not enter the water supply. They are recycled into the production process immediately. Minerals absorbed into skin. Seacell® produced in Germany.
Plant pulp + kelp extract	Yes	N/A	Lyocell w/ special mineral features	Closed cycle	N/A/Yes	
Corn	Yes	Synthetic fertilizers/pesticides in crops	PLA fiber	Closed cycle	N/A/Yes	Corn is already grown for food, energy, and now fiber. Yet to be determined if pesticides and other chemicals are being controlled on nonfood corn crops.
Kenaf	Yes	No	PLA fiber	N/A	N/A/Yes	Crop is now being planted for automobile interior fabrics by Toray for Toyota and others.
Bamboo	Yes (several crops per year)	No	A type of rayon	Closed cycle or toxic production	N/A/Yes	This raw material is a type of grass that can be harvested several times in a year. Produces a very soft, absorbent, and quick-drying fiber. Naturally antibacterial feature.
Soy (tofu by-products)	Yes	N/A	Soy (tofu by-products)	Closed cycle	N/A/Yes	Fiber seems to have a beneficial character by providing amino acids on the surface of the fiber to be absorbed into the skin.

TABLE 13-5. Comparison of new manufactured fibers to cotton

Fiber regenerated cellulosic	Hand	Luster	Drape	Resiliency	Abrasion resistance	UV resistance	Anti-bacterial	Wicking	Absorbency	Quick dry	Machine washable	Dyeability	Color fastness	Heat sensitive	Thermo-plastic	Comments
Lyocell Rayon Tencel®	Excellent	Poor	Excellent	Good	Fair	Yes	No	No	Good	Good	Yes	Excellent	Good	Yes	No	
PLA (fiber made from corn, sugar beets, cane sugar, etc.) Ingeo® by INVISTA/Cargill Ecodear® by Toray Lactron® by Kanebo	Fair	Poor	Fair	Good	Poor	Excellent	No	Very good	Fair	Very good	Yes	Excellent	Good	Yes	Yes	Accepts from disperse dyes, heat transfers possible. Yarns/fabric look/feel like cotton. Very lightweight fiber.
Bamboo China Bambro Textile Co.	Excellent	Fair	Excellent	Very good	Good	Very good	Excellent	No	Excellent	Very good	Yes	Excellent	Very good	N/A	No	Test for heat-set pleating. Excellent characteristics for hospitals, underwear, bath towels.
Compared to cotton	Fair	Poor	Fair	Poor to fair	Excellent	Poor to fair	No	No	Excellent	Poor	Yes	Good	Good	No	No	
Regenerated plant protein																
Soy Swicofil, Jiangin Jinda Textile Co., Ltd.	Excellent	Excellent	Excellent	Very good	Fair	Very good	No	No	Excellent	Very good	Yes	Excellent	Very good	Poor to fair	No	Cashmere substitute. Amino acids in the fiber, which may be absorbed into the skin—a beneficial health feature.
Compared to wool	Good	Good	Good	Very good	Good	Very good	No	Good	Excellent	Fair	No	Very good	Very good	Good	No	

Corn Trade name fibers of corn (fiber group PLA) include Ingeo®, Lactron®, ClarettaCorn, and Sorona, fiber group (tirexta). This fiber is very resilient and absorbent. Abrasion resistance is similar to cotton. It seems to also have good wicking ability and thermal insulation, similar to wool. It is also thermoplastic, which means heat-setting may be possible. It also has a soft hand and good drape (Dugan, 2000). Some consider PLA a good combination of polyester and cotton in one fiber. Again, when growing corn for non-food uses, chemical use may be uncontrolled. This point should be reviewed in more detail. Also, competition for corn as an energy source (i.e., ethanol) may make corn less available for fiber production.

Bamboo This very fast-growing grass can be cut and grown repeatedly in one year (Figure 13.2). Bamboo is pest-resistant and easy to grow in many climates. Rayon produced from bamboo has a lustrous, soft hand and many of the desirable cotton characteristics of strength and absorbency, but it is faster drying than cotton. This fiber is already in use for terry-cloth towels, bed linens, and apparel. Its natural antimicrobial characteristics and faster drying capability make it a wonderful choice over cotton, especially for interior design use ("Bambro Tex," 2003).

FIGURE 13.2. Bamboo is actually a generic plant name; there are hundreds of varieties of bamboo grown for a variety of end uses. (Courtesy Library of Congress)

Kenaf This stem fiber gained acceptance as a substitute for jute during the 1940s after hemp crops were banned in the United States (Figure 13.3). Kenaf has much of the same resistance to insects and mildew as ramie and hemp (ApparelSearch, 2007). Recently, Toyota, Ford Europe, and others have been experimenting with kenaf-based manufactured fiber as an alternative to nylon, polyester, and olefin fiber in automobile upholstery and other surfaces in the car interior. In 2003, Toray announced production of Ecodear® PLA fiber using kenaf as a raw material for certain textiles used by Toyota (Toray Group, 2003). Watch the development of kenaf fiber closely, as it could be useful in replacing or supplementing nylon or polyester oil-based fibers in interior, recreational, and industrial products.

FIGURE 13.3. Kenaf is a baste fiber that has great environmental advantages for paper production. (Photo by David Nance/Courtesy USDA)

Agricultural waste Not yet in mass production, there is an effort to create a regenerated cellulosic fiber from leftover grain crops such as rice stalks (Figure 13.4).

Protein Material

Protein material, either plant-based or animal-based, has also become a viable renewable raw material. So far, three protein raw materials have been used to manufacture fiber:

Soy Though a plant, soy is protein. Soy fiber is produced using the by-products of tofu production as the raw material source. The resultant fiber is extremely soft and has been useful as a cashmere or rayon substitute (Harvest SPF Textile Co., 2003). Nearly all research on this fiber source is being conducted in Japan and China.

FIGURE 13.4. Rice stalks, considered a type of agricultural waste, are being converted to fiber in Japan. (Photo by SUKREE SUKPLANG/Reuters/Landov)

Cow's milk Similar to soy, cow's milk fiber produces a very soft hand, but seems to be a weak fiber and easily wrinkles. The soft hand makes for a very appealing product, but more research is necessary to confirm the fiber's viability for apparel products. This fiber is being produced in several countries worldwide, but only in small quantities (Swicofil, n.d.).

Chicken feathers The keratin in feathers can be regenerated into polymers (i.e., fiber strands). It is too early to know how this new fiber source can be used in production (Comis, 1998).

Waste Material to Create Fiber

Studying the use of waste as raw material for fiber production is a new idea. Rice stalks, feathers, and other waste products could find new life in fiber form. As competition from energy and food producers for other crops (e.g., corn) put pressure on fiber resources, the creation of fiber from waste material is generating more interest.

Recycling Fiber Material

Recycling fiber from apparel or other fiber-based textiles has a long history. Wool products, for example, have been recycled into a fabric called melton wool. The US Navy peacoat is traditionally produced from recycled wool, which has a very thick, felted texture, making it an ideal fabric to protect against cold, wet ocean climates.

Oil, primarily produced for energy use, is now considered a non-renewable fiber resource. The cost of oil-based fiber production will continue to escalate as the amount of available oil decreases. In addition, petroleum-based products used in fiber production require high energy use (CO_2 production). But the need to reclaim oil-based fiber (e.g., polyester, nylon, acrylic, olefin, and spandex) makes the idea of recycling more motivating. There are efforts under way to discover ways to recycle these fibers. Patagonia, the outdoor apparel company, has led the apparel industry by selecting suppliers and their fabrics that can be recycled into new fiber and fabrics. Teijin Frontier fiber mill in Japan introduced a new fiber recycling program for Capilene® polyester. The two companies worked together to encourage the consumer to return the Capilene® garments to Patagonia and then shipped them to Japan for recycling into new polyester fiber and fabrics. According to Teijin Frontier's ECO-CIRCLE, the recycled polyester fiber is indistinguishable from new "virgin" polyester, but the recycled polyester requires 70 percent less energy to produce than new polyester. Now US fiber manufacturer Unifi and textile partners are also working with Patagonia with similar recycling programs (www.Patagonia.com).

The fiber recycling concept of oil-based fibers is just beginning, and it is an important step toward conserving the amount of these fibers currently available worldwide.

Recycling today's manufactured fibers is complicated, particularly since many fabrics are often blended fiber content and have applied chemical finishing that may not be possible to separate from the fiber. It is now possible to extract polyester fiber from a cotton/polyester blended fabric. Teijin Frontier has invented such a recycling process. Research is ongoing to perfect recycling manufactured fiber.

Other fabrics, especially those that cannot be recycled into new fiber, must go to landfill. Therefore, the idea of biodegrading or composting into simple, organic compounds is now another consideration if chemically recycling fiber is not possible. However, much more research is necessary to establish healthy and clean composting of natural fiber textile products, due to the chemicals applied to the textile product. It is possible that the Permaculture Institute's encouragement of practices to introduce certain species of mushrooms that break down complex metal compounds in toxic soil could be one solution to successfully composting natural fiber fabrics. In 2002, mycologist Paul Stamets successfully partnered with the Washington State Department of Transportation to mycoremediate (break down) hydrocarbon fuel using mushrooms (Baker, 2002).

ideas in action

New awareness of fiber recyclability into new, high quality fiber is causing the athletics industry to review its use of spandex. Nearly all sports attire uses elastomeric fiber blended with wicking polyester fiber for function in active sports. Spandex, in all its trade name forms, cannot be recycled. Yet other elastomeric polyester-based fibers (which can be chemically recycled, like all polyester) are gaining recognition. Nike and other athletic apparel companies are investigating alternatives to spandex in order to create fully recyclable athletic apparel. A polyester fabric that is blended with spandex cannot be recycled. However, a polyester fabric that is blended with a polyester elastomeric fiber (such as elasterell) can be chemically recycled. While Invista is now introducing bio-based Lycra® spandex (meaning it is produced using one-third plant raw material and the remaining two-thirds petroleum raw material), the fiber does not seem to be recyclable into new fiber-like polyester fibers.

The Brave New World: Fibers by Design

With the invention of polyester microfibers back in the early 1980s, fiber production crossed the line of simply imitating nature and moved on to manipulating fiber for specific functions. Manufactured fiber today is created for specific products, such as Nike's fabrics that wick moisture away from the body, dry fast, and kill bacteria.

Though polyester microfiber was originally intended to imitate silk, the process of creating microfiber opened the way to manipulating the fiber-making process and created classes of manufactured fiber that go beyond imitating nature (Figure 13.5). Fibers are being created that fulfill the expectations of performance-based athletic and other functional apparel. By changing the fiber structure, particularly polyester, it has become possible to create manufactured fibers that can:

* *Wick moisture away from the body without absorbing moisture into the fiber.* This means that fabrics can keep the body warm and dry

without extra weight in extreme weather conditions and help prevent muscle injury during and after athletic performance.

- *Create water absorbency in non-absorbent fiber.* Polyester fibers are hydrophobic, or *non-water-absorbent*, but new fibers have been developed that actually absorb moisture, while still retaining many of the positive characteristics of the original polyester fiber.
- *Resist static electricity.* Adding certain chemicals to the pre-fiber stage, fibers that are usually poorly resistant to generating static electricity can become highly resistant.
- *Resist oil absorption in fibers that absorb oil easily.* Normally oleophyllic, fibers have been developed to resist oil absorption and to prevent unsightly oil stains from body oils and other environmental circumstances.

Today, fiber and textile producers design their products to the lifestyles of consumers who demand convenience, comfort, and fit: very lightweight, warm and dry or cool and dry, wrinkle-resistant, quick-drying, and colorfast. Designers and merchandisers are now able to

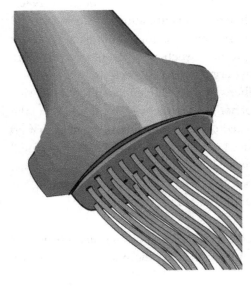

FIGURE 13.5. The size and shape of the holes on the head of the spinneret determine the dimensions of synthetic fibers like polyester. (Courtesy Fairchild Publications, Inc.)

specify how they want the fabric to look and function, and textile mills can design the fabrics using fibers and yarns to fulfill their customers' expectations.

One of the more interesting developments in textiles is the use of nanotechnology. In the case of fiber production, the use of tiny molecules at the fiber level (i.e., nano) has eliminated some of the negative aspects of the usual chemical finishing process on textiles. By reducing the molecular size of a functional (e.g., antibacterial or water-resistant) finish, it has become possible to make this finish undetectable by hand, yet the performance is very good to superior and the life of the finish is very durable. Yet to be understood are potential negative aspects of nanofinishing, such as the environmental impact of extremely small molecules absorbed into the skin, added to the wastewater, or released into the soil. In the meantime, fiber producers are using the nanofinishes with very positive performance results.

The Categories of Fiber by Design
We can now divide these fibers by design into several categories. All the time, new developments are being created; therefore the following introduction to this new fiber world is a partial list.

Pre-Fiber and Fiber Enhancements
As mentioned in discussing petroleum-based fibers that are not resistant to static electricity (e.g., polyester), it is possible to introduce new function chemical structures at the fiber solution level before the extrusion into fiber or to existing fiber. By adding performance function before the fiber is extruded or to existing fiber, more traditional (i.e., often more toxic) fabric finishing methods are avoided. The resultant fiber has a highly durable extra fiber property that is highly resistant to static electricity; highly resistant to bacteria, in some cases destroying bacteria; and water-resistant.

Intelligent Fiber

Using new chemical components, manufactured fiber can respond to temperature changes by expanding or shrinking in length and diameter. The result will be fabrics that can keep us warm or cool as the air temperature changes (Agrawal et al., 2005).

Fiber Morphology

This development of changing the physical structure of textile fibers is opening a new world of fibers and textiles, not only for apparel, but for power and light generation, as well as digital transport of data. We are just beginning to see the possibilities of these new uses for fibers, some of which are further described below.

Carbon Nanofiber Nanotubes

This microscopic fiber construction allows for heated or cool air, moisture, light, or electric charge to move along inside a mass of fiber for various purposes (Singh et al., 2004). Beginning with optic fiber in the 1960s, the idea of fiber as transport has gained momentum. There is research going on now to consider how to create electronic products that don't depend on specific wiring for power. For example, carbon fiber nanotubes may find uses in creating conductive surfaces, replacing traditional yarns or wire. By using the concept of microscopic hollow fiber tubes as the transporter, research is ongoing to create new classes of fiber and the resultant textiles for heating, cooling, light, energy, and digital transport (Kem & Lewis, 2003). Georgia Institute of Technology is one of many research labs that are working on this important new textile development (Toon & Kumar, 2004). There is discussion about using carbon fiber to create anti-gravitational features. The impact of textiles that generate power or light, provide communication, defy gravity, or provide heating and cooling can be enormous.

Composite Fiber

Enhanced fiber, created from existing manufactured fiber or natural fiber through a variety of methods and composites, include the following:

Nanocomposite fiber Used to create bioactive fabrics that will "regenerate or replenish chemical coatings and chemically active components" (National Textile Center Report, 2000).

Layered fiber Each layer is positioned for a different purpose, and the final fiber combines several features in one fiber. These fibers are designed for specific functions. The interior core is the base fiber and the outer layer is functional (e.g., water-resistant, antimicrobial, antistatic, heat-retaining, cooling). While many of the applications are on fabric finishing, there is ongoing research at the fiber level as well (US Patent 4756958).

Bicomponent fiber Bicomponent fiber is created by splitting fibers to contain more than one type of fiber. In a split fiber, chemists can place PLA (e.g., corn) and polyester, for example, within a single fiber structure, thereby combining the benefits of both fibers.

Encapsulating Fiber

By enclosing, or *encapsulating*, fibers within a fabric, it is possible to extend performance enhancement. EPIC (Encapsulated Protection Inside Clothing) by Nextec Applications, Inc. provides fabrics that breathe but are highly wind- and water-resistant. This new field of encapsulating fiber is just beginning, and further developments will emerge to enhance existing fiber with additional performance properties (Anderson, 2006).

Ultralight Fiber

There is a continuing effort to create fiber that has a very low specific gravity yet maintains all expected fiber properties (Toon & Kumar, 2004). The US military, for example, has focused on creating an ultralight army uniform and gear. Fabric has played an important role in reducing the weight of the uniform, and efforts are ongoing to lighten fabric weight even further. The early polyester and later nylon microfibers introduced us to lightweight yet functional products. However, by comparison, these early developments will seem heavy as these new fibers become more available and we understand how to use them. For example, corn-based PLA fiber has a much lighter weight than polyester (Dugan, 2000).

Genetically Engineered Fiber and Now a Synthetic Fiber

This fiber is a combination of naturally occurring sources that amount to a new raw material fiber source. For example, goat's milk, enhanced with a spider gene, has created a new, very strong yet lightweight fiber. This new fiber shows promise to replace Kevlar®, a very strong yet heavy fiber used in bulletproof and fire-resistant garments. Yet the quantity produced through goat's milk is too small. In March 2014, AmSilk, a venture capitalist-backed private company, announced it was about to begin commercial production of a synthetic version of spider silk (Scott, 2014).

Medically Enhanced Fiber

Manufactured fiber, such as lyocell rayon fiber, is produced carrying seaweed minerals along its surface to provide for absorption of those minerals through the skin. Cornell University has developed clothing for thymic cancer patients to wear that encourages absorption of needed minerals via clothing produced from specially manufactured fiber (Foundation for Thymic Cancer Research, n.d.). We are just beginning to realize the scope of medical applications using fiber as the carrier of health benefits and for tissue engineering (Abel et al., 2003).

Conclusion: What are the Fashion Industry's Next Steps?

In presenting how fiber choice is expanding and changing fabrics, designers and merchandisers must make it their priority to ask several important questions when sourcing fabrics. Is natural fiber important? If so, can chemical-free fiber, as opposed to organically grown fiber, be used, or perhaps a less-known natural fiber? What are the new manufactured fibers? What are their positive features and drawbacks? How can the use of these newly enhanced fibers add value to products?

Could the textile and fashion industry market a globally recognized logo that communicates "good fiber choice for the environment," similar to the internationally recognized care symbols required on all apparel? As the fashion industry is globally sourced, produced, and sold, international symbols that are recognized throughout the world would be of great help in promoting positive fiber choices by suppliers, designers, merchandisers, and consumers. The standards must be developed to include the following: organically grown fiber, chemical-free fiber, closed-cycle production fiber, biodegradable fiber, and recyclable fiber (see Figure 13.6).

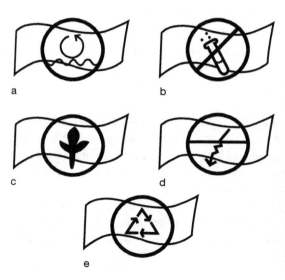

FIGURE 13.6. Graphic symbols, functioning like current international care symbols, could be developed to represent: (a) closed-cycle fiber production; (b) toxic chemical-free fiber production; (c) organically grown fiber; (d) biodegradable fiber; (e) recyclable fiber, fabrics, and garments. (Illustrations by Kristina Berberich-O'Toole from symbols courtesy of Mark Baugh-Sasaki)

Ongoing fiber research has acknowledged the need to change the way fiber is produced. Apparel fabrics have moved from simple protection and adornment uses of fiber into a world of fiber manipulation for both aesthetic and performance designs, with an enhanced definition of body adornment. Fiber is again the engine for change in textile production. From the new fiber information provided in this chapter, it is obvious that the fashion industry has many options from which to choose. The fashion industry, previously focused on pure aesthetics, must develop a new standard in defining fashion with an environmental sensitivity and an artistic balance.

Discussion Questions

1   *Alternative fiber choice*: What fiber options, based on absorbency and ability to dry quickly, could be alternative choices to absorbent fiber that must be dried in a dryer?
2   *Chemically recycling fiber option*: When designing athletic performance apparel, what fiber can be chemically recycled into new fiber? Briefly describe the process.
3   *Adding additional performance functions to fiber*: How can a fiber mill create a manufactured fiber with new performance characteristics?

References

Abel, T., Cohen, J. I., Escalera, J., Engel, R., Filshtinskaya, M., Fincher, R., Melkonian, A., & Melkonian, K. (2003). New trends in biotextiles: The challenge of tissue engineering. *Journal of Apparel, Textile, and Management*, 3(2). Retrieved February 18, 2007, from http://www.tx.ncsu.edu/jtatm/volume3issue2/vo3_issue2_abstracts.htm.

Agrawal, A. K., Jassal, M., Save, N. S., Periyasamy, S., Ghosh, A. K., Ramasubramani, K. R. T., Vishnoi, A., Palanikkumaran, M., & Gupta, K. K. (2005). Environmentally responsive smart textiles—II. Retrieved

February 18, 2007, from http://www.expresstextile.com/20050515/hiperformance01s.html.

Allen, W. (2004). Cotton subsidies and cotton problems. Organic Consumers Association. Retrieved March 26, 2007, from http://www.organicconsumers.org/clothes/224subsidies.cfm.

Anderson, K. (2006). Innovate or disintegrate: The latest in textile finishes. Retrieved February 18, 2007, from http://www.techexchange.com/thelibrary/innovateor.html.

ApparelSearch description of kenaf fiber. (2007). Retrieved February 18, 2007, from www.apparelsearch.com/kenaf_description.htm.

Approved Certification Bodies. (March, 2014). Retrieved June 8, 2014, from http://www.global-standard.org/certification/approved-certification-bodies.html.

Baker, L. (2002, November 25). How mushrooms will save the world. *Salon.com*. Retrieved August 21, 2014, from http://www.salon.com/2002/11/25/mushrooms/.

Bambro Tex's description of bamboo fiber patented manufacture and fiber characteristics. (2003). Retrieved February 18, 2007, from http://www.bambrotex.com/second/bamboocenter_nab.htm.

Baugh, G. (2011). *The fashion designer's textile directory: A guide to fabrics' properties, characteristics, and garment – design potential.* New York: Barron's Educational Series.

Better Cotton Initiative Annual Report. (2013). Bettercotton.org. Retrieved June 8, 2014, from http://bettercotton.org/wp-content/uploads/2014/04/BCI-Annual-Report-2013-web.pdf.

Bio-polyester used in mass-produced electric cars. (2012, November 26). Innovation in Textiles. Retrieved June 10, 2014, from http://www.innovationintextiles.com/biopolyester-used-in-mass-produced-electric-car/.

Borromeo, L. (2014). Technology could allow hemp and flax to break cotton's global hold on textiles. *The Guardian*. Retrieved November 10, 2014, from http://www.theguardian.com/sustainable-business/hemp-flax-bast-cotton-crailar.

Comis, D. (1998). Chicken feathers: Eco-friendly "plastics" of the twenty-first century? United States Department of Agriculture. Retrieved February 18, 2007, from www.ars.usda.gov/is/pr/1998/980209.htm.

Dodes, R. (2011). Hemmed in by cotton, Hanes eases into flax. *Wall Street Journal*. http://online.wsj.com/news/articles/SB10001424052748703696704576222800474866630.

Dugan, J. S. (2000). Novel properties of PLA fibers. Fiber Innovation Technology, Inc. Retrieved February 18, 2007, from www.fitfibers.com/publications.htm.

Foundation for Thymic Cancer Research. (n.d.). Protective clothing initiative. Retrieved February 18, 2007, from http://www.thymic.org/clothing/initiative.htm.

Harvest SPF Textile Co., Ltd. (2003). Soybean protein fiber description and history. Retrieved March 26, 2007, from www.spftex.com.

Invista unveils renewable, bio-based Lycra material. (June 2, 2014). The Living Principles. Retrieved June 9, 2014, from http://www.livingprinciples.org/invista-unveils-renewable-bio-based-lycra-material/.

Kem, Y. K. & Lewis, A. F. (2003). Concepts for energy-interactive textiles. Materials Research Society. Retrieved March 26, 2007, from www.mrs.org/s_mrs/sec_subscribe.asp?DID=168004&CID=2985&SID-1&VID=113&R.

McCollough, D. G. (2014, April 25). Deforestation for fashion: getting unsustainable fabrics out of the closet. *The Guardian*, UK. Retrieved August 5, 2014, from http://www.theguardian.com/sustainable-business/zara-h-m-fashion-sustainable-forests-logging-fabric.

National Organic Program's Labeling Packaged Products Table. (2003).

National Textile Center Report, Project #M00-D08. (2000). Nano-composite fibers. Retrieved February 18, 2007, from http://www.ntcresearch.org/pdf-rpts/AnRp00/m00-d03.pdf.

NCLS (National Conferences of State Legislatures). (September, 2014). State industrial hemp statutes. Retrieved November 1, 2014, from http://www.ncsl.org/research/agriculture-and-rural-development/state-industrial-hemp-statutes.aspx.

Organic Consumer Association. (July 31, 2014). *Cotton: From the field to your closet*. Retrieved February 17, 2015, from https://www.organicconsumers.org/news/cotton-field-your-closet.

Rainforest News. (2013, October 31). Retrieved June 10, 2014, from http://www.salvaleforeste.it/en/become-active/3672-la-deforestazione-%C3%A8-di-moda-rayon-e-viscosa-sotto-accusa-2.html.

Scott, A. (2014, March 3). Spider silk poised for commercial entry. *Chemical and Engineering News, 92*(9), 24–7. Retrieved August 21, 2014, from http://cen.acs.org/articles/92/i9/Spider-Silk-Poised-Commercial-Entry.html.

Singh, K. V., et al. (2004). *Applications and future applications of nanotechnology in textiles*. Retrieved March 26, 2007, from www.utexas.edu/centers/nfic/fc/files/nanocot.pdf.

Sustainable Table's definition of organically grown crops and certified organic labeling. (2014). Retrieved June 8, 2014, from http://www.sustainabletable.org/issues/organic/.

Swicofil AG Textile Services milk fiber characteristics. (n.d.). Retrieved February 18, 2007, from www.swicofil.com/products/212milk_fiber_casein.html.

Toon, J. & Kumar, S. (2004). New class of fibers: Composites made with carbon nanotubes offer improved mechanical & electrical properties. Georgia Research Tech News, Georgia Institute of Technology. Retrieved February 18, 2007, from http://gtresearchnews.gatech.edu/newsrelease/nanofibers.htm.

Toray Group press release. (2003). Toray starts production of automobile upholstery material. Retrieved February 18, 2007, from http://www.toray.com/news/fiber/nr030513.html.

United States Department of Agriculture. Retrieved March 26, 2007, from http://www.ams.usda.gov/nop/ProdHandlers/LabelTable.htm.

United States Patent 4756958. (n.d.). Fiber with reversible enhanced thermal storage properties and fabrics made there from. Retrieved March 26, 2007, from http://www.freepatentsonline.com/4756958.html.

USDA OK's Organic Textile Labeling Including GOTS. (2011). Retrieved June 8, 2014, from http://www.organicnewsroom.com/2011/06/usda_oks_organic_textile_label.html.

SHONA BARTON QUINN is an apparel industry executive currently serving as the Sustainability Leader at Eileen Fisher. This chapter examines how ethical, social, and environmental issues are addressed by apparel companies. Ms. Quinn holds a Master's degree in Industrial Ecology from the Yale School of Forestry & Environmental Studies.

CHAPTER 14

Sustainable Sourcing

Shona Barton Quinn

From design considerations through production and distribution, fashion industry executives make many decisions that impact the environment. By incorporating sustainable sourcing practices into the business plan, a holistic strategy emerges that capitalizes on system-wide teams, supply chain relationships, raw material assessment, geographical location, and cost analysis.

Connecting Sustainability and Sourcing

It's Fashion Week in New York. Design students love it. They dress models backstage and look for famous people. Meanwhile, designers and CEOs cross their fingers and hope that buyers and writers like the show. Much inspires these shows; even planet Earth is a source of inspiration. But the link between fashion and Mother Nature typically stops on the runway. Sustainable sourcing strives to inspire design and production decisions across the entire supply chain to justly link sustainability with brand identity.

"But," one may say, "sourcing is complicated enough without sustainability." That response is a fair one. Sourcing managers have to contend with price, quality, time, vendor relations, and regional issues.

Yet incorporating environmental issues into these criteria may simplify sourcing strategies while adding value to the brand. Fashion executives who want to incorporate sustainability into their decision making must fully understand where products come from, how they are processed, and where they go when the customer is finished with them.

Executives might start by asking this question: *Is our company meeting the needs of the present without compromising the ability to meet our needs in the future?*

The question is adapted from the official United Nations definition on Sustainable Development (Brundtland et al., 1987). When considered appropriately, it should lead executives to contemplate the areas of their supply network that rely on environmental and social capital.

This exploration can lead to a logical conclusion: While it is important to have goals, it is challenging to create garments that have no negative impact on people and the planet. Accordingly, sustainable sourcing is best considered an ongoing practice with ever-increasing possibilities; a journey toward innovative ways of making, using, and recycling clothing. It is complex, never-ending work that can add value and improve business metrics if applied correctly.

Viewing Business Strategy Holistically

Over the last decade the apparel industry has gone through a transformation in its business strategy. Many large retailers are competing over who can sell the most units at the lowest price. While lowering prices may drive revenue and appeal to a larger customer base, it may also be undermining social and environmental standards farther up the supply chain. Sustainable sourcing requires a shift in strategy. Manufacturers must look beyond getting the most fashionable and lowest-priced garments to the selling floor, and adjust to a more connected world, building trust and creating a sourcing strategy that works for the long term.

Legitimate sustainable sourcing managers understand the importance of the *who, what,* and *how* of sourcing as opposed to *more* and *cheaper.* Additionally, a sustainability executive is not only aware of the customer's needs and the supplier's capabilities, but also views a garment in holistic terms, considering all aspects of its life cycle (Figure 14.1). This includes raw material extraction, manufacturing process, consumer use and reuse, and recyclability or compostability. Each stage of the life cycle will have environmental, social, and economic impacts, such as the availability and efficient use of materials, energy, and water. In addition, availability of workers and wage rates at field and factory level is continually shifting, affecting family and local community dynamics.

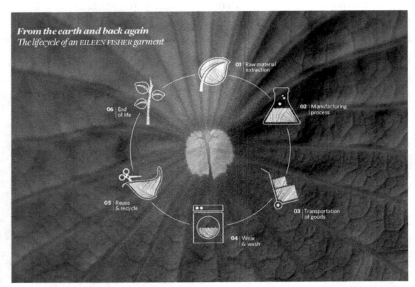

FIGURE 14.1. Life cycle clothing flow chart. (Drawing adapted from T. E. Graedel & B. R. Allenby [2003], *Industrial Ecology,* Prentice Hall)

Why Sustainable Sourcing Matters

The emergence of sustainability within the fashion industry is happening for many reasons, which include a rising awareness of: environmental stresses, human rights, legal risk mitigation, government regulations, and Internet connectivity (Esty & Winston, 2006). This section considers the role these issues play in the development of sustainable sourcing in the fashion industries.

Building Environmental Awareness

The concept of sustainability is not an invention of the late twentieth century. It is deeply rooted in many previous cultures. Societies on every continent in the pre-industrial era, from Senegalese farmers to European foresters, understood the importance of nurturing the conditions on which life depends (Grober, 2012).

Yet the twentieth century stands out because it was a time of major technological and scientific progress. World population grew from 1.6 billion in 1900 to 6 billion by 1999 (US Census Bureau, n.d). Transportation evolved from horse and buggy to automobiles, high-speed trains, and commercial air travel. Through developments in information technology, people became more connected and aware of social and environmental issues impacting the world.

In 1962, Rachel Carson published *Silent Spring*. For Americans, this helped to establish the environmental movement of the late twentieth century. Mainstream US culture in the early 1970s was exposed to many forms of environmental media—Dr. Seuss's book *The Lorax*; Keep America Beautiful's Public Service Announcement about pollution featuring a Native American; Joni Mitchell's song "Big Yellow Taxi" with its chorus, "They paved paradise to put up a parking lot"; and movies like *The China Syndrome* and *Soylent Green*.

In 1987, the UN's World Commission on Environment and Development published "Our Common Future," raising the level of urgency for action around environmental issues (Herrmann et al., 2014, p. 472).

By the late twentieth century, scientists, corporate leaders, politicians, and civil society were beginning to see the linkages between big issues—population growth, economic growth, energy needs, air pollution, water pollution—and depletion of resources. Concerns around the planet's natural capacity, limits of growth, and human health impacts were now understood by a wide range of people.

Yet, unfortunately, today sourcing managers still face pressure to respond to a growth-oriented business model, ignoring the limits of growth. Beyond cost-cutting initiatives, like reducing waste through efficiencies, many social and environmental issues are kept at arm's length from the core business strategy. But businesses interested in long-term viability will need to put sustainability issues within the core decision-making process or face future risks to both business and the broader society.

Stepping on the Shoulders of Social Responsibility

In the early 1980s many US retailers and brand labels began shifting their production to developing countries to take advantage of lower labor costs. Unfortunately, most of these companies were unaware of or uninterested in the factory environment in which their goods were produced. Labor advocacy groups began researching and publicizing the exploitation of factory workers and pinned responsibility on brands like Nike and Wal-Mart's Kathie Lee Gifford. Hastily, legal departments at apparel companies created codes of conduct to protect themselves from the liabilities associated with labor rights violations within their supply networks. Additionally, brands invested in factory audits to protect their corporate reputations. The focus on labor issues also brought increased awareness and growth of sustainable initiatives.

Today, apparel companies with established sustainability policies are proactively reducing risk by encouraging suppliers to look at the entire system of activities and resources linked to their business, including but not limited to management, processes, raw materials, and workers' needs. This holistic approach better enables factories to manage both social and environmental compliance issues and run more efficiently.

Mitigating Risk and Regulatory Barriers by Being Proactive

Governments at all levels dramatically influence the behavior of businesses—through laws, policies, taxes/subsidies, country-wide goals, and as large buyers of goods. In addition, governments at all levels are incorporating sustainability into new regulations. If a company's sourcing department does not follow developing international policies, it may lose business in the regulated region when products don't conform to the law. For example, due to the complexity of textile chemical regulations worldwide, EILEEN FISHER became a member of Bluesign Technology. One membership benefit is regular updates on emerging chemical regulations that help EILEEN FISHER keep suppliers informed of new governmental laws.

Building Societal Trust

Acting as both consumers and producers, businesses should hold themselves accountable by understanding their role in conserving resources (Figure 14.2). Corporations build trust within society by embracing sustainability.

Communication through the Internet has changed the playing field. Traditionally, companies had control of their message. Today they do not. The Internet offers a broader scope of information to society, both good and bad. Media has helped put environmental issues on center stage. Brands can only overcome negative attacks by being honest and transparent about their interests in contributing to society. By looking after this aspect of its reputational capital, a company creates a motivating work environment, a loyal supply chain, and a trusted image.

FIGURE 14.2. Few companies are fully aware of their carbon emissions, but full disclosure is essential if greenhouse gas emissions are to be constrained. (Photo by Paul Ellis/AFP/Getty Images)

The first sections of this chapter have covered what sustainable sourcing is and why it has emerged within the fashion industry. The next section reviews key components of environmental stewardship and sourcing.

Key Components to Environmental Stewardship and Sourcing

A sourcing executive's decision on where to produce clothing is based on several key criteria: individual commitment, company commitment, strong supply networks and partnerships, access to materials, cost of goods, and location. This section shows how each of these criteria can be incorporated into sustainable sourcing practices.

The Depth of Commitment: Individual, Company, and Supply Network

For positive change within a supply network to happen, mind-sets need to change. This includes an individual's mind-set, a company's mind-set, and the mind-set of the broader supply network. No easy task.

As a sustainable sourcing manager, one cannot underestimate the power of mind-set and building trusting relationships. As part of creating big shifts, there will be a strong need for collective seeing, learning, and doing (Kania et al., 2014). But before we discuss collective impact, let us consider the individual.

Individual Commitment

> *"A significant part of the pleasure of eating is in one's accurate consciousness of the lives and the world from which the food comes."*
>
> —Wendell Berry, "The Pleasure of Eating"

Individual mind-set connects to sustainability in many ways. Here are two examples:

- knowing our connection to the Earth's natural systems;
- understanding our real desires as humans.

Sometimes we forget that "with every breath and every mouthful of water, every one of our cells is in contact with the Earth" (Grober, 2012). We're in need of Earth. Earth is not in need of us. It is the human race that needs to be concerned about survival, not Earth. So, when considering what to do about environmental problems, slow your thinking and go deeper—down to each cell in your body. After some reflection about one's place within the natural world, perhaps each individual can begin to contribute to a sustainable society (Grober, 2012).

In *Good News for a Change*, David Suzuki and Holly Dressel share:

We reflected on what had brought each of us the most personal
happiness in the past. This exercise made us realize that, beyond
the very basic levels, our separate experiences of satisfaction,
contentment and joy had very little to do with material
consumption and comforts. They had more to do with
connections with others, with feeling useful and, amazingly
enough, with sharing everything – from food and feelings to
ideas and beliefs. (Suzuki & Dressel, 2002)

Company Commitment

> "Until we have a reasonable idea of where we want to go, we are unlikely to get there."
> —David C. Korten, *The Post-Corporate World*

At the corporate level, sustainability starts with a company's
commitment to the issue. Once the commitment is made, staff must
be educated about sustainability and its link to corporate growth.
Although staff members may understand there are some environmental
impacts linked to the fashion business, they may not tie it directly to
their jobs. Developing a training program will give staff a clear
understanding of the components of sustainability and how they can
contribute to a greener supply network. This should include a
sustainability plan that takes a systemic approach to business and
product development by reviewing all aspects of the company's
environmental footprint, including the life cycle of garments produced.

When taking a holistic approach to sustainability and corporate
development, people from within the organization as well as the firm's
network of stakeholders should be considered. One of the most
important areas is design. Engaging designers in the process allows a
company to filter out many of the toxic compounds that might be used
in its products and incorporate greener substitutes at the point of product

creation. There are many issues to consider when creating a garment, such as corporate image, consumer needs, price, quality, and innovation. Layering on environmental aspects may overwhelm a designer unless a thoughtful approach is taken. Because designers are often detached from the environmental impacts of a product, it will be important to create a system-wide team that includes experts from other product stages to tackle these challenges. Sustainable sourcing requires a more thorough knowledge of the supply chain, therefore educating designers will be an important aspect of its success (Lofthouse & Bhamra, 2000).

System-wide sustainability teams may have two or three layers: the core team, the extended team, and the external stakeholders. The core team includes a sourcing executive, a manufacturing engineer, a designer, and a sustainability expert. The extended team may include a market researcher, a legal counselor, a logistics manager, a sales manager, and key suppliers. For example, a chemical supply company may play an important role within the extended team by offering green chemistry alternatives to the core team and ultimately to the dye and finishing houses within the supply network. External stakeholders may include non-profit groups, government agencies, trade associations, and local communities. Fostering collaboration among industry businesses through external stakeholders, such as trade associations and non-profit groups, has allowed companies to share results of factory assessments, reducing the number of audits per factory, making both the supplier's and the buyer's job easier.

Figure 14.3 is an illustration of structure of a system-wide sustainability team. The links among system-wide teams can be demonstrated through the most common design elements. For example, connections among chemical companies, designers, and dye houses will be one of the new dynamics to selecting finishes; this connection will allow the designer to evaluate fabric options not only on aesthetics but also with respect to environmental impacts. As part of creating a sustainable supply chain, the core team should assess their current business relations, product categories, and marketing strategies with the following tactics:

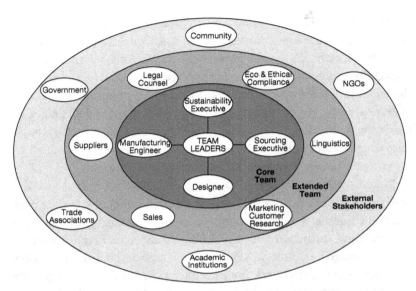

FIGURE 14.3. Structure of a system-wide sustainability team. (Adapted from T. E. Graedel & B. R. Allenby, *Industrial Ecology* [2003], Pearson Education)

1   Rank current suppliers by importance and identify potentially green suppliers. Would creating a smaller, simpler supply chain allow the company to build a sustainable supply chain more effectively and efficiently?

2   Rank fabrications based on importance and sustainable traits. Then brainstorm on how to incorporate sustainable characteristics into each fabrication.

3   Review customer satisfaction polls and SKU (stock keeping unit) counts. If the company can satisfy customer demand by making fewer quality garments that sell with a higher margin than many styles with the same functionality but a lower margin, the company will succeed in generating equivalent or higher profits using less material. Additionally, there may be a market segment the company is missing that can be filled through eco-innovative products or services.

The core team should then consider these questions when reviewing the sustainability of its supply chain:

1   Is this the right product for our customer?
2   Where do the raw materials for the product come from?
3   If it is a natural or regenerated fiber, is the supplier using sustainable practices to produce and extract the raw material?
4   If it is a synthetic fiber, what percentage of the raw material is made of high quality recycled content?
5   Does the supplier have a successful management system (e.g., the International Organization for Standardizations environmental management standards—ISO14001) in place with an appointed compliance manager?
6   How energy-efficient is the machinery used in the production process?
7   Are green chemistry concepts being used to pretreat, dye, and finish the fabric?
8   Is the dye house investing in closed-loop water systems?
9   How many miles does the fiber travel throughout its life cycle (i.e., from raw material extraction to production process to retailer to consumer)?
10   What mode of transportation is being used?
11   Can the same high quality garment be produced with less material?
12   What percentage of fabric waste is produced when making a product?
13   Are workers' rights respected? (See International Labour Organization's website for example of standards: www.ilo.org/ public/english/standards/norm).
14   Can this product be returned to the retailer, repaired, recycled, or composted by the consumer?

This series of questions should foster ideas within the sustainability team, allowing the company to consider which strategy it will take to develop a sustainable sourcing plan. The questions will also allow the team to contemplate alternative strategies for sourcing, such as location and product miles. The next part of this section addresses supply chain relationships.

EILEEN FISHER: Focusing on the First and Last Mile of a Garment

Where does this shirt come from? And where will it go? At EILEEN FISHER, we explore these questions every day. The design, merchandising, manufacturing, and sales teams all understand the significant environmental and social opportunities linked to our product.

EILEEN FISHER staff continually strive to leverage its strengths around intentional design, high quality natural materials, and well-being to create a clothing line that our customers are proud to wear over and over again.

FIGURE S14.1. EILEEN FISHER garment. (Courtesy EILEEN FISHER)

The EILEEN FISHER supply chain is big and complex, so a few priorities are set. One is to focus on the first mile of a garment—the raw material. About 90 percent of EILEEN FISHER raw materials come from farms and forests.

It is at this first mile where the perceived limitless expansion of clothing will face the realities of a limited world. These land-reliant materials can be the focal point of conflict—over land, water, and other resources. This is where the sourcing manager sees an industry's dependency and impacts on ecosystems (Meyers, 2011).

The Business Planning Department tracks EILEEN FISHER's annual growth of environmentally preferred materials. Over ten years of slow and steady progress, environmentally preferred materials grew to account for over 40 percent of the company's product line.

More recently, EILEEN FISHER began focusing on the last mile of a garment with a take-back program called GREEN EILEEN. Gently used garments may be returned by customers for credit toward a new purchase. Some used items are resold, extending the useful life of the garment.

Currently, we are researching how to recover cellulose from plant-based worn-out clothing to make new clothes, thereby reducing EILEEN FISHER's impact at the first mile by using resources recovered from the last mile.

Building Relationships within Supply Networks

Beyond deciding where to source material or produce garments, fashion executives need to engage with suppliers on the importance of incorporating sustainability into management plans. Important components of this are high level commitment, open communication, trust, and a genuine interest to build a sustainable supply network.

Unfortunately, the apparel industry does not have a good track record of building long-term relationships within the supply chain. Factories and textile regions go out of fashion as quickly as the latest skirt length. Suppliers believe, for good reason, that buyers see low cost as a priority over building deeper, long-term relationships.

It's helpful when brands acknowledge their own shortcomings—like inconsistent buying practices and its impact on a supplier's operations. A buyer's habits of constant price pressure, a noncommittal policy, incessant requests for shorter order cycles, and frequent changes in orders need to be relayed to corporate executives as a serious business disadvantage for both parties (Bremer, 2005).

When companies build stronger ties within their supply chain, factories have a clearer understanding of the brand's direction and can make proactive business decisions (Liker & Choi, 2004). Contradictory to this, if the relationship is superficial, it will only lead to temporary improvement. A supplier may try to be compliant with a company's code of conduct, but if there is no real commitment to managerial change from the supplier level, the effort will dissipate or, worse, lead to cover-up (Hurst, Murdoch, & Gould, 2005).

Brands should view supplier relationships as collaborative and value the importance of long-term mutual benefits. The supply network should create time for collective learning and doing, exchanging knowledge and developing shared goals that will define their system-wide approach to a sustainable business partnership.

Once these kinds of positive relationships are created, the supplier will achieve results that go beyond just lowering costs. Additional benefits may include technology upgrades, flexibility with changing conditions, quicker turns, and higher quality products (Liker and Choi, 2004).

Coordination throughout the supply chain is a key component for all companies, but for sustainable sourcing, it is crucial. A clear communication channel should be established and each member's interests incorporated into the sustainability strategy. This approach converts the supply chain into a knowledge network and allows each member to understand the common threads linking sustainability to the supply network (Goldbach, 2002).

Figure 14.4 demonstrates various stakeholders within a supply network. It is important for brand or retailer to go beyond their primary supply chain partners and engage deeper into the supply

FIGURE 14.4. Finding common ground. (Adapted from A. Ionescu-Somers & U. Steger [2008], *Business Logic for Sustainability: A Food and Beverage Industry Perspective*, Palgrave Macmillan, p. 39)

network to understand the common environmental or ethical issues. Eventually independent transactions become a part of a highly coordinated network (Goldbach, 2002).

There are two different but related aspects to supply chain management. One is focused on the overarching common issues among stakeholders. The other is the focus on the operational management at one specific facility within the supply network and the potential for sharing this knowledge with supply chain partners.

The Supply Network

Brands know that when considering the entire supply network engagement, coordinating stakeholders can be complex. But it offers an opportunity to partner in new ways, defining objectives and creating efficiencies. It also encourages suppliers to test new ideas and become confident around sustainability issues. Trade associations and non-profits can help facilitate engagement among brands and suppliers. Two examples of non-profits engaging in this work are the Sustainable Apparel Coalition (SAC) and Textile Exchange (TE).

Following are two questions when considering sustainable sourcing:

1   What sustainability issue common to all stakeholders in the supply chain may be worth addressing as a group?
2   Why might it be important to allow different supply chains to use different solutions to solve the same environmental problem?

Facility-based Issues

Well-managed operations within a manufacturing facility are a key value to business partners and should be recognized—specifically by the buyer or brand downstream. If an agent is between the brand and manufacturing facility, it may create a communication barrier. Therefore, it is important for brands to reach out beyond the agent and engage with the supply network.

A well-managed facility will most likely be engaging in some or all of the following management practices:

- Tracks operational inputs and the potential for using renewable inputs.
- Tracks outputs and develops processes for reuse.
- Implements energy, water, and material conservation practices.
- Invests in more efficient and/or sustainable technologies (example: closed-loop technologies).

- Practices lean management techniques—finding and eliminating waste. This includes reducing process time, defects, and inventory levels.
- Finds linkages between operational, quality, and sustainability management systems and standards.
- Engages in a continual process improvement to become more flexible and aligned with buyer's needs.
- Engages in earlier development steps with buyer (example: pre-production coordination).

In addition, a progressive brand may also be reviewing product life cycle issues and considering how to coordinate forward and reverse flows of their products. Examples can include extending a product's life through repair and reuse, and later, at the end-of-life stage, pursuing partnerships with suppliers developing technologies that will create value from end-of-life products through remanufacturing.

Fiber Sourcing Options

"Our foresters have studied economics, but they haven't studied the forest ecosystem, which is the basis of the whole thing."
—Merv Wilkinson, Forester and Landowner

Knowing the *where* and *who* of sustainable sourcing is important, but one also needs to consider the *what*. What materials are being sourced? Choosing fabric has many environmental aspects attached to it. Ranking tools, like Made-By's *Environmental Benchmark for Fibers* or the Sustainable Apparel Coalition's *Material Sustainability Index (MSI)* are helping designers review material options.

Within one fiber classification, like cotton, there can be many options a designer can choose from. Incorporating social and environmental issues within cotton fiber production generally proceeds in one of three scenarios: a fair-trade standard that focuses on social issues, an organic standard that addresses environmental issues, or best management practices (BMP) that may focus on environmental, social, and economic issues. A company's goal may be to capture all three aspects of sustainability (i.e., social, environmental, and economic) with one standard, but each system has specific strengths.

The fair-trade standard aims to make sure farmers are paid a fair wage. While fair trade also has an environmental component, it focuses on the well-being of the farmer. Alternatively, organic and BMP farming promote ecologically sound growing methods. Still, organic and BMP differ as well. Organic production focuses on the avoidance of synthetic chemicals and genetically modified organisms. BMP encourages the reduction of chemical use but may not ban it. Additionally, BMP tends to be neutral regarding genetically engineered crops. For example, if a chemical company develops a seed considered "drought-tolerant," it may be acceptable for production under BMP guidelines. It is important to a sourcing manager to review all these options and decide which standard makes sense for his or her sustainability goals.

A New Resource: Recycled Fibers

As mentioned earlier, waste can be recycled into new products. Governments may be the initiators of this new resource. The European Union introduced regulations for producers known as Extended Producer Responsibility (EPR), requiring producers to take back goods from consumers after their useful life is over. Although many companies see this as simply another forced policy initiative, it is intended to act as a market incentive that will encourage companies to find innovative ways to create new products from old materials (Mayers, France, & Cowell, 2005).

US citizens are the largest consumers of products and, therefore, the largest producers of waste. But most US companies do not view waste as a resource for new raw materials. Teijin and Toray, two Japanese polyester and nylon textile producers, have found a profitable way to recycle material and produce new material. However, it is important to note that when using recycled content in new products, one must be aware of the quality and source of the recycled material. Companies do not want products that contain harmful toxins. For the textile industry, there are opportunities to create technologically advanced recycling plants that classify waste, identify fibers, and test for hazardous compounds.

Bar code or radio frequency identification (RFID) tags, containing information about where the garment came from and its physical and chemical characteristics, could also aid in the end-of-life stage. Beyond helping corporate buyers trace their products or use as a marketing tool, these tags could identify fibers and garments, sorting and recycling them based on quality or fiber content.

Costing Corporate Values

The wise and moral man
Shines like a flower on a hilltop
Making money like a bee
Who does not hurt the flower.
The Pali Canon (500 BC)

"How much will it cost?" is an important question, yet many fashion executives spend little time researching the answer. Direct costs, which include materials and labor, have always been the focus of costing. Indirect costs (i.e., everything but materials, labor, and trim) are less well understood and therefore sometimes missed. David Birnbaum, author and apparel industry consultant, created a flow chart showing 101 steps needed to produce a style. He says that only 15 percent of these steps are direct costs; the other 85 percent are indirect costs, such as the employment of designers, sales staff, and website developers (Birnbaum, 2003). Birnbaum points out the importance of finding the critical cost drivers of a business by looking beyond how much fabric costs and what sewers make.

For sustainable sourcing, this entails looking at not only the garment's costs but at the entire supply chain, pinpointing critical cost drivers, and using specific accounting measures to analyze the problem.

For example, currently the retail price of organic apparel is higher than conventional apparel because the social and natural investments associated with organic fibers are not valued by many brands. Organic cotton farmers are paid more for their product than conventional cotton farmers. The higher premium is much deserved because organic farming is labor-intensive. In addition, organic farming protects environmental resources, like water, air, soil, and biodiversity, yet many businesses are still reluctant to incorporate social and natural capital into their costing analysis.

The higher cost of organic at the fiber level is multiplied at each stage of production and ends up creating a large gap between the retail prices of organic versus conventional apparel, referred to as the "multiplication effect." By looking at the entire chain, a sourcing manager can identify this magnification of raw material costs and partner with suppliers to reduce the inflated price (Brooks, Davidson, & Palamides, 1993).

In addition, the cost of resources—like materials, energy, water, and chemicals—will continue to increase as resources are constrained. These increases will promote operational improvement to capture and use by-products that are currently wasted. But in order for manufacturing facilities to upgrade technologies and capture waste, they may also need access to more capital. As new financial models are explored, brands may consider being a guarantor of funds to suppliers investing in sustainable technologies. So perhaps beyond asking, "How much does it cost?" a company might consider asking themselves, "What sustainability values should be embedded in our costs?".

Location: Global and Local Options

Based on statistics from panjiva.com, over 70 percent of the world's countries are part of the textile and apparel sector. The industry is both global and local. But due to widespread dispersion of apparel supply networks, global is more the norm and clothing companies are built upon that reality.

Furthermore, when considering plant and animal based fibers, due to natural adaptation and/or societal choices, there are specific regions where certain plants or animals thrive. For example, most alpaca fiber comes from Peru and cotton needs a specific climate to flourish.

Finally, as a result of Internet technology, supply networks spanning the globe are much more connected. Moving materials halfway around the world is easier as shipping companies build networks that flex with buyers' needs; meanwhile, concerns about miles traveled is left in the hands of company personnel measuring carbon emissions.

Mapping Regions to Mitigate Risk

Water, one of the global economy's most vital resources, is at risk, especially in developing countries. In general, there are three sectors in the apparel industry that use large amounts of water: agriculture, dyeing and finishing, and home washing. While the textile industry doesn't want water to be a limiting factor of doing business, it is slow to respond. Companies are just beginning to classify supplier locations by water use and efficiency potential.

Large corporations interested in a long-term supply of raw materials can assess drought risk of farm or forestry regions using new mapping technology. For example, tracing and overlaying a company's cotton production map over a drought map will allow a company to see where the hot spots are and prevent a future risk in the deficiency of raw materials due to water scarcity.

Here are a few questions one might wish to consider, if using raw materials from farms or forests:

Understanding the Difference between Transparency and Traceability

A supplier may be willing to verify through documentation where a product comes from but for competitive reasons be more resistant about sharing the location of specific sources of materials. When facilitating supplier relations, it is helpful to be aware of these concerns.

Traceability is the ability to verify the history, location, or application of an item by means of documented recorded identification (ASME Boiler and Pressure Vessel Code, n.d.).

Transparency implies openness, communication, and accountability. Transparency is operating in such a way that it is easy for others to see what actions are performed. It has been defined simply as "the perceived quality of intentionally shared information from a sender" (Schnakenberg & Tomlinson, 2014).

1   In what region of the world is the firm's raw material grown/raised?
2   Is the region at risk of water scarcity?
3   Are fields rain-fed or irrigated? If irrigation is used, is it done efficiently (e.g., drip irrigation)?
4   If a tree plantation, does growing trees significantly impact the local water table?

Sourcing Locally

Towns across the world have historically been built around an industry, and the apparel trade was a key driver of this movement. Mill towns developed near factories producing textile products. Today, global supply networks are more prevalent than local but some sourcing executives are considering the advantages of local industry, referring to them as supply chain cities and bioregionalism.

Supply Chain Cities

The supply chain city was the brainchild of Henry Tan, CEO of Luen Thai, a vertically integrated apparel company, and Chris Chan, a vice president with the Liz Claiborne company in Asia. The city in Dongguan, China was conceived to support everything from design concept to fabric development to finished products, giving buyers a total supply chain solution. One advantage of having many processes within one area is a highly organized vertical operation that reduces the turn time of product development from one year to twelve weeks (Luen Thai, n.d.).

India refers to this close grouping of industrial facilities as clusters. Tirupur, located in southern India, is referred to as a cluster but offers the same opportunity as a supply chain city.

Because of the vertical platform used by supply chain cities, the opportunity to incorporate sustainability into processes exists at both the facility level and the municipal level. By using eco-industrial parks as a template, waste is sent back upstream, solar panels create energy, water is recycled, and transportation emissions are reduced when suppliers are located in close proximity to one another. Thus, the supply chain city reduces the garment turn time and develops the product using sustainable business practices. This business concept has a better chance of gaining acceptance when governments at the local and national level support such initiatives by offering incentives such as eco-tax rebates, training, and technical assistance.

Bioregionalism

Another alternative to a global supply chain is making clothing closer to the market. This is referred to as bioregionalism. Bioregionalists develop products through the local population within a naturally defined region using local renewable materials and waste reduction strategies (Desai & Riddlestone, 2002). Bioregionalism maintains that the homogeneous consumer culture has lost its understanding of its dependency on the natural world. Supporting local economies results in reduction in various business and environmental costs, such as transportation costs, carbon dioxide emissions, infrastructure costs due to reduced truck-to-port miles and sea or air miles, and financing costs due to lower insurance and warehousing requirements.

Bioregionalists seek to minimize product miles, a relatively new idea in the debate about sustainability. Typically, product miles are defined as the distance it takes for a product to get from the field to the end consumer. By reducing transport miles, greenhouse gas emissions linked to transport can be reduced. Additionally, reducing product miles may also reduce the time between producing a product and selling it, thereby improving a garment's chance of success in the trend-oriented fashion industry.

The University of Cambridge recently released a report (Allwood et al., 2006) comparing three different scenarios for apparel production:

1   Production is moved from China closer to the UK market, thereby reducing product miles and greenhouse gas emissions.
2   Production is moved closer to the market, and high technology knitting equipment would be used to reduce the labor cost increase caused by relocating production from China to the United Kingdom.
3   Production is moved closer to market, high technology knitting equipment would be used to knit equipment, helping to eliminate production steps, and recycled material would be taken advantage of as a raw material resource.

The researchers discovered that each of these scenarios reduced overall global environmental impacts. But the first scenario of simply shifting production closer to the market did not yield much environmental benefit and the environmental impact in the United Kingdom actually increased because of increased production within that region. Additionally, each scenario has a negative social impact on sewing operators in China. If production is moved from China to the United

Kingdom, Chinese sewers would be out of work. The third scenario, moving production using high-tech knitting equipment and using recycled material, had the lowest global environmental impact because the local industry is using recycled fiber instead of extracting and transporting new fiber (Allwood et al., 2006).

The Bioregional Development Group, a non-profit organization in the United Kingdom, did a feasibility study on growing, processing, and making hemp apparel within the United Kingdom. Hemp was chosen because it can grow in the United Kingdom's climate without much water and using no pesticides. Although this was only done on a small scale, bioregionalists believe local communities all over the world can take advantage of this concept (Blackburn et al., 2004).

Conclusion

On a daily basis, the fashion industry interprets society's interests concerning clothing. One of those interests is the environment. Leading companies need to consider how their products will represent this societal issue, whether by changing a store light bulb or creating sustainable products. For some companies, it will mean equipping their staff with a new set of skills based on an understanding of sustainability, why it's important, and how to implement responsible sourcing practices.

Sustainable sourcing takes many players within the supply chain, each bringing their own expertise to the team. Companies, and the broader society in which they do business, will benefit by taking advantage of these collaborative efforts.

Discussion Questions

1 If you were a company leader, how would you align your company's core business strategy with the sustainability strategy?

2   How could sustainability values be imbedded in costs? And how
    might natural capital metrics help?
3   What would be some ways brands and suppliers could build a
    shared sustainability strategy for long-term mutual benefits?

References

Allwood, J., Laursen, S., Malvido de Rodriguez, C., & Bocken, N. (2006). Well
    dressed? The present and future sustainability of clothing and textiles in the
    United Kingdom. Cambridge: University of Cambridge Institute for
    Manufacturing.

ASME Boiler and Pressure Vessel Code, Glossary, Section III, Article NCA-
    9000. (n.d.). In Wikipedia. Retrieved August 15, 2014, from http://en.
    wikipedia.org/wiki/Traceability.

Berry, W. (1989). "The Pleasure of Eating." Retrieved from http://www.
    ecoliteracy.org/essays/pleasures-eating.

Birnbaum, D. (2000). *Birnbaum's global guide to winning the great garment war.*
    Hong Kong: Third Horizon Press.

Birnbaum, D. (2003). 101 steps to producing a style: Flow chart. Retrieved
    November 1, 2006, from www.fashiondex.com/globalguide/index.html.

Blackburn, K., Brighton, J., James, I., Riddlestone, S., & Scott, E. (2004,
    November). Feasibility of hemp textile production in the UK. Retrieved
    November 21, 2006, from Bioregional Development Group website at
    http://www.bioregional.com/.

Bremer, J. (2005, June 21). *Kenan institute initiatives in China.* American Apparel
    and Footwear Association Annual Meeting, New York.

Brooks, P., Davidson, L., & Palamides, J. (1993, February). Environmental
    compliance: You better know your abcs. *Occupational Hazards, 123.*

Brundtland, G., Khalid, M., Agnelli, S., Al-Athel, S., Chidzero, B., Fadika, L.,
    et al. (1987). *Our common future.* London: Oxford University Press.

Desai, P. & Riddlestone S. (2002). *Bioregional solutions: For living on one planet.*
    London: Green Books.

Environmental Protection Agency, (n.d.). Clean energy-environment
    partnership program. Retrieved December 10, 2006, from Environmental

Protection Agency Web site at http://www.epa.gov/cleanenergy/ stateandlocal/partnership.htm

Esty, D. & Winston, A. (2006). *Green to gold*. New Haven: Yale University Press.

European Commission's Environment Directorate-General. (2006). Registration, evaluation, and authorization of chemicals (REACH) regulations. Retrieved November 15, 2006, from European Commission Web site at http://ec.europa.eu/ environment/chemicals/reach/reach_ intro.htm.

Goldbach, M. (2001). *Managing the costs of greening: A supply chain perspective*. Proceedings of the 2001 Business Strategy and Environment Conference, September 10–11, 2001, Leeds, UK, pp. 109–18.

Goldbach, M. (2002). *A conceptual framework for green supply relationships: The example of green cotton chains*. Conference Proceedings of the International Expert Workshop, May 16–17, 2002, Fontainebleau, France.

Graedel, T. E. & Allenby, B. R. (2003). *Industrial ecology*. Upper Saddle River, NJ: Prentice Hall.

Grober, U. (2012). *Sustainability: A cultural history*. Devon, UK: Green Books.

Herrmann, C., Hauschild, M., Gutowski, T., & Lifset, R. (2014). Life cycle engineering and sustainable manufacturing. *Journal of Industrial Ecology*, 18(4), 471–7.

Hopkins, L., Allen, D., & Brown, M. (1994). Quantifying and reducing environmental impacts resulting from transportation of a manufactured garment. *Pollution Prevention Review*, 4(4), 491–500.

Hurst, R., Murdoch, H., & Gould, D. (2005). *Changing over time: Tackling supply chain labour issues through business practice*. Retrieved December 10, 2006, from http://www.impacttlimited.com/site/casestudy_item. asp?CS_ID=9.

Kania, J., Hanleybrown, F., & Juster Splansky, J. (2014). Essential mindset shifts for collective impact. *Stanford Social Innovation Review*. Retrieved August 15, 2014 from http://www.ssireview.org/supplement/collective_ insights_on_collective_impact.

Korten, David C. (2000). *The Post-Corporate World*. Berrett-Koehler Publishers.

Liker, J. & Choi, T. (2004). Building deeper supplier relationships. *Harvard Business Review*.

Lofthouse, V. A. & Bhamra, T. A. (2000). Ecodesign integration: Putting the "co" into ecodesign. In S. A. R. Scrivener, L. J. Ball, & A. Woodcock (Eds), *Collaborative design* (pp. 163–72). London: Springer-Verlag.

Luen Thai Holding Limited. (n.d.). Supply chain cities. Retrieved November 25, 2006, from http://www.luenthai.com/supplychain.htm.

Mayers, C., France, C., & Cowell, S. (2005). Extended producer responsibility for waste electronics. *Journal of Industrial Ecology, 9,* 169–89.

Meyers, D. (2011, December 16). The first mile. [blog post]. Retrieved from https://www.2degreesnetwork.com/groups/2degrees-community/resources/first-mile/.

Nike's corporate responsibility report. (2004). Retrieved January 15, 2007, from http://www.nike.com/nikebiz/nikebiz.jhtml?page=29&item=fy04.

Organization for Economic Co-operation and Development. (2004). *The development dimension of trade and environment: Case studies on environmental requirements and market access.* Paris: OECD Publications. Retrieved October 24, 2006, from http://www.oecd.org/dataoecd/23/15/25497999.pdf.

Schnackenberg, A. & Tomlinson, E. (2014). Organizational transparency: A new perspective on managing trust in organization–stakeholder relationships. *Journal of Management.*

Suzuki, D. & Dressel, H. (2002). *Good news for a change.* Vancouver, Canada; Greystone Books.

US Census Bureau. (n.d.). Statistical abstract of the United States. Retrieved August 15, 2014 from http://www.census.gov/population/international/data/worldpop/table_history.php.

HÉLÈNE DAY FRASER is an Associate Professor at Emily Carr University of Art and Design, Canada. She is a founding member of the ECU Material Matters research cluster, a member of the Emily Carr DESIS Lab, the International Local Wisdom research network, and Creatives with Intent (an Emily Carr based sustainability initiative). She is the Lead Investigator on the cloTHING(s) as conversation research project and co-investigator and a Research Fellow with the Brooklyn Fashion and Design Accelerator. Hélène holds a BAA Fashion and an MAA Design. Her creative practice and research consistently engages in reimagining textile product possibilities—exploring analogue and digital forms of making through art/design and interdisciplinary-based collaborations.

CHAPTER **15**

Challenges and Propositions: Alternative Approaches to Design and Engagement

Hélène Day Fraser

Adaptive Garment Systems?

Change

A Declaration: The fashion industry has been built on a notion of change that is contingent on the new (new look, new you, shiny new) and the ever-continuing perceived need for refinement through replacement.

An Observation: The reality of climate change places us as individuals and social beings in a position where we must actively reconsider our assumptions and reprioritize our actions. Rather than continuing on the prescribed route and being satisfied with a dangerous status quo, fashion designers have the opportunity to consider something that the industry does incredibly well—offering up opportunities for change and new means of self-projection. Reframing this asset may allow us to align our field in a way that is reflective of the times and indicative of the difficult adjustment contemporary society needs to make in order to live sustainably. Contemporary society's assumed need for the new—and, more importantly, our ability as fashion designers to extract insight about how this functions in the clothing arena—are integral to this space of re-evaluation.

Resilience

There is an increasing recognition in contemporary society that potent insights can be found in the organizational structures found in our natural environment. In particular, understandings of the qualities and actions of resilience occurring in the natural world are being applied to a diverse range of areas responsible for our social and constructed environment. From fields such as technology and social media (Stevens, 1981) to design for sustainability (Manzini, 2013), resilience is being considered as a site and means of reframing how we go about our everyday life.

The "resilience perspective" emerged out of the field of ecology in the late 1960s and since the early 1970s has been linked to multi-stable states and non-linear responses to change (Folke, 2006). It has had a significant effect on our contemporary understanding of social-ecological systems and in turn has affected policies in a wide range of areas outside of ecology. A deeper, informed understanding of resilience in natural systems has shifted how society deals with change. An early focus on resilience as a means of absorbing shocks while maintaining function (keeping things stable / as is) has evolved (Berkes, Colding, & Folke, 2003; Folke, 2006; Smit & Wandel, 2006). Today organizations in many different fields of expertise, including design, are attempting to address their own capacities for renewal, regeneration, reorganization and development (Berkes et al., 2003; Folke, 2006; Gunderson & Holling, 2002). In embracing disturbance and change, a new set of strategies have emerged. These attempt to make use of and establish methods for distributed, non-hierarchical, networked systems of communication, production, and enterprise in order to tackle a wide range of complex social, environmental, and economic challenges.

While big and unwieldy in scope, it is important to recognize that these maneuvers are very relevant to the fashion schema. Clothing helps us navigate our everyday and is in effect part of a broader human social ecology. This chapter asks you to consider **renewal**, **regeneration**, and **reorganization** in relation to the ways we design, produce, and use clothing. It reflects on the dynamic between **change** and **resilience** in conjunction with notions of the **incomplete**. It provides examples of this at play in design solutions and social scenarios from within the domain of both fashion and its environs. It intends to allow you the space to consider how we might act as fashion designers to re-evaluate the ecologies of fashion and clothes. Context, experience, and systems of connection all play key roles in this.

Incomplete?

Traditionally when we design an article of clothing we concentrate on "it" and not so much on the periphery. We consider the hand, drape, color of the fabric, the style lines and the interplay between the *skin* we are creating and the body structure that it is intended to hang on. This is a detailed and intense process and one that is very much about refinement of details: fit, pattern construction, notions. Refinement leads to an end product and a finished garment. And we, as fashion designers, send it out as a statement for others to consider and pick up. Presented on the catwalk and in show rooms, moved onto the retail floor it is a finished object. Take it or leave it. These are the colors, this is the sizing—*hopefully you will like it.*

When designing an artifact or piece of clothing in this manner, the only way to encourage change is by offering up a new option, a new statement—a new article of clothing for the user to consume. Beyond the obvious issue from a sustainability standpoint—this is a system of planned product obsolescence, rooted in the production of too much, in the creation of waste, and recognized as having a problematic capacity to facilitate a significant depletion of resources and energy (Fletcher, 2013a)—this viewpoint offers a limited understanding of what change can entail. It is contingent on always producing the new and assumes that we as designers must finish the product, ready for consumption.

Consider a different alternative. What if the design you created was almost complete, if aspects were not quite finished and intended to be this way? If instead of offering up a statement to be consumed, your clothing was in fact a suggestion, an offering, the first part of a sentence, a conversation for the user (who will invariably end up wearing the article of clothing) to be picked up and continued? Something that can be added to, adjusted, and changed? What if that article of clothing (as part of a conversation) came back to you at a later date for you as a designer to reconsider and pick up and change again? What if it was understood to be in an ongoing state of development (Fraser, 2008)? How would you do this? What are the implications for you as a designer and a wearer of clothing and for the industry you are connected to?

The design of incomplete artifacts is evidenced in many areas of design. Take, for example, the coloring books designed by Japanese children's book illustrator and writer Tarō Gomi. First published in French in 2001, *The Doodle Book: Draw! Colour! Create!* introduces the user to the first gestures of a drawing and then asks the participant to interact and complete the illustrations. Rather than merely filling in the enclosed, delineated spaces with color the user is invited to apply their own creativity. This is a very basic example of incomplete design at play. In industrial and communication design, the Do It Project in the Netherlands treated designed artifacts in a similar way (Klaassen & Troxler, 2011). As a genre of work these design solutions are not just shots in the dark. They are deeply rooted in innate cognitive processes that are connected to meaning and engagement (Sennett, 2008). Design research initiatives such as work by the Eternally Yours Foundation, and investigations looking into the non-intentional design of everyday objects and the built environment (Brandes, Stich, & Wender, 2013) and Craft of Use practices linked to the clothing we wear (Fletcher, 2013b), are examples of design-led research that offers up solid grounding for new design practices (Figure 15.1). Conducted by interdisciplinary teams that have included design experts from the fields of industrial, interaction, communication, and fashion design, these projects are helping to identify both the opportunities for

FIGURE 15.1. The International Local Wisdom Network headed by Kate Fletcher has documented and categorized a plethora of ways that people adjust and become attached to their clothing over time. These Craft of Use practices are now available as a resource for designers working in sustainability. (Photo by Jeremy Calhoun)

reframing and the pitfalls connected to open-ended design propositions. They provide solid resources that are worth considering if we, as fashion designers, acknowledge that there is a need for a change in how we approach our work and the designed outcomes we facilitate.

Distributed

Non-linear Routes—New Narratives

Our tendency for millennia has been to treat systems of making in linear, hierarchical terms. For the contemporary garment trade, linear systems, routed in the Industrial Revolution, have consisted of actions of design and production in which different components (textile production, notions, etc.) feed into the cut–make–trim process— invariably leading to the creation of a garment that is then packaged and sold. An individual's inevitable use of it is understood and assumed to be part of the equation but is addressed only nominally and rarely considered to any great extent by conventional fashion practices.

Today, however, we communicate in a very different way than we did even ten years ago. We are connected via distributed, non-hierarchical systems or networks. As nodes in the network we have the capacity to reach one another and engage in a manner and to an extent that has never been experienced before. President Obama's first election campaign and its use of social media, in which there was a direct back-and-forth dialogue between the presidential candidate, his team, and the American constituency, is an example of this (Crawford, 2009). More radical social movements such the Arab Spring or the Occupy Wall Street protests illustrate fluid, dynamic modes of engagement that are also significant. While these examples are social, cultural, and political in nature, they do have links to the way we make and consume physical artifacts such as clothing. The ways in which we are connecting have changed—ergo, the ways in which we make are being affected.

Current clothing production systems are a hybrid of the analogue and the digital. There is a significant human and political element to this form of making. Factory floors are comprised of large numbers of people participating in mechanical actions of assembly and individual acts of decision making and production. This analogue system is deeply connected and modulated via distributed networks of digital communication, software and task-specific technologies for garment styling, patterning, grading, marker making, laser cutting, etc. An increased relevance of 3D software in conjunction with recent developments in 3D printing and additive manufacture is also at play in the design and production of clothing styles and notion development. The dynamic between traditional production systems and new technologies for production is significant when applied in conjunction with the digital networks that we use to communicate. They allow designers and producers to circumnavigate old routes and ways of getting things done. The systems are no longer uniquely linear.

Non-linear systems shake up our notions of what constitutes a finished product. This is because they open up processes to a wider number of stakeholders, giving them the capacity to shift and adjust how, when, and by whom any given product is made. The beginning, middle, and end narrative of conventional practices no longer applies.

Mechanisms for Feedback

With the increasing prominence of non-linear distributed systems in the contemporary landscape, new routes of making and engagement are being piloted and established.

Rediscovering the Individual

A Choice

Circumventing old routes. Beyond affecting the systems that connect designers, producers, and retailers, distributed networks of communication invite the user into the picture as never before. The growing numbers of clothing-based companies trying to establish new, online models of customization and personalization are indicative of this.

While it can be argued that user online customization services offered by sportswear giants such as Nike and Adidas continue to propagate assumed, problematic conventions connected to the consumption of material goods, they have also served to illustrate and help seed new mechanisms for individual users to connect with the previously opaque back end of the garment trade. Both the NIKEiD and Adidas Customize programs, as well as the extension of bespoke into the digital arena by Burberry, are propositions that enable users to modify and interact with the object's final aesthetic prior to production and at locations far from the sites of manufacture. In facilitating acts of "re" design they move the user from the role of a passive player to one involved in active participatory feedback loops that previously did not exist. These conditions point to the potential for increasingly meaningful, active, and reciprocal dialogues between designers, producers, and users.

A Connection
It is worth considering the implications of changing the modes of engagement we have with the artifacts we own and the clothing we wear. If resilient, distributed systems of connection are not based on clear beginning, middle, and end narratives, how do we continue to establish and create meaningful links across time and place?

In 2005, futurist Bruce Sterling coined the term *Spimes* to describe a new type of manufactured artifact that might be tracked through time and space and exist as part of the internet of things (Sterling, Wild, & Lunenfeld, 2005). Within a very short period of time evidence of this concept began turning up in the sphere of design. Early examples relevant to fashion include the work of creatives such as Christien Meindertsma, who began exploring the possibility of connecting users directly to the makers/producers of clothing they wore. In 2005 Meindertsma's project the One Sheep Cardigan consisted of three cardigans each knitted from the wool of one sheep and accompanied with that particular sheep's identifying ear-tag, a passport (containing specific information about the cardigan's lineage and origin), and a trophy ribbon (Meindertsma, 2005).

Several years later, in 2009, Meindertsma developed the Flax Project, aiming to expose the links "from the seed to the end product" (Meindertsma, 2009). This work and others that sought to expose the back end of the product life cycle has evolved. Moving from the conceptual space, the imperative has been taken up and applied to much larger, global, commercial initiatives. The IOU project began in 2011. Its online space provides a means of establishing an evocative narrative that facilitates connections between the makers and wearers of each article of clothing found in the IOU collection. Through videos and photos, the site links artisans in India (who made the cloth) to artisans in Europe (who constructed the garment) to proud wearers and owners of specific IOU garments. This transparent, traceable "prosperity chain" extends around the globe and is intended to empower both the artisans and the users (IOU, n.d.). It is a wonderful example of the social imperative becoming a value proposition that is tightly connected and integral to the physical qualities of the clothing itself.

If it is not already obvious, this work that looks at open traceability has the potential to further evolve into a space where clothing producers and design houses allow people access not only to the previously opaque "back" story that occurs as clothing is conceived and produced, but also to narratives that evolve out of and are attached to articles of clothing after the point of purchase—that occur through our use, care, and reuse of clothing. Through similar digital systems and visual devices employed by the Flax and IOU projects, it is conceivable that the space for narratives (connected to the making of a product) could be extended in a meaningful and active way through the continued/shared stories of use in the post-purchase arena. A recent video by Patagonia's Common Threads Program has users speak about where they have been in their Patagonia clothing and the adaptations they have made to their garments over time (Common Threads Program, n.d.). Imagine similar ongoing narratives being shared and attached to specific articles of clothing in a proactive manner. Patagonia's work points to the potential of open narratives that rely on the communication of how an individual object has been used, where it has been, who has worn it. By documenting and adding emotional and social value to articles of clothing over time via processes that tag and develop poignant narratives, fashion/clothing based companies and designers have the opportunity to actively facilitate positive new value systems connected to the ongoing cycling of clothing through the user space. The old imperative to chuck out and start completely anew might be circumvented.

Rediscovering the Local

The Role of Place

An interesting connection to the notion of *Spime* and its conceptual use as a mechanism for exposing clothing histories are the other narratives and resilient approaches being taken to address clothing production concerns. Although the examples above occur and connect people across vast distances, they are also distinctly about the local. Distributed systems and their means of connecting to the local have opened up other conversations about closed-loop production, specifically to approaches that attempt to circumvent the distance conundrum (Sinha et al., 2010). Two examples of initiatives that seek to address local production, consumption, and knowledge transfer are the Sustainable Cotton Project and Fibershed. Both are based in California.

The Sustainable Cotton Project, as its name implies, deals specifically with the implications of cotton-based production. It seeks to decrease the toll that the "soil-to-shirt" cotton production process has on Earth's air, water, and soil, as well as the health of people in cotton growing areas (Sustainable Cotton Project, n.d.). Through its Cleaner Cotton campaign the group connects the stakeholders in the farms, mills, and local communities where California cotton is produced and processed. It provides a channel to increase the supply and demand for local, ethically produced cotton products.

Fibershed takes a different tack, aiming to demonstrate a bioregional clothing model that is tightly connected to its geographical landscape. Using its California base and local wool production as a case study, Fibershed acts as a hub and online resource for other similar regional textile supply chain initiatives and communities that wish to take on or reintroduce systems of local, connected cooperative-run production (Fibershed, n.d.). The organizations of Fibershed and the Sustainable Cotton Project and the regional textile supply chains that they inform are deeply connected to local rules of interaction. As systems of confluence deeply rooted in sense of place and people, they have an ability to change and adapt to a range of ecological, social, and political factors. Non-linear and local in nature, they generate new paths of dependency that align with work done by socio-ecologists looking into the resilience perspective (Folke, 2006).

Taking on and rediscovering the local and the small-scale changes how we think about the design of any particular garment. Not only does our sense of responsibility shift; so too do the narratives we attach to any given outcome. Connections to the ways in which natural resources are processed and affected by human contributions can be made more apparent. Our expectations of what the clothing might, and should, look like also shifts from models of standardization to ones that are open to and celebrate the contributors (environmental, human, and technological factors) of any given outcome. In the wine industry there is a French term, *terroir*, which speaks to a humble honoring of the specific qualities of a wine—of the time and site of its origin. Connected to a sense of place, it is understood that the qualities of any particular bottle of wine is contingent on where the grapes were grown, the particular terrain (slope of hill, quality of earth, water drainage); that this, along with the weather, the timing of the harvest, and the intuition of the winemaker, all affect and add value to the final outcome. This production is regional specific but also individualized in nature and contrary to mass-produced models that treat outcomes as necessary exact replicas of one another. Clothing understood and celebrated in a similar manner allows for a redistribution of value that has arguably long been needed.

Rethinking Conventional Approaches: Engaging in Acts of Making

Repair
Tightly connected to ideas of designing for change and the incomplete artifact is the imperative that designers have a strong understanding of the cumulative effects of time and use on an object. In the case of

clothing, fabric wears out, it snags, it gets torn. It traps odors as we sweat in it. Outdoors or in work and play environments it collects residue such as salt and dirt, which accumulate and erode its surface. With all of this wear comes the need for repair.

Acknowledging the significance of use shifts the assumed design directive. Repair needs to be considered as part and parcel of the route of any designed object. It needs to be addressed not only as a response mechanism and afterthought but also as a proactive route for extending a product's life cycle indefinitely. Systems-based thinking is essential to this tenet.

There are a growing number of precedents and designed responses that acknowledge this and offer considered, adroit propositions. These are often examples of repair that work on a functional level (fixing something that has been broken) but also examples that make use of a key part of the designer's skill set—that employ visual messages and poetics in order to shift conventions of behavior and perspective.

Artifact—You Can Do It ...

From the field of industrial and product design come examples of work by groups such as the French design studio 5.5 and a design project called Réanim (Réanim, n.d.). Réanim was developed in 2003 and riffs off of the green Pharmacy signs, which are a prominent marker in the French urban environment, and the French word *réanimation* which is connected to notions of intensive care and resuscitation. Developed as a kit of parts, Réanim consists of a series of articles (e.g., spare chair legs, spare seats, thread, and connection units) all in the affiliated French "Pharmacy" green. This design is intended to be understood and used as a means of mending, and of aiding otherwise damaged goods to be repaired—to get well. While not textile based, this mashing together of cues from the existing built environment (artifacts) along with fixing tools (and their implicit modes of action) is an effective example of broken objects being reinterpreted (through their design and repair) to be used again with a new, embedded gain in value. Once users have applied parts of the Réanim toolkit to their broken article of furniture, the design proposition invariably extends beyond the green "fix it" piece and becomes also the object that has been resuscitated/Réanim.

Another design more easily applicable to the fashion context that addresses the possibility of reviving and reconstituting both the function and value in a broken artifact is Woolfiller by Droog designer Heleen Klopper. Like Réanim, Woolfiller is a kit of parts, in this case one that works with "the tension between material and the object" (Woolfiller, n.d.), and that provides us with the means to repair holes and hide stains in our wool sweaters, jackets, and carpets—facilitating revived function and affecting our resulting attitudes toward once damaged artifacts.

Beyond extending our understanding of what constitutes a design and allowing us to reconsider when the act of designing actually stops, design propositions such as Réanim and Woolfiller give rise to an *I can do it/I want to do it* mentality. These "designed affordances" (Norman, 1988) have the ability to lead people to reconsider how they can engage and take action. It is important to recognize that the design work is concentrated not solely on the artifact but also on facilitating a particular relationship to it. Altruistic motivation aside, both Réanim and Woolfiller are examples of designed affordances offering up a sense of satisfaction to the user that are routed in the kinesthetic and ritual. They are routed in practices of ritual and action that get us past issues of cognitive dissonance and the negative qualities of affect—that allow us to move a designed object from one stage to the next—to add new value (Fraser, 2008). They help us instigate and produce something new.

Knowledge

Actions—We'll Help and ...
Facilitation of the "fix it" mentality is also connected to maker culture and, of course, the DIY movement. The sense of satisfaction afforded to

individuals who take on acts of making not only comes through design propositions such as Réanim and Woolfiller, it also extends to independently driven projects. It is particularly effective when built on and supported both in terms of material supply and distributed systems of connection. Websites such as Fixperts and the iFixit platform that Patagonia encourages are examples of this. The Fixpert platform provides face-to-face interactions with its Fixpartners and demonstrates how people can take on the repair. Fixfilm-makers capture this process and translate the conversations and experiments into short documentaries to be shared with others in the online space (Fixperts, n.d.). The iFixit platform, on the other hand, is a more conventional teach/knowledge supply model that provides guides and "how to" directives that can be viewed and downloaded (iFixit, n.d.). In both cases, the means to forgo sending "broken" objects to the landfill site are provided.

Dialogue

Facilitating repair culture is not just about making information accessible; it is also very much about the tactics used to share, show, and motivate. The Dutch design group Platform 21 has played with conventional messaging and tools for motivation in order to reveal the process of making and repair and to connect amateur and professional creativity. This has entailed hosting online design competitions, such as their 2009 effort called Remarkable Repairs, or producing a Repair Manifesto which "opposes throw away culture and celebrates repair as the new recycling" (Platform 21, n.d.).

Space

Providing physical space is also key to reframing our assumptions. Events/gatherings/hubs are integral to reconstituting a mending-minded repair culture. Symposiums and groups such as MEND*RS at Lancaster University in the United Kingdom invite people to collect, reflect, and mend textile-based artifacts together (MEND*RS, n.d.) While not quite the same as the quilting bee phenomenon of 1800s North America society, these models of engagement are tightly connected to specific social constructs and provide forums for re-engagement with making. In addition to collective acts of gathering and construction, growing numbers of tool libraries and open access maker labs are turning up in urban centers. These sites are providing people with the technologies and direct connection to individual makers well versed in what it takes to construct and fix. Within North America, however, there is a lack of maker sites that are able to provide the equipment and expertise connected to the making and repair of textile-based goods (sewing machines, sergers, walking foots, and irons are generally not listed). While disappointing, the upside of this gap points to an opportunity for designers interested in taking on issues of repair of textile-based artifacts.

There are some key elements found in the burgeoning make/use environments discussed above that should move from sitting on the periphery of the fashion agenda. They are all comprised of sharing, open systems, kits of parts and formulas for new forms of engagement, and they inevitably support, bolster, and underpin new notions of value (see the discussion of upcycling below). As resilient modes of engagement they offer up opportunity for renewal, regeneration, and reorganization of the existing and unsustainable fashion system.

Value

Proactive Approaches
Not all acts of repair are about bringing something back to the condition it once was in, to the function it once had. Proactive approaches often attempt to grapple with regeneration and the constituents that catalyze, amplify, or shift notions of value that we attach to cloth through reframing past expectations of how things are made/look/act.

Upcycling
Arguably upcycling resides in this reframe space. Upcycling is the process of moving waste materials and products on to a new stage where there is an increase in the perceived value of the item (Fletcher, 2013a). It is a process of adjustment in which value judgments are realigned through material, semiotic, and emotional reconfiguration. Designs and systems that facilitate this move need to be resilient—able to take on and adjust to a broad array of artifacts with a range of different physical attributes. The task is not a simple one. Post- and pre-consumer waste require different approaches. Likewise they offer up different opportunities. Moving the waste material or artifact from one stage to the next, upwards toward higher revalue, requires that the designer is able to adequately understand and acknowledge the nature and narrative and everyday use of the artifact and material that is being realigned. Context is everything. Moving beyond the notion of design as a single statement output is the imperative.

Consider textiles (an artifact of human production): fabric waste off the factory floor (pre-consumer waste) comes to the upcycle process with a different set of conditions than artifacts of clothing that have been worn and washed numerous times (post-consumer waste). The configuration and roles of material possibility (size, shape, textures, molecular structure, etc.), semiotic variables (general wear and tear that causes things to be ripped, stained, smell, etc. affect the way we respond and attach meanings—both positive and negative—to designed things), and emotional connection (developed through narratives/stories connected to the designer, makers, users who have had contact with the object) vary with each given scenario.

Pre-consumer Waste—Recycling of Raw Materials
As anyone who has visited a factory cutting room floor or looked at the negative space around pattern pieces on a pattern marker will be aware, the leftovers created by conventional systems of clothing production are

highly irregular. Adding value to this pre-consumer waste poses its own unique set of issues and approaches. As it is often difficult to conceive how scraps of cloth can be slotted back into streams of production efficiently, a pragmatic approach is often taken. This looks to the reconstitution of the material by going back to its base components— back to the fibers themselves. The task is a difficult undertaking and fraught with issues of physical degradation. Nonetheless, approaches such as the Eco-Circle fiber-to-fiber recoiling system by Teijin (Fletcher, 2013a; Scaturro, 2008) are evidence that chemistry developments are providing means of effectively reconstituting the physical nature of recycled materials so that they can be reconstructed as "new" textiles and (subsequently) new "valued" articles of clothing. Because these recycle systems go back to base elements, they also play a significant role in the post-consumer waste arena.

Systems Approaches

Although textile-centric developments and innovations are outside the direct sphere of influence and field of expertise of the fashion designer, this does not mean that we are afforded the space to relinquish responsibility—all of our decisions invariably affect the cyclical routes of the material streams we are connected to. Efficient and effective regeneration of fibers in the post-waste arena means that the design and subsequent production of clothing needs to facilitate material separation. Added components such as embroidered circuits, fused layers of cloth, and notions such as snaps and zippers are rarely the same fiber content as the textile substrate (the garment) they are connected to. They need to be removed in order for the garment's fibers to be regenerated. This forces us to reconsider and explore how our designs might be constructed to address larger system requirements. Redirected to look beyond the artifact of our design (a garment) in order to address material stream issues changes our perspective and offers up new possibilities and new creative modes of expression.

Frugal Narratives

Other tactics taken to add value to pre-consumer textile waste include its direct application to new sets of artifacts that are derivatives of the production chain they were initially connected to. Textiles can be used for a wide range of outcomes. Many of these are not clothing related. Disassociating post- and pre-consumer waste from its original task/function allows for opportunities to renew in previously unconsidered ways—for the construction of entirely new designed propositions. An example of this can be found in design efforts such as those connected to Pepe Heykoop's 2011 Skin Collection (Heykoop, n.d.). The Skin Collection is a set of furniture consciously designed to make use of leather waste produced by the furniture industry. The combination of previously abandoned chairs, armoires, and lamps (post-consumer waste) and the scraps of discarded leather (pre-consumer waste) provide new value to both the soft and hard elements that constitute the design.

FIGURE 15.2. Pepe Heykoop's Skin Collection is designed to make use of leather waste. (Courtesy of Pepe Heykoop)

Changing Contexts

Altering the placement/position of an artifact/object in relation to its surroundings changes how we respond to it, and often this is also linked to changes in its perceived value. As an act of deterritorialization (Semetsky, 2003) these changes affect our emotional, semiotic, and material value judgments. Work by designers such as Katherine Soucie is exemplary of this. The Sans Soucie line is built on a specific technique of fabric regeneration (Sans Soucie, n.d.). Through a process of dyeing, cutting, and silk-screening regular-grade nylon hosiery, "waste" is stabilized and transformed into a material that can be used to create skirts, shirts, and jackets. Katherine's line of clothing made out of her hosiery regeneration process consciously emulates elements of the bioregional connections demonstrated in the Fibershed model discussed above. Production remains small scale and local—closely linked to the people who purchase her products and the mills that provide her with the damaged goods for repair.

FIGURE 15.3. The Sans Soucie clothing line uses a hosiery regeneration process developed by Canadian designer and artist Katherine Soucie. (Photo by Shimon Karmel)

Hacks = Agency

Work by Andrea Crews and Otto Van Busch demonstrates clothing-based repair/hack initiatives that have wielded regeneration as a tool for imbuing textile-based artifacts with agency. The articles they have played with do not reside in the same functional, semiotic, and emotional space that they originated from, nor do they change entirely. Rather they are contingent on acts of making (interventions) that adjust and shift value. Whether or not this is connected to upcycling is open for debate. What is clear is that the clothing artifacts they deal with, and the subsequent acts of remaking that have evolved from the precedents they have set, have triggered new venues for the regeneration of textile-based artifacts. Space has been provided for programs such as the UK-based TRAID charity that works to stop clothes from being thrown away—offering circular and sustainable approaches to tackling waste disposal, production, and consumption (TRAIDremade, n.d.).

Sharing

Our social relations and aspirations play a significant role in how we perceive value. While prestige and power pull money into the value equation, belonging, kinship, and connection are equal contingents in the picture. We connect narratives that are associated with these qualities to the objects we own and wear and this in turn imbues them with specified value.

Narratives turn up in spaces where artifacts and actions of sharing align. Examples of this can be found in multigenerational approaches to artifacts that are passed on from one individual or group to the next. One could consider this in relation to a piece of clothing that has belonged to a range of family members (see the Local Wisdom Network website for documentation of examples) but other spaces also facilitate this. Cloth swaps among friends and within organizations encourage an intimate space of shared ownership. Values connected to clothing will shift depending on who is sharing and how. A clothing library system based in Western Australia that provides unemployed people clothing for crucial job interviews (The Clothing Exchange, n.d.) facilitates a different value from projects such as the Wear Worn project of the Local Wisdom Network, where a small group of design students developed and tested a system for sharing preferred articles of clothing amongst a small group of friends.[1]

Sharing also has a place in contexts more closely connected to conventional fashion practices, at the back end of the production cycle. Estonian fashion designer Reet Aus's "UpCycled" collection and proposed waste-mapping database Trash to Trend could potentially shift how fashion deals with its material flows (Aus, n.d.). Based on her doctoral thesis, Aus's tracking system aims to connect designers to

FIGURE 15.4. The Wear Worn project explored design approaches to sharing clothes—sizing, emotional attachment, care required, and systems of distribution were integral to this. (Courtesy of Jean Chisholm and Emanuel Ilagan)

mass-produced production leftovers (offcuts and roll ends). Though yet to be launched, the tracking system she has developed to deal with this type of material is an example of organized principles of sharing being proposed to encourage transparency and create new routes for post- and pre-consumer textile waste to flow back into existing production routes.

Resolution?

Non-linear systems and the new mechanisms for feedback that they encourage pull us in different directions. They open up the space for us to reconsider acts of making (both individual and social) as a viable/ desirable means of engagement with the objects around us and, of course, the clothing we wear. They trigger new value systems and narratives that celebrate and are contingent on notions of renewal, regeneration, and reorganization. They demand that the larger social, ecological, and political context of any given clothing scenario of use be addressed.

Dynamic in nature, these approaches to the designed world involve risk. They necessitate a stepping outside of the stable boundaries and defense mechanisms that we have historically and repeatedly constructed. They ask us to look beyond singular acts of solve and resolve. While daunting, they are also inherently about agency. They offer up new possibilities and ways of addressing otherwise seemingly insurmountable odds. They call us into action and lead us to design approaches that have the possibility to work in concert with our natural environment and our built world.

Discussion Questions

1   Can you reimagine your design process so that it is consciously made up of elements of renewal, regeneration, and reorganization?

If your process already contains these elements, where does this appear? Who are the stakeholders that play a part in the acts of renewal, regeneration, and reorganization?

2   How might you apply resilience theory to your designed outcomes? If your design is more than a garment in isolation, how do you connect to larger systems? How do you design garments that are meant and understood to have the capacity to adapt over time?

3   How can you design clothes with intentional mechanisms for feedback? How do you imbed connection and choice into the artifact/piece of clothing?

4   If you were to do a survey of local infrastructure—farmers, makers, users etc.—and used this as the starting point for your design outcome, what would it look like? What does it mean to design for looped cycles based on close proximity?

Note

1   This initiative offered the university students the opportunity to add more variety into their limited student wardrobes and to cut back on their individual clothing consumption patterns. It also forced them to contend with issues related to wearing other people's clothes; to consider how to address comfort levels related to cleanliness and care, and size and gender differentiation. This helped the design students identify the choice of clothing that could effectively be used in this type of clothing share system. It also helped the designers identify the parameters for a new set of clothing forms, which could function within the share system's limitations.

References

Aus. R. (n.d.). Trash to trend. Retrieved August 27, 2014, from http://trash-to-trend.myshopify.com/collections/reet-aus-in-bangladesh.

Berkes, F., Colding, J., & Folke, C. (Eds.) (2003). *Navigating social–ecological systems: Building resilience for complexity and change*. Cambridge: Cambridge University Press.

Brandes, U., Stich, S., & Wender, M. (2013). *Design by use: The everyday metamorphosis of things*. Walter de Gruyter.

The Clothing Exchange. (n.d.). Retrieved September 1, 2014, from http://clothingexchange.com.au/index.php/about-us.

Common Threads Program, Patagonia. (n.d.). Retrieved August 1, 2014, http://www.patagonia.com/ca/common-threads/.

Crawford, K. (2009). Following you: Disciplines of listening in social media. *Continuum: Journal of Media & Cultural Studies, 23*(4), 525–35.

Fibershed. (n.d.). Retrieved August 2, 2014, from http://www.fibershed.com/.

Fixperts. (n.d.). Retrieved August 2, 2014, from http://fixperts.org/.

Fletcher, K. (2013a). *Sustainable fashion and textiles: Design journeys*. Routledge.

Fletcher, K. (2013b). Craft of use. [Online] Available at http://craftofuse.org/ (accessed January 10, 2013).

Folke, C. (2006). Resilience: The emergence of a perspective for social–ecological systems analyses. *Global Environmental Change, 16*(3), 253–67. Through Emily Carr University of Art + Design Library website http://scholar.google.ca.ezproxy.eciad.ca:2048/schhp (accessed August 28, 2013).

Fraser, H. (2008). Exploring change: The object–identity–consumption dynamic. Master's thesis, Emily Carr University of Art + Design, Vancouver. Retrieved June 28, 2014, from http://issuu.com/designdegreeecuad/docs/fraser2008.

Gunderson, L. H. & Holling, C. S. (Eds.). (2002). *Panarchy: Understanding transformations in human and natural systems*. Washington, DC: Island Press.

Heykoop, P. (n.d.). Retrieved August 20, 2014, from http://www.pepeheykoop.nl/en/works/skin-collection.

iFixit. (n.d.). Retrieved August 2, 2014, from https://www.ifixit.com/patagonia.

IOU Project. (n.d.). Retrieved June 1, 2014, from http://iouproject.com/.

Klaassen, R. & Troxler, P. (2011). Do it with Droog. *Open Design Now*. Retrieved June 12, 2014, from http://opendesignnow.org/index.php/article/do-it-with-droog-roel-klaassen-peter-troxler/.

Manzini, E. (2013). Resilient systems and sustainable qualities. *Current: Design Research Journal,* 4, 11–14.

Meindertsma, C. (2005). One sheep cardigan. *Flocks.* Retrieved September 1, 2014, from http://www.christienmeindertsma.com/index.php?/projects/one-sheep-cardigan/.

Meindertsma, C. (2009). Flax project. *Flocks.* Retrieved September 1, 2014, from http://www.christienmeindertsma.com/index.php?/projects/flax-project/.

MEND*RS. (n.d.). Retrieved July 15, 2014, from http://mendrs.net/.

Norman, D. A. (1988). *The psychology of everyday things.* New York: Basic Books.

Platform 21. (n.d.). Remarkable repairs. Retrieved July 15, 2014, from http://www.platform21.nl/page/5621/en.

Réanim. (n.d.). Retrieved August 2, 2014, from http://www.5-5designstudio.com/fr/projet/2004-55designers-reanim.

Sans Soucie. (n.d.). Retrieved August 20, 2014, from http://www.sanssoucie.ca/.

Scaturro, S. (2008). Eco-tech fashion: Rationalizing technology in sustainable fashion. *Fashion Theory: The Journal of Dress, Body & Culture,* 12(4), 469–88.

Semetsky, I. (2003). The problematics of human subjectivity: Gilles Deleuze and the Deweyan legacy. *Studies in Philosophy and Education,* 22(3–4), 211–25.

Sennett, R. (2008). *The craftsman.* New Haven: Yale University Press.

Sinha, P., Dissanayake, D., Mahwera, D., & Kahabi, C. (2010). Creating a global vision for sustainable fashion. In *87th Textile Institute World Conference 2010.* Manchester, UK: Textiles Institute, pp. 247–75.

Smit, B. & Wandel, J. (2006). Adaptation, adaptive capacity and vulnerability. *Global Environmental Change,* 16(3), 282–92.

Sterling, B., Wild, L., & Lunenfeld, P. (2005). *Shaping things.* Cambridge, MA: MIT Press.

Stevens, C. H. (1981). *Many-to many communication.* [Online] Cambridge, MA: Center for Information Systems Research, Alfred P. Sloan School of Management Issue. Available at http://hdl.handle.net/1721.1/48404 (accessed March 1, 2013).

Sustainable Cotton Project. (n.d.). Retrieved August 1, 2014, from http://www.sustainablecotton.org/pages/show/cleaner-cotton-marketing-cmpaign.

TRAIDremade. (n.d.). Retrieved September 1, 2014, from http://www.traid.org.uk/traidremade/.

Woolfiller. (n.d.). Retrieved August 2, 2014, from http://www.woolfiller.com/wolplamuur.nl/index.php?lg=en&.

Peg and Awl: To Make Things out of Other Things

Interview by Janet Hethorn, September 30, 2014

Many ideas were expressed in this section that address the need to find more environmentally sustainable ways to develop fabrics and fashion products. Beginning with a call to reframe the fashion system, through the opportunities occurring within textile and fiber development, challenges and options were presented. Then guidance was provided in the form of sustainable sourcing suggestions and models. Completing the section, we were inspired by many examples of design explorations with a focus on engagement and innovation.

Included throughout the chapters within this section were several case studies and stories of best practices to achieve these goals. However, one may still be left with the question, "How do I start?" For this reason, I wanted to close our book by highlighting a company whose story provides inspiration for action. Peg and Awl is a business involved in creating products for everyday use that give new life to found materials. Thus their mission: To make things out of other things. They create items for the home, kitchen, office, and the garden. They make bags of all sizes and functions to carry things in and items to store other things in. "Treasures built from abandoned materials," is their tagline.

In 2012, Peg and Awl moved from a home-based shop to a larger space in the Port Richmond neighborhood of Philadelphia, PA. What began as a way to make useful things for themselves is now a thriving design/make business. As stated on their website, http://pegandawlbuilt.com, "Our work is made from olde things, treasures found and recovered from misfortune and neglect, relics of the unusual, the confused and the macabre, cut and pulled and built

into wearable curiosities, inscribable keepsakes and useable, long-lasting treasures."

I had the privilege of interviewing Margaux Kent who, along with her husband Walter Kent, are the founders of Peg and Awl. Following are her comments and my elaborations.

Where Does the Name "Peg and Awl" Come From?

"Peg and Awl" is the title of a song by the Carolina Tar Heels. Margaux reflects, "It's a song that I liked about shoemaking and also takes us back to a time when things were made well." The Peg and Awl logo contains a Hagal rune symbol, meaning (in part), "what happens after the destruction." This also symbolizes continuous change and creative building. Both their name and visual messaging, via marketing and social media, reflect their values of quality and renewal. It was clear from the start of the interview that this is a company that is carefully crafted and authentic. What a great foundation for a business that is taking meaningful sustainable action.

How Did You Move from Making Things for Yourself to Making Things for Others?

"It all started with the Black Spot Books. I made journals." She then tells of a time when she was traveling, and her journal was stolen. Needing to make a new one, she went scavenging around Amsterdam for materials. Not wanting to buy new leather ("it's a vegetarian thing"), she found a bindery and an upholsterer up the street. There she found used materials to make what she needed, and created a new journal. "Anywhere we went, people wanted it." So, she made more for her friends.

I asked Margaux to explain how Peg and Awl is rooted in their values and vision. She told me about Walter's background in making things: "Walter has eleven siblings. They always did projects where they used bits and pieces—to be able to afford what they wanted to make. He came from a thrifty background, but he also worked with his Dad, a cabinet maker and builder, in his workshop. Walter's mom is a historian and home schooled everyone with this focus. He had historical information and a love for history."

So, both Margaux and Walter had a love for creating/making and a respect for things from the past. It seems predetermined that they would create a company together with a focus on making new things from old things. But, according to Margaux, "The real trigger to using antique materials was the Amsterdam experience."

Where Do You Find the Materials that You Work With?

In making a commitment to using reclaimed material, the challenge then becomes one of finding. "We have always gone to flea markets, always made things, and we do find sources out and about. One day we came across a general store, run by a husband and wife. The supplies they had for sale were actually from his grandfather." There they found, and with some coaxing purchased, a whole stash of vintage zippers. Everything they had. And here it is important to explain how outlook and opportunity connect. As Margaux explained, she believes in happenstance: "If your eyes are open, anything is possible. I have this way where I see the world as malleable. My eyes are open for it. It happens enough to sustain a business."

They have made a firm choice to use reclaimed material, whether it is antique notions found in a general store, vintage fabric from a flea market, or leather that is reclaimed, such as the bag straps made of World War II gun slings. "Every item bears marks of a not-fully-known and not-quite-finished past." The wood used in their wares comes from torn-down buildings, circa 1800s, finds of scrap wood, and storm-downed trees.

They make things with things with a prior life under human hands. Everything has a story. The waxed canvas is new, sourced from a local company. All of the leather is reclaimed. Lining fabric is from aprons, bedding, pinafores, shirts, and seed sacks.

"Everything we make has an element of something that is reclaimed," states Margaux. "Planned obsolescence. We are working against this horrible concept. The world is too big. People keep buying junk. It's depressing. We are encouraging a non-throw away item, something that you'll have for a long time."

How is Your Company Involved in Sustainable Practices?

"Through the reuse. We incorporate antique materials and make things that endure, are worth saving, and look better with wear. In this way, you start to show the history of how you are living," Margaux explains.

It was so refreshing and encouraging to listen to Margaux express her positive outlook. "Whatever it is, the one thing I have confidence in is that things will work, and if they don't then something else will work. It's so tricky.

When I think about what we live on, we don't live on much. Our pay check is what we need to get by. We don't go shopping every season. When you have this mind-set, you live it. Living your values, this is an important distinction. We evolve and go through many things. We are always evolving. This naturally comes out of who we are and what we believe. We are not thinking about what will sell better, but instead, what will go with one's lifestyle."

It is obvious that the design ideas behind Peg and Awl's products evolve from need. They create things that resonate with values. Some words of encouragement from Margaux: "Know about making, think about what you want. Build it. Come up with products. Think big. Create new worlds. I find magic in places where people find mold and stink."

What is Your Most Innovative Action or Aspect?

Margaux explains to me the real core of their creative process. She clearly understands (lives and breathes) the simple connection between need and building solutions that address that need, no more, no less. "What we are doing is so basic, connecting one thing that we like to what we discover. Simple dots. It's easy to me. Why isn't everyone doing this? I don't know."

Looking at history, and culture production over time, people make things that they need. Getting things from a store is not always an option. For Peg and Awl, the creative process is embedded within what they value and how they live their lives on a daily basis. "We just think about how to garden, what clothes to wear, how to make something to eat off of. There is so much discovery in basic life. Follow your dreams and what you are passionate about. It is going to happen. Sure we are going to run out of vintage zippers, but then there will be a strange detour to take us somewhere else."

What is the Most Challenging?

"The balance between work and life. Time management," Margaux explains. "I have a motor that didn't quit before, but now I tire. At a certain point, you have to put so much time into your work that it results in losing out on other things." And then there is the real concern about sourcing, when the development of products is based on finding reclaimed materials to make them from. When I asked her about this, she remained positive while acknowledging the concept of materials actually going away. "New ideas will always come about (I believe). What's next? We have so many ideas." That alone can be challenging! "It's hard to figure out when to make new things, when to implement, and knowing when to go in what direction. The challenge becomes how to go about selecting and acting."

What are the Possibilities for Sustainable Futures? New Directions?

Margaux explains, "I feel like since I was in high school, I have always had the understanding that things are very wrong. I think we had a weird turn-off in humanness with the Industrial Revolution. That was the wrong road. We need to keep learning and understanding how to do things better and better. When I think about the world, there are so few people who are going to go out and be brave, but so many other people will just follow suit. There are people who are making the right decisions, and others will follow. If the right people are convinced, the rest will follow."

Margaux introduced me to a TED talk that she had recently listened to, "The Best Stats You've Ever Seen," by Hans Rosling, 2006. It is about the statistics of perceptions regarding sustainability. He explored the question, "Is the world headed in a sustainable direction?"

Turns out that the world is going in a much more positive direction than we are aware of, but the perspective of people is that the world is in disaster mode. Because of the negative perception, we are not able to see the statistics of the positive. We never hear how things are changing.

Somehow, I believe that Peg and Awl will continue to innovate and model this positive direction. Their approach to designing and making, rooted in deep values of long-lasting quality, informed by necessity and opportunity, and embedded in the creative process, is at the core of driving this change. As we consider the question, "What's next?" it is critical not only to look forward, but also to look within; to find the passion and value that will fuel the actions you take to bring about positive change. Don't accept anything less.

Page numbers followed by 'n' refer to notes.